Endorsements for *Social Emotional Lea*
and Out-of-School Time: Foundations and Futures

The social and emotional development of our nation's youth is a common, essential concern of those working in school and out of school. This volume will be the catalyst for long overdue conversation, collaboration, and synergy. It is essential reading for practitioners, researchers, and policy makers in both contexts who are concerned with preparing children for the tests of life, and not a life of tests.

—Maurice J. Elias, PhD
Rutgers University, Co-Director of the Academy
for Social-Emotional Learning in Schools and After School Settings
(SELinSchools.org)

Social Emotional Learning and Out-of-School Time: Foundations and Futures is an extremely important and timely publication. The scope and depth of this work makes it a must read for any serious Out-of-School Time or K–12 educator. In 2014 California identified social emotional learning as the most promising bridge to bring coherence between expanded learning programs and the school day. (*A Vision for Expanded Learning in California—Strategic Plan 2014–2016*) I have found this to be the exact case. All across California, school day and Out-of-School Time professionals are having deep and authentic conversations about youth-centered collaborative efforts. We also know that providing social emotional development opportunities is a cornerstone for any high quality Out-of-School Time program. I plan to share this publication widely with K–12 educators, policy makers, parents, and so many others.

—Michael Funk, Director
Expanded Learning Division
California Department of Education

Youth thriving rests on the development of life skills and on using these skills to contribute positively to self and society. Out-of-School Time (OST) programs that enhance social and emotional learning (SEL) are key foundations of such positive youth development for millions of young people across the nation. Elizabeth Devaney and Deborah Moroney have brought together researchers, practitioners, and policy makers in a timely and singularly important volume that creatively and convincingly integrates the knowledge base documenting the linkages between OST programs and SEL and, as well, provides a compelling vision for advancing research and evaluation, improving program quality, and creating policies promoting youth thriving through scaling and sustaining effective OST–SEL relations. This book is required reading for all people seeking resources for enhancing the well-being of the diverse young people of our nation.

—Richard M. Lerner
Bergstrom Chair in Applied Developmental Science and Director
Institute for Applied Research in Youth Development
Tufts University

As someone who has helped shape and define out-of-school time as a field—which has standards of practice, a credible evidence-base, workforce and leadership development, leadership and grassroots advocacy, and systemic supports—I am proud to see this volume push the field to more intentionally articulate the work we already do to support the whole child. While the book's title clearly indicates its focus on SEL practice in OST programs, two statements made in the Foreword and Closing Commentary remind us to liberate ourselves from talking about SEL in the context of specific settings and, instead, focus on how learning happens in those settings. In the Foreword, Mahoney and Weissberg encourage us to shift our attention from which setting is best for SEL, and instead examine how different settings can work together to best implement SEL. This calls for a more nuanced examination of when and where SEL happens, to consider the formal and informal learning settings even within schools where SEL can be named, taught, and practiced. One only has to spend 10 minutes on a playground to see children and youth practicing their SEL skills. Similarly, in the Closing Commentary, Pittman reminds us, based on lessons from the U.K., that youth work is "setting and activity neutral." It meets young people where they are and the "specific activities are merely a medium through which the experience which leads to personal and social development is offered." This suggests that even within the OST sector, settings vary greatly, and Section II on Research-Informed SEL Practice helps us get to that more nuanced understanding of SEL and settings, even within the OST sector. Together, the two statements are a reminder to place youth in the center of what we do and surround them with a variety of settings that support SEL in- and out-of-school.

—Priscilla M. Little, Consultant

As a leader in a nonprofit that cares deeply about supporting young people's social, emotional and academic development, I'm excited to see a book that comprehensively explores the many contributions of out-of-school time programs. This volume has much to offer—from making sense of the various SEL frameworks and how they intersect with youth development to offering practical approaches for improving practices and policies. OST programs provide a unique space to nurture the development of skills, mindsets and capacities that support healthy development and academic success. As a field, our capacity to support SEL has grown significantly over the past several years, building off of our history in positive youth development. We've become more intentional in our approaches to building SEL skills, more sophisticated in elevating youth voice, and better at investing in the adults that work with young people to hone their own social and emotional skills. I hope this book will spark additional interest in SEL and be a catalyst for schools and OST providers to work collaboratively across systems in service to youth.

—Brenda McLaughlin, Chief Strategy Officer
Building Educated Leaders for Life

Whenever two previously separate fields begin to interact and potentially start to merge—as is happening today with OST and SEL—it is a moment of both promise and peril. The best ideas and practices from each field might be combined into a coherent new approach that produces both improvement and innovation. Alternatively, the strengths of both fields might be diluted or lost altogether amidst a confusing and often contradictory jumble of terms, frameworks, and practices. This volume is an invaluable resource for practitioners, researchers, funders and others who want the interaction of OST and SEL to take the first rather than the second path forward. From a diverse array of perspectives, the authors demonstrate that with clear thinking and clear language, the merger of SEL and OST can result in a whole that is even greater than the sum of its two powerful parts.

—Kent Pekel, EdD, President and CEO
Search Institute

This volume's authors—a veritable "Who's Who" of individuals in the youth work profession/youth development field—have been thoughtful trailblazers for many years, so it's no surprise their collection of essays provides a practical, multifaceted view. Ever since Robert Halpern's seminal "Confronting 'The Big Lie': The Need to Reframe Expectations of After-School Programs," we, in the field, have been working to articulate what we do and what we should be held accountable to when given needed support for planning and professional development. Throughout, and especially in Karen Pittman's concluding exhortation to focus on the "what and how," this volume renews our focus and drive to achieve greater intentionality in our practice. Well-constructed and comprehensive, this publication rightly directs our attention to the importance of engaging in data-informed and child-centered continuous improvement processes. Our focus on SEL must include skill building through hands-on group learning—and through reflective developmental experiences both for the children we work with and for ourselves as well, as models and co-learners standing shoulder-to-shoulder with young people.

—Dara Rose, Senior VP, Strategies & Program
HORIZONS NATIONAL

Having spent all of my adult life working with, and advocating for, high-quality youth programming, I understand the critical role Out-of-School Time (OST) programs play in the social and emotional development of young people. As the Executive Director of the New York State Network for Youth Success, *I am thrilled to see such a comprehensive view of current best practices and research on social-emotional learning (SEL) in OST programs.* It is exciting and encouraging to see so much documented progress with SEL in OST condensed into one comprehensive book that furthers understanding of both research-informed practices and systems building around policy. This book, edited by two leading researchers in the field, Elizabeth Devaney and Deborah Moroney, should be required reading for any practitioners, policy makers, and educators in the field. Both the editors' and contributors' emphasis on making SEL an "intentional practice" is the exact conversation we all should be having right now.

—Kelly Malone Sturgis, Executive Director
New York State Network for Youth Success

Social and Emotional Learning in Out-of-School Time

A volume in
Current Issues in Out-of-School Time
Helen Janc Malone, *Series Editor*

Social and Emotional Learning in Out-of-School Time

Foundations and Futures

edited by

Elizabeth Devaney

Children's Institute, University of Rochester

Deborah A. Moroney

American Institutes for Research

INFORMATION AGE PUBLISHING, INC.
Charlotte, NC • www.infoagepub.com

Library of Congress Cataloging-in-Publication Data

A CIP record for this book is available from the Library of Congress
http://www.loc.gov

ISBN: 978-1-64113-384-5 (Paperback)
978-1-64113-385-2 (Hardcover)
978-1-64113-386-9 (ebook)

Printed in the United States of America

Dedicated to all the frontline staff who have devoted their lives
to working with and for young people and
to the American Educational Research Association Out-of-School Time
Special Interest Group

CONTENTS

SECTION III

SEL SYSTEMS AND POLICY

SECTION IV

SEL RESEARCH, MEASUREMENT, AND ASSESSMENT

SECTION V

CONCLUSION

FOREWORD

SOCIAL AND EMOTIONAL LEARNING IN AND OUT OF SCHOOL BENEFITS YOUNG PEOPLE

Joseph L. Mahoney and Roger P. Weissberg

Over a decade ago, our colleagues undertook a review of research on social and emotional learning (SEL) programs (Durlak, Weissberg, Dymnicki, Taylor, & Schellinger, 2011; Durlak, Weissberg, & Pachan, 2010). Initially, one goal of the review was to include evaluations carried out in school and in out-of-school settings to understand the combined effects of SEL across these contexts. There was particular interest in SAFE programs with (a) *sequenced* step-by-step training, (b) *active* forms of learning, (c) a *focus* on social and emotional skill development, and (d) *explicit* SEL goals. However, an insufficient number of studies examining SEL across the settings made it impossible to assess their combined impact. As a result, two separate reports were published: one on school-based SEL (Durlak et al., 2011) and the other on out-of-school SEL (Durlak et al., 2010). This volume shows that since these reports were released, great progress has been made with respect to how programming and systems support SEL across learning contexts.

Social and Emotional Learning in Out-of-School Time, pages xiii–xx

It is an exciting time for SEL, following a surge of interest in recent decades (Durlak, Domitrovich, Weissberg, & Gullota, 2015). Educators show strong support for SEL (Bridgeland, Bruce, & Hariharan, 2013; DePaoli, Atwell, & Bridgeland, 2017), and school and out-of-school settings alike are implementing SEL programs and practices around the world. Hundreds of research studies with rigorous designs conducted within and outside the United States on a variety of SEL programs reach the same general conclusion—namely, that these programs produce positive benefits for participating youth on a range of important outcomes (Mahoney, Durlak, & Weissberg, 2018). SEL is also cost-effective (Belfield et al., 2015), and federal, state, and local policymakers are backing the SEL movement with increased funding (Goldberg, Sharvit, & Singh, this volume; Price, 2015). The National Commission on Social, Emotional, and Academic Development was recently formed with the purpose of engaging communities to "... fully integrate the social, emotional, and academic dimension of learning in K–12 education so that all students are prepared to thrive in school, career, and in life" (The Aspen Institute, 2017, p. 1). Finally, the Assessment Work Group is a new partnership between the Collaborative for Academic, Social, and Emotional Learning (CASEL), the RAND Corporation, Harvard University, the CORE Districts, Transforming Education, and XSEL Labs to establish practical social and emotional competence assessments of preschool to high school youth in and out of school ("Assessment Work Group," n.d.).

OUT-OF-SCHOOL TIME SETTINGS AS CONTEXTS FOR SEL

In an expanding field characterized by numerous frameworks and terms (Berg et al., 2017), it is important to define what is meant by SEL. We define SEL as the processes by which children and adults:

> ... acquire and apply the knowledge, skills, and attitudes that can enhance personal development, establish satisfying interpersonal relationships, and lead to effective and ethical work and productivity. These include the competencies to understand and manage emotions, set and achieve positive goals, feel and show caring and concern for others, establish and maintain positive relationships, and make responsible decisions. (Weissberg, Durlak, Domitrovich, & Gullotta, 2015, p. 6)

In the context of a growing SEL movement, this volume makes a major contribution to the field. The chapters show the important role out-of-school time (OST) plays in developing social and emotional competencies for all young people and highlights that OST has much to offer the future of the SEL field. At the same time, the volume represents a timely opportunity for the OST community to take advantage of the collective knowledge available on SEL.

As a starting point, the chapters in this volume contribute to our understanding of a broad and modern view of education. The volume makes it clear that OST staff understand the important role of SEL in children's development. Indeed, OST providers have historically maintained a broad view of education as a way to help young people navigate their social environment and actively develop the skills needed to function successfully in a multicultural and changing world (e.g., Section I of this volume, "SEL in OST: Background and Frameworks"; Blyth, Chapter 2, this volume; Devaney & Moroney, Chapter 1, this volume). Adults in OST and school settings agree that these skills are needed for young people to be successful in school, college, career, and in life.

It is also important to note that SEL is a field anchored by strong research. Several of the chapters show that OST settings are important contexts for SEL by expanding and applying this scientific knowledge base (e.g., Section II of this volume, "Research-Informed SEL Practice"; Noam, Allen, & Triggs, Chapter 14, this volume). OST's historic emphasis on positive youth development (PYD), where all young people are viewed as assets to be nurtured, fits well with the goals of SEL (e.g., Devaney & Moroney, Chapter 1, this volume; Taylor, Oberle, Durlak, & Weissberg, 2017). Specifically, the focus on whole-child development, fostering strengths such as character, citizenship, and positive cultural identity, supportive relationships, and equitable learning opportunities cultivated through active and experiential learning make OST programs well suited for promoting SEL. As Blyth (Chapter 2, this volume) notes, both youth development and SEL programming enhance the competence of young people so they are better able to manage themselves, engage in constructive relationships, and contribute responsibly to society.

However, as the field of SEL expands across OST and other settings, it is critical that a systemic approach be taken to provide intentionally aligned and coherent SEL practices across contexts. Elsewhere we have described systemic SEL as a multi-layered system of programming and relationships that fosters and integrates SEL synergistically across contexts and over time. These conditions are enhanced through the use and continuous improvement of evidence-based practices that actively involve all youth, reinforce social and emotional competencies, and create equitable learning opportunities across school, family, and community settings (Mahoney, Weissberg, et al., 2018).

From a systemic view, partnerships and relationships are at the core of effective SEL. A shared focus on SEL opens up a point of communication and collaboration in, for example, a school–community partnership. Aligning goals, strategies, and practices across settings also helps to avoid fragmented or even contradictory experiences that can diminish efforts to foster social and emotional competence. As such, attention should not be focused on which setting is best for SEL, but rather how different settings can work together to best implement SEL (see, for example, Brohawn and Traill [Chapter 7, this volume] on the ExpandED Schools partnership model).

CHALLENGES AND OPPORTUNITIES FOR THE FIELD

This volume describes several important challenges and opportunities for the field of SEL. Next we comment on four of these areas. Our insights reflect learnings from this volume, past research and practical experience in the field, and ongoing collaboration in the Partnership for Social and Emotional Learning Initiative (PSELI), supported by the Wallace Foundation ("Social and Emotional Learning," 2018).

1. *SEL goals are in line with the PYD perspective, but the approaches to learning and skill development in OST and school settings are often different.* OST settings do not have the constraints of a time-consuming school curriculum, and youth often participate on a voluntary basis. As a result, a youth-centered approach to programming that emphasizes informal learning processes has been common. This approach emphasizes learning through social interaction and relationships that take place in the context of active and experiential learning projects and activities. In contrast, schools more often foster SEL intentionally through explicit instruction and more broadly through academic instruction and improvements in climate and culture.

   The different approaches to learning in OST programs and schools need not be points of contention or conflict. In fact, a key challenge and opportunity for the field involves establishing coordinated OST and school programming. Each setting has a great deal to offer the other, and the complementary nature of these settings represents an opportunity for connection and collaboration to improve the lives of all young people through SEL programs and practices. However, this requires that staff in the two settings understand, respect, and support their different approaches to learning and development (e.g., Brohawn & Traill, Chapter 7, this volume). Joint professional development and programming—with school and OST staff working side by side—may provide opportunities for schools and OST programs to align practices around common goals in ways that produce more positive outcomes for young people. It may also provide opportunities for OST and school staff to discuss shared data; learn from each other, and about each young person's strengths and needs across contexts; and support each other's efforts to continuously improve. From a systemic perspective, an aligned and collaborative partnership guided by a shared vision, common language, and common emphases for SEL will support implementation and achieve developmental outcomes most effectively (CASEL, 2017).

2. *Regardless of context, SEL programs and practices need to be intentional to be fully effective.* Historically, OST settings have maintained a focus on developing and improving high-quality programming at the point of service by creating safe, supportive, and productive environments where youth can thrive (e.g., Smith et al., 2016). High-quality OST settings are, in turn, linked to positive developmental outcomes for young people (e.g., Vandell, Larson, Mahoney, & Watts, 2015).

   However, a focus on PYD and point-of-service quality may not be intentional about SEL (Devaney & Moroney, Chapter 1, this volume), and being intentional is critical to program effectiveness (Blyth, Chapter 2, this volume). For example, a meta-analysis of OST programs and SEL (Durlak et al., 2010) found that only SAFE programs with a combination of sequenced and developmentally appropriate activities, opportunities for active learning and feedback, and a focused and explicit effort to promote SEL were associated with significant improvements in self-perceptions and bonding to school, positive social behaviors, school grades, and levels of academic achievement, and with significant reductions in problem behaviors. Chapters in Section III of this volume, "SEL Systems and Policy," describe an evolution in some of our large OST systems from a focus on quality programming, *per se,* to quality with explicit efforts to foster social and emotional skills in youth and in adults.

3. *To have a consistent and coherent approach to SEL, evidence-based programs and practices should be used and aligned across settings.* Several chapters in Section II describe a growing awareness that developing social and emotional competence in OST settings requires a clear and consistent language of SEL and a corresponding set of evidence-based practices (e.g., Brackenridge, Chapter 11, this volume). There are relatively few evidence-based SEL programs designed specifically for OST settings (Jones et al., 2017). SEL programs can and have been carried out effectively in OST settings (e.g., Laird, Logan, & Meste, this volume), but they may be less common due to the more informal and project-based approach to learning in OST settings, the diversity of OST program types, and the fact that school-based SEL programs have received greater attention from researchers. It may also be that OST practitioners have viewed youth development as a proxy for SEL and so believe they are already carrying out this work. In addition, finding the resources to implement developmentally appropriate curricula and professional develop-

ment for school-based SEL programs may be challenging for OST settings. For example, OST programs often serve a broad age range of youth simultaneously with variable attendance patterns. They also tend to experience high rates of staff turnover and may operate with modest budgets. Given these challenges, some OST settings may benefit from a flexible set of evidence-based practices.

To that end, other evidence-based approaches have been used in OST contexts to promote SEL. For example, several of the chapters in Section II discuss the Weikart Center's model for continuous quality improvement at the point of service (Smith et al., 2012). Likewise, in the PSELI, some OST programs are using a version of the Weikart Center's Youth Program Quality Assessment tool that includes strategies designed to support SEL (e.g., Bednar et al., this volume; Smith et al., 2016).

4. *SEL programs and practices require professional development for adults.* Many of the chapters in this volume underscore the need for adults who interact with children to have social and emotional skills that permit them to effectively communicate, teach, and model the competencies they want children to develop. However, some OST staff may lack social and emotional competence themselves, the knowledge and skills needed to foster SEL in their youth, or both.

   Like some school-day teachers (Schonert-Reichl, Kitil, & Hanson-Peterson, 2017), OST staff often do not receive regular opportunities for the SEL-focused professional development (PD) needed to foster adult social and emotional competence. Unlike school-day teachers, there is no national credentialing system of education and training for OST staff (Mahoney & Warner, 2014). Existing approaches to PD in OST settings must also account for staff turnover, a part-time workforce, and variable youth attendance. Despite some of these barriers, chapters in this volume describe approaches to SEL-focused PD and professional learning communities for the OST workforce (e.g., Brackenridge, Chapter 11, this volume; Brohawn & Traill, Chapter 7, this volume). In this work, efforts to use shared data to guide the PD and continuously improve programming are critical (e.g., Noam, Allen, & Triggs, Chapter 14, this volume).

The chapters in this volume emphasize that effective partnerships, relationships, and intentional competence-enhancement efforts are at the heart of well-implemented, effective, and sustained SEL. Best research and practice suggests that these are critical components to benefit young people. This volume lays the groundwork for critical research, practice, and policy directions to establish beneficial, coordinated, and intentional SEL efforts across OST settings, whether partnered with schools or as stand-alone programs. These programs can provide young people with the opportunities they need today to become healthy and productive adult citizens who contribute positively to the world of tomorrow.

—Joseph L. Mahoney
Senior Research Scientist

—Roger P. Weissberg
Chief Knowledge Officer,
Collaborative for Academic, Social, and Emotional Learning (CASEL)

REFERENCES

Assessment Work Group. (n.d.). Retrieved from the Collaborative for Academic, Social, and Emotional Learning website: https://casel.org/assessment-work-group/

Belfield, C., Bowden, B., Klapp, A., Levin, H., Shand, R., & Zander, S. (2015). *The economic value of social and emotional learning.* New York, NY: Center for Benefit-Cost Studies in Education.

Berg, J., Osher, D., Same, M. R., Nolan, E., Benson, D., & Jacobs, N. (2017, December 18). *Identifying, defining, and measuring social and emotional competencies.* Washington, DC: American Institutes for Research. Retrieved from https://www.air.org/resource/identifying-defining-and-measuring-social-and-emotional-competencies

Bridgeland, J., Bruce, M., & Hariharan, A. (2013). *The missing piece: A national teacher survey on how social and emotional learning can empower children and transform schools.* Washington, DC: Civic Enterprises.

Collaborative for Academic, Social, and Emotional Learning. (2017). *Key insights from the Collaborating Districts Initiative.* Chicago, IL: Author.

DePaoli, J. L., Atwell, M., & Bridgeland, J. (2017). *Ready to lead: A national principal survey on how social and emotional learning can prepare children and transform schools.* Washington DC: Civic Enterprises and Hart Research Associates for CASEL.

Durlak, J. A., Domitrovich, C. E., Weissberg, R. W., & Gullotta, T. P. (Eds.). (2015). *Handbook of social and emotional learning: Research and practice.* New York, NY: The Guilford Press.

Durlak, J. A., Weissberg, R. P., Dymnicki, A. B., Taylor, R. D., & Schellinger, K. B. (2011). The impact of enhancing students' social and emotional learning: A meta-analysis of school-based universal interventions. *Child Development, 82,* 405–432. doi:10.1111/j.1467-8624.2010.01564.x

Durlak, J. A., Weissberg, R. P., & Pachan, M. (2010). A meta-analysis of after-school programs that seek to promote personal and social skills in children and adolescents. *American Journal of Community Psychology, 45,* 294–309. doi:10.1007/s10464-010-9300-6

Jones, S., Brush, K., Bailey, R., Brion-Meisels, G., McIntyre, J., Kahn, J., . . . Stickle, L. (2017). *Navigating social and emotional learning from the inside out: Looking inside and across 25 leading SEL programs: A practical resource for schools and OST providers (elementary school focus).* New York, NY: Wallace Foundation. Retrieved from http://www.wallacefoundation.org/knowledge-center/Documents/Navigating-Social-and-Emotional-Learning-from-the-Inside-Out.pdf

Mahoney, J. L., Durlak, J. A., & Weissberg, R. W. (2018). *An update on social and emotional learning outcome research.* Manuscript in preparation.

Mahoney, J. L., & Warner, G. (2014). Editors' notes: The development of the afterschool workforce. *New Directions for Youth Development, 144,* 1–10.

Mahoney, J. L., Weissberg, R. P., Shriver, T. P., Greenberg, M. A., Bouffard, S., & Borowski, T. (2018). *A systemic approach to social and emotional learning.* Manuscript in preparation.

Price, O. A. (2015). Financing and funding for SEL initiatives. In J. A. Durlak, C. E. Domitrovich, R. P. Weissberg, & T. P. Gullotta (Eds.), *The handbook of social and emotional learning: Research and practice* (pp. 114–131). New York, NY: The Guilford Press.

Schonert-Reichl, K. A., Kitil, M. J., & Hanson-Peterson, J. (2017). *To reach the students, teach the teachers: A national scan of teacher preparation and social and emotional learning.* Vancouver, BC: University of British Columbia.

Social and Emotional Learning. (2018). Retrieved from The Wallace Foundation website: http://www.wallacefoundation.org/how-we-work/our-work/pages/social-emotional-learning.aspx

Smith, C., Akiva, T., Sugar, S., Lo, Y. J., Frank, K. A., Peck, S. C., . . . Devaney, T. (2012). *Continuous quality improvement in afterschool settings: Impact findings from the Youth Program Quality Intervention study.* Washington, DC: The Forum for Youth Investment.

Smith, C., McGovern, G., Peck, S. C., Larson, R., Hillaker, B., & Roy, L. (2016). *Preparing youth to thrive: Methodology and findings from the social and emotional learning challenge.* Washington, DC: Forum for Youth Investment.

Taylor, R., Oberle, E., Durlak, J. A., & Weissberg, R. P. (2017). Promoting positive youth development through school-based social and emotional learning interventions: A meta-analysis of follow-up effects. *Child Development, 88,* 1156–1181. doi:10.1111/cdev.12864

The Aspen Institute. (2017). *About the Commission.* Washington, DC: Author. Retrieved from https://assets.aspeninstitute.org/content/uploads/2017/12/FINAL_About-the-Commission_11.2.17.pdf

Vandell, D. L., Larson, R. W., Mahoney, J. L., & Watts, T. R. (2015). Children's activities. In W. F. Overton & P. C. M. Molenaar (Series Eds.), *Handbook of child psychology and developmental science (7th edition). Volume 4: Ecological settings and processes in developmental systems* (M. H. Bornstein & T. Leventhal, Vol. Eds., pp. 305–344). New York, NY: Wiley.

Weissberg, R. P., Durlak, J. D., Domitrovich, C. E., & Gullotta, T. P. (2015). Social and emotional learning: Past, present, and future. In J. A. Durlak, C. E. Domitrovich, R. P. Weissberg, & T. P. Gullotta (Eds.), *Handbook of social and emotional learning: Research and practice* (pp. 3–19). New York, NY: The Guilford Press.

SECTION I

SEL IN OST: BACKGROUND AND FRAMEWORKS

CHAPTER 1

FOCUSING AND FRAMING SEL IN OST

An Introduction to the Volume

Elizabeth Devaney and Deborah Moroney

This is an exciting time for the out-of-school time (OST) field. It seems like everywhere you turn, school staff, community leaders, physical and mental health service providers—and even, dare we say it, some politicians—are talking about the importance of the very skills OST has been championing for decades. Rather than having to make the case for how we support academic achievement, we are now in a position to communicate how we can contribute to, and even lead, efforts to support social and emotional learning (SEL). All of a sudden, the world has finally realized that in order for our children (and, quite frankly, our adults) to thrive, and for our society to function, we need to be able to take on other perspectives, rather than dismissing them, when someone has a different point of view. We need to be able to identify our hot buttons and use strategies to manage them. We need to be able to communicate, work in teams, set goals, manage our time, and pick ourselves up when we fail. This is not new information for many

Social and Emotional Learning in Out-of-School Time, pages 3–14

of us who have been working to support the development of these skills in young people for many years. Nonetheless, we have work to do, both to build upon our strong history of supporting youth development, and to share our story so we can be leaders in the SEL movement.

We chose to bring together the narratives in this volume precisely because of this growing SEL movement. While it is, in many ways, a good thing that SEL has begun to receive the attention it deserves, drawing both focus and funding to such an important body of work, there is also a downside. We see a danger that SEL will be perceived as simply the latest trend in education—something that could disappear at the whim of key leaders, rather than something that is foundational and historically embedded in the work of high-quality educators and youth workers. As we have written about elsewhere (Devaney & Moroney, 2017; Moroney & Devaney, 2017), the OST field was founded on a youth development approach that focuses on creating environments where youth can be the drivers of their own development and success. We believe it is essential to have a conversation about how SEL fits within that youth development philosophy. In particular, it is essential to understand what lessons we can draw from more than two decades of research and practice in creating positive environments for youth that contribute to their overall development, and how that can translate into high-quality SEL. This book is an opportunity to do just that—to reexamine, reframe, reenergize, and perhaps remind those both in and out of the field that OST is deeply rooted in practices that promote SEL.

FRAMEWORKS AND DEFINITIONS

We are often asked to help sort out the various definitions and frameworks related to SEL in OST, such as 21st-century competencies, grit, growth mindsets, noncognitive factors, character, foundations for young adult success, and so on. We wanted to share some of that thinking before readers dive into the chapters that explore or exemplify these issues more deeply.

In the OST field, there have historically been two approaches to defining the skills and competencies that OST programs promote and foster. One approach has been for researchers and thought leaders to study, frame, and define skills and competencies in a way that is accessible to practitioners and researchers, so they can find a conceptualization that fits their mission and vision for how to support positive development. The value in using one of these frameworks is that the developers have taken the time and care to ensure the skills and competencies are clearly defined, grounded in research, and malleable through practice. There is also some benefit to a field sharing a common framework for communication, workforce mobility, and general field consistency. Finally, there is a practical efficiency in picking something that already exists, in order to avoid wasting valuable resources on a framework development process.

A second approach has been for systems and programs to develop and fine-tune their own, localized skills framework, often based on the nationally developed versions. There are quite a few examples of this approach in this volume. There are also benefits to this approach. Bringing stakeholders together to sort through skills and competencies and determine their value in a local context and program vision builds engagement and buy in. This approach works best when locally grown framework developers take some time to crosswalk their framework with an established one (e.g., CASEL's framework) to check that the skills they have identified in their framework are grounded in research, clearly and accurately defined, and malleable. Regardless of the approach, frameworks are important because they are fundamentally communication vehicles for system-building efforts and have great value in that role.

We are not the only ones thinking about these issues. One of the authors in this volume, Dale Blyth, is leading an effort to sort through the frameworks dilemma as part of a national SEL Assessment Workgroup led by CASEL (Blyth & Borowski, 2018). In addition, our colleagues at American Institutes for Research (AIR), Juliette Berg and David Osher, explored over 130 social and emotional competency frameworks from across multiple fields of study and made some important contributions about where there is overlap and where there are some pretty significant gaps in how we are thinking about skill building (Berg et al., 2017). This study highlights just how complicated it can be to identify key skills to focus on, choose a framework, and communicate to and gain buy in from key stakeholders across a community.

Perhaps controversially, we are not in the camp that believes the field as a whole needs one framework. Although that would be convenient for clarity, it would take away significantly from the various ways in which OST practitioners, programs, and systems get to the SEL table. In addition, trying to reach common agreement about a framework can sometimes paralyze the work, and can even build siloes as people become focused on defending their specific framework to the detriment of finding common ground. However, we do share the belief that a program or system of programs will benefit from a framework for visioning, communication, and ideally, implementation.

You can see by the framing of this volume that we chose to use the term SEL to talk about the *process* of social and emotional skill building, and that we talk about social and emotional skills or competencies as the *outcomes* of that process. We based our framing and presentation on the recent Wallace Foundation-funded study that found the term SEL to be the most widely used and accessible, and on our own experience that it is being widely used in practice (Loeb, Tipton, & Wagner, 2016). We are not dismissing the many other valid framings, and we hope you see a variety of approaches depicted in this volume. Ultimately, what we are talking about is skill building—creating environments that allow young people to develop core skills they need to be successful in life. The work Stephanie Jones and colleagues are doing around kernels of practice will help us achieve this goal (Kahn, Brush, & Bailey, 2017). In fact, it is an essential next step if we are to be successful.

The second big question we get asked is how SEL relates to youth development. In Chapter 2, Dale Blyth gives his take on SEL and youth development, along with some background on the development of the field. He describes what he sees as the differences between SEL and youth development and discusses how OST programs may need to reconcile those differences in order to do both well.

We have also done a bit of writing and thinking on this (e.g., Devaney & Moroney, 2017; Moroney & Devaney, 2017) and we share our perspective here. A youth development approach fosters a safe and supportive environment, where relationships can flourish and youth can engage in learning experiences of all kinds (e.g., science, technology, engineering, and mathematics, or STEM; SEL; arts) to explore their interests. These are the absolute foundations of a high-quality youth development program. Many of the practices that OST providers employ in implementing high-quality youth development programs promote social and emotional skill building. For example, much of the STEM programming in OST settings requires hands-on exploration and problem solving in small groups. When done well, these types of activities allow young people to develop relationship- and team-building skills, promote critical thinking, and foster problem solving (Moroney & Devaney, 2017). There are dozens of examples like this of how SEL is perhaps *unintentionally* happening in OST programs through high-quality youth development practice.

Going forward as a field, we believe we need to make SEL an *intentional practice* built into high-quality youth development programs to support participants' social and emotional skill building. This could take the form of intentional SEL instruction, the same way we would recommend building STEM or arts into a high-quality youth development program. Alternatively, it could take the form of embedded SEL practices, infused throughout any content. OST programs can weave in both approaches to intentionally include SEL in their offerings. In fact, OST programs are especially well poised to foster SEL (and many already do) because high-quality OST environments are built to support youth development. However, we want to ensure that OST systems acknowledge that in order for their staff to intentionally foster SEL, they will have to invest in staff preparation. Many of the chapters in this volume present innovative strategies for supporting staff in implementing SEL in high-quality OST programs that take a youth development approach.

OVERVIEW OF THE VOLUME

This volume was designed to intentionally address the issues we raise in this introduction from a variety of perspectives. There are chapters written by practitioners, policymakers, and researchers. By large city-system builders and individual program leaders. By veterans in the OST field and those who are newly minted. By those serving preschool children through high school-age youth. By those in small and large cities on each coast and in the middle of the country. By those who are leading large grant-making initiatives and those who are working on their own. Because the authors and what they write about are so varied, so too is the tone, style, and information each chapter contains. Rather than try to correct this, we have opted to allow this diversity of tone and style to serve as a reminder of—and tribute to—the variety and diversity of the OST field. The breadth and variety of the book is designed to highlight how widespread SEL is in OST, and how the approaches and even intended outcomes vary, while still driving toward the same result: improved social and emotional development for success in school, work, and life.

The book is divided into four sections. The first section serves as an introduction, discussing the founding of the OST field and how it has shifted to embrace an SEL lens that is grounded deeply in its youth development roots. The next three sections address SEL practice, policy, and research in the OST field. Readers will find on-the-ground stories about how individual programs and systems alike have incorporated SEL strategies. They will also get a bigger picture perspective on how SEL and OST align with other movements like college and career readiness, school-based SEL, and quality improvement. Finally, readers will find chapters that touch on how OST is tackling the sticky question of how to measure our success in building young people's social and emotional skills.

Section I: SEL in OST—Background and Frameworks

In the second chapter of the introductory section, Dale Blyth takes us through the foundations of the OST field, highlighting the evolution of SEL in OST from skills that were primarily "caught" through effective instruction and well-facilitated programs to skills that are now intentionally "taught." He talks about the importance of both approaches and offers a framework for how OST programs might think about this caught/taught distinction. We hope readers take from this section a grounding in youth development, an understanding of how SEL is evolving in our field, and some new (and potentially boundary-pushing) ways to think about the intersection of positive youth development and SEL.

Section II: Research-Informed SEL Practice

In Section II, leaders from five OST programs and systems share how they are approaching SEL implementation. Each chapter offers a slightly different perspective. Leaders from the Greater Rochester After-School Alliance and WINGS for Kids talk about the youngest children, focusing on how they have built SEL programming for elementary youth, including prekindergarten youth. In Rochester, the SEL work has evolved organically out of the city's intensive quality improvement system. At WINGS, SEL has always been an intentional focus from the day the program opened its doors. Next, the Providence After School Alliance and Boston After School & Beyond describe how SEL has become a core component of their summer learning programs for middle school youth. They explore how SEL and STEM are intertwined and the importance of hands-on learning to both STEM and social and emotional skill development. Leaders from After School Matters in Chicago then discuss their high school system and how they see SEL as an important aspect of their work to help high school youth discover and practice their interests in preparation for the future. To round out the age spectrum, the next chapter turns to college and career pathways and discusses how the American Youth Policy Forum and others have envisioned SEL as a component of preparing youth for their postsecondary lives. Finally, in the last chapter in this section, ExpandED Schools shares the evolution of its model, which pairs schools and community partners for a full day of learning, using SEL as a key strategy to build common language and strategies among school-day and OST staff. Readers should finish this section feeling energized by the wide variety of approaches OST programs and systems are using to implement SEL, and struck by the common themes that emerge despite their variety of approaches. Most notably, we think readers will see SEL as both embedded in and evolving out of quality improvement initiatives.

Section III: SEL Systems and Policy

Section III moves from practice to systems change and policy development. In this section, both system and policy are defined broadly. That is, we look at both citywide and statewide systems, as well as capacity building and funding networks. Likewise, the policy discussions include both federal and state political contexts, but also look at how we approach and think about cross-sector collaboration, systemic changes that influence practice, and key influences on policy at all levels. The first chapter in Section III describes how the New York City Department of Youth and Community Development (DYCD) has developed a common framework that successfully incorporates SEL while honoring DYCD's core values of youth development and youth leadership. The framework has provided an umbrella under which all of DYCD's programming, professional development, and evaluation efforts can be organized. The next chapter focuses on how the Connecticut Afterschool Network has incorporated SEL into its statewide efforts to drive quality improvement and professional development and gives examples and perspective on other statewide after-school networks grappling with this work. Next, the Partnership for Children and Youth describes a technical assistance system they built (360°/365°) to provide supports for staff on a variety of topics, including SEL. They share how they used professional learning communities as the catalyst for in-school and OST professionals to share effective SEL practices. The Afterschool Alliance discusses opportunities and challenges for SEL in OST from a policy perspective and examines how federal and state policies facilitate the implementation of SEL in OST. Finally, funders from Grantmakers for Thriving Youth share their interest in promoting collaboration across the school day and OST to successfully support social and emotional skill development, as well as lessons learned from their work to date. We hope that readers will come away from this section with a better understanding of how SEL fits into the larger context of citywide and statewide OST systems, as well as core policy developments and professional development efforts that are leading to greater connections between in-school and OST practitioners.

Section IV: SEL Research, Measurement, and Assessment

The last section in the book focuses on measurement—specifically, how the OST field is grappling with the key questions of how to assess and measure our success in supporting social and emotional skill building in OST programs. The section looks first at measurement of adult outcomes (i.e., improved instructional practices) through a description of the David P. Weikart Center for Youth Program Quality's work over the past decade and beyond. We then turn to measurement of youth outcomes (i.e., improved social and emotional competencies), with a chapter from the Youth Development Executives of King County and AIR, which have collectively developed an assessment process for measuring social and emotional competencies in older youth. Finally, leaders from the Program in Education,

Afterschool and Resiliency (PEAR) discuss a systems approach to measurement that looks at the uses of assessment data and discusses how to create a comprehensive measurement system that promotes continuous improvement, helps to understand individual youth, and examines summative outcomes. We hope readers walk away from this section able to ponder some of the key questions in determining whether and how to assess SEL practice and participants' social and emotional competencies, and knowing more about existing tools, methods, and resources for employing measurement strategies in support of continuous quality improvement and improved youth outcomes. This section barely scratches the surface of this big and important topic in the SEL field, and we recognize that many others are thinking and writing about assessment. For example, as noted earlier, CASEL is leading a national work group on the topic (see measuringsel.casel.org) and AIR has created the *Ready to Assess* suite of tools to help practitioners determine how and when to begin assessing social and emotional skills (Moroney & McGarrah, 2015).

The volume ends with a conclusion from Karen Pittman that serves as both a summative statement and a charge for the field as we look to the future. In this closing, Pittman encourages us to learn from other fields and disciplines but also demonstrate and own what OST practitioners do well by defining the "what" and "how" of our work.

Core Themes of the Volume

As noted earlier, one of the key reasons for developing this volume was to capture and synthesize what SEL looks like in OST, and how it might differ from SEL in formal settings. We knew that programs and systems across the country had begun this work and were grappling with how to define, shape, implement, and measure their SEL approaches as the rest of the country caught up with the importance of SEL as a foundation for youth success. We have talked to colleagues, heard presentations, and been involved in various projects across the country. We weren't exactly sure what we would learn as we developed this volume, but when we read through the chapters as they began to come in, we observed that most chapters emphasized the importance of adult SEL as a precursor to being effective in implementing SEL practices and programs with youth. We think this is an important contribution and likely key to the success of local SEL efforts. For the most part, the chapter authors emphasize a strengths-based (as opposed to deficit-based) approach in their SEL efforts. This is congruent with the youth development movement we discuss earlier and also cornerstone to high quality, universal SEL. In the following section we describe five core themes that clearly emerged for how SEL has evolved in the OST field. We discuss each below briefly and then offer, in a limitations section, some key ideas that did not end up as central to the volume.

- *Focusing on social and emotional skill development is good for everyone.* Although OST programs have been fostering social and emotional skill building through high-quality programming for years, those outcomes have been hard to define. For at least the past decade, OST programs have set aside those goals and spent more staff and leadership time understanding, defining, and thinking about how their programs support academic achievement and success in school. The argument has often gone something like this: OST programs that use high-quality youth development practices stimulate youth interest, engage youth more in learning, promote curiosity, perhaps build confidence and a sense of efficacy, and therefore, improve academic achievement. By necessity, this emphasis on academic outcomes has meant that programs were not thinking about, or spending time improving, how they supported social and emotional outcomes. That has now changed. The research clearly shows that social and emotional competencies are critical for success in life. By incorporating SEL into OST more intentionally, we are now building opportunities for youth to develop skills that will serve them well across the developmental pathway and especially as they move into college and career, and that's good for young people.
- *The field's foundation in youth development has made SEL a natural fit.* For most OST practitioners, SEL has been an easy sell. Unlike school-day staff, who may feel that SEL is a new or unexpected part of their job, most OST practitioners are relieved to finally be able to acknowledge that the development of social and emotional skills is not only an acceptable side effect of high-quality programming, but a legitimate and important outcome in and of itself.
- *SEL is widely supported and provides opportunities for alignment between sectors.* Supporters of education and OST, including funders, policymakers, intermediaries, and capacity-building organizations, have an emerging but clear agenda to ensure that all children and youth have opportunities for SEL in school and in OST. There are now multiple initiatives across the country at the local and national level—several of which are shared in this book—that are building bridges between schools/school systems and OST using SEL as a catalyst. This shared vision for positive development and common language provides the opportunity for professionals across sectors (education, workforce, OST, mental health, to name a few) to create a common agenda and mechanisms to coordinate on behalf of children and families.

- *OST builds young people's social and emotional competencies through experiential learning and practices.* The practice chapters clearly show that OST practitioners to date have been more likely to use instructional practices than to implement specific SEL programs or curricula. In many cases, this has evolved out of the OST field's preference for hands-on learning that takes place through play, exploration, high-interest activities, and practical applications of academic content. A few programs (e.g., ExpandED Schools) have begun to explore implementation of evidence-based SEL programs (e.g., Second Step). In most cases, however, this is because of a partnership with a school where SEL curricula may be valued over instructional practices.
- *SEL practices have been honed through quality improvement initiatives.* In many cases, the evidence-based practices that most practitioners appear to be using to foster social and emotional skill development have emerged organically out of quality improvement initiatives. Almost all of the practice and several of the systems chapters touch in one way or another on the evolution from quality improvement efforts focused on intentional, high-quality youth development practices to SEL efforts focused on intentional, high-quality SEL instruction. There is a natural connection here, in that many of the practices these quality improvement systems promote are also strategies and practices that can promote social and emotional skill building. In fact, Chapter 15 tackles this subject head on by describing how the Weikart Center for Youth Program Quality studied SEL instructional practices in OST, connected them to their program quality assessments, and have now created a new observational assessment focused on the intersection between quality and SEL.
- *The focus on SEL has started to shift practice.* This change in emphasis to more intentionally focus on SEL practice and measure social and emotional outcomes is leading to changes in how OST programs and providers approach skill building. Rather than focusing solely on academics (knowing that social and emotional skill building was happening as a side effect), practitioners are now intentionally building strategies into their programs that foster these skills. They are also measuring how well those strategies appear to be working by looking at improvements in social and emotional competencies in youth participants. At the same time, OST systems are fostering intentional capacity-building efforts around SEL. And yet, despite all of these new efforts and the intentional focus on SEL, it is clear from reading the chapters in this volume that, ultimately, SEL in OST still comes from a foundation in positive youth development practice and the creation of high-quality environments and opportunities.

Limitations

As we have described, the volume is rich with important information on the state of SEL in OST, but it is only a first step in the conversation toward supporting all young people in their social and emotional development, both in schools and in OST settings. We acknowledge the presentation of SEL practices in this volume focus primarily at the systems and program level and on the adults who work within them. This was intentional in order to capture the big picture and core themes for how SEL is emerging in OST programs across the country. But we recognize that because of that choice, youth voice is not represented in this sea of adult perspectives on SEL. Further, we do not explore deeply or fully the SEL experience for young people by race and ethnicity, primary language, gender identity, or ability. In fact, current SEL frameworks and associated practices are inadequate in addressing SEL for all youth across all settings, and so this is where the movement needs to focus (Berg et al., 2017). Secondly, we know that SEL happens in the context of families, schools, and communities where youth are living, learning, and playing. This volume focuses on SEL practice in OST programs and systems, but we acknowledge that the primary actors in a young person's SEL are their family members, peers, and other adults in their lives and are a reflection of where they live. Finally, as Blyth points out in the following chapter, SEL is criticized as having a dominant culture lens on youth experiences and development. We assert that many of the chapter authors in this volume explore and implement SEL in a participatory way with youth, families, schools, and communities but acknowledge that the field as a whole should continue to push a social justice lens on how we describe and implement practices that build all people's positive development, across settings, and with youth as the drivers and agents of their own trajectory.

CONCLUSION

It has been our privilege to work with the authors in this volume, to gather their stories and hear about the work they are doing to intentionally build SEL into their programs, systems, policies, and research. We think they collectively tell an important story about how SEL has evolved in the OST field, and where it is going. We come away from reading these chapters energized by the work, and with a clear understanding that our next big step as a field is to focus on the adults—to dive deep on what SEL practice looks like in OST programs, and to prepare staff through a concerted professional development effort to implement them. Happy reading!

REFERENCES

Berg, J., Osher, D., Same, M., Nolan, E., Benson, D., & Jacobs, N. (2017). *Identifying, defining, and measuring social and emotional competencies.* Washington, DC: American Institutes for Research.

Blyth, D., & Borowski, T. (2018). *Frameworks, frameworks everywhere—What are practitioners to do?* Retrieved from https://measuringsel.casel.org/frameworks-frameworks-everywhere-practitioners/

Devaney, E., & Moroney, D. (2018). Out-of-school-time learning and 21st century skills: Building on the past to shape the future. In H. J. Malone & T. Donahue (Eds.), *The growing out-of-school time field: Past, present, and future* (pp. 245–265). Charlotte, NC: Information Age.

Kahn, J., Brush, K., & Bailey, R. (2017). *Kernels of practice for SEL: Low-cost, low-burden strategies.* Cambridge, MA: Harvard Graduate School of Education.

Loeb, P., Tipton, S., & Wagner, E. (2016). *Social and emotional learning: Feedback and communications insights from the field* [Slide presentation]. New York, NY: The Wallace Foundation. Retrieved from http://www.wallacefoundation.org/knowledge-center/pages/sel-feedback-and-communications-insights-from-the-field.aspx

Moroney, D., & Devaney, E. (2017). Ready to implement? How the out-of-school time workforce can support character development through social and emotional learning: A review of the literature and future directions. *The Journal of Character Education, 13*(1), 67–89.

Moroney, D., & McGarrah, M. (2015). *Are you ready to assess social and emotional development?* Retrieved from https://www.air.org/resource/are-you-ready-assess-social-and-emotional-development

CHAPTER 2

THE CHALLENGES OF BLENDING YOUTH DEVELOPMENT AND SOCIAL AND EMOTIONAL LEARNING

Getting More Intentional About How Competencies Are Both Caught and Taught in Out-of-School Time

Dale A. Blyth

The out-of-school time (OST) field is indeed at a pivotal moment in history, as noted in the first chapter and in Devaney and Moroney (2018). As the visibility and value of social and emotional learning grows, OST must work to both position itself as the major contributor to the development of social and emotional competencies for youth that it has always been as well as work to improve the intentional ways it does so.

Both a youth development (YD) approach to practice and a social and emotional learning (SEL) commitment to building the social and emotional

Social and Emotional Learning in Out-of-School Time, pages 15–31

competencies that all young people need are essential components of high-quality learning and development opportunities. The fields of YD and SEL present a logical, complementary fit—especially in OST. There is much overlap and agreement between the two. In practice, however, the relationship between SEL and YD can become complicated by challenges arising from five differences—differences in (a) underlying philosophy and values; (b) the settings from which they primarily emerged; (c) how learning and development are approached; (d) how they deal with culture, race, and context; and (e) how they typically see and use data. These differences are not barriers but challenges that both create new opportunities for demonstrating the value of YD as well as create ways to improve OST practices.

This chapter is about how the OST field and its programs and practices can capitalize on the new energy around SEL and become more intentional about combining SEL with the YD practices that have come to shape OST. It offers the reflections from my many years of diverse experience as a university educator, researcher, program director, trainer, field builder, writer, volunteer, and administrator of YD programs in OST. I am deeply invested in this work and the young people it impacts. This chapter offers reflections on how OST systems and programs can get optimally intentional about building young people's social and emotional competencies as a central part of their practice, using the best of both YD and SEL approaches. In doing this, I believe the systems and programs in the OST field will find new ways to increase and balance intentionality around how these competencies are both *caught* and *taught*.

THE IMPORTANCE OF BOTH "TAUGHT" AND "CAUGHT"

The metaphor of skills being taught and caught highlights two critical dimensions of learning that are both present in the acquisition of most competencies: intentionality and experience. In simple terms, taught refers to intentional efforts to pass on knowledge from one, usually older, experienced person to a younger, less knowledgeable person. Commonly the young person is tested to make sure that the intended subject matter has been learned. Caught, on the other hand, refers to learning discovered from doing—learning extracted from personal experiences both accidental and intentionally planned to provoke learning. Taught places more emphasis on teaching content and caught emphasizes creating opportunities for youth to catch or build skills. Effective learning techniques—and most effective practitioners, whether teachers or youth workers—use both processes. Attending a summer camp provides good examples. Much adult effort will go into teaching a young person canoeing skills, or how to safely build a fire. At the same time, other skills are more caught: figuring out how to settle a disagreement, to have empathy with a homesick friend, or to take initiative to clean up the campsite. An evening conversation reflecting around the campfire can add intentionality to what was actually learned during the day.

Larson and Walker (2018) provide an excellent review of how learning theories have evolved over time to reflect this. They discuss how classic learning theories reflect a developmental continuum from "I teach, you learn" to "let's tackle this together" to "help me learn about this from your perspective." They illustrate how the field of learning theory initially focused on adults teaching and shaping young people—approaches that tend to emphasize the content or skill to be learned, the role of the adult practitioners in teaching it, and assessment to validate whether the young person has learned it. Later constructivist views emphasized the role of the child or youth as producers of their own development. From this perspective, young people are seen constructing, or at least co-constructing, their own development by "catching on" to how things work, and are not just viewed as empty vessels into which adults pour content. This growing understanding underlines that most competencies are both powerfully caught and taught.

Additionally, Larson and Walker (2018) point out that scholars have explored how the acquisition of new competencies is supported through relationships with others, as well as through norms and identities acquired through social interactions. Collaborative learning theory focuses on guided participation and the interactions between the leader and the learner that use scaffolding approaches to help develop mastery. Relationship theories emphasize caring relationships and connections that provide a secure base for learning and development, particularly in the area of SEL. Sociological theories consider the way norms, social constructs, culture, and context shape learning and identity development.

Contemporary developmental theories emphasize that the young person actively constructs competencies from life experiences, relationships, social interactions, and engagement with adults, and SEL emphasizes that there are things adults can do to actively shape and help youth reflect on these experiences to form specific skills. Furthermore, the growing field of neurobiology (Blair & Raver, 2015) adds new understanding about how emotions are intimately tied to learning. Combined, there is emerging consensus that learning and development does involve the learner and their emotions, and that it is influenced by experiences and how they are processed—not simply by what is taught. This is particularly true for the variety of social and emotional competencies now recognized as critical for success in school, college, work, and life.

In essence, learning and development are increasingly seen as both taught and caught in an interactive process. Neither is the leader/instructor the source of all knowledge, nor the learner an empty vessel; both are active in creating the conditions where learning and development occur. Some things cannot be taught until a young person has mastered certain basic competencies. Catching on to new or more nuanced competencies often depends upon what they already have been taught or have experienced. Similarly, teaching approaches that label what has been learned through experience can often enhance the use of that labeled skill in different contexts.

Social and emotional competencies grow in response to experiences loaded with emotions, relationships, and goals—both experiences that are naturally occurring as well as ones that are intentionally created. The experiential and flexible nature of OST in shaping opportunities makes it an ideal place to build such social and emotional competencies. Increasing intentionality about how these competencies are both taught and caught in OST requires understanding the foundations of YD as well as reflecting on five key challenges that emerge when combining YD and SEL.

THE HISTORICAL FOUNDATIONS OF YOUTH DEVELOPMENT

Although the terminology is different, community-based nonformal learning involving adult leadership and voluntary participation of children and youth roughly 6–19 years old has been a feature of American life for nearly 200 years. The diversity of clubs, groups, troops, teams, societies, lodges, and other associations designed by adults specifically to engage and influence young people has prospered and expanded, offering voice, choice, fun, and friendship (Quinn, 2005).

Historically, although the precise focus of organizational efforts differed, these varied youth organizations shared many common features. Paid and volunteer adults and young people organized around gender, faith, neighborhood, vocational interests, cultural pursuits, hobbies, outdoor interests, sports, civic engagement, and much, much more. Older youth frequently led younger children. Groups featured adults engaging young people in social and learning activities for fun, friendship, personal growth, and civic life. Project work was popular, as it challenged individuals as well as groups to learn a part, organize swimming lessons, plant a community garden, or do public speaking. The end goals most often focused on individual and group efforts to demonstrate moral strength, physical fitness, social adeptness, character development, and emotional expression, as befitting of citizens in a democratic society. Note that many of the broad goals behind these efforts are essentially about providing opportunities and support to help youth acquire what today would be identified as desirable social, emotional, and civic competencies. They were seen as voluntary but important opportunities. Often efforts were made to assure that society's "at risk" youth and adults engaged in such opportunities to nurture their development as productive workers and good citizens. In short, these efforts were then—and are today—contributing to SEL.

Success in attaining organizational and personal goals was marked by public competitions and demonstrations of accomplishments, with rewards like badges, beads, patches, and recognition ceremonies marking mastery, accomplishment, and contribution as a leader, a productive family member, a friend, or a civic activist. In these settings and programs, lessons learned and competencies gained were more often seen as caught than taught. The language of active learning or experiential learning was common. Group reflection by members acknowledged accomplishments but was less prescribed and formulated than "taught methods" associated with schooling, grades, and tests. Often these efforts were seen as supporting character development in young people by helping them experience and co-construct the activities. Seldom were skills tested for in any serious way; nor were people held accountable by a third party for whether these skills were learned. Rather, for most of these programs, accountability was placed with the youth and with the volunteers, families, and donors who made them possible.

THE UNIFYING CONCEPT OF POSITIVE YOUTH DEVELOPMENT

The concept of positive "youth development" (YD) emerged in the 1970s in response to the need for orienting practitioners and applied research to the processes of adolescent development. It was quickly adopted by many youth organizations as a unifying term—a descriptor that "fit" for the majority of OST organizations serving middle-school-aged and older youth. The growing acceptance of the YD term and concept as an expression of their core values over time united the field in support of YD principles, YD practice (youth work), and YD research. It represented a shift from focusing on understanding how adolescents develop to focusing on using what is known to support youth as they develop. This shift to a more applied, practice-oriented approach that goes beyond studying development is at the core of YD.

Initially the term *youth development* was confusing; it was often used in three different ways (Hamilton, Hamilton, & Pittman, 2004, p. 3).

- First, youth development refers to a *natural process* of growth over time—young people develop.
- Second, youth development refers to a set of *principles* and values that links learning to development and the active engagement of the young person.

- Third, youth development is a set of *practices* of youth workers (professionals and volunteers) that involves adults and young people in experiences and activities that stimulate and support positive development.

The focus in the last of these is not on particular outcomes for youth. Rather, the focus is on processes, principles, values, and practices—things that when done well (with what is now called "high quality") should create a positive difference in the lives of youth broadly—including building specific competencies that could be assessed.

Features of the YD ethos and practice (Walker, Marczac, Blyth, & Borden, 2005) have laid the foundation for the approaches that drive most discretionary OST programs today—at least for those that target middle school and high school ages. YD established itself as a strength-based, universal practice, in contrast to the deficit-focused, treatment orientation common in the 1980s in programs to address drugs, alcohol, sexual promiscuity, and antisocial behaviors, which labeled young people in negative ways. That said, YD also maintained a special heart for engaging disadvantaged youth and addressing social justice issues. YD became distinct from early childhood education, childcare, and school-age care—in particular, establishing a more active role for young people in the creation and conduct of learning experiences. Over time the continuum has grown from simple youth participation to youth engagement to youth leadership to more specialized aspects of youth organizing and community development.

YD efforts in OST generally remained more focused on process than data or specific youth outcomes. Russell (2018) talks about the evolution of OST evaluation efforts around both quality and impact. The work on quality improvement in particular evolved from the development of quality standards to the use of quality assessments such as the Weikart Center's Youth Program Quality Assessment (Smith et al., 2012). This use of data, both self-report and externally generated ratings, focuses on the process at the point of service, not youth outcomes, and is generally well received and supported by practitioners. Use of evaluation data on impact has also evolved, and has made significant contributions, as noted by Russell (2018), but in our view does not overly dominate the way YD is practiced.

On a separate but related level, data gathering and use within YD expanded to population and community levels, going beyond evaluating specific programs and interventions. In the 1990s, the Search Institute Developmental Assets framework introduced a focus on measurable outcomes and supports. It delineated both internal assets that young people need as well as external assets that support their development (Benson, Leffert, Scales, & Blyth, 1998). This framework provided data to communities on the presence or absence of positive assets in the lives of youth in communities, versus the results of specific programs.

At roughly the same time, efforts to examine different youth interventions, coming primarily from a prevention research perspective, studied evidence-based approaches to youth outcomes (e.g., Hawkins & Catalano, 2005). Later on, the "Five C's of Positive Youth Development" framework, emphasizing competence, confidence, connections, character, and contribution, was refined and studied by Richard Lerner and colleagues (Lerner, Phelps, Forman, & Bowers, 2009). The point here is not that there is not solid research about YD but rather that YD as practiced is not primarily driven by data on outcomes or the use of formally studied evidence-based programs. This is both a strength and a limitation of the field.

THE EMERGENCE OF SEL

Next, I look briefly at the emergence of SEL and the forces shaping it. While social and emotional dimensions of development are not new, and even stretch back thousands of years (Humphrey, 2013), SEL as an explicit term emerged, like YD, in the early 1970s. SEL emerged as a "conceptual umbrella" that connects developmental experiences and capabilities "found across a broad set of studies focused on what personal and social capabilities produce adequate functioning in school and interpersonally" (Tolan, Ross, Arkin, Godine, & Clark, 2016, p. 218). Evidence from many places supports the relationship between these social and emotional competencies and a variety of measures of success, from better achievement test scores, to more positive and fewer negative behaviors, to improved mental health (Weissberg, Durlak, Domitrovich, & Gullotta, 2015).

In the foreword to this volume, Mahoney and Weissberg offer a definition of SEL that appropriately separates the process of learning (SEL) from the actual competencies themselves. Just like YD, SEL is about the process of learning—but as we will see, SEL typically approaches it in ways that are slightly, but meaningfully, different.

The field of SEL emerged to help capture the process of learning a set of competencies that have been empirically demonstrated to be important for success. It is now the name applied to the movement to improve and assess those skills. To date these SEL efforts are often perceived as grounded in school contexts and addressing skills and content that are considered appropriate to be taught as universal competencies that all young people need. These characteristics often mean SEL approaches typically favor the *taught* side of the caught–taught continuum, though clearly many specific SEL program efforts balance caught and taught approaches differently, just as do different OST programs.

SEL programs' efforts to create processes that intervene in and build these competencies are more deeply rooted in research and evidence-based approaches than is typical in OST YD practice, as noted above. Furthermore, the interventions designed to create these competencies in children and youth are also increasingly well documented, with many now meeting the standards required of "evidence-based" programs (e.g., see "2015 CASEL Guide," n.d.; Jones et al., 2017). The next section discusses the differences between YD and SEL approaches broadly on five factors, and then elaborates on the challenges these present in practice—especially for blending the two approaches together in OST programs primarily driven by strong YD principles and values.

FIVE CHALLENGES TO INTEGRATING YD AND SEL APPROACHES IN PRACTICE

Table 2.1 provides a quick overview of five differences between typical YD and SEL approaches and names the resulting challenges practitioners face. I see these as challenges, not barriers, and with each comes opportunities. Many are challenges OST practitioners would face in any event. The OST field and the programs and practitioners that make it up need to consider these challenges if OST is to optimally integrate both approaches and become more intentional about the ways social and emotional competencies are both caught and taught.

The Challenge of Selecting Competencies

The initial challenge for OST as a field and for its intermediary systems and programs is to select the specific set of social and emotional competencies that will guide efforts to become more intentional. While SEL is more competence focused, the growing multitude of frameworks, the inconsistent use of words, and each framework's specific list of competencies make it hard to know which to select (e.g., see Jones et al., 2016). YD, with its youth-centric approach, prefers specific competencies to emerge from the interactions with the youth. Some specific points to consider:

- There is no one perfect framework or one set of competencies universally agreed upon for OST as a field, or for specific types of programs to adopt. Not all OST programs need to become intentionally focused on competencies, even if almost by definition all are contributing to SEL.

TABLE 2.1 Comparison of Youth Development and Social and Emotional Learning Approaches: Differences, Similarities, and Challenges for OST Practice

Area	SEL	Commonalities	YD	Challenges for OST Practice
Foundations	Competence focused—finding ways to improve the teaching and learning of SE competencies	Recognition that SE competencies are both *taught* and *caught* through experiential, relationship-based, and collaborative approaches	Youth focused—creating ways for children and youth to choose opportunities that support their development, including development of SE competencies	Selecting specific social and emotional competencies
Settings	More often used in schools, which emphasize a formal learning/taught approach	Recognition that responsibility for SEL is shared with families, cultural groups, and the communities in which youth live	More often used in nonformal and informal settings where youth are given opportunities to learn and develop (i.e., opportunities to catch)	Finding a new balance of *taught* and *caught*
Developmental Roots	More often informed by studies of early childhood and elementary-age youth as well as college and career transitions	Shared recognition of needing approaches that cover the full age range	More often informed by work with early, middle, and later adolescents, where the young person's role in own development is critical and there are more complex social and community contexts and forces at work	Supporting developmentally appropriate approaches
Sociological Roots	Provide universal approaches to building critical competencies and provide extra supports where needed to reduce existing inequities—culture and race are too often not a focus	Both increasingly see the need to address inequities in the learning and development of young people and the settings, structures, and processes that contribute to these competencies and may support inequities	Engage youth "where they are" and utilize culture, civic, and social justice approaches to confront and address inequities	Proactively addressing cultural, racial, and income differences
Data Use	Historical more publically and system-funded, with emphasis on using data to identify critical competencies and evidence-based practices	Growing awareness from implementation science and new ways of using data that limiting data use to proving impact is less effective than using data to improve impact by moving practice	Historically mixed and unstable types of funding, with uneven but increasing pressure to use data to improve quality and demonstrate desired outcomes	Expanding use of data for improvement and accountability

- Consider the frameworks already used in the community and check out what frameworks are used in schools. Also see if state standards exist, as more states are adding standards around social and emotional competencies.
- Rather than search for the perfect framework and set of competencies to embrace, it is probably more important to select a set of competencies that includes both social and emotional dimensions (or what some refer to as both intra- and interpersonal competencies) that fit together well and fit with the program, setting, and youth involved.
- Selecting and using clear language around specific types of social and emotional competencies is critical to increasing intentionality. Ultimately it is consistent alignment of well-defined competencies/skills, strategies, practices, and measurement that is likely to enhance impact.

Embracing this challenge includes taking intentional steps to *frame* the social and emotional competencies youth need to build; *name* them specifically so there is a language to use; *claim* them as a clear part of what the program is about; and finally, *work* them into the way the program is designed, the ways staff are prepared, the environment created, and the program's daily practices.

The Challenge of Balancing Taught and Caught

Youth development approaches in OST settings have long relied on high-quality experiences and strong relationships, using an experiential education approach to learning that is active, conversational, reflective, youth-centric, and focused on youth as co-creators of their own development to ensure skills are caught. As noted above, SEL efforts, particularly as seen in schools, tend to use a more formal taught approach, with specific content and curriculum designed to help all youth learn and practice critical competencies largely identified by adults rather than the young people. That said, educational settings are increasingly paying attention to the importance of school culture, teacher preparation, and cultural competence in these areas—factors critical to supporting a more caught approach.

- High-quality programs and the emphasis on measuring and continuously improving quality have enhanced the likelihood that OST programs are good places where social and emotional competencies can be caught. This does not in itself, however, mean they are

as intentional about developing critical SEL competencies as they could and should be.
- The challenge is to find a new balance point in how OST programs and practices help ensure these competencies are caught as well as intentionally taught. To be clear, I am suggesting a moderate shift toward intentionally teaching these competencies, not a radical shift that sees these competencies as just content that must be taught in school-like ways. Some of the ways specific OST programs have increased their intentionality around social and emotional competencies are documented in chapters in the second section of this book.
- When an explicit set of competencies is selected, the OST efforts will be better able to become intentional in the ways it prepares its staff, designs programs, creates learning environments, uses youth and adult routines, and defines what it seeks to measure and improve. Some programs will incorporate significantly more efforts to teach; others will concentrate on strategies to assure competencies are caught. All should do so from a strength-based, youth-centric approach in which the choices and voices of youth drive the work.

Schools and OST programs need to identify and implement ways they can become more intentional in both teaching these competencies and helping youth experience catching them during the opportunities they have each day. In many cases, professionals from each setting have talents that could benefit the other professionals as well as the youth served.

The Challenge of Developmentally Appropriate Approaches

Much of SEL originally emerged from early childhood and elementary experiences—particularly the belief in a universal, strength-based design for all children and youth. SEL approaches to middle school and high school programs sometimes become focused more on addressing deficits in social and emotional competencies—including addressing disciplinary and mental health issues.

In contrast, YD emerged from work with older youth (age 10–24 in some countries), and emphasized support for the role young people actively play in co-constructing their development. Some YD approaches also promote an explicit social justice perspective that not only "meets youth where they are" but also seeks to help them change the world through service learning, community development, and youth organizing efforts. Such efforts are often less about just developing competencies to cope with an existing situation and more about learning ways to change things that are unjust.

These differences lead to the challenge of finding developmentally appropriate ways to utilize the foundational skills youth have while helping them stretch into new areas. By intentionally focusing on a specific set of competencies it is possible to strengthen and continually improve the ways those competencies are both developed and used.

Based on these different developmental roots and the challenge of finding and using developmentally appropriate ways to help youth stretch and build their social and emotional competencies, I offer the following reflections:

- The OST field, especially at the front line, often has an educated but highly mobile workforce made up of both paid and volunteer staff (Hurd & Deutsch, 2017). Preparing and supporting staff in OST programs to become more socially and emotionally aware, competent, and effective will allow them to also become more developmentally intentional about these competencies. Investments in staff are needed to help accomplish this.
- As youth are developing all the time, deciding what is developmentally appropriate often means stretching them in new areas. Adults may underestimate young people's skills rather than stretch them. Creating scaffolding learning opportunities is a key to supporting both learning and development. It is important for mastery as well as exposure to the next level.

While OST and YD broadly have a long history (if not always fully developed practices) of challenging and supporting youth's development, focusing on a clearly defined set of social and emotional competencies represents an important way to further support young people's development.

The Challenge of Culture and Context

YD approaches and the OST field work to reduce the opportunity gap by providing enriching and challenging opportunities that are both accessible and popular (since these opportunities are by definition voluntary, not mandated). SEL approaches often seek to create a level playing field where all youth can acquire the critical competencies they need to succeed. Increasing SEL and building social and emotional competencies is seen as a tool or process for reducing or eliminating inequities. In some districts, SEL efforts and equity efforts are explicitly combined. The challenge for both YD and SEL efforts is how to support the development and learning of social and emotional skills in culturally, racially, linguistically diverse children and youth who are also diverse in gender identity and abilities. This means embracing the challenge of helping youth develop their own ways of being while also understanding and respecting others' ways of being.

Too often, American SEL frameworks come primarily from a Western, individualistic set of values and do not do enough to discuss how culture, context, income, and race impact SEL.

In an effort to understand how OST providers in Minnesota's Twin Cities talked about social and emotional competencies, over 20 focus groups were convened to discuss what competencies youth needed and what competencies programs were trying to nurture (LaCroix-Dalluhn, 2017). While over 180 different terms emerged, they all boiled down to essentially the common competencies in most frameworks—with three notable exceptions. The categories of cultural respect, cultural healing, and cultural identity development stood out and are differentially important for youth of color.

Considering the major implications of this challenge for OST programs, I offer the following reflections:

- Youth workers need to better understand and support grounding the development of SEL in the sociological factors that shape differences and similarities in the competencies needed by different groups.
- Training in cultural competence and examining one's own cultural roots and biases is essential.
- In our diverse society, all youth—not just minority youth—need to be able to code switch and become "socially and emotionally multilingual."
- Practitioners working with youth, whether teachers or youth workers, need to learn about how differences inform and shape competencies and their use, as well as how different competencies relate to individual as well as collective success.

Both YD and SEL approaches need to become more explicit and proactive in understanding, supporting, and respecting the wide range of differences, and not try to impose a "one size fits all" set of competencies or ways in which those competencies are taught and used. Critically, a focus on SEL and competencies should enhance and advance these conversations—not be used to impose one group's way of being and doing on anothers.

The Challenge of Using Data for Improvement and Accountability

While SEL has been born out of evidence and empirical studies demonstrating the importance of social and emotional competencies, as well as strong results from evaluations of the interventions designed to build these competencies, YD has been shaped more by practice, wisdom, and beliefs about what works that are informed by research but not primarily driven by it. There are many reasons for this, including the voluntary nature of youth work and the wide variability of what occurs in these programs. The most recent and prominent use of data in OST utilizing a YD framework is the growing use of data on quality for continuous improvement in ways that are motivating versus judgmental—data as a tool versus as a weapon.

Differences in the pressure to use data for accountability are significant. SEL's heavy presence in schools and their use of public funds and too-often high-stakes accountability approaches create a very different environment for data and data use. Most YD programs feel accountable to their youth, families, and donors first, then to the public or taxpayers, because most receive limited public funding. Accountability in YD is more often judged by success stories and rich qualitative data from practice rather than rigorous experimental data from comparative evaluations.

Based on existing differences and the rapidly changing nature and use of data in our society, I offer the following reflections on the challenge of using data to improve intentionality in building social and emotional competencies:

- OST programs and the intermediaries that support them need to take advantage of new approaches for gathering and using data for accountability and continuous improvement. Many programs are now getting more systematic about assessing quality and participation/dosage as well as surveying participants about their experiences and looking at ways to connect data of different types. Measures of social and emotional competencies can and should be part of the data collected and used to both improve practice and demonstrate impact.
- The time for OST programs to primarily focus on reducing the burden of data collection is over; it is now time for a new focus on maximizing the benefits of data use relative to the burden of data collection. Improving this ratio means making sure to understand and use data to benefit young people, improve practices, and make the case for the benefits of what we do and how we do it, versus primarily working to reduce the burden on young people and staff. When benefits exceed burdens, our field will be on the track to more effective data collection and powerful use. To be clear, this is not a call to increase the burden, but rather to look at data issues in a different way.
- Given the importance of youth cocreating their own development, I particularly encourage efforts to design assessment and collection efforts with youth, and to actively share data back with young people to enhance understanding.

The importance of this challenge is also heightened by the fact that expectations for using data more fully and effectively have both increased and broadened in society as a whole. The OST field should become more accountable for using data well to improve what we do and how we do it, as well as to demonstrate that we can and do make a difference in building these competencies. This broader emphasis on seeing things through data, along with the OST field's generally positive experience with data on quality improvement, have created an opportunity for OST programs to rethink the ways we collect and use data; to move toward using data in ways that are more compatible with SEL; and to become more intentional about collecting data related to youth competencies, sharing the data with youth and families, and using the data to improve intentionality.

A CALL TO MOVE FORWARD INTENTIONALLY

Capitalize on the opportunity and meet the challenges! This is indeed a pivotal time for the OST field to reaffirm its commitment to experience-based, youth-centric learning and to take seriously the growing need to support a better-understood and critically important set of social and emotional competencies. Working to take advantage of this to make OST even better is too good an opportunity to ignore.

Remember that families, schools, communities, and OST programs all share a fundamental commitment to the learning and development of young people. Each may identify what they feel to be the most important factors for success in life and in school. For the field and for individual programs and practitioners in OST, these similarities and differences need to remain in the forefront of our thinking, especially in light of the inequities in access to the opportunities we offer and the active hardships and discrimination too many youth and families face.

YD and SEL advocates must commit to learning from each other. School settings currently may well lean too heavily on the taught side and see these competencies as content to be delivered, learned, and tested in ways that allow systems to be held accountable. In the process of focusing on teaching them, schools may not pay sufficient attention to school climate, relationships, and other factors that affect whether youth are in environments with relationships for optimally catching positive social and emotional competencies.

When YD and SEL bump up against each other intentionally, caught and taught tend to complement each other. It is easy for OST programs to rely on quality improvement, but there is now a reasonable expectation that complementary and more intentional efforts within OST programs can support and enhance the learning and development of valued social and emotional competencies.

The OST field viewed broadly is increasingly responsible for high-quality experiences and using data to inform outcomes and improvement related to how SEL and YD are carried out. The trick is in addressing the challenges and finding the right point on the taught–caught continuum for our field as a whole, as well as for individual programs and practices.

I hope it is clear that I am arguing neither for simply getting on the SEL bandwagon nor for a wholesale shift in what OST is or does. Nor am I arguing OST should become driven by a narrow, predetermined set of key competencies and become accountable for making sure every youth has them. Rather, I hope I have made a case for the important role that OST as a field can and should play—to varying degrees and in varying ways—in becoming more intentional about both the teaching and catching of the social and emotional competencies that are key to success in school, college, work, and life. Doing so represents a critical and logical next step that will position our field as important and successful, instead of simply following another funding stream or educational fad.

REFERENCES

2015 CASEL Guide: Effective Social and Emotional Learning Programs—Middle and High School Edition. (n.d.). Retrieved from the Collaborative for Academic, Social, and Emotional Learning website: https://casel.org/middle-and-high-school-edition-casel-guide/

Benson, P. L., Leffert, N., Scales, P. C., & Blyth, D. A. (1998). Beyond the village rhetoric: Creating healthy communities for children and youth. *Applied Developmental Science, 2*(1), 138–159.

Blair, C., & Raver, C. C. (2015). The neuroscience of SEL. In J. A. Durlak, C. E. Domitrovich, R. P. Weissberg, & T. P. Gullotta (Eds.), *Handbook on social and emotional learning: Research and practice* (pp. 65–80). New York, NY: Guilford.

Hamilton, S. F., Hamilton, M. A., & Pittman, K. (2004). Principles of youth development. In S. F. Hamilton & M. A. Hamilton (Eds.), *The youth development handbook: Coming of age in American communities* (pp. 65–80). Thousand Oaks, CA: SAGE.

Hawkins, D., & Catalano, R. (2005). *Investing in your community's youth: An introduction to the Communities That Care system.* Retrieved from https://www.communitiesthatcare.net/userfiles/files/Investing-in-Your-Community-Youth.pdf

Humphrey, N. (2013). *Social and emotional learning: A critical appraisal.* Los Angeles, CA: SAGE.

Hurd, N., & Deutsch, N. (2017). SEL-focused after-school programs. *The Future of Children, (27)*1, 98–115.

Jones, S., Bailey, R., Brush, K., Nelson, B., & Barnes, S. (2016). *What is the same and what is different? Making sense of the "non-cognitive" domain: Helping educators translate research into practice.* Boston, MA: Harvard Graduate School of Education EASEL Lab. Retrieved from https://easel.gse.harvard.edu/files/gse-easel-lab/files/words_matter_paper.pdf

Jones, S., Brush, K., Bailey, R., Brion-Meisels, G., McIntyre, J., Kahn, J., . . . Stickle, L. (2017). *Navigating SEL from the inside out: Looking inside & across 25 leading SEL programs: A practical resource for schools and OST providers.* Report prepared for the Wallace Foundation. Retrieved from http://www.wallacefoundation.org/knowledge-center/Documents/Navigating-Social-and-Emotional-Learning-from-the-Inside-Out.pdf

LaCroix-Dalluhn, L. (2017). *Propel SEL: Findings & recommendations.* Report for Sprockets, City of Saint Paul Afterschool Network. Retrieved from https://www.sprocketssaintpaul.org/sites/default/files/downloads/page/Sprockets%20Propel%20SEL%20Recommendations_final%20%281%29.pdf

Larson, R. W., & Walker, K. (2018). Processes of positive development: Classic theories. In L. Caldwell & P. Witt (Eds.), *Recreation and youth development,* 2nd ed. Urbana, IL: Venture.

Lerner, J. V., Phelps, E., Forman, Y., & Bowers, E. P. (2009). Positive youth development. In R. M. Lerner & L. Steinberg (Eds.), *Handbook of adolescent psychology: Vol 1. Individual bases of adolescent development* (3rd ed., pp. 524–558). Hoboken, NJ: Wiley.

Quinn, J. (2005). Building effective practices and policies for out-of-school time. In J. L. Mahoney, R. W. Larson, & J. S. Eccles (Eds.), *Organized activities as contexts of development: Extracurricular activities, after-school and community programs* (pp. 479–495). Mahwah, NJ: Erlbaum.

Russell, C. (2018). The growth, evolution, and state of OST evaluation. In H. J. Malone & T. Donahue (Eds.), *The growing out-of-school time field: Past, present, and future.* Charlotte, NC: Information Age.

Smith, C., Akiva, T., Sugar, S., Lo, Y. J., Frank, K. A., Peck, S. C., . . . Devaney, T. (2012). *Continuous quality improvement in afterschool settings: Impact findings from the Youth Program Quality Intervention study.* Washington, DC: The Forum for Youth Investment. Retrieved from http://www.cypq.org/content/continuous-quality-improvement-afterschool-settings-impact-findings-youth-program-quality-in

Tolan, P., Ross, K., Arkin, N., Godine, N., & Clark, E. (2016). Toward an integrated approach to positive youth development: Implications for intervention. *Applied Developmental Science, 20*(3), 214–236.

Walker, J., Marczak, M., Blyth, D., & Borden, L. (2005). Designing youth development programs: Toward a theory of developmental intentionality. In J. L. Mahoney, R. W. Larson, & J. S. Eccles (Eds.), *Organized activities as contexts of development: Extracurricular activities, after-school and community programs* (pp. 25–48). Mahwah, NJ: Erlbaum.

Weissberg, R. P., Durlak, J. A., Domitrovich, C. E., & Gullotta, T. P. (2015). Social and emotional learning: Past, present, and future. In J. A. Durlak, C. E. Domitrovich, R. P. Weissberg, & T. P. Gullotta (Eds.), *Handbook on social and emotional learning: Research and practice* (pp. 3–19). New York, NY: Guilford.

SECTION II

RESEARCH-INFORMED SEL PRACTICE

CHAPTER 3

FROM QUALITY TO SEL

A Community in Motion

**Christina Dandino, Luiz A. Perez,
and Carla Stough Huffman**

It is not unusual for providers of before- and after-school, summer, and expanded learning time opportunities to collectively identify themselves as youth development programs, while simultaneously defining their differences by the time or setting in which their programs take place. Rochester, New York, has traditionally been no exception. There are many influences that contribute to this silo mentality, including funder priorities, multiple programs operating in the same participant space, and an ever-changing resource pool that sometimes rewards competition over collaboration. The factors that can create connection include a collaborative vision, shared language, and common framework. Influenced by several community-wide collective impact initiatives and supported by the many members of the Greater Rochester After School Alliance (GRASA), a more connected landscape is emerging in Rochester. Something as simple as accepting a collective identity, and recognizing that all of our programs fit under the umbrella of out-of-school time (OST), has begun to build unity and excitement as we

Social and Emotional Learning in Out-of-School Time, pages 35–51

work diligently to embed program quality and inform social and emotional learning (SEL) practices across systems and sites engaged in OST youth development programs.

THE STORY OF GRASA

Throughout the past 5 years, GRASA has engaged in much of the work described above, first as a committed group of volunteers representing funding, policy, program implementation, and evaluation, and more recently as an intermediary, with the addition of an advisory board and a small paid staff. GRASA's mission is to unite the community to ensure that all youth in Monroe County, New York, have access to high-quality OST programs on their journey to successful adulthood—a commitment shared by all its members.

Beginnings

Beginning in the 1990s, Rochester Area Community Foundation (RACF) convened community leaders to create an initiative that supported the development of high-quality early childhood programs by championing accreditation, quality standards, and capacity building to improve outcomes. Today, the Early Childhood Development Initiative (ECDI) is a strong, successful model that continues to inform work with this age group. Foundation leaders soon recognized that a similar coordinated effort did not exist for school-age youth development programs that provide enrichment and prevention programming during out-of-school hours.

Following the same process, GRASA was established in 2001, as an initiative of RACF, to improve the quality, quantity, and accessibility of afterschool programs. The initial goals of the early founding members—RACF, United Way of Greater Rochester, Rochester City School District, City of Rochester Department of Recreation and Youth Services, and the Rochester-Monroe County Youth Bureau—included developing a communitywide common framework, principles, language, outcomes, and practices across youth development and OST. The first 5 years of GRASA's evolution focused on the following activities:

- conducting an OST inventory to learn what existed in the community,
- supporting efforts to secure 21st century community learning center funds and increase state funds,
- surveying families and youth, and
- exploring quality standards and tools in OST.

At that time, the National Research Council and Institute of Medicine published their report on *Community Programs to Promote Youth Development* (Eccles & Gootman, 2002), which set in motion a chain of additional research that furthered growth in youth development and OST knowledge and practice. Around the same time, the David P. Weikart Center for Youth Program Quality was in the process of validating an observational quality measure for OST. Rochester began piloting that measure—the Youth Program Quality Assessment (YPQA)—in 2005. From 2006 to 2010, GRASA held public meetings with OST programs to introduce youth program quality standards and the accreditation process that was then available through the National Afterschool Association (formerly the National School Age Care Association). RACF then became the first local funder to incentivize participation in program quality improvement and program accreditation processes for OST in their proposals. GRASA hosted the development of the Rochester after-school plan and model (a common framework and essential elements for programs), with facilitation assistance from The After School Corporation (currently ExpandED Schools; The After School Corporation, 2008). Finally, a cadre of trainers with youth development expertise participated in the Weikart Center's "youth work methods" training of trainers to support quality instructional practices.

Creating Quality

Through the lens of a newly developed strategic plan and partnerships with RCSD, the Ford Foundation's More and Better Learning Time initiative, and The Wallace Foundation's summer learning initiative, GRASA adopted and brought to scale the Weikart Center's comprehensive Youth Program Quality Intervention (YPQI) in 2011. The YPQI was launched with comprehensive, system-wide supports, including observation with the Program Quality Assessment (PQA) and associated planning with data, coaching, training, and technical assistance based on a continuous quality improvement cycle: assess, plan, improve. All of these processes have led to improved quality of programming across GRASA member organizations over the past 4 years, since the intensive YPQI implementation began (Helegda, Roy, Smith, & Macleod, 2017; Sniegowski, Newman, & Devaney, 2016). In 2016, confident that the community was moving in the right direction, RACF added staff to assist with GRASA's continued development.

SEL IN THE OST COMMUNITY: GRASA'S POINT OF VIEW

History

The Rochester community has a long history of focus on social and emotional well-being. As early as 1957, a faculty member in the psychology department at the University of Rochester, Dr. Emory L. Cowen, was one of the first to study the notion of wellness in mental health. As part of that work, he developed a prevention program for children having adjustment difficulties in school called the Primary Mental Health Project. The project began in one Rochester elementary school and has since been implemented in hundreds of schools across the country. It is currently overseen by Children's Institute in Rochester.

In addition, evidence-based SEL programs have been championed over the years by numerous local groups, including The Children's Agenda, a local advocacy group for children's well-being. In particular, various programs were introduced in the community in the 1980s and 1990s, including Nurse Family Partnership, Parent Effectiveness Training, Promoting Alternative Thinking Strategies (PATHS), Coping Power, and Second Step. In the mid-1990s, a community-wide collaboration led to the implementation of a comprehensive Developmental Assets® initiative (in partnership with the Search Institute) that is still evident in various communities. At that time, the late Dr. Peter Benson was invited to Rochester, heightening interest in the assets model. Within 8 years of his visit, all 18 school districts and communities throughout the county and city were engaged in youth asset building. In 2009, the city school district was awarded a six-million-dollar Safe Schools/Healthy Students grant that allowed for the expansion of several evidence-based programs, including PATHS, Coping Power, and Olweus Bullying Prevention, as well as the introduction of "Trauma-Informed School Cultures" training.

Current Efforts

Building on this rich history, GRASA has worked over the past few years to broker relationships across numerous sectors that are actively engaged in SEL efforts. For example, a strong partnership with Rochester City School District has resulted in school-day expanded learning opportunities that embed enrichment, while improving quality practices and program content during the school day. Likewise, Rochester's cradle-to-career collective impact initiative, ROC the Future, utilizes GRASA's expertise to lead its Expanded Learning Opportunities Collaborative Action Network, which focuses on using OST as part of the strategy for improving outcomes for young people in the city. Finally, the Greater Rochester Health Foundation's Initiative for Children's Social and Emotional Health Implementation Task Force (ITF), on which GRASA is represented, has as its mission "to challenge the status quo and inspire action that will significantly improve the social and emotional health of children throughout the Greater Rochester Region" (Greater Rochester Health Foundation, n.d.). The ITF's promotion/prevention workgroup identified the need for a common lens and language for children's social and emotional health and well-being, across and within child-serving settings. Although the issues and context may have changed, the Rochester of today continues to prioritize SEL and well-being. As a result, GRASA's work has always held SEL as a priority outcome.

Further, because GRASA views SEL work as a natural progression of, and partner to, the quality improvement process embodied through our YPQI work, we have built a close collaboration with Children's Institute that, as noted earlier, has a history of support for SEL in children. In addition, Children's Institute has been a long-term partner with GRASA in supporting our robust quality improvement process and providing an adaptable data collection system. Specifically, for more than a decade, Children's Institute has collected PQA data on OST programs for RACF and GRASA, overseeing certified external assessors and the collection and input of scores into the Weikart Center data portal. Children's Institute also connected GRASA to COMET—an online relational database that allows data entered by providers to be sent to a centralized location, analyzed by Children's Institute, and then reported out to partners. By linking new and existing data sources, COMET collects and manages data electronically for multiple levels of information. United Way of Greater Rochester (UW) and Children's Institute partner to use COMET in all UW-funded OST programs, in adherence to the community's Rochester after-school plan and model.

GRASA has also formed a partnership with the new SEL Center at Children's Institute, with a collective focus on building the capacity of OST providers to implement SEL strategies for youth in intermediate, middle, and high school. Together, our goal is to focus on cross-setting alignment of systems, improving program models, improving social and emotional competence for youth, and improving relationships for families.

A common concern across all our systems is action related to promotion and prevention. The goal is to have all systems engage in universal promotion activities, strategies, and practices. All of the above partners are working together toward alignment and advocacy with SEL. Along with connecting and aligning these resources, GRASA provides professional development and coaching through its capacity building network.

Identifying and Measuring Outcomes—A Community Effort

GRASA sought to pinpoint our community's most-desired youth-level outcomes for OST programs, compare them to national research, and roll them out to the community for endorsement, use, and measurement. During 2013–2014, focus groups were held with over 200 community members, including youth and families, for input into identifying youth-level outcomes for OST programs. A scan of the national research was also completed and reviewed. GRASA ranked and determined the following local community outcome priorities for OST:

- academic competencies,
- engagement,
- health and wellness,
- intrapersonal development,
- life and career skills, and
- social relationships (peer and adult).

As a next step in the quality improvement work, GRASA began exploring ways to better measure outcomes. Based on a 2007 meta-analysis conducted by Joe Durlak and Roger Weissberg (Durlak, Weissberg, Dymnicki, Taylor, & Schellinger, 2011), and other research pointing to the importance of OST in contributing to social and emotional outcomes, GRASA and its partners decided to focus on measuring social and emotional competencies and improving the capacity of youth workers to deliver evidence-based SEL practices.

The GRASA Quality Working Group reviewed eight different social and emotional measures in use nationally and assessed multiple categories for consideration, including: cost, outcomes assessed by the tool, reliability, validity, user-friendliness, availability of both individual and aggregate data, and the ability to be used with COMET for a single point of data entry and analysis. The quality working group also conducted telephone and in-person interviews with the designers of several tools to learn more about options, and partnered with a local graduate student to analyze the research literature on OST outcomes. Based on that review, the group chose to pilot the Devereux Student Strengths Assessment (DESSA). This tool is research-based, comprehensive, and inclusive—all elements that are important to our community (Naglieri, LeBuffe, & Shapiro, 2014). In addition, the DESSA appealed to GRASA partners because of its alignment with educational standards and its strength-based perspective, as well as its simplicity, which promised to make it accessible to different populations with little training. By design, the DESSA appeared to be a tool that could support our collective needs.

Since 2015, GRASA has used the DESSA-mini, a short, eight-question version of the full measure, with children in Grades K–8 participating in OST programs in the Rochester community. The assessment was piloted in 2014–2015 and was expanded to include more GRASA member organizations in subsequent years. Now in the fourth year of implementation, GRASA still considers the data to be in a preliminary stage. It is clear that creating a community-wide measurement system for OST programs requires patience, collaboration, and a fair amount of trial and error.

Challenges

Implementing a community-wide data collection process of this kind has presented GRASA with a range of challenges that need to be addressed before the data can be considered reliable. The process has improved each year, and OST providers using the instrument are becoming more comfortable with its administration. However, we still consider it an emerging process.

Some of the challenges that have arisen over the past several years may provide useful lessons for other communities attempting to develop similar common measurement systems (Zimmer, Devaney, Embt, & Lotyczewski, 2017):

- *Staff turnover* is high in youth programs, which makes it difficult for some programs to have the same staff member complete both the pre- and post-DESSA at the beginning and end of the year. The instrument is designed so it can be used by different staff, but the results may be more reliable when the same person completes both.
- *Staff–youth interaction* may not be consistent throughout the year, even when staffing is stable. The very nature of programs designed to give youth voice and choice means that youth typically move around from one activity to another and may have interactions with many staff members.
- *Youth participation* is not necessarily consistent throughout the year. For example, youth may participate in the fall, but not in the winter or spring, which means that they are no longer attending by the time the post-DESSA is completed. In programs with open enrollment, the program staff may not have completed a pre-DESSA for late entries. Getting a pre- and post-assessment of a child, completed by the same staff person, was challenging.
- *Program schedule variation* means that some begin in sync with the school year while others do not start until October. Some end in May; others end in June. There are sometimes only a few months

between the pre- and post-DESSA, which may not be enough time to see change.

- *Initial training gaps* were identified as everyone became more familiar with the instrument. Although GRASA and COMET conducted training on how to use the DESSA, they did not realize the importance of facilitating conversations among program staff about how to come up with consistent definitions for terms. For example, the rating scale for the DESSA-mini is "*never–rarely–occasionally–frequently–very frequently*," but different staff from the same organization may define "*rarely*" and "*occasionally*" differently. It is also beneficial to discuss, as a staff, what the different questions mean and how staff interpret them, so that there is a common understanding of how they will be rated. GRASA and Children's Institute plan to develop and conduct training or facilitate meetings on these topics for the coming year's data collection.
- *Understanding the benefits* of conducting timely and accurate data collection is necessary if program staff and leadership are going to prioritize it. Although most programs have completed the process, it is not always timely. GRASA and Children's Institute are developing a "Planning With DESSA Data" workshop, modeled on the "Planning With Data" workshop for the YPQA that already exists. The hope is that this workshop will result in greater understanding of, and commitment to the use of, the DESSA for future years.

Future Directions

GRASA has been engaged in both quality and DESSA work for several years. Building on our community's historical grounding in SEL, strong partnerships across sectors, foundation in positive youth development, and desire to deepen our capacity in SEL, Rochester is well positioned to take its next steps. We hope to learn and share findings in three identifiable areas: data, process, and practice.

Data

Data are critical, both in their immediate ability to inform practice at all levels and their importance in sharing our story. Over the next 2 years, we will focus on the following areas:

- the effective use of DESSA data to inform SEL practice improvements in programs;
- the relationships among attendance, academics, and social and emotional competence data;

- the impact of quality improvement efforts on school climate at each site, as identified by the school climate survey; and
- the creation of a community baseline for social and emotional skills (using the DESSA), against which to measure progress.

Process

In a constantly changing environment, one way to build consistency is to create strong, effective processes that support priorities. Currently, GRASA is working on the following processes:

- creating a learning environment for adults who work with youth that can assist them in reflecting on their own understanding of SEL, help them develop their own self-awareness and self-management strategies, learn practices to reduce stress and burnout, and increase their own social and emotional well-being;
- identifying and developing effective processes and planning with school district professional development staff, their educational coaches, and GRASA staff and quality coaches to integrate SEL learning opportunities throughout the school district and community-based organizations;
- aligning and cross-walking schoolwide climate efforts with chosen evidence-based practices (EBPs);
- overcoming the challenges of implementation fidelity, data collection, and data tracking; and
- ensuring teaching and OST staff receive training credit for their time in professional development opportunities.

Practice

Knowing that the collection of data and creation of processes are only useful if they inform and improve the way programs are delivered, GRASA is hoping to learn how to achieve the following goals:

- blend evidence-based SEL programs and instructional strategies in a way that allows them to be embedded in any type of curriculum or programming, such as science, technology, engineering, and mathematics (STEM), literacy, social studies, sports, and so on;
- increase smooth transitions and handoffs between school and OST staff to better understand and support a young person's SEL needs; and
- enhance, expand, and embed paid professional development opportunities for both OST and school staff.

As a first step in these future directions, GRASA established a working group, with representation from across the community spectrum, that spent nearly 8 months engaged in a process designed to inventory current SEL training opportunities, identify gaps for future development, and create the foundation for shared language and vision. The group's work resulted in an infographic (see Figure 3.1) and mini slide deck designed to define social and emotional competencies and action steps across our community, and to help explain the connection between quality improvement and social and emotional skill building. The two documents can be used by anyone providing education or advocacy around SEL and social and emotional health and wellness. GRASA has an immediate goal of ensuring that programs and staff across sectors adopt and use these resources as we move forward so that we meet our data, process, and practice goals.

A CASE EXAMPLE—SEL IN SUMMER LEARNING

As Rochester's commitment to building its shared SEL vision grows, the ability to learn from one another becomes vitally important. While a number of programs have been doing exemplary work within their isolated arenas, children clearly benefit most from programs that are willing to share their experiences, both challenging and successful, with the broader community. The Greater Rochester Summer Learning Association (GRSLA), a member of GRASA, is one such entity.

Overview

GRSLA is a growing consortium of program sites (20 sites in summer 2017) serving early prekindergarten (EPK) to 11th-grade urban and rural youth in the Greater Rochester, New York, region. As a supporting organization serving as an intermediary, GRSLA systematically establishes and increases access to high-quality, evidence-based summer learning and enrichment. These programs level the playing field for youth from low-income families by stemming summer learning loss. Over multiple summers, this intervention closes the achievement gap for youth who are behind academically, placing program participants on a trajectory of success in school and in life.

Our affiliate programs are known as summerLEAP (Learning Enrichment to Achieve Potential), and our brand promise is to instill in our students a belief in their abilities, an understanding of their potential for achievement, and a joyous spirit of optimism about the future. Located on college campuses and in private independent schools and various community-based organizations, program participants across multiple years (EPK

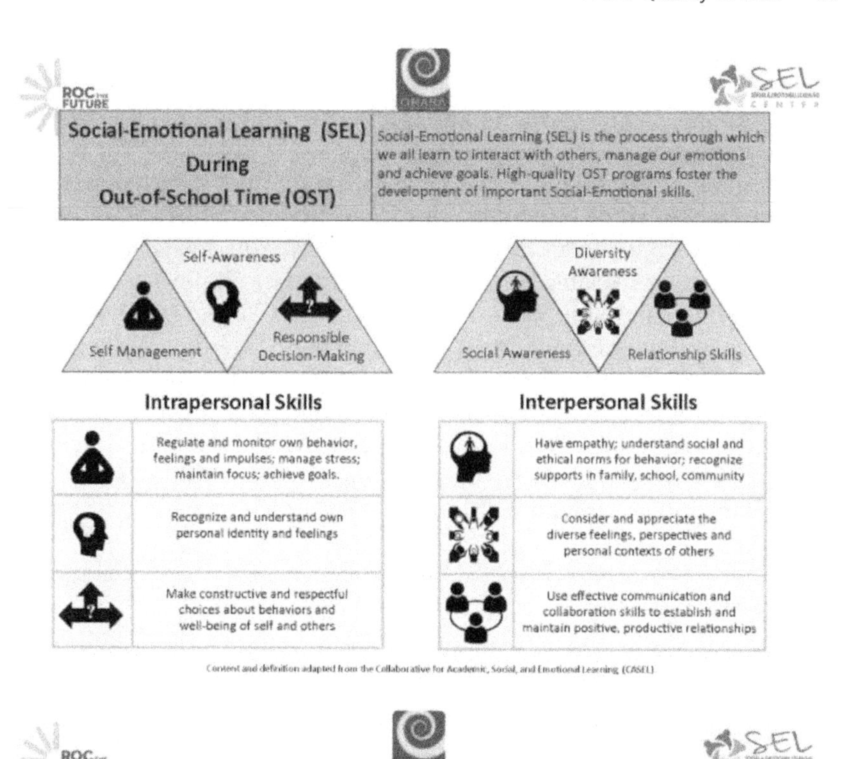

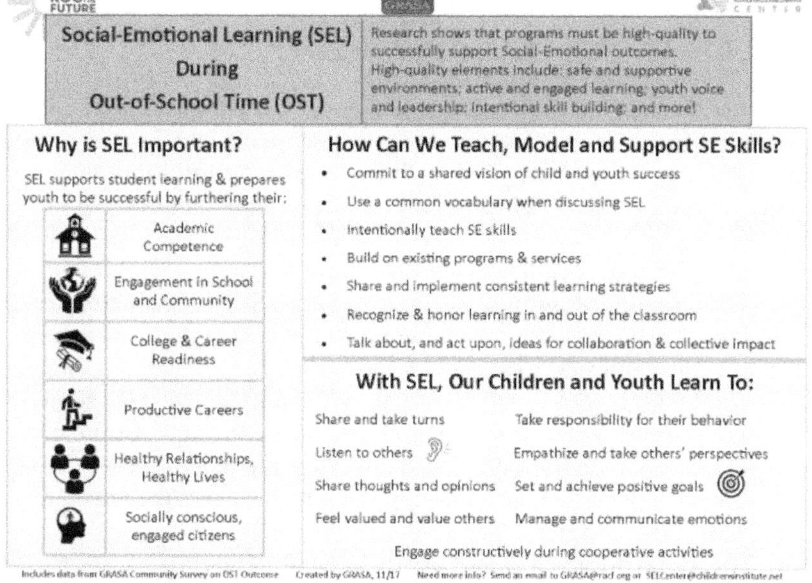

Figure 3.1 Community-wide SEL infographic, Slides 1 and 2. *Source:* GRASA, SEL Center, ROCtheFuture, SEL subcommittee, 2017.

to eighth grade) experience 6 weeks of project-based learning and enrichment that includes all youth learning how to swim. Small class sizes (15 youth) and a 1:5 adult-to-youth ratio facilitate a caring community with the ability to provide small-group and individualized instruction.

This small, safe community coming together summer after summer lends itself to embedded SEL practices and concepts that address the "whole" child. The primary focus at the program sites is highly academic, with defined outcomes related to literacy, kindergarten readiness, third-grade reading proficiency, and high school graduation. However, GRSLA takes advantage of the time youth are in the program to intentionally help them grow socially and develop emotionally. SummerLEAP OST programming presents a unique opportunity for providers to include practices and activities that result in SEL. That is, the programs are intentionally developing youth who are better decision makers, more engaged and aware citizens, and caring and empathetic individuals.

Program Approach

RULER

The primary strategy GRSLA uses to help youth develop their emotional intelligence is the RULER approach to SEL (www.ruler.yale.edu), developed by Dr. Marc A. Brackett at Yale University. Within our consortium of programs, two sites (Horizons at Harley and summerLEAP at The College at Brockport) have implemented the RULER approach, and one site (summerLEAP at Allendale Columbia School) has piloted it. RULER is an acronym that stands for recognizing, understanding, labeling, expressing, and regulating emotions. According to the Yale Center for Emotional Intelligence (n.d.), the RULER framework consists of four "anchors":

- The Charter—a collaborative document that helps classrooms/schools establish supportive and productive learning environments. The Charter is created by members of the class/school, outlining how they aspire to treat each other.
- The Mood Meter—an activity that helps youth and staff become more mindful of how their emotions change throughout the day, and how their emotions in turn affect their actions. The Mood Meter helps participants develop the self-awareness they need to inform their choices.
- The Meta-Moment—a tool that helps youth and staff handle strong emotions by encouraging them to pause and think before acting, which helps them make better decisions for themselves and their community.

- The Blueprint—a tool that helps youth and staff manage conflict effectively by considering a disagreement from the other person's perspective, as well as their own. Participants develop empathy by considering each other's feelings and working collaboratively to identify healthy solutions to conflicts.

The four anchors are built upon sequentially: The Charter is the first activity, followed by the introduction and use of the Mood Meter. Once these two anchors are in place, they facilitate use of the Meta-Moment and the Blueprint. The Charter is a collaborative document created by members of the classroom, outlining how they aspire to treat each other. Together, they describe how they want to feel at school, the behaviors that foster those feelings, and guidelines for preventing and managing unwanted feelings and conflict. By working together to build the Charter, everyone establishes common goals and holds each other accountable for creating the positive climate they envision.

Mood Meter

Although the GRSLA program sites implemented all four anchors, the Mood Meter was one of the favorite activities of participating youth. In morning circle each day, youth and adults (teachers, classroom assistants, support staff, and volunteers) charted themselves and got an opportunity to tell the whole group why they felt the way they did. This activity was powerful in many ways, but two, in particular, stand out. First, youth were each afforded the opportunity to, in a sense, "let out" why they were feeling a certain way, which was especially important if negative emotions were stirring. Even more important was that the teachers (and other adults) in the classroom received insight for the day on what a particular youth might be feeling. The stories that emerged as youth shared the genesis of their feelings or emotions sometimes involved happy occasions (birthdays, a family member returning from prison), but more often were related to violence, loss, or abuse that would instantly evoke empathy from their classmates, and put the adults on alert to use extra sensitivity around the child for the day. For example, one morning a child shared that his mom had been beaten by her boyfriend the night before, resulting in the mother being hospitalized and the boyfriend being jailed. During the morning Mood Meter check-in, he shared that he was feeling sad for his mother, afraid of the boyfriend, and angry and embarrassed about having to stay with relatives. Clearly there was a lot going on for this child as he commenced his day at the program. The Mood Meter activity provided him the opportunity to articulate his feelings (building his self-awareness skills), which resulted in him being embraced and comforted by his classmates (building their empathy skills), and being reassured by the adults of his safety and their concern (building relationships skills). Powerful interactions such as this were experienced on a daily basis and at all grade levels.

One challenge we encountered in using the Mood Meter was that some teachers, staff, and family members were not prepared, or were unwilling, to discuss their emotions. In response, we added additional in-program coaching for our faculty and staff, and made the RULER approach training available to family members and guardians. Our faculty and staff reported becoming more comfortable with the topic of emotions in their classrooms, resulting in stronger relationships with youth. Family members took advantage of the training and were grateful to learn, together with their children, strategies to communicate and understand each other better.

Feeling Words Curriculum

Although not one of the four anchors, another critical component of the RULER approach is the *Feeling Words Curriculum.* GRSLA found this aspect particularly compelling for our programs because of our focus on literacy. Arranged by grade level (Grades K–2 and 3–5), the Feeling Words Curriculum provides and expands the vocabulary through which youth can express their emotions. It empowers youth and adults to articulate and describe the full range of human emotions, rather than being stuck with an inadequate and limited vocabulary that does not fully describe what they are feeling. When the right words are not available, communication is not optimal, which can lead to children's feelings becoming confused, suppressed, or even displaced onto others. In learning new language to describe their emotions, youth automatically enhance their writing and critical thinking skills, while also developing the creativity and empathy needed to build mutually supportive relationships.

At the program sites, each classroom was provided the Feeling Words Curriculum for their grade level. Teachers would use this during the morning Mood Meter check-in, and strategically during the day when the conversation lent itself to helping youth describe their feelings. For instance, in the morning Mood Meter check-in, teachers would often ask for additional potential words to describe a feeling expressed by a child or an adult. For example, if a child uses the word "angry," the Feeling Words Curriculum provides additional words such as furious, irritated, frustrated, or tense, helping youth to more accurately choose the level of pleasantness (or lack thereof) and related energy (intensity) plotted on the Mood Meter. Several weeks into the program, youth would be using previously unknown words to express their emotions, and the idea of emotionally safe classrooms was in motion.

Early Outcomes

Since 2013, we have extended and expanded our summer work to include the youngest students in our community. In summer 2017, GRSLA ran a pilot with 70 EPK students (five classrooms) and another 255 prekindergarten students (17 classrooms). As in previous years, these cohorts grew in preparation for their next grade level (i.e., kindergarten readiness). As a result, they also demonstrated growth in the SEL domains emphasized by the High Scope curriculum used by our early childhood education community, measured by the corresponding Child Observation Record (COR) assessment. We also implemented the Teacher-Child Rating Scale (T-CRS) assessment for the entire EPK and prekindergarten cohort. The T-CRS is a 32-item objective rating scale completed by teachers to assess children's problem behaviors and competencies. Its scales measure four primary domains:

- task orientation (e.g., functions well, even with distractions; poorly motivated to achieve);
- behavior control (e.g., copes well with failure; disruptive in class);
- assertiveness (e.g., expresses ideas willingly; anxious, worried); and
- peer social (e.g., has many friends; lacks social skills with peers).

Teachers completed the T-CRS in the fall and spring of prekindergarten and near the end of the summer program. Administering the T-CRS at these times permits assessment of the growth of individual youth. Overall, the results were very promising, demonstrating statistically significant impact:

COR Advantage

- The Combined Group ($n = 230$) had statistically significant changes in the following areas:
  - social and emotional development (growth); and
  - language, literacy, and communication (growth).

T-CRS

- The UPK go Kindergarten Group ($n = 196$) had statistically significant growth in the following area:
  - peer social subscale.

Future Direction for GRSLA

Having identified SEL and growth as one of our key values in working with youth, GRSLA and summerLEAP will continue to highlight SEL in program guidelines, and to encourage all providers to continue incorporating activities that help youth and adults grow in this area. Just as we are committed to measuring and capturing the academic growth of our program participants to determine impact, and for program continuous improvement purposes, it is important to do the same for social and emotional growth and development. When necessary, we will provide training for faculty and family members, and we will continue to benchmark and make recommendations to consortium members about SEL programs and models appropriate for a limited (5–6 weeks) summer experience.

CONCLUSION

With its sustained efforts around SEL and program quality, and the current emphasis on collaborative action and collective impact, there is renewed excitement in the Rochester OST community. The GRASA network continues to expand, with new and nontraditional partners joining for the first time, and previous members who fell by the wayside returning to the table. Connections with intermediaries across the country allow us to learn from others who have gone before us down this path. Hopes are high, recognizing that we are starting the process with a solid and growing foundation that already reaches across sectors, draws on collective knowledge, and has a beginner's capacity to show success and share learning. Understanding that our whole will be stronger than the sum of its parts, Rochester will continue to commit its focused energy and efforts on behalf of all our children.

REFERENCES

Durlak, J. A., Weissberg, R. P., Dymnicki, A. B., Taylor, R. D., & Schellinger, K. B. (2011). The impact of enhancing students' social and emotional learning: A meta-analysis of school-based universal interventions. *Child Development, 82*(1), 405–432.

Eccles, J., & Gootman, J. A. (Eds.). (2002). *Community programs to promote youth development.* Washington, DC: National Academy Press. Retrieved from https://www.nap.edu/read/10022/chapter/1

Greater Rochester Health Foundation. (n.d.). The Greater Rochester Initiative for Children's Social and Emotional Health Implementation Task Force description. Retrieved from http://www.thegrhf.org/news-and-reports/reports/childrens-social-and-emotional-health/

Helegda, K., Roy, L., Smith, L., & Macleod, C. (2017). *Youth program quality intervention report: 2016–17 findings from the Greater Rochester After-School Alliance.* Ypsilanti, MI: The David P. Weikart Center for Youth Program Quality.

Naglieri, J. A., LeBuffe, P. A., & Shapiro, V. B. (2014). *DESSA-mini: Devereux Student Strengths Assessment K–8th grade. A universal screening and progress monitoring system for social-emotional competencies.* Charlotte, NC: Devereux Foundation.

Sniegowski, S., Newman, J., & Devaney, E. (2016). *Rochester Area Community Foundation education equity (youth) third party evaluation: Final report year 1: 2015–16.* Washington, DC: American Institutes for Research.

The After School Corporation. (2008). *The Rochester after-school plan: A report to Mayor Robert Duffy and Superintendent Jean-Claude Brizard from the working group of the Rochester after-school task force.* New York, NY: Author.

Yale Center for Emotional Intelligence. (n.d.). The Anchor Tools. Retrieved from http://ei.yale.edu/ruler/the-anchor-tools/

Zimmer, A., Devaney, E., Embt, K., & Lotyczewski, B. (2017). *Greater Rochester After-School Alliance (GRASA) 2016–2017 assessment report.* Rochester, NY: Children's Institute.

CHAPTER 4

SOCIAL AND EMOTIONAL LEARNING IN ELEMENTARY SCHOOL

Bridget Durkan Laird, Jolie Logan, and Elizabeth Mester

WINGS came into the picture in 1996, before many people were using—or had even heard of—the term *social and emotional learning* (SEL). As we started our work, we encountered plenty of skepticism about the value of social and emotional skills. We've come a long way since those early days, and thankfully for children all over the country, SEL is recognized, valued, and supported by ever-expanding research as an important contributor to behavioral improvements, academic achievement, and overall factors of long-term success.

Over 21 years, we've had many ups and downs, wins and losses. We've tried new things—some that worked and some that didn't. Through it all we have held tight to three core beliefs that have guided our work:

1. SEL starts with a positive culture and climate, and this type of environment doesn't happen by accident. It must be fostered with great intentionality and diligently maintained.

Social and Emotional Learning in Out-of-School Time, pages 53–71

2. SEL is fundamentally a "way" of teaching through your interactions, engagement, and relationships with children. It's not another workbook on a shelf or something to do in addition to teaching. SEL takes place when adults' social and emotional skills and practices are developed.
3. And because of number one and two, training and professional development of staff is a top priority.

In the first part of this chapter, we will share our journey as one of the earliest organizations on the scene and provide insights into how we've used these three beliefs to shape our unique approach to SEL. In part two, we will discuss the turning point that led us down the path of a 4-year randomized control trial, and what it means for the field and for our future direction.

PART I: BACKGROUND

The Inspiration

In 1995, WINGS founder Ginny Deerin attended a women's leadership conference and heard Johnetta Cole, then president of Atlanta's Spelman College, give a keynote address where she spoke about how girls and women often keep themselves locked up in small birdcages. Deerin recalls Cole urging the audience to envision themselves soaring beyond the cage—"the door is open, it's up to you to fly." During this same time, Deerin began recognizing a set of skills like empathy, individuality, and communication that could have guided her life differently if she had learned them early on. It was then that Deerin made a commitment to helping youth learn these skills. On a yellow legal pad she scribbled a list of the vital skills, using layman's words, and crafted a mission for what she wanted to achieve: "By the time that children are teenagers, they will know how to live joyfully, powerfully, and responsibly." Flying home from the conference, she happened upon a copy of *TIME* Magazine featuring Daniel Goleman on the cover. Goleman (1995) had just written the book *Emotional Intelligence.* Inside, Deerin found a list that nearly matched perfectly the one she'd sketched on the legal pad, enumerating the skills of an emotionally intelligent individual. But it was the Emily Dickinson (1983) poem "'Hope' is the thing with feathers" that pulled all of these moments together, inspired our name, and distilled Deerin's vision—to help children soar with WINGS.

And so, in 1996, after consulting educational experts and developing a set of preliminary learning objectives, Deerin launched a 1-week summer camp—WINGS for Girls—designed to help girls between the ages of 8 and 12 years old develop their emotional and social intelligence. The camp

"Hope" is the thing with feathers
by Emily Dickinson

"Hope" is the thing with feathers—
That perches in the soul—
And sings the tune without the words—
And never stops—at all—

And sweetest—in the Gale—is heard—
And sore must be the storm—
That could abash the little Bird
That kept so many warm—

I've heard it in the chillest land—
And on the strangest Sea—
Yet, never, in Extremity,
It asked a crumb—of me.

taught the girls skills like identifying feelings, introspection, self-acceptance, handling stress and releasing tension, personal decision-making, communicating with others, and conflict resolution. Similar to WINGS today, the camp model of one counselor for each small group of girls allowed developing relationships and establishing positive bonds to take center stage. More than 100 girls from diverse backgrounds participated. We quickly realized that 1 week of camp—even with intentional follow-up—wasn't enough time for us or the girls. Not only that, young boys needed all of the lessons and connections we were instilling in WINGS girls. When summer ended and the superintendent of schools asked for the WINGS model as an out-of-school time (OST) program for a Charleston, South Carolina, elementary school, the WINGS for Kids program was launched.

That program to give youth a comprehensive social and emotional education outside of school time was the start of WINGS for Kids. In the years since, the program has grown and evolved, continuing to develop and test strategies, hone teaching practices, and create new materials. What has never changed is our desire to instill those missing life lessons within a fresh and fun OST program so youth can live joyfully, powerfully, and responsibly.

Exclusive Focus on Low-Income Youth

Located in downtown Charleston, Memminger Elementary School was a failing Title I school where 95% of students received free or reduced-price meals. Memminger scored 96.11 out of 100 on the State of South Carolina's Poverty Index, placing it in the bottom 11% of all schools in the state (South Carolina Department of Education, n.d.). What became glaringly obvious from our initial year at Memminger was the lack of opportunities, particularly OST activities, available for low-income children.

Children living in poverty experience trauma at greater rates than their more affluent peers. As a result, they have an average 18-month lag in achievement behind their higher-income counterparts. Chronically elevated levels of stress associated with these circumstances can impact cognitive development and result in diminished executive function and self-regulation skills (van der Kolk, Roth, Pelcovitz, Sunday, & Spinazzola, 2005). Executive function and self-regulation are important mental processes for planning, focusing attention, remembering instructions, and juggling multiple tasks successfully. Reaching children early on fortifies them with the skills to stay in school and succeed in school—skills that are especially important because the elementary schools we serve feed into high schools that have been labeled by some as "dropout factories" (Balfanz & Legters, 2004). In order to help mitigate some of these challenges, not only did we seek out Title I schools, we intentionally focused on the children in these Title I schools who could benefit the most from WINGS: those who struggled with behavior issues, had failing academics, or lacked adult supervision after school.

From Day 1 that first year, we understood the powerful role college students could play as mentors in the lives of WINGS children. Likewise, because we served predominantly African American students, it became crucial we staff the program with role models who resemble our children. WINGS put a stake in the ground and decided to concentrate exclusively on reaching youth attending low-income schools. In doing so we could provide a safe place for them to go after school, and contribute to closing the opportunity gap by exposing them to extracurricular activities and caring mentors. Most important, we knew we could have meaningful impact by helping youth develop the skills to be resilient in the context of their environment. We are teaching skills that can radically change how they relate to others and behave in school. We are providing inspiration to do well in school and *stay* in school. We are fostering in them a belief in possibilities—and the hope for a bright future.

PART II: THE WINGS MODEL

Positive Culture

We are very intentional about our culture—the culture in the program as well as the culture of our administrative office—and it shows in all that we do: the language we use, the policies we set, the expectations we have of everyone on the team. We call it "WINGSY," and it is woven through every aspect of the organization. Language is an important element of our culture, and we take it to the extreme: we're always "flying high," we're "flappy" to see you, our meetings are "Soar Sessions," our corporate office is called "Soarporate," and we "let our wings out" when we meet new people. We embrace the "fun factor" at all levels of the organization because it's a notable element of our program, as we'll explain shortly. We are very serious about our work but also intentional about making sure to have fun from time to time. Our office (and all of our program offices) are equipped with a "compliment corner," a place for staff to praise other staff. We "stop, drop, and roll" when others need a hand or support. If you were to visit our office on a Friday, you would be invited to join us for "family lunch," our weekly ritual of gathering around the family table to share a meal together.

The WINGS culture is even more evident at our program sites. When you walk into a WINGS program there is an unmistakable energy; we call it a vibe. Similar to the family environment we foster at Soarporate, in our programs we want our children to feel like WINGS is their home away from home, a place where they belong, and feel safe and wholly cared for.

Culture is critical to creating a climate where SEL can thrive. Our goal is to create a supportive and engaging environment where youth can learn and soar. We do this in three ways:

1. Encouraging youth to become the best version of themselves.
2. Creating a community where everyone is valued.
3. Making learning fun!

Encouraging Youth to Become the Best Version of Themselves

WINGS is a safe place to learn how to take accountability for choices and actions, how to manage emotions, and how to deal with conflict. We help children identify their strengths and weaknesses, and feel empowered and inspired to participate, all while feeling supported and encouraged to be the best version of themselves.

Creating a Community Where Everyone Is Valued

WINGS is a community where all children feel like they belong. A place where children are free to make mistakes and try new things. We promote decision-making and uniqueness; we listen and pay attention. Our staff models kindness and fosters a deep sense of purpose and inclusiveness within each child.

Making Learning Fun

A WINGS program is *fun,* and a place where youth are comfortable: they can be loud or messy, laugh, use their imagination, and experience new and different things. Our focus on the "fun factor" is one of the ways we drive school attendance. If you don't attend school, you can't attend WINGS, and our youth don't want to miss WINGS.

Through innovation, growth, and creative activities, WINGS feels nothing like the school day. And we intentionally create this environment in big and little ways: we sit on the floor in groups, play music, have special handshakes, dance, and sing. Our focus on fun is also why we choose to reinforce and recognize positive behavior more than we correct negative behavior.

This kind of culture doesn't happen on its own, and it takes constant vigilance to maintain it. We carefully monitor culture through site visits and program assessments, but probably the most powerful way we maintain our program culture is through practicing what we preach by following the same guiding principles with our internal leadership and management practices—bringing out staff members' best, ensuring staff feel valued, and as we mentioned, injecting a little fun here and there.

When we establish a relationship with a new school or partner organization, culture is always front of mind. We look for partners who are willing to embrace our culture and understand its importance in producing meaningful outcomes for children.

Comprehensive Curriculum

All learning is social and emotional, and every interaction is a ripe opportunity for social and emotional skill development. Emotional intelligence refers to the ability to perceive, control, and evaluate emotions. Emotional quotient (EQ) is a measure of a person's adequacy in such areas as self-awareness, empathy, and dealing sensitively with other people and their emotions. Old beliefs only emphasized one kind of smart: book smart. Now, after years of research, brain science has shed light on a new perspective: paired together, emotions and intellect are the new smart. EQ is just as important as IQ, if not more so.

According to the Collaborative for Academic, Social, and Emotional Learning (CASEL), SEL is the process through which children and adults acquire and effectively apply the knowledge, attitudes, and skills necessary to understand and manage emotions, set and achieve positive goals, feel and show empathy for others, establish and maintain positive relationships, and make responsible decisions. Everything we teach at WINGS is rooted in the five core social and emotional competencies:

1. self-awareness (identifying emotions, accurate self-perception, recognizing strengths, self-confidence, self-efficacy);
2. self-management (impulse control, stress management, self-discipline);
3. responsible decision-making (identifying problems, analyzing situations, solving problems, reflecting);
4. social awareness (perspective-taking, empathy, appreciating diversity, respect for other); and
5. relationship skills (communication, relationship building, teamwork).

We've made these core competencies easy to understand and fun to learn with what we call The Creed (see Figure 4.1). The WINGS Creed provides a common language that is memorable and transferable to any situation or environment. It is our mantra, the epitome of our culture, and the

The WINGS Creed

I soar with WINGS. Let me tell you why. I learn lots of skills **that help me reach the sky.**

I love and accept **who I am on the inside and know my emotions are nothing to hide.**

Life's full of surprises that make me feel different ways. If I can control myself**, I will have much better days.**

I understand the choices I make **should be what's best for me to do, and what happens is on me and not any of you.**

I understand others are unique. I want to learn more about everyone I meet. I want to step into their shoes **and see what they are going through.**

I am a friend. I support and trust. Working together **is a must. Kind and caring I will be. I listen to you. You listen to me.**

I soar with WINGS. I just told you why. All of these things are why I fly high.

Figure 4.1 The Wings CREED.

foundation of everything we teach, and it serves as a compass for navigating all aspects of life.

In order to effectively teach social and emotional skills, you must first possess emotional intelligence. At WINGS, the first expectation of every employee is to live The Creed. We live The Creed in our interactions with one another and in our interactions with the youth in our programs. Reciting The Creed daily, our youth have come up with hand movements and interpretative gestures for each line. The result is a high-energy recitation, similar to a camp song or a rally cry that starts each program day.

The WINGS Creed is made up of seven verses, five of which align directly to each core competency, or skill. Our explicit teaching of these social and emotional skills is done through The Creed and 10 specific social and emotional lessons. Each lesson has a learning objective and a tip or technique to aid in teaching (see Figure 4.2).

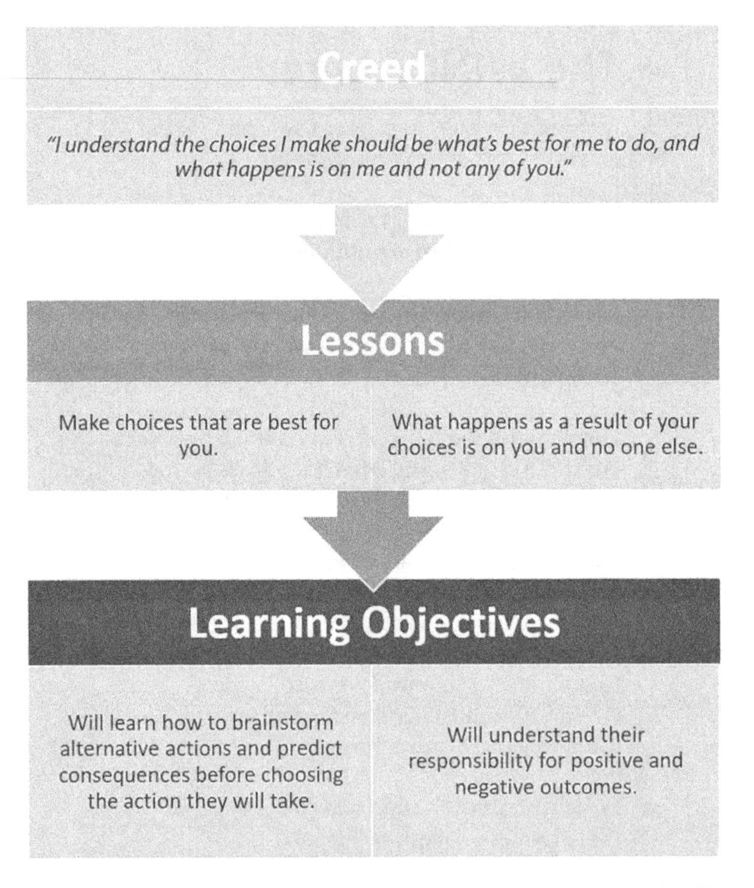

Figure 4.2 Example lesson and learning objective corresponding with a line of The Creed.

While curriculum is an important element for any program, it's how we teach that matters most:

1. We integrate SEL into all program activities.
2. Lessons are reinforced in small teachable moments that occur throughout the day.
3. We model social and emotional skills in the way we engage with youth and interact with our peers.

Integrating SEL Into All Activities

Each week focuses on one or two lessons. These lessons allow staff to use a universal language when teaching children social and emotional skills. Weekly lessons are first introduced during *Community Unity*, which starts each day. As a community, staff and youth discuss the week's lesson, play games, and reflect upon moments when this lesson was in action; recite The Creed; and participate in positive recognition. For example, when the lesson of the week is "accept responsibility for what you do," staff use the teaching tip "Show Your ID." Show your ID encourages young people to own up to things without placing blame by stating what "I did . . . " to contribute to either the positive or negative outcome. After playing a game, say Telephone, staff guide youth in a discussion with prompting questions like, "Can you show your ID for something good you were responsible for during the game?" or "Does anyone want to show their ID for blaming others during the game instead of taking responsibility for yourself?"

Academic Center provides homework assistance and the opportunity to further build ELA, STEM, and math competencies, all while staff reinforce The Creed and the weekly social and emotional lessons. Staff might use the "Show Your ID," technique when a child says their teacher didn't give any homework, when in fact the homework was left in the classroom, to encourage accountability. Or a staff member might say "show your ID" to a student who helped her peer with a tricky math problem and provided words of encouragement. It's moments like these that can plant confidence or lessen anxieties, creating space for academic learning to happen.

Enrichment Time exposes our children to extracurricular activities and free play—real-time opportunities to continue capitalizing on The Creed and contemplating the weekly lesson. When youth participate in activities such as soccer or lacrosse, cooking, art, or music, staff have ample occasions to tie in the weekly lesson and The Creed by reflecting on teamwork, participation, creativity, or focus. Continuing the "Show Your ID" example, staff and youth can discuss the role each member of the winning team played, how an individual youth finished his or her art project, or what each member of the dance team accomplished.

The week's lesson culminates in *Wild WINGS*: a celebration of the social and emotional lesson and an opportunity for staff to play and interact together, on the children's level. We intentionally make Wild WINGS high energy, relevant to our children's interests, and packed with new experiences.

Teachable Moments

Teachable moments happen in real time, all the time. Staff look for situations where they can reinforce The Creed or weekly lessons in group or individual settings. When staff capitalize on teachable moments, WINGS youth hear and internalize The Creed—*in real time*—helping to develop their social and emotional skills. Beyond utilizing language from The Creed, staff are encouraged to show thoughtfulness through three approaches:

- Acknowledging behaviors: Pointing out the positive socially and emotionally smart behaviors that you want to see happen again.
- Conversation prompts: Engaging the child in a conversation that deepens SEL—it can be a question you ask, maybe to reflect or think about something with a different perspective, or it may just be a statement to get the conversation started.
- Assigning tasks: Giving the child a task that will help build any of the SE skills.

From trips to the bathroom, walking the hallways, and lining up to transition to the next activity—these moments are rich with opportunities to acknowledge positive behavior, have a social and emotional skills-based conversation, or assign a task that builds social and emotional skills. It can take years of experience for a staff member to learn how to incorporate lessons into these small moments, but with The Creed, staff can infuse these teachable moments quickly and easily because they have a vocabulary to pull from.

Modeling

We believe you can teach more with your attitude and actions than you can with your words alone. In order to effectively teach social and emotional skills, staff must model these skills by using positive body language, making responsible decisions, taking accountability (showing their ID), and encouraging the display of social and emotional skills in others. Simply put—staff are role models to each other and to WINGS children.

We have a saying, "Let your WINGS out," which encourages staff to display, act, and live the lines of The Creed. Are you showing the world your wings by being kind and caring? Are you listening, trusting, and willing to compromise? "Let your WINGS out" is a quick way to model positive behavior and have a positive attitude.

One of the most significant concepts we model is to take responsibility for both positive and negative outcomes. Using the technique, "Show your ID" one more time, if a staff member has been curt or shown frustration with a child, the staff member can use this as an opportunity to be accountable to the group and admit the mistake: "Hey guys, can I show my ID? I didn't explain things very well and that got us all a little frustrated. Next time I'll make sure to really think through the instructions before we start."

When children hear staff naming emotions to describe how they feel, admitting a weakness and asking for help, or not rattling off excuses but instead taking responsibility, they feel valued and respected. When youth see staff taking a moment to breathe, using their manners, working as a team, or taking the time to listen to them without getting distracted, they feel safe and supported. And these feelings of value and support are not exclusive to our children. When the staff models social and emotional skills with each other, they learn from one another, feel empowered, are challenged, and are filled with new ideas and opportunities.

Training Is a Top Priority

From very early on, we recognized that the staff who interacted with children were the magic-makers, the link from our curriculum to our impact. In order to teach emotional intelligence skills you first have to possess the skills yourself. In our early years, annual staff training was a camp of its own—a week long and overnight. The training was packed with sessions during the day and group bonding activities in the evenings. This was possible with a staff of only 12. Now, with a full-time staff of 42 and a part-time staff of 108, we can no longer pull off the overnight format. But the overall approach we took in the early years remains at the core of how we conduct annual staff training today. Each year, the full-time staff kicks off the new school year with a full week of training, honing our own social and emotional skills. Over the course of the year, full-time staff come together for quarterly "Soar Sessions"—the time to further the lessons introduced at training.

We invest heavily in recruiting, hiring, and training—especially for the staff who work directly with youth. And our experience has shown that investing in the training and development of staff pays huge dividends for our children. Each summer after full-time training, part-time staff, some of whom are returning from the year before and some of whom are new hires, participate in two full weeks of training—all before the programs even start. Pre-service training includes 80 hours on topics like "Empowering Kids in Poverty," "Using Behavior Techniques With Empathy," and "Implementing Social and Emotional Skill Building Through Teachable Moments." Staff begin to learn how to internalize and then model the five social and emotional skills, with the goal of supporting, engaging, and teaching children.

At the core of our training is empathy: stepping into the shoes of our children. Daily sessions teach staff how to get on their level to enable them to be children. From start to finish, training is hands-on, high-energy, engaging, and inspiring—laying the foundation for the culture and climate of the WINGS program. We intentionally replicate the energy, support, and engagement we want the youth in our programs to experience. Our talented training team provides an experience unlike traditional trainings. New staff feel safe to learn about themselves and their social and emotional competencies, all while having fun and bonding with team members.

Additional training and professional development happens over the course of the year through ongoing trainings with sessions like "Child Development Levels," "Kid Play," "When Consequences Don't Work," and "Teach by Being a Role Model." Weekly staff meetings also provide time for program leaders to coach their team and provide constructive and positive feedback in a small group setting. Quarterly staff evaluations determine whether staff members are in fact positive, encouraging, fair, trusting, empathetic, and good listeners, and identifies strengths and weaknesses. Through ongoing feedback and constant coaching, staff continue to learn and grow their own skillset throughout the year, positively impacting their effectiveness as a mentor and role model.

Staff are a significant investment—but are 100% what makes the program unique. When you walk into a WINGS program, you feel it through the positive energy, the kid-friendly environment, and the family vibe. That doesn't happen with a program model alone. It's only when the adults have developed their own social and emotional competencies and have internalized the WINGS "way" of teaching that children soar.

PART III: INNOVATION DRIVEN BY RESEARCH AND DATA

Early Results

From our beginning, we have been committed to collecting data and engaging in research. In 2005, we were feeling great about the work we were doing on the ground with young people. Yale University conducted preliminary research on our program that showed positive results for a sample of children who participated in the program compared to those who did not participate. The research found greater academic achievement (Ivcevic & Brackett, 2005) and increased self-esteem and higher satisfaction with school (Ivcevic, Rivers, & Brackett, 2004). In addition, children were engaged and loved the program, staff and families were raving about it, and the staff were witnessing (and experiencing) life-changing moments every day. Excited about the potential, we were anxious to spread our own WINGS to reach more and more youth.

Our first attempt at growth was a middle-school leadership academy. The thought was that this would help us stay with our children for a longer period of time. After 2 years, we realized that our expertise and strength was elementary school, and that to deliver the most impact, we needed to focus on one thing and do it really well. Our second attempt at growth was through the WINGS Development partner program. This program was aimed at partnering with others to infuse SEL into their existing programs. Although the partners enjoyed using the WINGS activities and working with us, we did not feel our work with them was truly impacting children.

From the outside looking in, what we were doing appeared successful. We had eight partners and had even grown across state lines with partnerships in Washington, DC. We also had the positive findings from Yale University. But we were uneasy. The positive outcomes were not necessarily things we had intentionally set out to achieve. We were essentially casting a wide net, trying a lot of things, and then happy that the data indicated that good things were happening as a result of our work. We weren't sure that we could explain exactly how we were getting positive results. We were feeling uncertain and not sure how to move forward. We engaged a consultant, who introduced us to the "theory of change" concept and led us through the process of defining our specific theory of change. In order to grow in a meaningful way, it was necessary to first figure out what it was that we were intentionally trying to achieve. What specific impact did we truly want to have on the youth in the program? How would we measure it? We answered these questions in a four-day intensive session that included board members, senior staff, and direct-service staff. The session was brutal, and forced us to make some very hard decisions. One of the hardest decisions was to step back from the partnership work in order to test and refine our theory of change through our direct-service programs. It was tough to pause on our expansion but we knew if we wanted to be successful in the long run that we needed to take this time to step back and build a strong foundation.

With a theory of change in hand (see Figure 4.3), our next steps were to codify our current program, create a performance management system to track our progress towards our short-term goals, and then expand our direct service to additional schools in our area. Our goal was to open one new school in Charleston per year for the next 3 years. The intention here was to have enough children in the program for a full-scale evaluation. The evaluation would start with an implementation study to look at the fidelity of our program delivery, and end with an impact study to evaluate the outcomes youth were achieving as a result of participation in WINGS. Essentially, we wanted to know that we were really doing what we claimed to do.

Original Theory of Change

When children get WINGS for two years, they:

- Develop strong social and emotional skills.
- Improve behavior and school attendance in elementary school.

Which leads to:

- Positive behavior and school attachment in middle school.
- A future hope and expectation of graduating from high school and avoiding jail and teenage parenthood.

Figure 4.3 Original theory of change.

We documented every piece of our program procedures and training so that each program site could operate in exactly the same way. Deciding what to include in the performance management system was even tougher.

We had two key short-term goals: for youth to know and understand social and emotional skills, and to use them in their everyday lives. Initially we measured their knowledge and understanding of the skills by their ability to recite the WINGS Creed. This later evolved into a more thorough Objective Knowledge Assessment to measure each child's knowledge and comprehension of the learning objectives taught during the preceding period. Initially, to measure how they were using the skills in everyday life, we asked them to provide a meaningful example of using The Creed at home or in the classroom. We would eventually use the Devereux Student Strengths Assessment (DESSA) to capture classroom teacher and staff observations of behavior. Measuring observable behavior has proved to be a more meaningful way to measure outcomes than a child's own perception of their behavior.

Our approach to performance management has come a long way. Getting to where we are today is based on a continuous learning process. Initially we tracked every data point we could come up with. While we took this "capture everything" approach for a couple of years, it eventually proved too cumbersome and too scattered to be meaningful. It was also extraordinarily time consuming and resulted in an overwhelming amount of data to interpret. Learning and adapting is an operational value we are proud of, so we continuously refine our goals and key measures, along with our approach to performance management.

Along the way we've also learned that measuring SEL is not an easy thing to do. Fortunately, as we have evolved so has the field of SEL; helpful new field-tested tools, such as the DESSA, continue to emerge. In addition, we've learned to focus our performance measurement on the things we are intentionally trying to impact—social and emotional development, behavior, and school attendance. We've stopped trying to capture data that fall outside the scope of our theory of change. For example, our theory of change does

Current Theory of Change

When children get WINGS for two years, they:

- Develop strong social and emotional skills.
- Improve behavior and school attendance in elementary school.

Which leads to:

- Positive behavior and strong attachment to school in middle school.
- A future hope and expectation of high school graduation.

This current version shows our continuous evolution and refinement based on learnings from research and data.

Figure 4.4 Current theory of change.

not specifically include academic achievement. There is a growing base of research that supports the link between well-developed social and emotional skills and improved academic achievement (Durlak, Weissberg, Dymnicki, Taylor, & Schellinger, 2011). While we know that academic improvements are a benefit of the work that we do, and our program has academic components, our specific goals are to develop social and emotional skills, improve behavior, and improve school attendance. While it's not easy, having a focused theory of change helps us stay true to what we are trying to accomplish and avoid the trap of trying to be all things to all people (Figure 4.4).

Randomized Control Trial

Once the program model was fully codified, we developed our performance management system, and grew to a total of four schools in Charleston serving over 450 children, we were ready to begin a formal impact evaluation. Fortunately, we had established a relationship with the University of Virginia when one of their research teams used our program for a small study on the use of a fine motor skill intervention. Dr. David Grissmer led the fine motor skills study and was eager to dive deeper into evaluating the WINGS program after seeing it in action several times. Grissmer and his team wrote and received an Institute of Education Science grant from the U.S. Department of Education to conduct a full randomized control trial (RCT) of the program. About two years into the study, WINGS received a Social Innovation Fund grant from the Edna McConnell Clark foundation to expand the scope of the project by adding an implementation study. A team of researchers at the University of Virginia, College of Charleston, and Portland State worked together to complete the impact and implementation aspects of the study.

The study was aimed at using our theory of change and testing whether or not we were in fact having an effect on children's social and emotional skills and behavior (Figure 4.5). The study was a four-site, three-cohort, block-RCT, in which entering kindergartners were randomly assigned by gender to 24 implementation blocks: child-level random assignment to WINGS or to the control group was determined by gender within each school and within each of three entering cohorts of eligible kindergartners whose parents or guardians had applied for enrollment in the program. Both qualitative and quantitative data were collected, including child assessments, teacher observations during the school day, parent or guardian interviews, and fidelity observations.

Preliminary results show that children randomized into WINGS have statistically significant ($p < .05$) or marginally significant ($p < .10$) positive effects on ten important measures of teacher-rated classroom behavior and individual tests of children's developmental and academic skills. Multiple teacher-rated measures show a broad pattern of reduced negative behavior and improved quality of the relationship with teachers. The significant or marginally significant measures include executive function, naming

10 Questions the RCT Study Set Out to Answer

1. Does assignment to WINGS have a positive impact on children's person-centered competencies?
2. Does assignment to WINGS have a positive impact on children's relationships and behaviors in the classroom and at home, and if so, what mediates this effect?
3. Does assignment to WINGS have a positive impact on children's school outcomes (social and academic), and if so, what mediates this effect?
4. What are the impacts of WINGS on children's person-centered competencies, relationships and behaviors, and school outcomes after 1 year, 2 years, and 3 years?
5. Does assignment to WINGS impact the social school outcomes to a greater or lesser extent than academic school outcomes?
6. Does the impact of WINGS on children's person-centered competencies, relationships and behaviors, and school outcomes after 1 year, 2 years, and 3 years vary for children with different characteristics?
7. Does the impact of WINGS on children's person-centered competencies, relationships and behaviors, and school outcomes vary across the different sites within which random assignment was conducted?
8. Is variation in the impacts of assignment to WINGS related to children's attendance and engagement in the program?
9. Do the effects of assignment to WINGS vary across implementation blocks, and if so, is this variation related to implementation fidelity?
10. What are the family characteristics and home experiences of all children in the study and the out-of-school time experiences of children who are not randomly assigned to WINGS?

Figure 4.5 Ten questions the RCT study set out to answer.

vocabulary, letter-word ID, and improved classroom behavior (closeness, less hyperactivity and bullying, and self-regulation).

Lessons Learned

Results aside, some of our most important learning has come from challenges related to conducting an RCT within a low-income demographic—challenges related to transiency rates, dosage, and disparity in how schools measure behavioral issues.

Disparity in School Behavior Data

There is no consistent standard among schools for defining what constitutes a behavior referral, and great disparity in what kind of information is tracked at the school level. Some elementary schools maintain school behavior grades while others do not. Additionally, depending on what data the school tracks, in some cases behavior-related data were considered health information and therefore subject to privacy considerations.

High Transiency Rates

Children in low-income households move frequently, which made it difficult for the researchers to track them over the entire study period. As a result, we now evaluate school attendance prior to WINGS enrollment, targeting students who have been present for multiple years.

Dosage

A condition of enrollment in the WINGS program is to attend every day. Children who do not maintain full-time attendance are dismissed from the program, allowing a child on the waitlist to fill the full-time spot. To maintain the integrity of the study, we made exceptions and allowed children assigned to WINGS as part of the study to stay in the program even if they were not meeting our attendance requirements. However, only children who received the minimum dosage of 100 days were factored into results, and since not all original participants maintained full-time attendance, preliminary results indicate the power of the study was diminished based on the number of qualifying children.

The implementation study also provided valuable lessons about the quality of our program and ways in which we could improve on the model. As a result of the study we made small but important changes to the program. For example, some activities have been modified or are being developed to address the needs of different ages of children in the program. We have also started pairing staff for some program components as a way to provide additional support to them.

Finally, to address the high transiency rate of children entering the program at different points during the school year, we reorganized our learning objectives and teaching sequence to accommodate both new children entering the program and the children who started the program at the beginning of the year.

We are committed to quality and impact. While the RCT methodology is rigorous and the challenges mentioned made it an imperfect process, it did help advance our efforts to deliver the highest quality program possible and to produce meaningful outcomes for the children we serve. We look forward to sharing the final results of the research and contributing to the growing evidence base in the field. We also believe our lessons learned can be of value to others, by inspiring others to utilize what we've learned and, equally as important, highlighting areas that would benefit from additional or deeper study via future research projects.

Future Direction

The intensity with which we train front-line staff, as we've shared here, and the many years we've had to hone our approach provide a strong foundation for our next phase of learning—testing and evaluating training methods to effectively foster adult social and emotional skill development. We plan to work with other OST programs, nonprofits, and school districts by providing training and technical assistance around integrating SEL. As we further this work we will be gathering and analyzing data to contribute to best practices in professional development as it relates to teaching children social and emotional skills. By continuing to share what we're learning, our hope is that others will benefit from our experience and use our lessons learned to create meaningful impact for more children.

CONCLUSION

SEL is important work—life-changing work. Creating a culture where SEL can thrive, modeling social and emotional skills and teaching in a way that is supportive and engaging, and always learning is the WINGS way of accomplishing this. We firmly believe that SEL can't be reduced to a checklist of things to teach; it is an ongoing process of adults leading by example in small and big ways—again, and again, and again. Only when we as adults build and enhance our own skills can we better create a supportive and engaging environment where children can learn and soar.

REFERENCES

Balfanz, R., & Legters, N. (2004). *Locating the dropout crisis: Which high schools produce the nation's dropouts? Where are they located? Who attends them?* Baltimore, MD: Center for Research on the Education of Students Placed at Risk, Johns Hopkins University.

Dickinson, E. (1976). "'Hope' is the thing with feathers." In T. H. Johnson (Ed.), *The Complete Poems of Emily Dickinson* (p. 116). Cambridge, MA: The Belknap Press of Harvard University Press.

Durlak, J., Weissberg, R., Dymnicki, A., Taylor, R., & Schellinger, K. (2011). The impact of enhancing students' social and emotional learning: A meta-analysis of school-based universal interventions. *Child Development, 82*(1), 405–432.

Goleman, D. (1995). *Emotional intelligence.* New York, NY: Bantam Books.

Ivcevic, Z., & Brackett, M. (2005). *WINGS for Kids evaluation study for academic years 2001/02, 2002/03, 2003/04, and 2004/05: Academic outcomes.* Unpublished report, Department of Psychology, Yale University, New Haven, CT.

Ivcevic, Z., Rivers, S., & Brackett, M. (2004). *WINGS for Kids evaluation study for academic years 2001/2002, 2002/2003, and 2003/2004: Social and emotional outcomes.* Unpublished report, Health, Emotion, Behavior Laboratory, Department of Psychology, Yale University, New Haven, CT.

South Carolina Department of Education. (n.d.). *South Carolina Department of Education Poverty Index.* Retrieved from https://ed.sc.gov/data/report-cards/state-report-cards/2015/

van der Kolk, B., Roth, S. Pelcovitz, D., Sunday, S., & Spinazzola, J. (2005). Disorders of extreme stress: The empirical foundation of a complex adaptation to trauma. *Journal of Traumatic Stress, 18*(5), 389–399.

CHAPTER 5

A COMBINED APPROACH TO SUMMER, SEL, AND STEM IN BOSTON AND PROVIDENCE

Hillary Salmons and Chris Smith

TAKING LEARNING OUT OF ACRONYM SILOS AND INTO REAL LIFE

Until recently, the terms STEM (science, technology, engineering, and math) and social and emotional learning (SEL) represented discrete ideas in education circles. Increasingly, however, youth workers, educators, researchers, and funders recognize that these terms have more in common than initially thought. In fact, further study has demonstrated that rather than being mutually exclusive, these learning processes are deeply entwined.

STEM encompasses four interrelated disciplines that help us understand how things work. The STEM domains teach us to analyze evidence, seek input from others on ideas, and identify new paths forward when things don't work out.

Social and Emotional Learning in Out-of-School Time, pages 73–86

SEL is an ongoing process that begins at birth, in which *learning* is the key word. Social and emotional skills help us manage our emotions, work with others, and navigate opportunities and challenges. They enable us to think critically, show empathy, work purposefully in pursuit of a goal, and persist in the face of setbacks. SEL also helps us interpret and navigate the nuances and complexities of relationships between people, concepts, and processes, and to understand why things work. Emotions impact young people's academic engagement, work ethic, commitment, and school success, and emotional processes affect how and what we learn (Durlak, Weissberg, Dymnicki, Taylor, & Schellinger, 2011). Social and emotional competencies make up the intricate, often unconscious web that supports us in all that we endeavor to do, and practice over time is needed to improve these competencies.

Looking beyond the jargon and acronyms, it is clear that STEM and SEL have a lot in common. Both are fundamental to solving open-ended problems and exploring real-world ideas, and improving both STEM skills and social and emotional skills requires practice, experimentation, and working with others. Research also shows that active learning—which requires youth to engage in hands-on activities where they think critically about what they're doing and learning—increases academic STEM achievement (Freeman et al., 2014).

This chapter focuses on how two citywide out-of-school time (OST) systems builders, Boston After School & Beyond (BASB) and the Providence After School Alliance (PASA), evolved their summer learning programming to help young people develop social and emotional competencies and STEM skills in tandem with one another. Key to this work has been each organization's use of assessments recommended by Every Hour Counts, a national organization of which BASB and PASA are founding members. Every Hour Counts developed a common measurement framework for the OST field (Every Hour Counts, 2014). This framework, developed in collaboration with American Institutes for Research (AIR) and with support from The Wallace Foundation, defines a set of system-, program-, and youth-level outcomes that citywide expanded learning systems should aim to achieve. Over the past decade, the Every Hour Counts national network, which includes PASA, BASB, and more than 20 other cities and regions, has accumulated a wealth of practical experience and data from after-school and summer programs to make a case that the STEM and SEL fields benefit from a merging of their respective best practices.

BASB and PASA began to deepen this approach in 2011 after Every Hour Counts and its New York City partner, ExpandED Schools, launched the Frontiers in Urban Science Education (FUSE) project, with support from the Noyce Foundation. This project aimed to scale access to high-quality STEM learning for youth in OST programs, building on lessons piloted in New York City by ExpandED Schools. As part of the FUSE project, PASA and BASB focused on using summer to expand standards-aligned STEM learning experiences in field-based learning environments.

A TALE OF TWO CITIES LINKING STEM AND SEL

Providence and Boston were two of five cities funded by The Wallace Foundation in 2004 to build quality after-school systems to reach youth from low-income families at scale. Funding resulted in the formation of two citywide OST intermediary organizations, BASB and PASA, both of which were tasked with improving youth access to each city's OST programs. Rather than focusing on remediation or homework help, both cities focused on providing young people with the types of OST experiences that many low-income families are unable to afford: high-quality enrichment programs in arts, music, and sports, and rigorous but fun project-based learning programs. Recognizing the wealth of local resources already present in each city, from youth-serving environmental organizations to museums and stand-alone program providers offering music and art lessons, PASA and BASB knew that reinventing the wheel was unnecessary. Instead, each worked to better coordinate its city's program providers.

Since 2004, PASA and BASB have worked to build year-round, citywide after-school and summer learning systems that are rooted in youth development practices and standards. These learning systems complement the school day by exposing youth to experiences that can help to address the opportunity-driven learning gap that exists for youth in low-income communities (McCombs, Whitaker, & Yoo, 2017).

In Providence, PASA brought together a network of community-based STEM, arts, and sports program providers and united them through a single system of programming called the AfterZone. Offered to middle school youth throughout the city, each of the city's five middle schools serve as AfterZone sites and offer program menus from these providers. Providers receive professional development, undergo regular program quality assessments, benefit from data collection and sharing, and share best practices with one another. In Boston, BASB leveraged the strengths of its program providers through convening and communication, policy development and coordination, research and analysis, and program demonstration and partnerships.

Both organizations brought programming into school buildings to nurture relationships between community-based providers and school-day teachers and administration. Both organizations also understood that tracking youth-level data is critical to achieving high-quality programming, and both use an online data-tracking tool developed by Cityspan to track attendance and retention and engage in independent program observations to rate program learning environments. These ingredients—cross-sector relationship building, data collection, investments in instructor practice improvement, and regular program observations and evaluations—have been key to the success of SEL-driven STEM learning in both cities.

Summertime and the Livin' Is STEM-y

In Boston and Providence, the creation of citywide summer learning strategies followed multi-year efforts resulting in high-quality after-school systems in both cities, with BASB focused on youth in elementary and middle school and PASA focused exclusively on youth in middle school. In both cities, the expansion into summer programming was inspired by a national effort to address the findings of a Johns Hopkins research study on summer learning loss among youth from low-income families (Alexander, Entwisle, & Olson, 2007). This study triggered major investments by The Wallace Foundation and the Walmart Foundation focused on preventing summer learning loss. The Johns Hopkins study also prompted mayors across the country to focus on addressing the summer learning gap.

Both PASA and BASB received multi-year funding (PASA from the Walmart Foundation and BASB from The Wallace Foundation) to design summer learning strategies that could stem or reverse summer learning loss for youth in each city. Efforts to create effective summer learning strategies involved each city's mayor, the local philanthropic community, school district administration, and the organizations that were already involved in BASB's and PASA's after-school learning systems. The city teams worked to build high-quality, engaging "fifth quarter of learning," as BASB Executive Director Chris Smith calls it.

These efforts paid off, and summer quickly emerged as the ideal time to explore classroom content in STEM in dynamic, community-based environments that are playful and fun, and that incorporate problem-solving and the arts. The combination of warm weather and outdoors-oriented programming immediately lent itself to hands-on STEM programs in community settings, much like the summer camp experiences of more affluent young people.

Thanks to the fact that many teachers desire summer employment, summer also became the perfect time to bring together school-day educators and staff from community-based STEM programs to learn from one another and share best practices. Program staff shared youth development-centered, hands-on approaches like those used in museums and environmental education organizations, while school-day educators shared content knowledge and classroom management approaches.

This approach was supported by multi-year research conducted as part of The Wallace Foundation-funded RAND study entitled "Learning from Summer: Effects of Voluntary Summer Learning Programs on Low-Income Urban Youth" (Augustine et al., 2016), which points to the value of converting summer remediation strategies into youth development-oriented experiential learning programs. A forthcoming report from AIR drawn from a summer of data gathering in Providence and Boston will examine this connection further.

IN PROVIDENCE, CREATING A CITYWIDE SUMMER STEM CAMP POWERED BY SEL

By the time PASA delved into summer programming, it had spent 5 years developing a core set of youth development skills in all of its programs using the Weikert Center's Youth Program Quality Assessment (YPQA) tool, as well as the Survey of Academic and Youth Outcomes Youth survey (SAYO-Y) and Teacher survey (SAYO-T), both developed by the National Institute for Out of School Time (NIOST). These assessment tools made it clear that PASA's programs were garnering positive youth outcomes around SEL, including in its hands-on STEM programs.

In light of these findings, and with a 2-year start-up grant from the Walmart Foundation, Providence designed a summer learning strategy in 2012 that focused on using youth development and SEL approaches within the context of hands-on, community-based STEM learning settings that encourage experimentation, collaboration, and trial and error. PASA partnered with the Providence Public School District to align programming with the Common Core State Standards and Next Generation Science Standards, and to recruit school-day teachers who could codesign and co-deliver summer programming alongside some of the AfterZone's highest quality STEM program providers. What resulted was the AfterZone Summer STEM Camp, which was designed to meet three goals:

- Provide field-based STEM learning programs that offer dynamic, hands-on learning experiences to youth who rarely get to be in the woods, rivers, oceans, photo labs, or design-build workshops, and give these youth opportunities to work with real-world professionals so that they have a chance to make connections between their interests and future career opportunities.
- Deepen the inquiry-based youth development practices of Providence's school-day educators and staff from community-based STEM programs by allocating time for them to learn and reflect

together, co-lead programs, and design an integrated, project-based summer learning curriculum.

- Build partnerships between PASA, its STEM program providers, and the city's middle school faculty and principals in a way that promotes the social and emotional competencies that youth need time and space to develop.

With the support of the Noyce Foundation-funded FUSE grant through Every Hour Counts, PASA initiated a 30-hour professional development series that brought together school-day educators and staff from community-based STEM programs to explore best practices and design summer curricula that connected experiential learning and SEL approaches with classroom content and national and state standards. This approach offered young people who were struggling in math and science the opportunity to participate in rigorous, field-based STEM learning experiences that felt and operated more like a camp experience. The AfterZone Summer STEM Camp replaced the district's summer remediation program, making it possible to stop focusing on test scores as an end goal, and instead focus on deepening the set of measurable social and emotional competencies that directly support school-year science and math learning over the long term.

To complement young people's school-year classes, AfterZone Summer STEM Camp programs contextualize scientific principles and integrate applied mathematics through fun and engaging activities, field trips, and experiences. Within their programs, youth work with professional designers, environmental scientists, engineers, and district teachers. Twice a week, youth do fieldwork and engage in hands-on learning led by the teaching teams. On the remaining days, youth move into the classroom for instruction in STEM subjects. The instruction is collaboratively led by the certified teachers and staff from the community-based STEM programs and is directly related to data the youth collected during their fieldwork.

For example, youth in the 2017 "buoyancy lab" program with Save the Bay spent 5 weeks working with two Save the Bay instructors and a district teacher to learn how and why things float. The youth focused on learning the correlation between mass, volume, density, and an object's ability to float, with plenty of hands-on opportunities to experiment with manipulating the volume of objects to create the right density for flotation. Their final project for the program combined these lessons with a real-world engineering challenge: Construct a vessel using cardboard and duct tape that is able to not only float in the bay, but that can carry two seventh and eighth graders and can be successfully rowed from one dock to another as part of a race. This program embodies the natural connection between SEL and STEM. Youth had to learn the kind of STEM concepts they would learn in a classroom, but they also had to experiment with those concepts in order to apply them to a real-world problem, persevere when their designs didn't work, and work as a team to design, build, and race an unsinkable boat. Some teams ended up wetter than others, but the point was in the learning process and the willingness to risk applying what they had learned in a real-world setting.

From Summer SEL and STEM to Long-Term Youth Engagement

After 6 years of development, the AfterZone Summer STEM Camp acts as the driver for PASA's STEM and SEL practices throughout its middle and high school learning systems, year round. The summer provides time for district educators and staff from community-based STEM programs to deepen their practices, learn from one another, and experiment with new approaches. It also helps youth truly begin to connect how their program interests and social and emotional competencies are tied to STEM subjects and careers. This, in turn, facilitates a deepened understanding of their academic and career opportunities, and of their own personal strengths when it comes to communicating, working with others, taking initiative, and sticking with problems until they solve them.

To further help young people, program providers, and school staff better connect the SEL, STEM, and career dots, PASA used its summer programming to pilot the use of STEM badges. PASA's badges are a 21st-century update of the concept pioneered by Girl and Boy Scouts—iPhone learning adventure app meets youth outcomes data. Assessment results from the SAYO-T consistently showed that youth in PASA's youth development-oriented summer STEM programs were developing a core set of five social and emotional competencies: problem-solving, teamwork, communication, engagement in learning, and perseverance. To better demonstrate the connection between these competencies and STEM learning, PASA developed a system of badges that are directly linked to SAYO-T assessments and rooted in training around SEL for staff. PASA's STEM badges reflect where youth shine when it comes to those five measurable social and emotional competencies within STEM learning contexts. AfterZone Summer STEM Camp participants choose their own programs, which means that badges reflect each young person's particular interests, emerging passions, and skills. For example, if a young person earns a communication badge in a STEM program, the badge denotes that he/she effectively expressed his/her understanding of the program's STEM content. Multiple communication badges within multiple STEM programs throughout middle school can indicate a special passion for and understanding of STEM. After a successful summer pilot, followed by a successful full summer rollout, PASA implemented its badge strategy throughout its school-year AfterZone STEM programs.

In Providence, these SEL-linked STEM badges (initially developed through the summer programming) have begun to help AfterZone staff and school guidance counselors better serve eighth graders as they begin their high school OST program selection process. Because badges are visual, they have also provided youth with new ways of understanding their own interests, future possibilities, and inherent strengths and areas for growth in ways that are not possible with the grades and test scores of a science or math classroom. As a result, Providence has seen youth and staff engaging in fresh conversations about why social and emotional competencies matter in the types of workplaces they might be interested in, and how these competencies can benefit them throughout life.

THE CITY AS CLASSROOM IN BOSTON

Like PASA, BASB's foray into summer programming followed many years of work within the after-school space in Boston. Launched in 2010, the Boston Summer Learning Project (SLP) aimed to reverse summer learning loss among high-need youth through 5-week summer programs delivered by certified academic teachers and staff from community-based programs in diverse locations across the city. Since Boston's Mayor Walsh set the goal of dramatically expanding access to summer learning in Boston in 2015, BASB's summer efforts have expanded into a citywide coalition of programs that collaborate to provide high-quality experiential learning opportunities for Boston youth. These hands-on learning opportunities are helping to close achievement and opportunity gaps by equipping youth with the knowledge, skills, and experiences necessary for every aspect of their lives. But it really does take the whole village.

That's not a problem in Boston, where school-year educators and staff from community-based programs work together to recruit Boston Public School (BPS) youth from low-income families in high-need populations, including early readers and English language learners. They then co-deliver 5-week, full-day summer learning experiences that blend rigorous academic content with hands-on, exciting enrichment activities at a wide array of locations across the city. All programs aim to stem summer learning loss, close opportunity gaps, and empower youth with competencies and learning experiences that set them up for success in the ensuing school year.

For example, at the summer learning classroom at Thompson Island Outward Bound Education Center (TIOBEC) in Boston Harbor, the essential question posed to youth in the 2017 summer program was: "How can we reduce the human footprint on the environment?" By design, this question doesn't have an easy or short answer. Instead, TIOBEC chose an open-ended question that requires a thoughtful approach and is relevant to real life, not just theoretical. The program required that youth, their teachers, and program staff address this question together as a way to encourage collaboration and create links between academic subject matter and enrichment activities while exploring the island.

Over 5 weeks, youth worked together to gather data, build a credible case, and produce evidence to support their findings, which they presented publicly. As you might imagine, not everything worked out as planned. Youth had to adjust, redirect their work, and persist until they produced a final presentation. That process is at the heart of scientific discovery and STEM learning, as well as SEL. To gain social and emotional competencies like persistence, you have to fail occasionally in order to learn to try again. Having to build a case and present it publicly also helps build English language arts (ELA) skills, as well as confidence and public speaking skills.

Building on this successful summer learning model, BASB expanded its focus to enhance year-round STEM learning opportunities through the BoSTEM initiative, which it launched in partnership with United Way of Massachusetts Bay to ensure that every middle school BPS student has access to high-quality STEM learning experiences. BoSTEM acknowledges that girls, youth of color, and youth from low-income families also face complex sociocultural barriers to STEM careers. In response, BASB and United Way created a year-round approach that integrates culturally responsive STEM OST programming with in-school curricula to prepare high-need middle school students for post-secondary STEM education. Specifically, BoSTEM focuses on increasing engagement and interest in STEM learning and careers, effectively using a culturally responsive SEL instructional approach to address systemic STEM education inequities.

The Path From Summer School to Summer Learning Is Through SEL

BPS officially adopted BASB's model as its flagship "summer school" in 2017, rebranding it as the Summer Learning Academies (SLA) to reinforce how a demonstration project became an institutionalized approach to summer learning—one where the entire city is the summer learning classroom. Boston's Summer Learning Community includes SLA sites as well as additional programs across Greater Boston, featuring a range of program models and offerings that include leadership development, enrichment, and work-based learning. Through the SLA, youth learn in new settings, such as community centers, college campuses, and natural preservations. A typical day for an SLA youth includes breakfast; 3 hours of project-based learning that focuses on math, ELA, and science; lunch; and enrichment activities including arts, swimming, or internships. This type of programming empowers youth to hone skills like teamwork and communication within a wide array of academic content areas.

The 2017 Boston Summer Learning Community involved 61 organizations operating at 132 sites serving 11,000 students—the biggest Boston coalition focused on high-quality summer learning to date. BASB remains an integral co-implementation and co-management partner for the SLA, collaborating with BPS on youth recruitment criteria, teacher hiring, training, evaluation, operations, and fundraising. To further the coalition's learning and growth, BASB continues to convene the Boston Summer Learning Community regularly throughout the year to conduct trainings on youth skill development, brainstorm strategies for addressing common challenges, and share best practices from the field. Data findings from the preceding year directly inform the content and format of these convenings.

For example, for one convening, BASB contracted Harvard's Program in Education Afterschool and Resiliency (PEAR) and the Museum of Science's Engineering is Elementary team (EiE) to design and deliver training modules focused on Next Generation Science Standards and SEL for partner organizations implementing the FUSE approach that summer. PEAR and EiE each delivered a general training for all summer site managers, focused on the Power Skills and Next Generation science and engineering practices, respectively. The two teams then collaborated to deliver an integrated, two-part training on teaching Power Skills in the context of Next Generation-aligned STEM programs for all middle school site staff, which consisted of the teacher/program staff teams.

Weaving Together Summer, STEM, and SEL in Continuous Improvement

As in Providence, measurement for continuous improvement is key to BASB's approach to making the connections between SEL and STEM—and indeed any academic content area—visible, and demonstrating how program quality is the only way to get there. BASB uses NIOST's SAYO-T tool and the PEAR Institute's Dimensions of Success tool (which defines 12 indicators of STEM program quality in OST programs) to assess individual youth-level SEL and STEM outcomes, as well as program quality. In line with the OST field's dedication to youth voice, BASB sites also employ NIOST's SAYO-Y to rate program quality from the young person's perspective. This approach creates a detailed picture of how well BASB's network is progressing in SEL and STEM, and where there is room to improve. Informed by the results of these evaluations, all summer sites receive a

Program Report for Improvement & System Measurement (PRISM) in the fall, which shows a program's specific results across all measurement tools and compares them to the summer network as a whole. Importantly, these data serve as the foundation for a robust continuous improvement cycle. BASB utilizes the previous years' findings to tailor the content of professional development sessions and identify future areas for improvement. By working together, BASB and its partners have made learning more relevant, rigorous, and engaging.

BASB is already seeing the fruits of its labor. From 2011 to 2017, youth participating in the SLA/SLP have consistently demonstrated positive growth on academic and college readiness skills. In summer 2017, for example, teachers rated youth as significantly improved in math, ELA, and all six social and emotional competencies measured by NIOST's SAYO-T: critical thinking, communication, perseverance, relationships with adults, relationships with peers, and self-regulation. Likewise, 2017 results from PEAR's Holistic Student Assessment (HSA; a student survey of skill strengths) identified strong improvements in critical thinking, perseverance, and assertiveness—all competencies associated specifically with STEM career success.

After refining this continuous improvement process, BASB developed the Achieve, Connect, Thrive (ACT) Skills Framework to provide a common vocabulary that bridges education and youth development, as well as school, after-school, and summer learning. The ACT Framework codifies the social and emotional competencies necessary for college and career success, while incorporating a wealth of practical experience, evidence, and resources drawn from and for the OST field. As a result, Boston is finding it easier to create shared goals that span the OST and K–12 environments, all to the benefit of the city's young people.

Through an in-depth alignment of the ACT Framework and Next Generation science and engineering practice standards, BASB was also able to identify the criteria for its own badges. In the summer of 2015, BASB piloted the use of its digital badges in order to unite the city's often fragmented learning ecosystem, and to supply young people with a new currency for demonstrating progress and mastery of social and emotional competencies both in and out of school. BASB's badging initiative aimed to validate young people's growth and achievement in four essential competency areas tied to both short- and long-term success and achievement, identified through their ACT Framework and relevant to the Next Generation Science Standards: critical thinking, communication, perseverance, and teamwork. Badges are awarded based on a minimum attendance criterion of 80%, in addition to a pre-post teacher assessment of youth skills using the SAYO-T. BASB has two types of badges: Achievement badges represent consistently strong performance in a skill, while growth badges represent a youth's notable improvement in a skill.

Following the successful 2015 badge pilot, BASB and Cityspan have established a digital badging infrastructure that includes valid, reliable measurement tools and a shared, citywide database in order to ensure the quality, uniformity, and transferability of badges. BASB's badges enable program providers to customize the learning experience to target specific skills critical to youth success, while providing youth with a visual representation of growth and achievement on the road to college and career. For youth, BASB hopes these efforts will continue to advance badging currency to demonstrate growth for multiple audiences, including their peers, teachers, college admissions officers, and employers. Across the city of Boston, digital badging is also helping to establish a more holistic representation of a young person's learning experience—one that goes beyond attendance and grades and acknowledges the learning and growth that occurs in any number of settings across Boston.

FOR SYSTEMS BUILDERS INTERESTED IN SEL, PRACTICE MAKES PERFECT

The success that Providence and Boston have seen with regard to creating and measuring connections between SEL and STEM has been largely due to support provided through the FUSE initiative, led by Every Hour Counts, with support originally from the Noyce Foundation (now the STEM Next Opportunity Fund). A key component of the *FUSE 3.0* model is a focus on enhanced collaboration between certified school-day teachers and staff from community-based programs. Partner agencies involved in the initiative provide professional development trainings to FUSE teams and then create conditions for educators and program staff to collaborate in a variety of ways, from aligning curricula to co-planning lessons to co-facilitating activities in the OST space. Participating intermediaries include: After School Matters in Chicago, ExpandED Schools in New York, PASA, BASB, and Nashville After Zone Alliance (NAZA) in Tennessee. Through FUSE, each of these organizations worked with a cohort of community-based programs to demonstrate successful strategies for building and scaling STEM enrichment programs that emphasize a collaborative approach.

Through the FUSE initiative, BASB and PASA worked together to examine how social and emotional competencies are articulated in the Next Generation Science Standards. Through that process, the city system builders learned that problem-solving, collaboration, communication, and perseverance are integral to the Next Generation science and engineering practices, allowing each to double down on existing efforts to improve SEL-connected program provider practices.

High-quality instructor practices rooted in youth development are at the heart of PASA's and BASB's approach to both SEL and STEM learning as systems builders, but they are also at the heart of K–12 academic standards. It stands to reason that the kind of experiential, inquiry-based learning that lends itself to STEM learning also helps youth build and deepen their social and emotional competencies. However, the youth development-centered and inquiry-based teaching practices that help young people build these competencies take time and training to learn and execute well. To ensure youth acquire a measurable set of social and emotional competencies, school-day educators and program staff need technical assistance, capacity-building support, data-supported and research-informed approaches, and ongoing feedback from an SEL-aligned assessment system that can help guide and improve their practice. In other words, in order for youth to solve real-world STEM problems and develop and demonstrate social and emotional competencies, programs must be intentional about the learning environment they create and the activities they design for their staff and youth.

Boston and Providence have both learned that ensuring programs are grounded in sophisticated, inquiry-based learning and youth development practices that focus on a manageable and measurable set of social and emotional competencies should be a priority for systems builders and program providers alike. Together, STEM and SEL represent the cutting edge of OST programming, which is increasingly demonstrating how to integrate these fields of study in order to deliver stimulating and engaging learning experiences for young people. In large part, this is because the OST field has long operated using a positive youth development philosophy. However, for youth outcomes to be consistent, there must be systemic investments that build capacity for program providers to deliver outcomes-oriented, SEL-rich programs. Furthermore, just as there is a culture of positive youth development in the OST field, there must be a culture of SEL outcomes. Building that culture through high-quality STEM programming is a natural place to begin.

ACKNOWLEDGMENT

This chapter was developed with the support of Every Hour Counts and Jessica Donner.

REFERENCES

Alexander, K. L., Entwisle, D. R., & Olson, L. S. (2007). Lasting consequences of the summer learning gap. *American Sociological Review, 72*, 167–180.

Augustine, C. H., McCombs, J. S., Pane, J. F., Schwartz, H. L., Schweig, J., McEachin, A., & Siler-Evans, K. (2016). *Learning from summer: Effects of voluntary summer learning programs on low-income urban youth.* Santa Monica, CA: RAND Corporation. Retrieved from https://www.rand.org/pubs/research_reports/RR1557.html

Durlak, J. A., Weissberg, R. P., Dymnicki, A. B., Taylor, R. D., & Schellinger, K. B. (2011). The impact of enhancing students' social and emotional learning: A meta-analysis of school-based universal interventions. *Journal of Child Development, 82,* 405–432.

Every Hour Counts. (2014). *Every Hour Counts measurement framework: How to measure success in expanded learning systems.* Retrieved from http://www.afterschoolsystems.org/content/document/detail/4060/

Freeman, S., Eddy, S. L., McDonough, M., Smith, M. K., Okoroafor, N., Jordt, H., & Wenderoth, M. P. (2014). Active learning boosts performance in STEM courses. *Proceedings of the National Academy of Sciences, 111,* 8410–8415. Retrieved from https://doi.org/10.1073/pnas.1319030111

McCombs, J. S., Whitaker, A., & Yoo, P. Y. (2017). *The value of out-of-school time programs.* Santa Monica, CA: RAND Corporation. Retrieved from https://www.rand.org/pubs/perspectives/PE267.html

CHAPTER 6

SUPPORTING SOCIAL AND EMOTIONAL LEARNING AMONG TEENS THROUGH INSTRUCTOR PRACTICE

Mary Ellen Caron and Jill Young

After School Matters (ASM) is a nonprofit organization that provides transformational out-of-school time (OST) opportunities to more than 18,000 Chicago high school teens (Grades 9 through 12) each year. In the organization's 25+ years of serving Chicago's teens, ASM has learned a great deal about social and emotional learning (SEL) in building positive futures for high school teens in OST programs. ASM's greatest gains in improving social and emotional skills have come from supporting instructors to foster these skills with teens through evaluation and professional development. This chapter provides an overview of ASM, an in-depth look at the organization's apprenticeship model, a summary of the evolution of SEL at the organization over the past 6 years, and recommendations and lessons learned.

Social and Emotional Learning in Out-of-School Time, pages 87–105

ABOUT AFTER SCHOOL MATTERS

Mission and History

The mission of ASM is to provide Chicago public high school teens opportunities to explore and develop their talents, while gaining critical skills for work, college, and beyond. The inspiration for ASM arose over 25 years ago from the desire of First Lady Maggie Daley to develop cultural activities for the city's teenagers. That first summer, 260 teens apprenticed under and learned from professional artists. With the support and leadership of its board of directors, ASM has grown since then; in fiscal year 2017–2018, ASM offered nearly 1,500 programs and approximately 26,000 opportunities at over 400 sites in the city of Chicago, ultimately serving 18,000 unique teens.

ASM achieves its mission by:

- Designing and delivering high-quality, hands-on, project-based apprenticeship programs in a variety of content areas, including the arts, communication, sports, and STEM.
- Engaging skilled professionals as instructors who support teens' growth and development in an intentional and meaningful way.
- Aligning and maximizing the resources of an extensive network of public–private partnerships—including Chicago Public Schools (CPS), the Chicago Park District, the Chicago Public Library, and hundreds of community organizations throughout the city—to coordinate and sustain investment in youth development through school- and community-based programming.
- Focusing on implementing continuous quality improvement, making data-driven and cost-effective decisions, strengthening skills to encourage improved academic outcomes, and generating positive impacts for teens, schools, and communities.

Core Program Components

ASM has identified five core program components to define the organization's work. The first component is advocating for teens and youth development. ASM does this by hosting teen showcases, collaborating with local and national media to highlight teen accomplishments, speaking to legislators on behalf of teens, and presenting on the organization's work with teens at national conferences.

The second component is building opportunities for teens through partnerships. Key partners include CPS, the Chicago Park District, the Chicago

Public Library, the Chicago Department of Family and Support Services, and the Chicago Department of Cultural Affairs and Special Events. Additionally, ASM operates as both an intermediary and a direct service provider for nearly 200 community-based organizations and 500 independent instructors, who are employees of ASM. Together, these partners provide safe and supportive community anchors throughout the city and facilitate access to neighborhood resources that allow ASM to deliver successful programs.

The third core component is engaging teens in skill development through the apprenticeship model, which focuses on project-based learning. ASM's approach to skill development, and SEL in particular, is discussed in greater detail later in this chapter.

The fourth program component is showcasing teen accomplishments. ASM does this by creating venues for teens to be publicly recognized through performances, demonstrations, and commissions in communities, organizations, and schools.

The fifth and final program component is disseminating research and best practices about OST for teens. ASM continuously engages in both internal and external evaluations, sharing those findings at local and national conferences. ASM also partners with Every Hour Counts, the national intermediary for expanded learning, to share with and learn from other national OST organizations.

THE APPRENTICESHIP MODEL

This section provides a look at how ASM engages high school teens in SEL through the apprenticeship model and project-based learning, as well as the expertise of ASM's instructors.

The Apprenticeship Model

The primary program model at ASM is the apprenticeship program. Apprenticeships are project-based programs, led by industry experts, that can provide a pathway to progress in social and emotional skill development and independence. According to Edutopia, project-based learning is "a dynamic approach to teaching in which students explore real-world problems and challenges... it inspires students to obtain a deeper knowledge of the subjects they're studying" (Edutopia, 2008, para. 1). In project-based learning, projects are central to the curriculum, focused on questions related to a discipline, youth-driven, realistic, and collaborative, and they involve youth in constructive investigation ("Why PBL?," 2009). Research has demonstrated that project-based learning produces positive outcomes in content knowledge and social and emotional skills such as collaborative skills, engagement and motivation, critical thinking, and problem-solving skills ("Why PBL?," 2009; Edutopia, 2008).

In apprenticeship programs, teens learn marketable skills from industry experts in an atmosphere approaching a workplace-like environment. These programs are typically provided at a 1:15 instructor-to-teen ratio. Teens complete final projects and participate in showcases, which increase in complexity across the apprenticeship levels so teens have the opportunity to expand their social and emotional skills. Teens must be at least 14 years old to participate. They must apply to the program and interview with ASM staff, and the selection process increases in complexity across the apprenticeship levels. Teens must also maintain professional standards of attendance, conduct, and dedication, providing them with maturity and knowledge as they prepare for college or the workforce.

ASM provides teens who successfully meet certain program requirements (including attendance and participation) with a monetary stipend. Stipends lower participation barriers, reinforce the importance of dedicated participation and hard work in programs, and have an economic impact on teens, their families, and communities. Providing stipends to teens empowers them and reinforces the value of their time and efforts.

ASM offers different levels of apprenticeships:

- *Pre-Apprenticeship*—An introductory, hands-on program that provides broad exposure to a specific content area and related careers. Teens who are ready and able to participate are prioritized for these programs, but dedicated space is held for teens with fewer resources who apply late.
- *Apprenticeship*—A hands-on program in which teens learn content-specific skills and work towards a culminating project or showcase. Teens who participate in these programs must interview with the instructor.
- *Advanced Apprenticeship*—An advanced, hands-on program in which teens refine their technical skills while producing a complex culminating project or showcase. Because these are more advanced programs, teens are required to provide a portfolio or audition for the program.

Additionally, ASM offers internships, which provide other opportunities for teens to practice and refine their skills. Teens must be at least 16 years old and are paid an hourly rate. These opportunities range from program assistance to schoolwide support for programming to outreach and engagement activities. They also include internship positions such as museum docent, camp counselor, corporate administration intern, and more.

Instructors are an integral part of the ASM apprenticeship model and are responsible for developing and delivering programming to teens. These instructors are skilled professionals in their fields who are also committed to sharing their knowledge with teens. From mural artists, advertising executives, engineers, and graphic artists to sports managers, journalists, and other dynamic professionals, these instructors build teens' technical skills and social and emotional skills.

ASM teens certainly learn technical skills in their selected content area as part of the apprenticeship model, but they also learn important career skills such as problem-solving, teamwork, leadership, and timeliness. Instructors are encouraged to introduce field experts, take college- and career-related field trips, provide mock interviews, build resume writing skills, help teens in the college search, and much more. As part of their apprenticeship programs, teens create a final product or performance, which they share with peers, family members, and communities through program showcases.

Youth Development

ASM considers itself to be a youth development organization, specifically focused on teens. ASM has identified the domains below as critical to teen development. As these domains indicate, ASM is focused on developing the whole teen, rather than skills for one specific context.

- *Social*—Gaining a sense of connection and belonging, and a well-developed support system.
- *Emotional*—Coping effectively with life and creating satisfying relationships with a broad range of people.
- *Intellectual*—Recognizing creative abilities and finding ways to expand knowledge and skills.
- *Physical*—Recognizing the need for physical activity, healthy foods, and sleep.
- *Environmental*—Occupying and creating pleasant, stimulating environments that support well-being.
- *Financial*—Knowing and addressing current and future financial situations with goals of satisfaction, security, and giving.
- *Occupational*—Experiencing satisfaction and enrichment from work while planning the steps necessary to achieve work goals in the future.
- *Ethical*—Expanding a sense of purpose and meaning in life that includes right action and supports human respect.

EVOLUTION OF SEL AT ASM

Though the very nature of ASM's model supports teen SEL, ASM has in recent years become much more intentional about fostering and measuring social and emotional skills. This next section provides a deep dive into several SEL initiatives that ASM has implemented over the last 6 years.

The ways in which ASM develops and supports instructors and teens in SEL has evolved over time (see Figure 6.1). These evolutions were primarily driven by two factors. First, ASM was ready for such an evolution; the organization had a robust and customizable data management system, leadership to champion and advocate for investment in SEL, and instructors who were dedicated to teens. Second, two external evaluations of ASM, conducted by the Erikson Institute and Northwestern University, pointed to the need to focus on SEL. ASM sought to better understand program quality in the context of apprenticeship programs and worked with the Erikson Institute to conduct qualitative observations of apprenticeship programs in the 2002 school year. Ultimately, the study revealed that ASM teens developed knowledge and skills in the discipline they were engaged in, skills in task interpretation and execution, the ability to work in groups, and the ability to identify self-effects. The study's authors also noted that the quality of the observed apprenticeships varied, and that those variations affected teens' skill development.

The ASM team reviewed the study to identify areas for improvement. To address the variance in program quality across apprenticeships, ASM adopted portions of the Youth Program Quality Intervention (YPQI)—a continuous quality improvement cycle for youth programs developed by the Weikart Center for Youth Program Quality. Specifically, ASM adopted the Youth Work Methods training modules to focus on professional development for instructors. The methods series includes topics such as structure and clear limits, reframing conflict, ask-listen-encourage, active learning, building community, cooperative learning, youth voice and choice, and planning and reflection.

Figure 6.1 Evolution of SEL at After School Matters.

Recognizing that the Erikson Institute's study was qualitative, ASM sought opportunities for an experimental evaluation of programs, ultimately working with Northwestern University in 2006 to study job readiness skill attainment, youth development impact, and academic impact related to participation in ASM programs. This experimental study followed Chicago public high school teens from 2006 to 2009. Teens who applied to programs were randomly assigned to either the treatment group or the control group. The study found that teens who participated in ASM programs as part of the treatment group had higher self-regulation, less problem behavior (including selling drugs or participating in gangs), and a stronger sense of connection to their school, and placed greater value on school and academics, compared to the control group. However, while the study found that teens were gaining critical career readiness skills, they were not able to articulate them in mock job interviews. These findings led to the first phase of SEL at ASM.

SEL 1.0: Adoption of a Framework and Assessment

The Northwestern study recommended that ASM focus more on transferable knowledge and skills that teens may gain through participation in ASM programs. To address this recommendation, communicate the importance of SEL, and establish a process for assessing social and emotional skills, ASM adopted a skills framework and assessment developed by the Chicago Workforce Investment Council (CWIC) and CPS. CWIC/CPS created the assessment using skills identified in existing employability assessment tools, such as ACT WorkKeys and Equip for the Future. The tool was designed for CPS high school classroom use by Career and Technical Education (CTE) teachers during the school year to formatively assess student skills and identify skills to target for improvement. The assessment, called the Employability Assessment, was designed to be (a) completed by a third-party rater, (b) free or low-cost to administer, (c) formative for developing skills in students, (d) practical and not overly burdensome, and (e) applicable to all occupational areas. The skills were categorized as fundamental skills, work ethic/character skills, problem-solving skills, interpersonal skills, and computer skills. Fundamental skills included appearance/hygiene, timeliness, and oratory/speaking. Work ethic/character skills included attitude, accountability/integrity, self-control, and ambition/initiative. Problem-solving included supervision, procedure/rule following, problem-solving approach, and information management. Interpersonal skills included verbal communication, active listening, feedback, and teamwork. Computer skills focused on computer literacy.

ASM chose to pilot the Employability Assessment with 10 programs in the spring of 2011 and created a cross-departmental working group to focus on SEL, including program curriculum, professional development, and evaluation. As part of the pilot, instructors and staff were trained in the Employability Assessment and asked to use the tool to collect and report data on the social and emotional skills of the teens in their programs. After the pilot, instructors, teens, and staff participated in focus groups and completed surveys. Results strongly suggested that instructors needed more guidance on introducing the skills, as well as integrating some of the skills into their program content. Toward that end, an instructor guide was developed and staff were trained on the assessment.

ASM planned to extend the pilot to Fall 2011 but received a grant to implement the initiative with all programs and develop data reports for the assessment in Cityspan, the organization's participant tracking system. The goals of the program were to foster the development of social and emotional skills with teens; implement a user-friendly tool that measures the skills of ASM teens; assess skills gained through ASM programs; and define, support, and celebrate teen successes. To meet these goals, ASM outlined several activities for instructors to complete over the course of the programs. In the first few weeks, instructors introduced the Employability Assessment tool, had teens use the tool to reflect and assess themselves on the skills, completed an assessment on each teen, and entered the results into Cityspan. In the middle of the program session, instructors printed the first assessment and conducted a one-on-one meeting with each teen to discuss the teen's self-assessment and the instructor's assessment, identifying skills teens were strong in and skills they could continue to develop together. Instructors also observed teens and integrated skills into their curriculum. In the last few weeks of the program, instructors completed a final instructor assessment of each teen and entered the results into Cityspan. In the last week of programs, instructors printed and distributed final assessments to teens. ASM also created an instructor guide based on pilot recommendations to help outline roles, processes, and timelines.

To evaluate the implementation of the Employability Assessment tool, process, and instructor guide, ASM observed programs and collected staff, instructor, and teen feedback through surveys. Staff and instructors noted several benefits of using the Employability Assessment. For example, it provided a basis for SEL conversations with teens. The one-on-ones were helpful for instructors because they offered a mechanism to connect individually with every teen. However, because ASM was building the assessment process, training, and data systems simultaneously, the organization ran into several challenges. There were issues with staff and instructor training and buy-in. Staff did not have enough time to adjust from a small pilot to a large-scale implementation and did not feel prepared to support instructors. Many instructors did not feel prepared to implement the assessment process and requested additional support. Specifically, instructors wanted additional training and resources to support SEL based on program content. Many instructors felt their program was too unique to adopt a standard assessment or framework.

There were also instructors who reported that not all teens were aware they were in an SEL program, so some did not see the point of focusing on SEL. Teens could not make connections to those skills outside of the program, and therefore did not take the assessment or process seriously. They also shared that the language on the assessment was not teen-friendly.

Staff, instructors, and teens also had concerns about how the data collected from the assessment would be used. Because of the timing of the pilot, no clear plan was in place for how to analyze, interpret, share, and utilize the data for different members of the organization, leaving many people uneasy. Teens felt like it was a test, and instructors were worried scores would be used to determine whether they were able to continue working with ASM. Additionally, there was no appetite yet to use the data outside of tracking compliance to the process for the purposes of implementation.

SEL 2.0: Increased Focus on Instructor Support

The problem remained that some instructors were not identifying the skills being taught, connecting the skills to the program content, or connecting the skills to life beyond the program. To help with this, ASM expanded and solidified the working group, with a primary focus on increasing the emphasis on instructor support in SEL and decreasing the emphasis on skills assessment. The initiative was renamed Skills for Success to indicate the shift in direction. In this new iteration, the working group decided to take a step back to identify ways to better support instructors in integrating skills into program content. The team developed a pilot where working group members were paired with instructors to provide SEL coaching for a program session.

Instead of focusing on the assessment and the process, 40 returning instructors with high-quality programs were asked to reflect on their curriculum to identify how they intentionally integrate SEL into program activities. The project team developed a program-planning tool and conducted observations to collect discipline-specific best practices and create resources for instructors to utilize across content areas. The goals were to help instructors incorporate social and emotional skills into programs by collecting best practices through instructor journals, program observations, and surveys. Ultimately, ASM wanted to identify the resources needed to incorporate SEL naturally into programs, and to create a mechanism for sharing those resources with instructors. The goals for teens during this phase were to provide them with an opportunity to self-assess, expose them to new careers, provide them an opportunity to learn about themselves, and build social and emotional skills.

At this time, ASM also began to connect the youth development methods in the YPQI to skill building. The YPQI is built around the research-validated Youth Program Quality Assessment (YPQA), an evidence-based tool that focuses on the four key areas of positive youth development: a safe environment, a supportive environment, interaction, and engagement. Scales on the YPQA align with the Youth Work Methods trainings ASM had previously adopted and focus on topics such as building community, planning, reflection, skill building, and youth voice and choice. Because the majority of ASM instructors are experts in their field, ASM prioritized professional development around youth development. The Youth Work Methods trainings were aligned with internal goals to support teen SEL through adult practice.

The working group developed several materials to support instructors based on instructor feedback and coaching sessions. ASM also shared five key tips for instructors to integrate SEL into program activities:

1. Plan and prepare program activities in advance to think through the activity's process.
2. Intentionally integrate and communicate social and emotional skills to teens when they have demonstrated the skill.
3. Incorporate Youth Program Quality (YPQ) methods such as planning and reflection, building community, and voice and choice into planning strategies.
4. Incorporate reflection strategies at the end of each day to make connections to real-world experiences.
5. Use additional resources to enhance learning and program content, such as supporting documents or field trips.

Based on instructor feedback, a prominent success was connecting skill building in programs to planning and reflection activities, and sharing YPQ Methods books with instructors to support those activities. Observations and instructor journals revealed that connecting social and emotional skills to program content most often happened in reflection activities that were planned before the start of the program. ASM was also able to create a small number of planning templates by content area.

While some instructors enjoyed having additional coaching support for SEL, not all instructors were receptive to feedback. The team observed programs that clearly developed social and emotional skills in teens but did not incorporate reflection activities and did not make the connection to real-world applications. Staff members were unclear about how they could specifically support instructors in SEL.

At the same time, the group that created the Employability Assessment began to rebrand the assessment and framework. The new framework helped clarify jargon, explaining that all of the different names for social and cognitive behaviors—employability skills, social and emotional skills, soft skills, critical-thinking skills, learning behaviors, habits of mind, 21st-century skills—were skills that youth could develop, and needed to thrive. The goal of the framework was to develop a toolkit of products and assessments that communicated, promoted, and benchmarked a targeted set of behaviors, skills, attitudes, and strategies deemed critical for college, career, and life.

SEL 3.0: A New Framework for Instructor Tools and Support

As a result of this work, MHA Labs was born. (MHA is an abbreviation for means and measures of human achievement.) The organization's focus is on building and translating the skills of young people towards personal, community, and economic success. Through extensive market research, MHA identified six building blocks of skills: personal mindset, planning for success, social awareness, verbal communication, collaboration, and problem-solving. These six building blocks consist of 35 skills. The framework was accompanied by an assessment that had three specific uses: a point-in-time tool for providing admissions officers and human resources managers with insights into the young person's skill readiness; a formative assessment used for providing teens with feedback and direction on skills improvement; and an employee performance appraisal used for retention, promotion, and performance pay increases.

The framework provided tools that could be adapted to any program or content, including flashcards, keychain cards, post-its, planners, basic trainings, guidebooks, and posters. ASM volunteered to pilot the use of materials and tools with programs. Instructors from eight programs were provided with the toolkit and asked to integrate it into their programs over the course of a program session. Instructors had complete freedom in how they incorporated the tools into their program, but they were asked to document those activities, as well as teens' reaction to the activities. Instructors who participated in the pilot focused on the following areas: planning and preparation, action and feedback, and reflection and improvement. Instructors had to plan and prepare for the social and emotional skills they wanted to incorporate into their daily program activities. They then had to incorporate those skills and provide feedback to teens by stating the goals of the day, delivering the lesson, and documenting evidence of the social and emotional skills being demonstrated by teens through multiple methods (post-its, journaling, photos, group critique, etc.). Finally, instructors completed reflection and improvement activities by conducting periodic, one-on-one feedback sessions with teens and presenting any evidence of growth in social and emotional skills that had been observed.

In a parallel process, ASM staff focused on the same three activities. For planning and preparation, staff scheduled site visits ahead of time to observe specific SEL activities. As part of action and feedback, staff collected data about whether the instructor explicitly stated or displayed the goals for the day; gave feedback to teens, and provided evidence for that feedback (e.g., post-it note, photo, work sample, etc.); and documented that evidence in the skill-building section of the YPQA. In reflection and improvement, staff shared feedback with the instructor based on all of the evidence that was collected during the observation and created an improvement plan related to skill building if necessary. The goals of the pilot were that instructors would have instructional tools and share promising practices for effectively integrating social and emotional skills, and that teens would receive specific feedback on how well they were progressing in their development of social and emotional skills.

Feedback on the toolkit was mixed. While some instructors enjoyed the freedom to incorporate the tools into their program as they saw fit, other instructors felt overwhelmed by the toolkit and sought more guidance and structure around how to use it. None of the instructors felt the framework conflicted with the mission of their program, which was an improvement over the previous skill-building initiative. There was some disagreement on the names of the skills. Instructors spoke about code switching and how it is imperative to teach teens about skills in their own language so they know how to talk about themselves, which better prepares them for the world. A success of the pilot was that staff felt they had reliable evidence of skill-building activities, and instructors felt more supported in connecting social and emotional skills to their program content.

SEL 4.0: Adopting a Quality Framework

Having found the right framework, ASM chose to move forward with implementing MHA with instructors by incorporating a formal training in MHA as part of new instructor institutes and professional development conferences, using instructors who were already engaged in the process and experts in SEL to lead the sessions with other instructors. Instructors were again given the freedom to explore the toolkit and integrate the social and emotional skills in ways that aligned with their programs. They were also encouraged to incorporate the assessment and provide ongoing feedback through an online survey.

Perhaps the most significant shift at this time was that ASM adopted the YPQI framework in its entirety as the organization's continuous quality improvement system. This meant moving beyond offering Youth Work Methods trainings and conducting YPQAs to also include planning with data sessions and coaching for quality improvement. The continuous quality improvement process helps ASM focus on enhancing the experience of teens and the skills of instructors. It also allows ASM to explicitly connect SEL to youth development and program quality, and to capture reliable and observable evidence of skill building, as well as other important areas of youth development. Finally, it provides a framework for supporting conversations about those observations, setting improvement goals, and supporting instructors through training and coaching.

Staff and independent contractors (called external assessors) use the YPQA to observe program activities and take notes, which are then used as evidence to score each area of youth development. Scores are combined with program administrative data and teen feedback to create a program quality profile that is used to drive program improvement efforts at ASM. All program providers who deliver apprenticeship model programs are led in a three-part sequence for continuous improvement. The process includes (a) an assessment using the YPQA, (b) a planning session to review the data and identify program areas of strength and opportunities for growth, and (c) a coaching plan to improve the program.

ASM chose the YPQI as its continuous quality improvement framework for several reasons: (a) the framework is research-based and rooted in youth development, (b) the assessment has strong technical properties and can be used with high school youth, (c) the framework is applicable across program types and settings, (d) there are available trainings and supports for staff and instructors who are included in the framework, and (e) the framework is widely used by ASM's local and national partner organizations.

ASM hires independent contractors to serve as external assessors, primarily during the summer. These external assessors are often youth development, education, or research and evaluation professionals. They must complete a rigorous 2-day training and pass a reliability test in order to be deemed reliable. External feedback is a critical part of validating results. ASM's external assessor program ensures program assessment scores are reliable and valid, and can be compared to national benchmarks. Not only does this program provide ASM with credible data, but it also allows staff to spend more time coaching for quality improvement.

SEL 5.0: Teen Voice and Using Data for Improvement

Though ASM adapted the MHA toolkits and trainings, feedback from instructors indicated that they were not prepared to implement the assessment tools for all program models. Instead, ASM implemented the assessment as part of the internship evaluation plan to allow teens in these programs and their adult partners to have performance evaluation conversations. However, this meant that ASM needed to assess social and emotional skills for the bulk of the organization's programs through alternative methods, because the MHA assessments were not logistically possible for most programs.

ASM decided to refine its post-program teen survey to lessen the burden of data collection on teens, instructors, and staff alike. Instructors had previously provided feedback that teens did not necessarily understand some of the skills in question until after they participated in the program, and teens had shared they were experiencing survey fatigue. Based on this feedback, ASM decided to pilot and then fully implement a retrospective pretest/posttest design for the teen survey to measure change in a subset of social and emotional skills (Young, 2016). In this design, teens complete their pretest and posttest questions at the same time during the posttest, ensuring teens have the same understanding of the skills in question at both pretest and posttest. This design was chosen to minimize the burdens of data collection and issues in missing data. The items of interest were leadership, teamwork/collaboration, problem-solving, public speaking and oral communication, meeting deadlines, and accepting constructive criticism. These skills were chosen based on literature on social and emotional skills for teens, commonly reported skills in ASM instructors' weekly plans, and teens' self-reported, open-ended comments about skills they learned in programs (Young, 2016). Up until this point, ASM had not actively engaged teens in talking about skill building. ASM conducted cognitive interviews with teens to determine whether the names for the skills were teen-friendly and applicable to all program types. In this exercise, ASM found that teens needed more context in the survey questions to better understand the skills and how they should assess themselves. ASM also determined that a retrospective pretest/posttest was the preferred design because teens did not know enough about the skills in question at the beginning of the program to provide valid responses for a traditional pretest. Teens provided ample evidence that their understanding of the skills changed drastically from the beginning of the program to the end of the program, rendering the traditional pretest meaningless. ASM continues to use the retrospective pretest/posttest design for measuring social and emotional skills gained.

Another development at this time involved training program staff to better support instructors through the continuous quality improvement process, with a specific focus on using data for program improvement and coaching. After ASM made an investment in observing programs using the YPQA and external assessors, it made similar investments in integrating different types of data into a program quality profile to inform conversations as part of Step 2 in the YPQI process, planning with data. The profile allows instructors to consider teens' feedback as feedback from an external assessor. ASM also invested resources in training staff in coaching and created tools to support them.

Additionally, professional development for instructors remained an area of focus. ASM created a training that outlined more specifically how to develop an engaging program session every day by integrating SEL and youth development best practices. ASM also created a program-planning tool to help new programs understand how to integrate SEL and high-quality youth development practices.

What's Next?

Though ASM has made great strides in thinking through how to foster social and emotional skills in teens, the work is not over. There are five main areas of focus in the next phase of SEL. ASM will continue to:

1. Immerse itself in the available frameworks on SEL, adapting elements that make sense for the organization's context and teens, and creating pieces that do not yet exist. Part of this work involves settling on names for the key social and emotional skills ASM wants all teens to acquire, while remaining flexible in the taxonomy so that the model is adaptable for different programs.
2. Refine its assessment strategy and measurement tools for social and emotional skills. This includes refining the skills ASM measures and aligning them more with ASM's youth development domains, testing the retrospective pretest to see how it correlates to external assessor ratings of skill building and teen reports of skills gained, testing new resources and tools, and making these resources and tools more accessible to instructors.
3. Create data tools and trainings to facilitate data-informed conversations to support SEL, instructors, and program improvement.
4. Consider additional audiences for sharing data. For example, schools post high-level report cards so families and communities can review information about the school. ASM needs to consider how it shares information about teens' skill development and quality programming to families and communities as well.
5. Provide training and coaching not only for instructors, but also for the staff who support them in program improvement.

RECOMMENDATIONS AND LESSONS LEARNED

This section provides key recommendations and lessons learned from ASM's evolving approach to SEL. ASM shares these in the hope that other organizations who serve youth, particularly teens in high school, can learn from ASM's experiences.

Lesson 1: Select an SEL Framework That Works for Your Organization

- *Young people and instructors need to be provided with the necessary language or framework to name skills.* The field's evolving terms for the set of skills (e.g., social and emotional skills, 21st-century skills, college and career readiness skills, etc.), and for specific skills that are of the greatest importance (e.g., critical thinking, problem-solving, etc.), make it difficult to teach and measure the skills. This is true for staff, instructors, and young people alike. To address this problem, organizations should identify the terms most appropriate for the work and provide ample training to embed the language in the programs.
- *Connect the SEL framework to a quality framework.* The SEL movement accelerated after ASM incorporated a continuous quality improvement process, which allowed ASM to collect observable feedback from reliable sources on skill development and other youth development factors, and provided a framework for program improvement and instructor training and support.
- *Accept that you may not find one SEL framework that meets the needs of your organization or your youth.* Borrow and adapt frameworks and measurement tools as needed to make it work for your organization. ASM has tried implementing frameworks wholesale and has not had success. Instead, ASM now incorporates pieces of MHA and YPQI, as well as creating homegrown tools, to meet the needs of its staff, instructors, and teens. These homegrown tools are informed by feedback from stakeholders through cognitive interviews.

Lesson 2: Focus on SEL Training and Creating Buy-In for Staff and Instructors

- *Be clear and reasonable with staff, instructors, and teens about expectations. Buy-in and training take time.* ASM set high (and unrealistic) expectations about the level of instructor and teen engagement in different

SEL initiatives. Staff and instructors were not always clear where the directives were coming from and did not always have time or training to adjust to the expectations. ASM only began to see changes in implementation when the organization set and communicated expectations and timelines that were more reasonable. ASM has made increased investments in instructor professional development to improve social and emotional skill development and program quality, including hosting an annual instructor forum as well as holding instructor orientation and kickoff meetings every program session.

- *Help instructors recognize that while their program is unique, there are social and emotional skills that are transferable across content areas.* Some frameworks have taken longer to catch on because instructors deeply believe that their program is different from anyone else's. They are right, but you can help instructors see the commonalities and provide them examples of how these skills may manifest themselves, especially in different content areas.

Lesson 3: Seek Regular Feedback From Your Stakeholders, Such as Youth, Instructors, Staff, and Board Members

- *Teens need the opportunity to reflect on skills they develop, not only through the self-assessment process, but also—and more importantly—by having a voice in framework and assessment development.* ASM learned the most about naming and defining skills through interviews with teens. These interviews also provided ASM with the knowledge that teens' understanding of social and emotional skills changed over time, which led to ASM implementing a more appropriate design to measure skill growth (the retrospective pretest/posttest).
- *Engage instructors regularly to get their feedback.* While ASM has focused the bulk of its SEL efforts on instructor support, that alone was not enough. ASM created an instructor advisory council made up of members who represent different content areas and geographic locations in the city to help guide ASM's thinking on organizational priorities and initiatives. ASM has more success implementing a new initiative when the organization treats instructors as partners and uses a flexible and collaborative approach to working with them.
- *Engage and educate your board members on SEL and quality improvement.* ASM's board created a program committee that includes board members, instructors, and staff. The committee meets regularly to identify organizational strategies, think through implementation issues, and discuss outcomes. The board members of the committee

are then able to articulate ASM's work in SEL to other board members and community members.

Lesson 4: Develop a Comprehensive Assessment Plan That Meets Everyone's Needs

- *Any assessment of social and emotional skills should incorporate both a formative and summative approach.* Formative assessments are low-stakes and provide a framework and language for instructors to have one-on-one meetings with teens to discuss social and emotional skills and set goals in the context of the program. They also help instructors identify and target the skills their teens need most. Summative assessments are often the desired outcomes of funders and external stakeholders, and having the opportunity to report summative assessment data helps demonstrate impact through skill growth.
- *Focus first on implementation, specifically developing the people who are fostering these skills in young people.* They need more support and time than one might expect. ASM made the mistake of implementing SEL initiatives and assessing teen outcomes too soon after pilots and with little instructor training. Supporting instructors through training, resources, and coaching gives them time to buy into the framework, integrate it authentically into their programs, and build their comfort in seeing themselves as skill developers. Do not focus on youth outcomes until implementation has been mastered.

Lesson 5: Develop a Plan for Data Collection and Utilization

- *Be clear about why you are collecting data and how the data will be used.* Have a process or plan in place for collecting, analyzing, interpreting, sharing, and utilizing data, and prepare use cases for different roles and training. ASM implemented a skills assessment tool without a plan for using the data collected. As a result, nobody knew what to do with the data once they were available, because nobody knew how they could be used. Now, ASM develops a data plan before data are collected to ensure the organization is not collecting more data than needed or overburdening staff, instructors, and teens.
- *Make a concerted effort to use data for program improvement purposes as well.* Initially, ASM focused on compliance rather than quality. The SEL initiatives were measuring success as completing the assessment process, rather than trying to understand what was working well and

what was a challenge. Because success was defined this way, data became an enemy rather than ally. ASM now disseminates a program profile that includes both quality and compliance indicators that support program improvement conversations and planning.

SUMMARY

ASM has focused intensely on fostering teen social and emotional skills and improving program quality over the last several years. The organization adopted various SEL frameworks and assessments, increased the focus on instructor support and training, adopted a quality framework, incorporated teen voice, and improved the utilization of data for improvement. ASM has learned a great deal through the several implementation phases of SEL, identifying both successes and areas for improvement. These initiatives (and the lessons learned) have created an organizational shift at every level in the organization—a shift that reinforces the mission of the organization to foster teens' social and emotional skill building through high-quality programs and instructor practice. ASM looks forward to continuing to learn and evolve in an effort to better serve Chicago's teens and partner with expert instructors.

REFERENCES

Edutopia. (2008). Why teach with project-based learning?: Providing students with a well-rounded classroom experience. Retrieved from https://www.edutopia.org/project-learning-introduction

Why PBL? (n.d.). Retrieved from the Buck Institute for Education website: http://www.bie.org/about/why_pbl

Young, J. (2016). *Retrospective pre/posttest design and response-shift bias in an urban after-school program for teens: A Mixed methods study* (Doctoral dissertation). Loyola University, Chicago, IL. Retrieved from https://ecommons.luc.edu

CHAPTER 7

SOCIAL AND EMOTIONAL LEARNING AND CONNECTIONS TO THE SCHOOL DAY

Katie Brohawn and Saskia Traill

Social and emotional learning (SEL) is an all-day, all-experiences process involving incredibly complex interactions between a person and her or his environment. To help understand the complexity of SEL, researchers work within disciplines such as neuroscience, childhood and adolescent development, education, and mental and physical health. This segmentation of the research perhaps increases the challenge of understanding SEL as a complex process that is happening throughout every waking hour and is highly integrated with academic and cognitive processes. As Camille Farrington and her colleagues describe so elegantly (Farrington et al., 2012), it is the integration of experiences into a holistic identity that is at the heart (and mind and body) of healthy development into adulthood.

Young people's learning days have also been segmented. For many young people in the United States today, the day starts with family or a caregiver,

Social and Emotional Learning in Out-of-School Time, pages 107–123

transitions to formal schooling, then moves to an out-of-school time (OST) program after school, and back to family or a caregiver before bed. The extent to which experiences in these different environments offer a coherent and meaningful sense of the world affects the development of social and emotional competencies. Such competencies need consistent reinforcing over time and across diverse settings.

ExpandED Schools works to help schools and OST organizations create a shared vision for working with young people so that children experience a more coherent learning day. This chapter describes how schools and community partners align their practices more deeply using ExpandED's model, and how they build on that alignment to develop social and emotional competencies more effectively than they would working separately. We describe how our training and professional development shifts the practices of teachers and OST providers, as well as our efforts to evaluate this work and engage stakeholders in continuous improvement of their strategies for supporting young people's SEL. We also offer examples of two New York City public schools and their OST partners, who have transformed their SEL supports for youth throughout the learning day by providing a more consistent and supportive learning environment.

BUILDING STRONG SCHOOL–COMMUNITY PARTNERSHIPS

At ExpandED Schools, elementary and middle schools partner with youth-serving community organizations that provide OST programs, such as settlement houses or community development corporations. The schools and community partners bring together their resources and expertise to give youth more opportunities to develop their talents, more support to overcome the challenges of poverty, and more time to achieve at the high levels essential for success in the modern workplace. Together, we

- *EXPAND the school day:* We add 2.5 to 3 hours each day to the conventional 6.5-hour school day, closing the learning gap by 450 hours/school year.
- *ENGAGE the community:* Through planning that includes teachers, families, and youth, we bring additional role models into the classroom, such as tutors, coaches, college students, and teaching artists. The teaching artists, sports coaches, and other supports that are a given in the lives of many children from middle- and upper-income families become part of an expanded day of learning for disadvantaged youth.
- *ENHANCE the learning:* We balance the curriculum with arts; sports; science, technology, engineering, and mathematics (STEM); and

> character-building enrichments. These learning opportunities broaden the curriculum and offer young people a clear picture of the exciting life ahead of them. Teachers are freed up to plan, collaborate, and deepen instruction, ensuring that classroom moments lead to insight and inspiration.

Our model of school–community partnership offers structures for integrated planning and developing a shared vision of success for young people, with enough flexibility to allow schools and OST providers to customize and take ownership of the model as it is implemented in their own community. Our schools are encouraged to tailor their extra time to young people's individual needs and interests. Some use extra time to offer an explicit focus on empowerment and equity—for example, through leadership workshops, public speaking and debate, or problem-based learning focused on the community surrounding the school. Some focus on adolescent literacy—for example, sixth graders participating in reading groups where youth choose books and read with peers, supported by a reading coach, to help boost their reading comprehension and engagement. Many of the schools and their community partners offer learning activities to build agency in young people, so that all children see a meaningful role for themselves in the adult world.

Schools and community partners co-plan during the summer months to align their activities and learning goals across the expanded school day. Their ExpandED Schools program managers (who act as coaches) offer information and support, with the necessary flexibility to enable teams to make choices about their plan based on their assets and needs. They consider the best use of school staff and those working for the community organization, and they compare the resources available through school and OST funds, often juggling multiple public funding streams to develop one seamless, comprehensive program. Teams plan for the integration of learning goals throughout the expanded day and determine how schools and OST providers will communicate and plan throughout the year to ensure continued alignment.

INTEGRATING SEL INTO SCHOOL–COMMUNITY PARTNERSHIPS

Based on the initial implementation of our evidence-based expanded learning model, we anticipated that school–OST teams would use the model to offer more opportunities for the development of social and emotional competencies. Indeed, in an early planning session, one principal noted that she participated in expanded learning planning sessions so she could "focus on more than test scores." We found that all young people participated in afternoon activities grounded in youth development—far more than we would expect in a typical school with an OST program. However, the intentionality of the SEL varied in afternoon activities, and because young people have choice over which activities they participate in, there was variation in the depth of their SEL experiences. We also noted that school and OST learning opportunities were often based on different SEL frameworks, resulting in youth learning different vocabulary and techniques to discuss and manage their emotions. These variations made it difficult for them to practice with adults and peers throughout the day.

Over the past few years, we have focused on the depth and integration of SEL to reach all young people in a school, and to add coherence across learning experiences. We found that a more intentional focus on SEL enabled school-CBO teams to

- build adult competencies to support their *own* social and emotional well-being,
- offer more time in the day for young people to develop and model social and emotional competencies through school-day and OST activity selection and lesson planning,
- support direct instruction to build youth's social and emotional competencies, and
- integrate practices throughout the learning day that promote SEL.

Discussions around how to align SEL goals and activities across the expanded learning day occur during the summer co-planning time. ExpandED Schools' coaches offer information so that teams can make informed choices. We encourage discussion and alignment to avoid competing programs within schools and OST programs, though we are careful to ensure solutions are generated by the group and have engagement and buy-in. For example, ExpandED Schools provides evidence-based SEL curricular materials to schools but we do not prescribe a single curriculum. We find that many OST providers have a program they already implement in the afternoon hours and many schools have curricula they offer during the day. Coaches facilitate the sharing of existing resources so that teams can discuss how to support each other's efforts, deepen their reach and impact, and avoid any possible confusion caused by competing frameworks. Teams plan for how SEL concepts will be infused throughout the expanded day through dual-purpose lessons (i.e., lessons aligned with academic standards and with SEL goals).

TRAINING AND PROFESSIONAL DEVELOPMENT

To realize the whole-child approach to SEL, ensuring that all young people receive the necessary opportunities to develop their competencies, adults with whom children interact need opportunities to build their own competencies. In our expanded learning schools, we offer professional development to all school-based personnel, including principals and school leadership, teachers, staff from community-based organizations, and other school staff. Teams consisting of two school staff and two staff members from community-based organizations attend train-the-trainer professional development in preparation for providing information to their communities. These individuals indicate their interest in becoming leaders for SEL implementation in the school and are in a strong position to do so, both through their named roles and the respect of their peers. In New York, school district representatives attend similar professional development through the central district, which facilitates further alignment. The train-the-trainer workshops also build the capacity of community organizations to introduce the approach in other partner schools, increasing the overall impact of our work over time.

Teachers and staff from community-based organizations then participate in a minimum of 30 professional development hours throughout the school year to hone their skills in teaching and applying SEL concepts. Professional development consists of sequenced workshops for multiple schools that take place in our centrally located offices, as well as school-based workshops for the full faculty from one school–OST partnership. These are supplemented with on-site observations, feedback, and continued co-planning sessions.

We focus on adult practices first for a few reasons. Ensuring that adults can model social and emotional competencies in their own behavior builds a strong SEL culture and recognizes the importance of modeled behavior in children's learning. We find that a focus on adult practice also allows time for belief and mindset shifts to occur among staff who are more reluctant than their peers to embrace a comprehensive vision of SEL. There are a few common areas that often require a shift in thinking. First, some OST providers may feel as if they are already experts in SEL and have little room to grow, due to the deep connections between SEL and youth development. Second, some staff may be concerned about a lack of time to develop SEL within classroom settings that already have tightly packed content and curriculum standards to address. Third, some staff may not have a growth mindset—that is, they may not believe that young people's social and emotional competencies can be developed over time, or that OST providers can play a key role in building these competencies. Finally, some adults may exhibit what could be described as "initiative fatigue"—that is, a belief that SEL may be the current focus of leaders but will soon pass as a priority. Enabling time for practices to evolve among adults is helpful in resolving some of these conflicts, which can otherwise inhibit the ability of the full faculty of the school and OST partner to engage in deep and meaningful implementation.

Our schools spent months focusing only on adult practice and began implementing with children slowly, only one or two classrooms at a time. The core team created demand among other adults to learn about what was happening, rather than generating pushback by requiring adults to implement something new in the classroom or new afternoon activities when they were not fully engaged and interested. Having adults focus on their own social and emotional competencies also builds a stronger school culture while new techniques continue to be integrated into the classroom. While there were late adopters at every school who were the most reluctant to implement new practices, the core team was able to maintain momentum and excitement as it built its own implementation and expanded to others.

EVALUATION AND CONTINUOUS IMPROVEMENT

ExpandED Schools approaches the use of SEL data in the same way it approaches the use of all other forms of youth outcome data (e.g., academics, attendance), using the data both for formative feedback and continuous improvement, as well as summative evaluation to demonstrate impact.

Selection of SEL Assessment Measures

Realizing that there are myriad SEL assessments available today, aligned with the many different, specific social and emotional competencies and overarching frameworks, our strategy is to first work with each site's program manager at the start of the year to document their SEL strategy. That information is then used to select the most relevant tool(s) for assessing the success of each site's SEL efforts. To the degree possible, we attempt to minimize variation in SEL assessment instruments so that we can explore patterns across our full network of school–OST partnerships.

When we originally launched our SEL data collection efforts in 2012–2013, we used the Character Lab's Character Card (formerly the KIPP Character Report Card; "Playbooks," n.d.) and the DESSA-mini (Naglieri, LeBuffe, & Shapiro, 2011). Adults complete both tools for the youth with whom they interact. As our network expanded to serve a larger proportion of middle schools, we added the option of a youth-completed tool, TransformED's MESH (Mindsets, Essential Skills, and Habits; Transforming Education, 2016). While there is value in using tools consistently over time for longitudinal assessment, especially from a research perspective, the field of SEL assessment is still relatively nascent. For this reason, it is important to stay up to date on the most relevant research in the field, and to select assessments that provide the best information to all key stakeholders, including school-day educators, staff from community-based organizations, and funders.

Formative Evaluation of Social and Emotional Competencies

In Fall 2013, ExpandED Schools sought to enhance the support provided by our coaches to help school–OST teams make stronger, data-driven instructional choices. We developed a multi-step data process to ensure that teams have the right tools and skills to analyze patterns of data, brainstorm together, and decide to pursue actionable strategies for change, highlighted by the Bridgespan Group in 2016 as part of its Research and Insights series (Brohawn, 2016; see Figure 7.1). First, ExpandED Schools' research staff facilitates the collection of data with all school–OST partners in the network. This includes enrollment and program and activity attendance data, the SEL measures (selected by the school–OST team and aligned with their SEL goals), and other information they may want to connect to social and emotional competencies, such as academic progress. The data are then analyzed by the research team and translated into a visual format that is easily accessible to a broad audience with varying data and research backgrounds. We find this step to be critical to holding engaging discussions around data interpretation and have invested significant time and resources in developing visually appealing and engaging data packets.

The research team convenes the group of ExpandED Schools' coaches at least monthly to walk through a sample site's results and ensure that all program managers feel capable of sharing their individual site's results and fielding questions that may arise from the school-CBO team. The research team then facilitates a discussion with all of the program managers about patterns *across* sites in order to uncover common challenges and successes. This analysis allows coaches to provide additional context to the data when sharing back with their school-CBO teams, pulling in information about what other OST programs are experiencing in their efforts to build social and emotional competencies, and about areas where they are struggling. This cross-site analysis also allows ExpandED Schools to identify school–OST teams that are especially successful so that they can serve as model sites to which others turn for best practices.

Equipped with this pre-analysis and cross-site review, program managers return to each school-CBO team to serve as data coaches, discussing the results and developing course corrections and future action steps. They solicit feedback regarding additional data that may be useful, given what

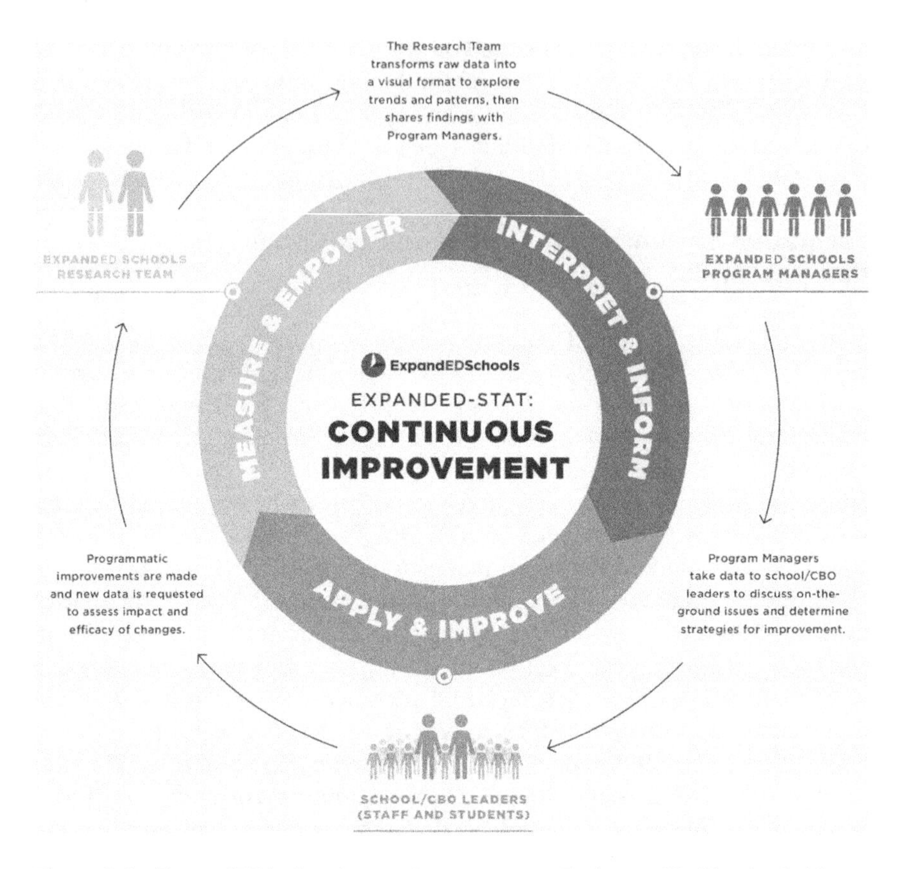

Figure 7.1 ExpandED's Continuous Improvement Cycle, profiled by the Bridgespan Group (Brohawn, 2016).

the current analyses are showing. This information is then shared back with the research team so that any new data that is desired can be collected in the next cycle. Program managers help ensure that the ExpandED Schools' research team is listening and responding to the voices of the school-CBO teams in order to meet their needs as they evolve, from the development of resources to aid in effective program implementation to the consideration of new measurement tools aligned with changes in strategy at the site level.

Summative Evaluation of Social and Emotional Competencies

As hungry as school–OST partnerships are for information that helps them target their continuous improvement efforts, there is also demand for summative evaluation as the SEL field and the body of related research evolves. Ever more, funders seek concrete evidence that programs are directly improving youth's social and emotional competencies. However, to date, the vast majority of assessments of such competencies have been subjective, either using adults as informants about youth or requiring youth to report on themselves. When we launched our data collection for social and emotional competencies in 2012–2013, we selected tools that adults completed about the youth with whom they interacted because of the younger age of our sample. These tools often ask questions about how often (or to what degree) adults see youth demonstrate certain behaviors, and there was a concern that there would be a disconnect between school-day teachers and OST staff serving as informants—that is, that the social and emotional competencies youth displayed during the afternoon hours would differ from those displayed during the school day because of different levels of interest in activities, different opportunities to develop adult–youth relationships, and so on. However, we found that in school–OST partnerships that sought to employ a cohesive SEL strategy, there were no significant differences in reported levels of social and emotional competencies when school-day educators and OST staff reported on the competencies of the same young people.

WHAT INTEGRATION OF SEL ACROSS AN EXPANDED LEARNING DAY LOOKS LIKE IN PRACTICE

In Fall 2016, ExpandED received a $1 million, 3-year grant from the New York Life Foundation to strengthen social and emotional competencies in middle school youth attending high-poverty schools. The funding enabled school–OST teams to receive training from the Yale Center for Emotional Intelligence in their RULER framework. RULER (recognizing, understanding, labeling, expressing, and regulating emotions) is an evidence-based approach that helps schools integrate emotional intelligence into their everyday teaching practice. Schools send teams to a 2-day institute, *The Anchors of Emotional Intelligence*, to train school staff on the model (with a minimum of three participants per school). We selected the RULER framework because it has a broad focus on emotions and emotional processes, rather than focusing on specific traits that may not match schools' individual focus areas (e.g., growth mindset, perseverance). We also believed the framework could be used with other, more specific curricula that school and OST staff may already be implementing, and our review suggested it could be used within both school and OST settings. Our schools brought OST staff as part of their teams to the introductory training, with the plan that they would bring the training back to their community together. Two of these school–OST partners' experiences are profiled below.

PS/MS 188 and the Educational Alliance

PS/MS 188, The Island School, is a K–8 school on Manhattan's Lower East Side serving nearly 450 youth. The school's demographics reflect the diversity seen across the boroughs: 95% of youth are Black and Hispanic, 14% are English language learners, 31% are youth with disabilities, and 100% are youth classified as living in poverty, including many who live in temporary housing/shelters.

PS/MS 188 has a long-held partnership with a community-based organization, Educational Alliance (Ed Alliance), and realizes the benefits of leveraging the skills and capacity of a local community-serving organization. Together, the school and Ed Alliance have implemented an expanded learning day where youth stay until 6:00 p.m. and OST activities are considered part of the learning day. A few years ago, the principal at PS/MS 188 commented to Ed Alliance leaders that youth could not sit in their seats and were acting out, which was hindering their learning. Ed Alliance knew that an SEL strategy would be most useful to help youth self-regulate and create an atmosphere that was more nurturing than punitive. The team was excited to partner with ExpandED Schools for coaching to implement the RULER framework across the expanded school day. Now, they have rolled out training for teachers and their OST staff on the framework and have created a common culture for implementation.

Ed Alliance was quick to acknowledge that schools have numerous demands and expectations (e.g., improved academics, strong attendance)—something they were able to learn firsthand through their work with the community schools network in which PS/MS 188 participates. As social and emotional competencies are not currently a direct accountability metric for schools, it can sometimes be difficult to raise the priority level for SEL relative to existing accountability measures (notably, test scores). However, as research continues to uncover the long-term benefits of social and emotional competency development for student academic achievement, Ed Alliance is eager to see SEL become a critical marker of success. As Ed Alliance's associate vice president, Chino Okonkwo, LCSW, stated, "It should be a marker because we know it's a part of the formula for student success" (personal communication, November 15, 2017).

Ed Alliance noted that creating buy-in among school staff was critical to the successful implementation of SEL across the expanded school day. As Chino noted, this buy in was "truly key because otherwise, consciously or unconsciously, efforts can be negated and progress can be hindered" (personal communication, November 15, 2017). As a result, when the school–OST teams rolled out RULER internally, they were slow and deliberate. They targeted a few school-day teachers who were seen as leaders within the school and who had influence with other faculty. The team also looked to gain buy in from certain personalities in the school, notably "late adopters." As Chino stated,

> It may not be intuitive to imagine, but some of the people who are typically slow to adopt a new strategy or approach can be your most helpful allies. Individuals who are typically late to adopt change can easily identify areas of concern that you may not anticipate. Engaging them early helps you shift the culture sooner. Having a mix of early and late adopters as part of your initial planning team ensures key stakeholders are empowered through the process. (personal communication, November 15, 2017)

The Results

The SEL data that are actively collected at PS/MS 188 highlight its successes. Youth continuously show gains in social and emotional skill development. Across the 2016–2017 school year, they demonstrated statistically significant gains in social and emotional skills across a variety of constructs aligned with the tenets of the RULER curriculum, including self-awareness, self-management, and social awareness. Further, youth at PS/MS 188 were more likely to be rated as socially and emotionally "strong" on a standardized assessment of social and emotional competencies (the DESSA-mini) than youth nationwide.

PS/MS 188 also consistently rates higher for school climate on the annual New York City School Survey than the majority of schools throughout District 1 (the section of New York City where the school is located), as well as across all five boroughs. On the most recent school survey (2017), 100% of teachers at the school indicated that the adults at the school did the following to address the social and emotional competencies of their young people:

- Help youth develop the skills they need to complete challenging coursework despite obstacles.
- Teach critical-thinking skills to youth.
- Teach youth how to advocate for themselves.
- Recognize disruptive behavior as SEL opportunities.
- Teach youth the skills they need to regulate their behavior (i.e., by focusing their attention, controlling their emotions, or managing their thinking, behavior, and feelings).
- Have access to school-based supports to assist in behavioral/emotional escalations.

These positive sentiments aren't limited to teachers. On the same survey, 99% of family members/guardians at the school indicated that their child's school would make them aware of any emotional or psychological issues affecting their child's academic performance. Further, 99% indicated that they felt respected by their child's teachers, that staff at their school worked hard to build trusting relationships with families/guardians like them, and that teachers and family members/guardians thought of each other as partners in educating children. The impact of this focus on parent engagement was also readily apparent in results from the 2015–2016 Quality Review Report of PS/MS 188, which noted: "School leaders consistently communicate high expectations and provide training to the entire staff. School leaders and staff have successfully partnered with families. Effective communication and partnership with families and staff create a culture of mutual accountability and support student progress toward expectations for college and career readiness" (New York City Department of Education, 2016, p. 2).

In the 2018–2019 school year, Ed Alliance is planning to expand into more schools in its network. It has also come to note the need for actionable data around social and emotional competencies, similar to data on academics and attendance. In 2016–2017, one of Ed Alliance's sites piloted the use of an online SEL data collection and reporting platform (Panorama). In 2017–2018, Ed Alliance devoted resources to rolling out this tool across all of its sites, including PS/MS 188.

Queens United and the Child Center of New York

Queens United Middle School serves 230 youth, more than 99% of whom are youth of color (85% Black, 6% Hispanic, 8% multiple races), 17% of whom are youth with disabilities, and 78% of whom live in poverty. The school opened in 2013, replacing the middle school grades of a failing K–8 school. Queens United has been partnering with its OST provider, Child Center of New York, as well as ExpandED Schools, since it first opened. As with PS/MS 188, Queens United quickly realized the value of a consistent OST partner to support efforts across an expanded learning day, especially in the development of social and emotional competencies.

Queens United takes a truly whole-child approach to the implementation of its SEL strategy, training formal educators, OST staff, and families alike. The school's prioritization of SEL is evident in its staffing structure—the dean of scholar affairs also holds the title of SEL coordinator. Further, the school's principal and guidance counselor actively participate in teaching classes with SEL goals for sixth graders, while the SEL coordinator teaches classes for seventh and eighth graders.

Like PS/MS 188, Queens United took a somewhat tiered approach to its SEL strategy, realizing the need to first ensure that staff members were fully engaged before rolling out strategies to youth. The first step involved a sit-down with all the stakeholders to build agreement on why they were focusing on social and emotional skill development. As the SEL coordinator explained, "if the adults don't know the reason, the kids are going to see that immediately" (M. Ogle, personal communication, November 20, 2017). A needs assessment quickly revealed that the RULER framework aligned well with the needs of this particular school.

For the first 6 months of the school year, the school–OST team focused entirely on implementing one element of RULER, the Mood Meter, with school and OST staff. The team wanted to ensure that staff felt comfortable talking about their *own* feelings before asking youth to talk about theirs. As the SEL coordinator noted, "You can't just do a [professional development session]" and consider your work finished; "A lot of educators don't think talking about feelings is part of their protocol; that's for the guidance counselor/social worker. Now we are asking educators to address it via an in-depth conversation and that's not easy to teach." In the first year, the school–CBO team held seven lessons on the Mood Meter, why it is important to introduce emotional vocabulary to youth, and how to do it. Now, visitors to Queens United can see evidence of widespread use of social and emotional vocabulary throughout the school day—over the loudspeaker in the morning, in math and English classes during the school day, and on the basketball court and in arts classes in the afternoon.

The seamless use of a common SEL framework across an expanded learning day doesn't stop when youth go home at 6:00 p.m. at Queens United. Last year, the school began introducing the RULER approach to families as well, so that it could be integrated into young people's home lives. Both the SEL coordinator and the school's guidance counselor held workshops within the parent–teacher association (PTA) meetings—activities around the Mood Meter and the second element of the RULER approach, the Charter—stressing the importance of consistent language at home and at school.

The Results

Queens United is already beginning to see the positive impact of its SEL focus in a number of outcome areas. The most recent NYC School Survey (2017) documented that Queens United scored above the average of other schools in its district in Queens on multiple measures of school climate, notably strong family–community ties, as well as effective school leadership and rigorous instruction. Further, 88% of family members/guardians indicated that Queens United makes them aware if there are any emotional or psychological issues affecting their child's academic performance.

The New York City Department of Education's 2016–2017 Quality Review Report on Queens United highlighted the school's focus on parent engagement in implementing its SEL strategies: "The school orchestrates ongoing events and creates multiple opportunities to partner with and engage families in the schoolwide culture of high expectations connected to college and career readiness... The Parent Teacher Association also engaged in multi-session training on the school's social emotional learning initiatives, including the RULER Approach and the Mood Meter system" (New York City Department of Education, 2016–2017, p. 7).

Data on social and emotional skill development collected directly by ExpandED Schools highlights Queens United's successes in this area as well. Young people at the school continuously show gains in social and emotional competencies. Across the most recent school year (2016–2017), they demonstrated statistically significant gains in social and emotional competencies across a variety of constructs aligned with the tenets of the RULER curriculum, including self-awareness, self-management, and social awareness. Further, youth at Queens United were significantly more likely to be rated as socially and emotionally "strong" on a standardized assessment of social and emotional competencies (the DESSA-mini) than youth nationwide.

LESSONS LEARNED ALONG THE WAY

Since ExpandED Schools began focusing on the importance of coherence in integrating SEL across the entire expanded learning day, we have learned many lessons.

Ensure Success in SEL Through Strong School–OST Partnerships

We found increased coherence, impact, and sustainability in building social and emotional competencies for young people by working with school–OST teams. To be successful, both schools and OST organizations need to recognize the benefits of working together and look for ways to partner on improving social and emotional competencies.

Take Time

From the outset, we envisioned that ExpandED Schools and their partnering community organizations would together redesign the entire school day and change school culture. These changes take time. Partnerships mature as they work toward shared goals and share accountability for results through collaborative planning, testing ideas, recalibrating, and reinvesting. Implementing changes in curriculum, enrichment activities, scheduling, and staffing takes multiple forms of communication, and takes time.

Allow time for questions from stakeholders, and for pushing past resistance to change. This calls for a phase-in strategy that focuses on one or two specific change areas at a time. These changes occur at the "speed of trust." ExpandED Schools continues to encourage partnerships to have planning conversations earlier and more often in order to align efforts and draw on the strengths each member brings to the partnership.

Build Engagement Among All Adults

Our most successful schools took time to build engagement among all adults, including the most reluctant, so that implementation would be effective. They focused on adult practice before beginning work with young people.

Focus on Continuous Improvement and Summative Assessment to Show Impact

We found it critical to have a multi-step continuous improvement process in which coaches and a research team help organize the collection of relevant data, analysis and presentation, and the development of future action steps. Researchers also collected and analyzed information on impact and outcomes to demonstrate the importance of SEL to leaders and other stakeholders.

Connect SEL to Content-Learning Goals

Once school-day teachers and OST staff were more comfortable implementing SEL framework elements and using emotional vocabulary, they began to integrate SEL into their lessons. Discussing social and emotional competencies or the feelings and behaviors of characters in fiction and nonfiction texts, or having explicit goals for building competencies as part of lessons, extended SEL throughout the learning day.

One content area particularly conducive to integration with SEL is STEM. The National Research Council's *Framework for K–12 Science Education* (National Research Council, 2012) makes clear the importance of the "affective domain" in learning science—that is, the importance of social and emotional competencies in scientific practice and engineering design. Research from Eric Jolly, Robert Tai, and others has clearly shown the importance of science engagement and interest in exploration to entrance into science-related careers. Thanks to the Noyce and Mott Foundations and others, STEM has emerged among OST providers as a critical area in which to offer learning activities, and many are now adept at using OST science curricula that engage and inspire, while also complementing school-day instruction. Advocates have been able to demonstrate how the youth development perspective in OST programs can help to address the affective challenge of STEM learning through explicit instruction in social and emotional competencies and learning activities that provide opportunities to build those competencies, such as group projects and presentations where youth explain the theories they have developed based on evidence they have collected.

Build System-Level Buy In

Coordinated SEL strategies require coordinated systems. In New York City, the city's Department of Education (DOE) and Department of Youth and Community Development (DYCD) oversee school-day and OST learning, respectively. Both have policies that encourage school–community partnership. For example, DYCD requires an education liaison from the school to be part of the OST staff. The DOE and DYCD have also both adopted the definition of SEL developed by the Collaborative for Academic, Social, and Emotional Learning (CASEL). DYCD went further, creating a framework called *Promote the Positive* to unite all DYCD-funded programs throughout the city (see Chapter 9 for a detailed description of DYCD's SEL work). This has helped to create a common framework for stakeholders throughout the city to talk about SEL and has accelerated the success of efforts by individual schools and OST providers.

CONCLUSION

In this chapter, we have offered a model for implementing SEL within school–OST partnerships. Even for those not implementing expanded learning as a model of school–community partnership, ExpandED's experiences offer interesting lessons in building elements of social and emotional alignment and partnership. Collaborating on SEL may allow greater partnership in other areas as well (e.g., family engagement, STEM, and literacy). Ultimately, SEL should cross over into all aspects of life, providing young people opportunities to practice and hone their skills in the largest array of contexts. This will help to create future leaders with the skills to seize opportunities, solve problems, and build stronger communities.

REFERENCES

Brohawn, K. (2016, October 31). *ExpandED Schools: Using process and talent to scale an initiative.* Retrieved from https://www.bridgespan.org/insights/library/organizational-effectiveness/expanded-schools-using-process-talent-to-scale

Farrington, C. A., Roderick, M., Allensworth, E., Nagaoka, J., Keyes, T. S., Johnson, D. W., & Beechum, N. O. (2012). *Teaching adolescents to become learners. The role of noncognitive factors in shaping school performance: A critical literature review.* Chicago, IL: University of Chicago Consortium on Chicago School Research.

Naglieri, J. A., LeBuffe, P., & Shapiro, V. B. (2011). Universal screening for social-emotional competencies: A study of the reliability and validity of the DESSA-mini. *Psychology in the Schools, 48*(7): 660–671.

National Research Council. (2012). *A framework for K–12 science education: Practices, crosscutting concepts, and core ideas.* Committee on a Conceptual Framework for New K–12 Science Education Standards. Board on Science Education, Division of Behavioral and Social Sciences and Education. Washington, DC: The National Academies Press.

New York City Department of Education. (2016). *Quality review report 2015–16* (PS 188 The Island School). Retrieved from http://schools.nyc.gov/OA/SchoolReports/2015-16/Quality_Review_2016_M188.pdf

New York City Department of Education. (2017). *Quality review report 2016–17* (Queens United Middle School). Retrieved from http://schools.nyc.gov/OA/SchoolReports/2016-17/Quality_Review_2017_Q289.pdf

Playbooks: Develop Character in Classrooms. (n.d.). Retrieved from the Character Lab website: https://www.characterlab.org/playbooks

Transforming Education. (2016). *Measuring MESH: Student and teacher surveys curated for the CORE districts* (Version 1.0). Retrieved from https://www.transformingeducation.org/measuring-mesh/

CHAPTER 8

HOW OUT-OF-SCHOOL TIME CAN SUPPORT COLLEGE AND CAREER READINESS THROUGH SOCIAL AND EMOTIONAL LEARNING

Jennifer Brown Lerner and Carinne Deeds

WHAT IS COLLEGE AND CAREER READINESS?

In order to thrive as adults, young people must be prepared to succeed in education, the workforce, and civic society. To accomplish this lofty yet achievable goal of preparing the next generation of successful young people, it is necessary to create a shared understanding of what it takes to become lifelong learners, find employment in a family-sustaining wage job, and engage with communities and civic society.

College and career readiness (CCR) is used within K–12 education as an umbrella term for the competencies graduates need in order to pass first-year, college-level courses or maintain a skilled job (Hooker & Brand, 2009). Although the term is widely used and has been adopted by policy

Social and Emotional Learning in Out-of-School Time, pages 125–144

makers—most recently, in the reauthorization of the Elementary and Secondary Education Act of 1965 (Every Student Succeeds Act of 2015 [ESSA], 2015–2016)—there is no consensus on the exact definition of CCR or the competencies it entails. In fact, according to a 2012 analysis by the National High School Center, more than 70 organizations focus on CCR and almost all have a unique definition or framework (National High School Center, 2012). Additionally, most states develop or adopt their own definitions of CCR or profiles of successful high school graduates (Career Readiness and Success Center, n.d.).

In 2009, American Youth Policy Forum (AYPF) operationalized a definition of CCR grounded in youth development. This broadened the field's understanding of readiness by naming the foundational competencies youth need in order to be prepared for college, career, and life. These competencies fall across the domains of knowledge, skills, abilities, and personal resources, with success defined through short-term, immediate, and long-term outcomes. Figure 8.1 outlines the central building block of AYPF's operational definition of CCR: "Foundations for learning and growth."

Knowledge, skills, and abilities (KSAs) are the fundamental academic, career-related, and contextual learning competencies that are vital to educational and professional advancement. Explicit instruction is the traditional mode of delivery for KSAs, yet the competencies listed under KSAs are not limited exclusively to academic knowledge or technical skills. Some KSAs are social and emotional competencies, such as communication skills, critical thinking, and teamwork.

Personal resources, a term often used in youth development literature, refers to the capacities, strengths, and developmental needs cultivated

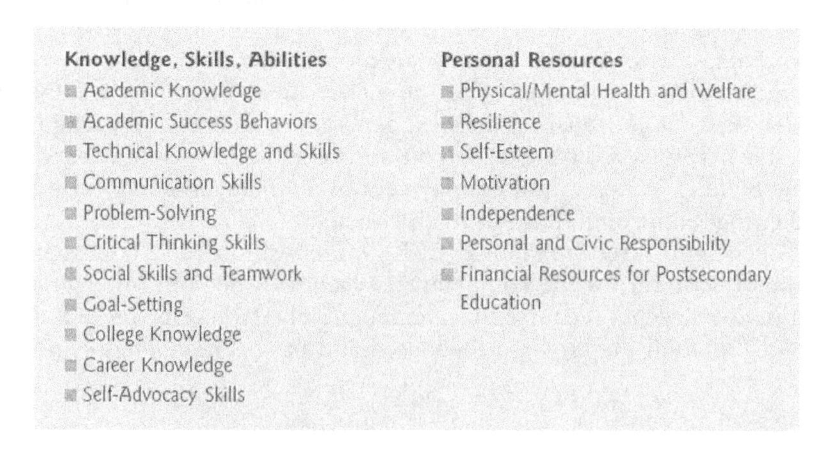

Figure 8.1 Foundations for Learning and Growth, AYPF's operational definition of CCR.

throughout a young person's life (Innovation Center for Community and Youth Development & National 4-H Council, 2003). Physical safety, positive mental health, flexibility, a strong moral character, creativity, and spiritual development underpin the personal resource competencies (Hooker & Brand, 2009). These competencies are typically developed through experiences and community participation. Personal resources such as resilience and self-esteem are also included in social and emotional learning (SEL) frameworks.

Although AYPF's operational definition of CCR separates KSAs and personal resources into two columns, it does not prioritize either set of competencies. Instead, it acknowledges that all are essential to readiness. Most importantly, it recognizes that all of these competencies (knowledge, skills, abilities, and personal resources) are malleable and can be developed in various settings, both within and outside of school.

Additionally, embedded into this operational definition is the notion that schools alone cannot be responsible for the development of all of these foundational competencies (Hooker & Brand, 2009). Figure 8.2 outlines a broad set of stakeholders who are responsible for equipping young people with the competencies outlined in AYPF's Foundations for Learning and Growth.

AYPF's operational definition of CCR and subsequent frameworks shift the perception of CCR to incorporate a broad set of competencies and

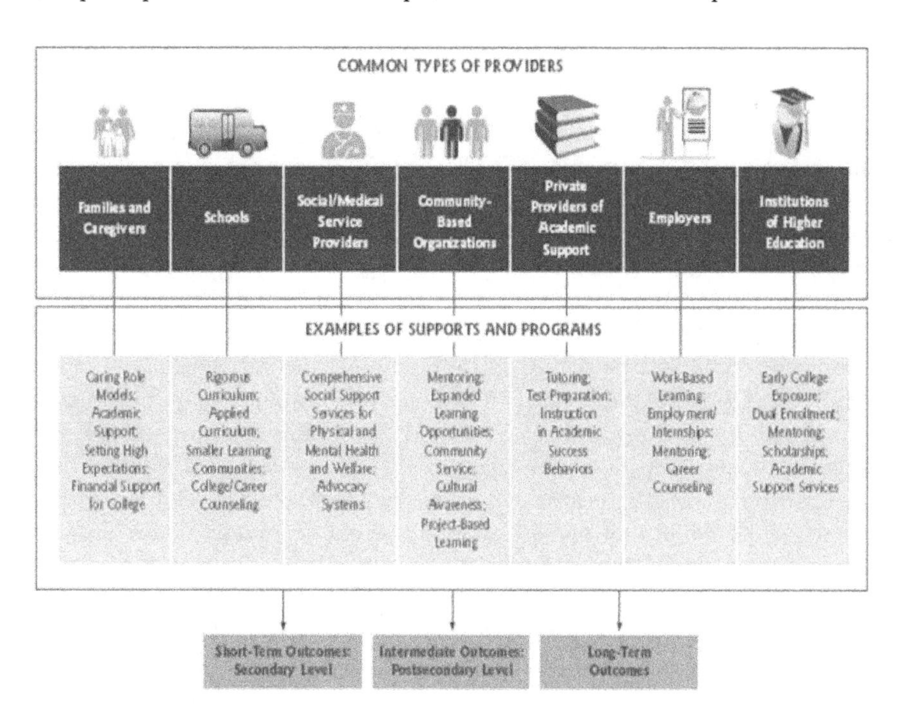

Figure 8.2 CCR stakeholders and outcomes.

underscore the role of community partners, including out-of-school time (OST) providers.

SOCIAL AND EMOTIONAL LEARNING: THE FOUNDATION OF COLLEGE AND CAREER READINESS

As outlined in AYPF's operational definition of CCR, social and emotional competencies are embedded in the knowledge, skills, abilities, and personal resources that are necessary for readiness. Though often thought of as separate, the development of academic and technical skills is complemented by a strong foundation in social and emotional competencies within AYPF's operational definition of CCR. Research indicates that skills like communication, problem solving, teamwork, and self-esteem are not only important for success, but are also important for enabling young people to become better learners in general. As a recently released report from the Council of Distinguished Scientists of the National Commission on Social, Emotional, and Academic Development at The Aspen Institute stated: "Social, emotional, and cognitive capabilities are fundamentally intertwined—they are interdependent in their development, experience, and use" (Jones & Kahn, 2017, p. 4).

In other words, learning is a social and emotional process. This idea, supported by extensive research in the field, reinforces the notion that social and emotional competencies are central to all types of learning and are an indispensable component of CCR. For instance, in both postsecondary education and workplace environments, young people need to be able to understand and regulate their emotions, communicate well with others, and make sound personal and social choices. Employers agree that social and emotional competencies are necessary for success and are essential for job seekers. A Forbes report on the skills that employers most want in their employees ranked these four social and emotional competencies at the top of the list: (a) the ability to work in a team, (b) the ability to solve problems, (c) the ability to make decisions, and (d) the ability to communicate verbally with people inside and outside an organization (Adams, 2014).

Research shows that social and emotional competencies can, over time, increase the likelihood of high school graduation, readiness for postsecondary education, career success, positive family and work relationships, better mental health, reduced criminal behavior, and engaged citizenship (Hawkins, Kosterman, Catalano, Hill, & Abbott, 2008). These competencies, along with other knowledge, skills, abilities, and personal resources, are what ensure that young graduates are ready for life after high school. Because of the importance and complexity of cultivating social and emotional competencies, a variety of institutions in the youth-serving ecosystem must play a role in ensuring all young people can obtain them.

HOW OUT-OF-SCHOOL TIME FOSTERS SEL TO SUPPORT COLLEGE AND CAREER READINESS

Schools alone cannot and should not bear full responsibility for ensuring that our nation's young people develop the competencies needed for college, career, and life. Although schools have always been a central component of the ecosystem of services for young people (Nagaoka, Farrington, Ehrlich, & Heath, 2015), efforts to better prepare youth for success should include a range of learning opportunities both inside and outside the classroom.

What the Research Says

Research overwhelmingly indicates that OST settings should play a role in the cultivation of social and emotional competencies. Leading researchers concur that developmental experiences occur in all settings, and that skill development is shaped by various environments (Jones & Kahn, 2017). Practitioners and thought leaders also agree that OST settings have an important role to play in supporting CCR. Around two thirds of organizations in the aforementioned National High School Center study highlighted the importance of facilitating engagement with community, families, postsecondary institutions, and other stakeholders, including OST providers, in their definitions of CCR (National High School Center, 2012).

OST systems (Browne, 2015) and providers have long worked to develop high-quality programs that support the development of knowledge, skills, abilities, and personal resources associated with CCR (Durlak, Weissberg, Dymnicki, Taylor, & Schellinger, 2011), and the evidence indicates that they have been largely effective, particularly in the development of social and emotional competencies ("Linking Schools and Afterschool," 2015). According to a 2007 meta-analysis of OST programs, high-quality OST settings have a positive impact on many "personal and social" skills, including problem solving, conflict resolution, self-control, leadership, responsible decision making, and self-esteem (Durlak & Weissberg, 2007). Embedded in AYPF's operational definition of CCR, social and emotional competencies provide an important foundation for academic development, are desired by employers, and are central to CCR.

How It Works

OST settings provide an ideal environment for fostering CCR because they allow for flexibility in the way social and emotional competencies (and other skills) are taught, acquired, and practiced. Specifically, high-quality OST programs provide flexible conditions for learning, encourage active youth voice, and facilitate positive relationships with peers and adults, all of which are important complements to the instruction that takes place within school walls. For example, youth participating in OST programs (OST youth) have the flexibility to learn in different physical places and spaces that may not be available to classroom teachers. Additionally, the OST sector is rooted in a positive youth development approach, which acknowledges that young people can and should contribute to their own development and success and provides various outlets for youth to have a meaningful voice in their learning (Hamilton, Hamilton, & Pittman, 2004). These conditions create a climate in OST settings that supports the development of social and emotional competencies (and other skills) that are central to readiness for college, career, and participation in civic society.

OST settings tend to cultivate SEL by providing a range of developmental experiences and occasionally using explicit instructional strategies (Blyth, Sheldon, & Mathias, 2014). SEL in OST settings is not a replacement for the SEL that occurs in schools, but it complements what happens in the classroom by reinforcing learning via engaging developmental experiences and additional instruction. As noted by Karen Pittman, president and CEO of the Forum for Youth Investment, these experiences in OST settings may not always be *called* SEL, but they are a critical part of the development of social and emotional competencies and, ultimately, readiness. According to Pittman, "project-based learning, deeper learning, service learning, STEM, career and technical education are examples of teaching/learning approaches and curricula that require students to practice the full range of social and emotional competencies in the service of mastering academic content" (Pittman, 2017, n.p.). All of these experiences are commonplace in high-quality OST settings and are ideal for providing youth opportunities to develop, practice, and demonstrate social and emotional competencies and other CCR competencies.

For example, OST youth often participate in developmental experiences such as project-based learning or career exploration that foster the development of readiness skills and expose them to various potential career pathways. Although college and career preparation is traditionally considered most relevant for youth in high school, OST settings often provide these experiences to youth in the middle grades, for whom skill development and college and career exploration is essential. Additionally, OST settings can connect young people (particularly older youth) to internships, apprenticeships, job-shadowing programs, and other experiences outside of the typical learning environment, allowing them to further develop and reinforce their skills. Through participation in an internship after school, for example, young people can develop skills like self-discipline, teamwork, and responsible decision-making, which are important to success within and outside of school and are often key strategies for staying engaged in learning.

In addition to providing engaging opportunities for the development of social and emotional competencies in a professional context, high-quality OST programs help familiarize young people with the processes of applying to and navigating college by taking them on visits to college campuses, working with youth and families to identify prospective colleges, providing assistance in the college application process, helping families navigate financial assistance, and providing mentorship to youth who may not get such support elsewhere (Brand & Kannam, 2017). With regard to efforts to build career awareness and college knowledge, it is important to note that there is value not just in the experiences themselves, but also in the relationships with caring adults and the built-in mentorship and guidance that allow many young people to explore their futures in a way that might not be possible otherwise (Gullotta, 2015).

Table 8.1 further explores the various developmental experiences provided in high-quality OST settings and what those experiences can look like

TABLE 8.1 Developmental Experiences in OST That Promote College and Career Readiness[a]

Experience	What It Looks Like
Project-based learning	• Engaging, hands-on projects
	• Application of academic/technical knowledge
	• Relevant to careers
Service learning	• Solving real-world problems
	• Engagement with community
	• Youth leadership
Work-based learning	• Internships
	• Apprenticeships
Career exploration	• Guest speakers from industry/business
	• Job shadowing
College navigation	• Identification of prospective postsecondary options
	• Visits to college campuses
	• Assistance with college application processes
	• Navigation of financial aid processes

[a] Developed by the authors.

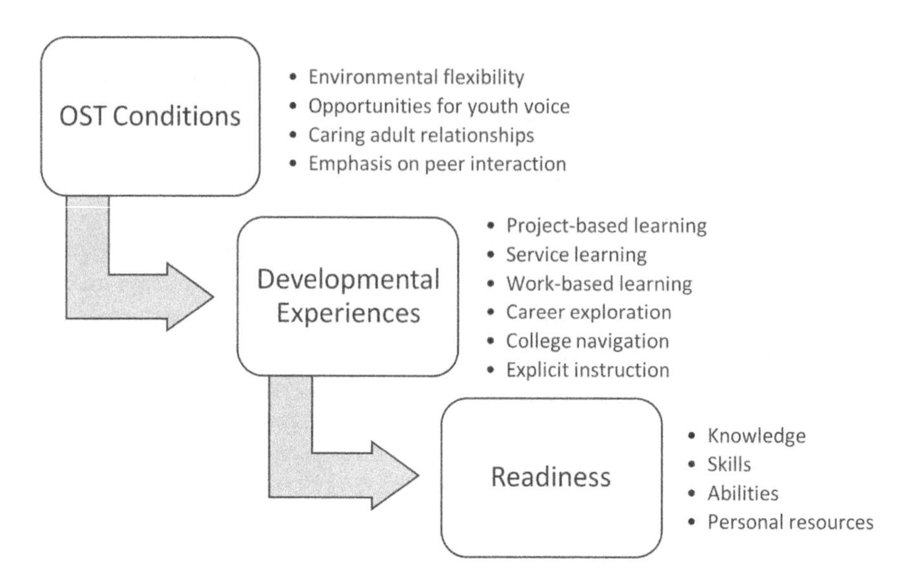

Figure 8.3 How OST supports college and career readiness.

in practice. These experiences provide opportunities for youth to cultivate the knowledge, skills, abilities, and personal resources necessary for CCR.

Ultimately, the conditions present in OST settings allow for a range of developmental experiences (including explicit instruction) that are uniquely positioned to cultivate CCR competencies, particularly social and emotional competencies (see Figure 8.1). Through participation in high-quality OST programs, young people can further hone, enhance, and practice their academic, technical, social and emotional, and other skills, giving them a greater opportunity to succeed in college, career, and life. Figure 8.3 illustrates the connections between the conditions present in OST settings, the developmental experiences provided by OST programs, and the knowledge, skills, abilities, and personal resources associated with readiness that are fostered by those experiences.

POLICY AS A CRITICAL LEVER AT THE INTERSECTION OF RESEARCH AND PRACTICE

In practice, OST providers across the country have aligned their strategies with the foundational competencies for CCR discussed in the opening section of this chapter. In these settings, SEL is both a foundation for academic and technical learning and a mechanism for ensuring young people have the social and emotional competencies they need to thrive after high school. Research has documented effective practices to promote SEL in

OST settings, as well as strategies to bring these practices to scale. For example, the SEL Challenge, managed by the Weikart Center for Youth Program Quality and the Susan Crown Exchange, demonstrated that effective and engaging OST programs provide developmental activities that foster the development of social and emotional competencies, from boat building to musical writing (Smith et al., 2016). By identifying the core elements of effective OST programming, research has also been able to drive the OST field toward scalability. Policy can complement these advances in research and practice by supporting the role of OST programming in developing CCR, as discussed in greater detail in Chapter 13 (Afterschool Alliance, 2016). The paragraphs below provide a brief summary of the ways in which policy at the federal, state, local, and even programmatic level can encourage CCR in OST settings.

Positioning

Policy can position OST programs as critical partners of K–12 education, and as an important component of the larger ecosystem of services for young people that supports CCR for all youth in a community, city, or state. For example, ESSA strengthened the language under Title I, Part A, to emphasize the importance of CCR for all youth. By naming OST programming as an allowable/acceptable use for these funds, policy drew a critical connection between after school and CCR. Additionally, policy makers' use of the bully pulpit is vital to communicating the importance of OST and its value in preparing youth for long-term success. This bully pulpit provides a critical opportunity for policy leaders at the national level, and also at the state and local levels. For instance, Betsy Price, the mayor of Fort Worth, Texas, and a longtime champion of the value of OST programs in her community, led a significant effort to coordinate OST programs in the city with all 14 local school districts, with the aim of ensuring that all young people have access to high-quality experiences that prepare them for college, career, and life. Mayor Price translated her words into actions by moving the coordinating functions out of the city and into a new nonprofit organization, Fort Worth SPARC, ensuring that OST efforts would be sustained after she left office.

Scale

Policy can also signal priorities and align resources (including providing additional funding) to promote the spread and sustainability of effective practices, from formal legislative and regulatory policy through to institutional or system-level policy. For example, 55,000 Degrees—a public–private partnership across education, business, and civic leaders in Louisville, Kentucky—aims to add 40,000 bachelor's degrees and 15,000 associate's degrees by 2020. To achieve this goal, the partnership is aligning its efforts with the significant work already underway in the community, including in the OST sector. Collectively, key stakeholders across government, business, and nonprofit sectors in Louisville have explicitly defined goals around CCR, while 55,000 Degrees and other community partners recognize OST programs as critical to achieving commonly agreed-upon metrics for youth outcomes, including CCR.

Access

Policy can also be a powerful promoter of equity by supporting systems-level coordination at the state or local level that expands access to college and career preparation activities for youth who may otherwise lack developmental opportunities. Research shows that OST programs have the greatest benefits for youth from low-income families and youth of color, who are less likely to attend high-quality K–12 schools, less likely to participate in extracurricular activities, and are traditionally underrepresented in postsecondary education (Afterschool Alliance, 2016). Youth from higher socioeconomic backgrounds tend to have greater access to learning opportunities outside of school through networks of family and community, but youth who are economically disadvantaged often have limited access to these opportunities and services. Policies that support the coordination of OST programming can enable greater and more equitable access to high-quality OST opportunities, which, in turn, can facilitate CCR for all.

CASE STUDIES

The following case studies demonstrate how the ideas discussed in this chapter can be put into practice. The OST systems described below (which include local, state, and national examples) use all three of the policy levers described above to effectively operationalize the connection between SEL and CCR.

Grand Rapids ELO Network

Grand Rapids' success in the OST space is a useful example of the power of coordination and the important role policy plays in positioning OST programs as critical partners in defining and building the KSAs necessary for CCR. Approximately 2 years ago, the Extended Learning Opportunities Network (ELO Network) and Believe 2 Become (B2B; an initiative of a local foundation) built the Imagine U toolkit. The goal of this resource is to help youth develop the mindsets, skills, future orientation, knowledge, and agency they will need for success in college and careers. The toolkit provides practitioners with the necessary language, strategies, and measurement tools to develop agency in children and youth, including setting goals, taking initiative, and persisting through difficulties ("Imagine U Toolkit," 2017).

Beginning with the academic research of Dr. Ronald F. Ferguson of the Achievement Gap Initiative at Harvard University, a broad coalition of stakeholders—including the ELO Network, B2B grantees across Grand Rapids, and Grand Rapids Public Schools—worked to define agency in the context of their community. As outlined in Figure 8.4, agency is explicitly inclusive of social and emotional competencies and also includes the range of knowledge, skills, dispositions, and abilities articulated in AYPF's operationalized definition of CCR.

Having established a common language and understanding of the desired outcomes for all Grand Rapids youth, a professional learning community composed primarily of local OST providers worked to develop activities and resources aligned with their definition of agency. Drawing on the available research base, the professional learning community also demonstrated

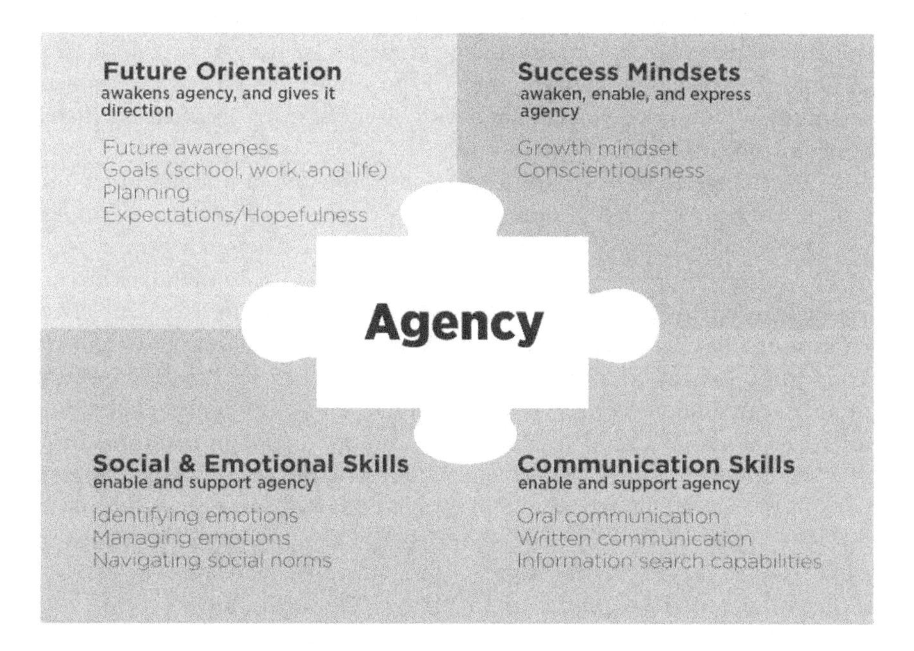

Figure 8.4 The components of agency. *Source:* Believe 2 Become, an initiative of the Doug and Maria DeVos Foundation.

the connection between learning environments and a young person's ability to acquire the desired skills, creating a common measurement tool across OST providers.

In the words of Lynn Heemstra, director of the ELO Network, "This initiative has been so successful that 97 percent of ELO providers have been involved, and the trainings have been the highest attended by youth development workers to date" ("Imagine U Toolkit," 2017, p. 5). This work in Grand Rapids illustrates the importance of community-wide alignment around common readiness goals and a broad acknowledgement of the foundational necessity of social and emotional competencies, developed both within and outside of the classroom.

Michigan After-School Partnership

Beginning in 2012, the Michigan Department of Education began a process of defining the characteristics of "career and college ready students," drawing on the best available research, garnering support from national organizations, and engaging with a range of stakeholders across the state. The resulting definition (see Figure 8.4) was then mapped across the state's academic standards ("Characteristics of Career," n.d.), and the state created tools and resources to help educators craft learning experiences to prepare youth to be career and college ready. By creating a clear definition of CCR, the Michigan Department of Education signaled to other youth-serving systems how they could align with their efforts to produce graduates ready for success beyond high school.

The Michigan After-School Partnership (MASP; the statewide after-school network) used this opportunity to create a pilot project entitled the Open Badges Project, in partnership with the Michigan Department of Education, the Michigan AfterSchool Association (the membership organization for youth workers in OST programs), Michigan State University Extension (MSUE) 4-H, and Eastern Michigan University's 21st Century Community Learning Center (21st CCLC) Bright Futures Program. Jointly, they ran three pilots focused both on student-level badges and credentials for youth workers. The MSU Renewable Energy Camp, an extensive summer learning program for middle and high school youth, was the badging pilot most closely aligned with Michigan's CCR definition. In addition to the in-person experiences offered during the camp, youth could work to earn complementary digital badges to further their learning and demonstrate competencies aligned with Michigan's CCR definition.

The MSU Renewable Energy Camp badges ("Digital Badges," n.d.) require a young person to conduct experiments, research new ideas, and explore innovative opportunities in the field of renewable energy via a complementary online platform while participating in the solar energy program. The badges are aligned with academic content standards and the CCR standards, but more importantly they ask youth to take ownership of demonstrating their learning and mastery through in-person and online tasks. These activities foster key social and emotional competences, including teamwork, time management, and communication in various modes (verbal, written, and digital).

Boys and Girls Clubs of America

Boys and Girls Clubs of America (BGCA) is a national OST provider network that serves over 4 million youth and teens around the country each year through local OST programs (clubs). Preparing young people for college and career is central to the mission of BGCA, whose educational programs are "designed to ensure that all Club members graduate from high school on time, ready for a postsecondary education and a 21st-century career" (Boys and Girls Clubs of America, n.d.). SEL (often referred to as character and citizenship or leadership development at BGCA) is central to the organization's youth development approach, which has led to success in clubs around the country. BGCA programs foster the development of competencies for readiness through a variety of programs, including those focused on character, citizenship, leadership development, and a variety of other college- and career-related activities, as described in AYPF's operational definition of CCR. A few of these programs are profiled below.

- *Diplomas2Degrees* is a BGCA college readiness program that helps teens develop both short- and long-term goals, while helping them better understand the landscape of postsecondary education opportunities through college campus visits, tours, and financial aid application assistance. The program centers on positive, supportive relationships with adult mentors, who offer guidance in transitions to and throughout the college experience.
- *CareerLaunch* encourages teens aged 13 to 18 to assess their skills and interests, explore careers, make sound educational decisions, and prepare to participate in the workforce, all of which cultivates self-awareness. Adult mentors help participants hone their job search and application skills and emphasize job readiness through online career exploration, college and job search information, and interactive job-shadowing and training activities.
- *The Torch Club* program for youth aged 11 to 13 focuses on strengthening social and emotional competencies (referred to primarily as "21st-century skills"), emphasizing the importance of integrity,

teamwork, and leadership. Torch Club participants work together to implement projects related to public service, education, health, and social recreation.
- *Ready, Set, Action* is a strengths-based SEL curriculum that fosters social and emotional skills and behavioral skills, developed by Partnerships in Education and Resilience (PEAR). BGCA partners with PEAR to help club youth cultivate supportive peer relationships and overcome adversity.

There are other, more specialized initiatives in state and local BGCA clubs throughout the country. For instance, clubs in the state of California are partnering with the University of California (UC) to improve CCR among club youth. As part of the partnership, UC will provide club members and their families with college and career information, campus exposure, and additional support as they apply to and enroll at UC schools. For example, "UC will train Boys & Girls Club staff to coach students. Participants will also have access to SAT prep workshops, tutorials on writing strong college applications and opportunities to visit UC campuses" (Freeling, 2016, n.p.). The partnership is part of Achieve UC, an initiative spurred by UC President Janet Napolitano to increase postsecondary enrollment among California youth, particularly among underrepresented student populations. OST providers are critical partners in this work to help ensure that *all* youth, not just those at well-resourced high schools, have access to the college knowledge needed to succeed in postsecondary education.

The Boys and Girls Club of Green Bay has also prioritized its college and career preparation work and received top national honors for its efforts ("National Awards," n.d.). Its Teens to Work (T2W) program is a multistep process. Teens must first participate in CareerLaunch, then in Money Matters (which promotes financial responsibility and independence), followed by Junior Staff (a club apprenticeship). Upon completion of this sequence, teens begin the final T2W component, in which the club matches young people with entry-level employment opportunities. National partnerships with employers and supplemental local funding enable this work.

Through participation in these and other BGCA programs, youth have the opportunity to cultivate deep social and emotional competencies. Whether through explicit instruction via the Torch Club or through practical relationship-building and decision-making experiences via T2W, programs provide a venue for youth to develop and practice the social and emotional competencies that are essential for CCR.

OPPORTUNITIES MOVING FORWARD

This chapter has explored the relationship between SEL and CCR and the ways in which OST programming can support the development of competencies needed for future success. However, we recognize that opportunities remain across research, practice, and policy to further develop these connections.

Establish a Common Understanding of College and Career Readiness Across Youth-Serving Systems

A shared definition of CCR, customized to suit the local context, provides the foundation for all the case studies shared in this chapter. This definition is typically accepted or adopted widely across youth-serving systems, including K–12 education and OST programs. A CCR definition (such as AYPF's definition) helps articulate the competencies a young person needs in order to be ready for success, including social and emotional competencies. While the OST sector has demonstrated that social and emotional competencies are core competencies necessary for success (Smith et al., 2016), more traditional education often limits CCR to academic success. A broader and shared definition is a necessary foundation for leveraging resources across youth-serving systems in support of CCR.

Position the OST Sector as a Critical Partner in the Youth-Serving Ecosystem Supporting CCR

In addition to including the OST sector in the shared definition or understanding of CCR, it must be positioned as a critical partner in the broader youth-serving ecosystems that work to ensure that all young people are prepared for college, career, and life. As articulated in this chapter, OST providers can deliver high-quality programs linking explicit instruction in social and emotional competencies with desired academic and technical competencies for CCR. OST settings allow for flexibility and innovations often not afforded to traditional K–12 schools, creating unique environments and experiences to help youth grow and develop.

While the OST sector is often considered a partner of K–12 education, its vital role in supporting CCR, especially for older youth, is not always articulated (Bowles & Brand, 2009). Demonstrating the value of the OST sector in support of CCR goals should and often does fall to state and local coordinating entities, such as statewide after-school networks or local OST intermediaries. Statewide after-school networks' ability to navigate across multiple youth-serving agencies at the state level can ensure that the OST sector is represented in key stakeholder conversations related to the development of CCR definitions, frameworks, or initiatives. Additionally, statewide afterschool networks can advocate for resources to be allocated to the OST sector in support of CCR goals. At the local level, OST intermediaries serve a similar role in community conversations and also function as an efficient mechanism for communicating state or local priorities to OST providers.

Engage Business and Higher Education as Partners With and Champions for OST Programs

As youth will ultimately enter higher education institutions and/or the workforce, these sectors are necessary partners in the work of CCR. At present, the OST sector does not always engage effectively with higher education institutions and business, but the shared goal of fostering CCR in all young people provides a unique opportunity to improve collaboration.

The case studies in this chapter describe partnerships of this nature at the local and state level. The challenge is to determine how best to move these initiatives to scale. Ideally, building a common definition of CCR will create a shared vision and understanding across sectors. However, there is limited research on best practices and policy conditions to support coordination between OST, higher education institutions, and business (with the exception of the college access field, which often is viewed as distinct from OST).

One concrete opportunity to connect the OST and workforce sectors around CCR is to further explore the relationship between social and emotional competencies and employability skills, where specific and noteworthy alignment has already been recognized. As a 2015 brief from American Institutes for Research (AIR) explains, "evidence suggests that we already know a lot about how to develop some key employability skills—we may just be calling them something else" (Devaney & Moroney, 2015, p. 3). A comparison of the Collaborative for Academic, Social, and Emotional Learning's (CASEL) SEL framework and the U.S. Department of Education's Employability Skills Framework found several related skills across both frameworks, including relationship skills, adaptability, self-regulation, and communication. This comparison can be taken one step further to explore the intersections with CCR competencies.

Realign Resources, Including Flexible Funding

Although there has been progress in demonstrating the value of OST programs in developing social and emotional competencies to support

CCR, the field must continue to innovate and explore new opportunities. Realigning resources (including funding, human capital, and political capital) would allow the OST sector to better coordinate with other youth-serving sectors. For example, access to federal funding associated with the Carl B. Perkins Act (1998) or Workforce Innovation and Opportunity Act (WIOA, 2014) could allow OST providers to create opportunities that capitalize on their expertise in developing social and emotional competencies but focus on developing critical technical skills or credentials through career and technical education or workforce training. Other opportunities around flexibility—such as the Performance Pilot Partnership (P3), which allows localities to lift restrictions on the allowable use of federal dollars in return for progress against common metrics—would allow the OST sector to function as a critical partner in the development of young people, ensuring they are ready for college, career, and life.

REFERENCES

Adams, S. (2014, November 12). The 10 skills employers most want in 2015 graduates. *Forbes.* Retrieved from https://www.forbes.com/sites/susanadams/2014/11/12/the-10-skills-employers-most-want-in-2015-graduates/#3922ec0b2511

Afterschool Alliance. (2016, August). *America after 3pm special report: Afterschool in communities of concentrated poverty.* Washington, DC: Author. Retrieved from http://www.afterschoolalliance.org/AA3PM/Concentrated_Poverty.pdf

Blyth, D., Sheldon, T., & Mathias, C. (2014). *Understanding social & emotional learning: Education and OST leaders' perspectives* [Slide presentation]. St. Paul: University of Minnesota, College of Education and Human Development, Center for Applied Research and Educational Improvement.

Bowles, A., & Brand, B. (2009). *Learning around the clock: Benefits of expanded learning opportunities for older youth.* Washington, DC: American Youth Policy Forum.

Boys and Girls Clubs of America. (n.d.). Education programs page. Retrieved from https://www.bgca.org/programs/education

Brand, B., & Kannam, J. (2017). Career and college exploration in afterschool programs in science, technology, engineering, and mathematics (STEM). In R. Ottinger (Ed.), *STEM ready America* (pp. 1–10). Flint, MI: The Charles Stewart Mott Foundation. Retrieved from http://stemreadyamerica.org/wp-content/uploads/2017/10/STEMReady_Article_Brand.pdf

Browne, D. (2015). *Growing together, learning together. What cities have discovered about building afterschool systems.* New York, NY: The Wallace Foundation.

Carl D. Perkins Vocational and Technical Education Act, Pub. L. No. 109-270 § 120 Stat. 683 (2005–2006).

CCRS Interactive State Map. (n.d.). Retrieved from the College and Career Readiness and Success Center website: https://ccrscenter.org/ccrs-landscape/state-profile

Characteristics of Career and College Ready Students. (n.d.). Retrieved from Michigan Department of Education website: http://www.michigan.gov/documents/mde/Characteristics_of_Career_and_College_Ready_Students_ADA_514673_7.pdf

Devaney, E., & Moroney, D. (2015). *Ready for work? How afterschool programs can support employability through social and emotional learning.* Washington, DC: American Institutes for Research. Retried from https://www.air.org/sites/default/files/downloads/report/Afterschool-Programs-Support-Employability-Brief-Dec-2015.pdf

Digital Badges. (n.d.). Retrieved from the Michigan State University website: http://www.canr.msu.edu/4_h_renewable_energy_camp/digital_badges

Durlak, J., & Weissberg, R. (2007). *The impact of after-school programs that promote personal and social skills.* Chicago, IL: Collaborative for Academic, Social, and Emotional Learning. Retrieved from http://www.adlit.org/article/20506/

Durlak, J., Weissberg, R., Dymnicki, A., Taylor, R., & Schellinger, K. (2011). The impact of enhancing students' social and emotional learning: A meta-analysis of school-based universal interventions. *Child Development, 82*(1), 405–433. Retrieved from http://onlinelibrary.wiley.com/doi/10.1111/j.1467-8624.2010.01564.x/abstract

Every Student Succeeds Act of 2015, Pub. L. No. 114-95 § 114 Stat. 1177 (2015–2016).

Freeling, N. (2016, October 4). UC partners with Boys & Girls Clubs to open college doors for California teens. *UC Newsroom.* Retrieved from https://www.universityofcalifornia.edu/news/uc-partners-boys-girls-clubs-america-open-college-doors-california-teens

Gullotta, T. P. (2015). After-school programming and SEL. In J. Durlak, C. Domitrovich, R. Weissberg, & T. Gullotta (Eds.), *Handbook of social and emotional learning* (pp. 260–266). New York, NY: Guilford Press.

Hamilton, S., Hamilton, M., & Pittman, K. (2004). Principles for youth development. In S. Hamilton & M. Hamilton (Eds.), *The youth development handbook: Coming of age in American communities* (pp. 3–22). Thousand Oaks, CA: SAGE.

Hawkins, J. D., Kosterman, R., Catalano, R. F., Hill, K. G., & Abbott, R. D. (2008). Effects of social development intervention in childhood 15 years later. *Archives of Pediatrics & Adolescent Medicine, 162*(12), 1133–1141. doi:10.1001/archpedi.162.12.1133

Hooker, S., & Brand, B. (2009). *Success at every step: How 23 programs support youth on the path to college and beyond.* Washington, DC: American Youth Policy Forum.

Imagine U Toolkit. (2017). Retrieved from the Believe 2 Become website: https://believe2become.org/documents/imagine-u-toolkit.pdf

Innovation Center for Community and Youth Development & National 4-H Council. (2003). *At the* table*: Making the case for youth in decision making.* New York, NY: Author.

Jones, S., & Kahn, J. (2017). *Evidence base for how learning happens: Supporting students' social, emotional, and academic development.* Washington, DC: Aspen Institute.

Linking Schools and Afterschool: Through Social and Emotional Learning. (2015). Retrieved from the American Institutes of Research website: https://www.air.org/sites/default/files/downloads/report/Linking-Schools-and-Afterschool-Through-SEL-rev.pdf

Nagaoka, J., Farrington, C., Ehrlich, S., & Heath, R. (2015). *Foundations for young adult success: A developmental framework.* Chicago, IL: The University of Chicago Consortium on School Reform.

National Awards. (n.d.). *National awards.* Retrieved from the Boys & Girls Club of Green Bay website: http://www.bgcgb.org/club-programs/national-awards/

National High School Center. (2012). *Defining college and career readiness: A resource guide.* Washington, DC: American Institutes of Research.

Pittman, K. (2017, July 24). *SEL, whole child education and student readiness: How do they connect?* Retrieved from https://www.huffingtonpost.com/entry/sel-whole-child-education-and-student-readiness-how_us_59761518e4b0545a5c3101ef

Smith, C., McGovern, G., Peck., S. C., Larson, R., Hillaker, B., & Roy, L. (2016). *Preparing youth to thrive: Methodology and findings from the Social and Emotional Learning Challenge.* Washington, DC: Forum for Youth Investment. Retrieved from http://www.cypq.org/SELChallenge

Workforce Innovation and Opportunity Act, Pub. L. No. 113-28 § 128 Stat. 1425 (2013–2014).

SECTION III

SEL SYSTEMS AND POLICY

CHAPTER 9

BUILDING A SYSTEM OF SEL

A Pathway to Change

Leona Hess, Denice Williams, J. Tyler McCormick, and Jessica Jackson

New York City (NYC) launched an initiative known as Out-of-School Time in September 2005. The Department of Youth and Community Development (DYCD)—the NYC agency responsible for out-of-school time (OST) programs and an array of other critical services, including youth employment—was tasked with implementing this new initiative.[1] The initiative extended access to structured programming (after school, during school holidays, and during the summer) to thousands of NYC youth in elementary through high school grades. At the outset, DYCD committed to investing in community-based organizations (CBOs) to run these programs, which would be located at public and private schools, community centers, parks, and NYC Housing Authority facilities. To support the initiative, DYCD invested in an online reporting and attendance-tracking system, commissioned a series of external evaluations, regularly convened stakeholders to gather their feedback, and developed various aids to support quality programming, including a significant investment in capacity building, the

Social and Emotional Learning in Out-of-School Time, pages 147–164

development of a program quality monitoring tool, and written guides on youth worker and supervisor competencies.[2]

In 2014, with a mayoral commitment to provide universal OST programs for middle school youth, the system exploded from 500 to 936 programs, with a budget of $325 million. The request for proposal (RFP) that catalyzed this expansion emphasized the importance of a commitment to positive youth development (PYD) and youth leadership.

DYCD leadership knew that the quality of programming could suffer as a result of expansion. To mitigate this risk, DYCD more than doubled the size of the team dedicated to supporting the OST programs; expanded its investment in capacity building where external technical assistance (TA) providers delivered program and organizationally focused support; and funded a new unit called Program Quality and Innovation (PQI), focused on preparing DYCD staff for the changes and identifying resources to share throughout the system of CBO providers. With support from Rescue.org and our opinionated NYC young people, the Out-of-School Time initiative was rebranded as the Comprehensive After School System (COMPASS), with a middle school portfolio named School's Out NYC (SONYC).

Simultaneous to this effort, DYCD Commissioner Chong formed the Planning Program Integration and Evaluation (PPIE) unit and appointed COMPASS Assistant Commissioner Denice Williams to be its first deputy commissioner. With similar growth in other program areas, PPIE's charge was to transform DYCD from 33 different program types (which were co-located but not otherwise integrated) into one agency with a common vision for community investment and commitment to holistic services, a common approach to program management, a unified data management system, and common measures of success.

PROBLEM SOLVING NEEDS SYSTEMS THINKING

During the early stages of the SONYC expansion, it became evident that DYCD needed to further define and articulate expectations regarding the youth leadership requirement for OST programs, as outlined in the RFP issued by DYCD to fund the new programs. This request came not only from CBO providers responsible for the programs, but also from DYCD staff who monitored and evaluated those programs. As an initial step, the PQI unit worked with TA partners to develop a youth leadership framework. However, PPIE recognized that a framework alone would not be able to adequately define and articulate expectations, impact program quality across a large system of providers, and effectively inform providers that had multiple DYCD-funded program contracts with similar RFP requirements about any changes. The only solution was to broaden the scope of our approach,

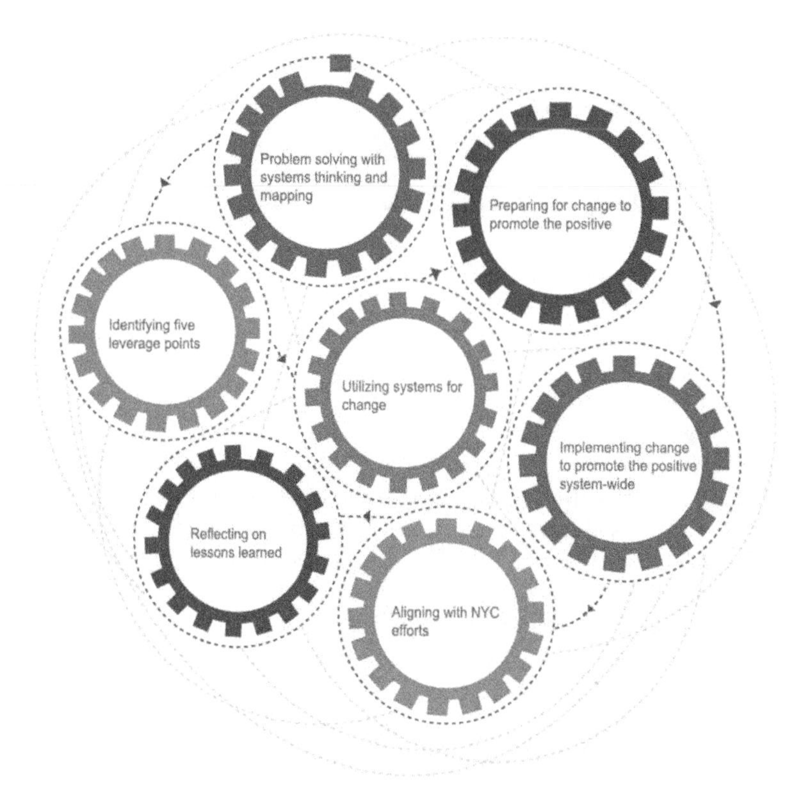

Figure 9.1 Path of change.

and we had just the unit to take on the task. Through a series of strategic planning sessions, PPIE reflected on what type of systems approach would effectively define and articulate expectations for diverse audiences. What type of communications would be sufficient? What types of training and supportive tools or materials should be developed? How could our approach promote and support program quality in the field? How does youth leadership fit with or accompany other RFP expectations and requirements that might be similar or related? How aligned are we with the most current literature and research on youth leadership and other related concepts, such as social and emotional learning (SEL) and PYD? More importantly, was the initial request from staff and providers a symptom of a larger, more complex issue? To answer these questions, we needed to shift our mindset away from seeing this request as an isolated event, and look at it as part of a bigger, interconnected picture. It required a holistic approach and a new, broader perspective. That led us to systems thinking, "... a set of synergistic analytic skills used to improve the capability of identifying and understanding systems, predicting their behaviors, and devising modifications to them in order to produce desired effects" (Arnold & Wade, 2015, p. 675). Our first step was to visually map our system in order to analyze and synthesize its elements and connections.

Systems Thinking in Practice Promotes Better Strategic Awareness

With systems mapping, we were not limited to looking at this single request to define and articulate youth leadership expectations, but could instead step back and identify the different patterns that this request was part of, the possible structures that might have prompted the request, and finally, the thinking that created those structures. Using this process, we were able to identify five leverage points where we could intervene and promote systemic change across the agency and provider network that would define and articulate expectations regarding OST programming for CBO providers and DYCD staff.

Leverage Point 1: Consistent RFP Language

Across DYCD program types, RFPs depicted youth leadership, PYD, and SEL as a requirement, an expectation, and/or an activity. The terms were also used interchangeably, rather than as three interconnected and interrelated concepts, reflecting disparate thinking among key DYCD program leadership and the agency's planning department (responsible for preparing all solicitations). Oddly enough, at this point there was no conflict because everyone was sure they were saying the same thing. This leverage point was identified as lower hanging fruit, because we could easily control what was written in RFPs, minimizing confusion and ensuring that providers with contracts from multiple program types received consistent messaging and a rationale for any variation.

Leverage Point 2: A Common Lens and Language

Beyond RFPs, we recognized the need to develop and effectively roll out a common lens, language, and visual frameworks in order to establish consistent definitions of key concepts across the agency and CBO provider network, regardless of program type. Building on the youth leadership framework developed by the PQI unit, PPIE worked to develop a common lens and language for all three interconnected concepts: youth leadership, PYD, and SEL. This common lens became known as *Promote the Positive*, and it provided a platform to articulate the relationship between PYD, SEL, and youth leadership. This leverage point was more involved than the first, as it required partnering with TA partners, DYCD program staff, and CBO providers to develop a common language. With multiple stakeholders involved in the development process and varying definitions of the concepts, we needed to dedicate time to collect, analyze, and synthesize the relevant information to determine the right fit for DYCD's common language and frameworks. Based on focus groups with CBO providers on their current practices, meetings with TA partners about what they were seeing and coaching on in the field, and reflection sessions with DYCD program managers on what they were evaluating and monitoring, we came up with a well-informed common language, as well as frameworks that reflected what was already happening in programs and aligned with best practices in the field.

Leverage Point 3: Communication Approach

In order to roll out any strategy, we would also need to create a communication approach to facilitate the exchange of information both internally within DYCD and externally with CBO providers. Internally, we needed to create a strategy that could reach all program areas and units providing program support (e.g., PQI, capacity building, PPIE, etc.). This leverage point would play a large role in the design of our implementation plan, and in the design of activities and roles that were developed to effectively communicate the common lens and language system-wide.

Leverage Point 4: Tailored Training and Capacity Building

In order for DYCD's program staff to be able to monitor, evaluate, and coach providers on how to implement Promote the Positive in the field—for example, identify and build social and emotional competencies, create the right factors and experiences that promote PYD, and identify the attitudes, skills, environmental conditions, and actions that support youth leadership development—we would need to build our internal capacity. This leverage point was critical and required ongoing support and an effective feedback loop to ensure staff acquired and built upon the necessary skills. First, we needed to determine our internal capacity to develop and facilitate the necessary trainings in-house. Second, we needed to develop the training content. Based on previous experiences training DYCD staff, we knew the trainings needed to be tailored specifically to job roles and functions. Externally, with CBO providers, we realized we also needed to ensure that the capacity-building trainings and one-on-one coaching from TA partners aligned with our common lens and language. Our intention was to be clear about what we expected of providers when it came to youth development, SEL, and PYD, and how we were going to hold them accountable when monitoring and evaluating programs.

Leverage Point 5: Consistent Evaluation and Monitoring

We recognized that if we were evaluating and monitoring programs on the quality of their implementation of Promote the Positive content, it made sense to use universal indicators, ensuring that all CBO providers would be held accountable to the same standards. This leverage point would require our evaluation unit to develop indicators that aligned with the common lens and language, as well as training materials and supportive tools to help reinforce consistent rating and ultimately improve the quality of all programming, not just SEL or leadership development activities.

Utilizing Systems Strategy to Promote the Positive

After identifying the five leverage points—that is, areas where we could intervene and focus our strategy—our next step was to develop an internal strategic planning and implementation workgroup that included different staff levels and roles. Similar to starting with oneself in order to enhance or build social and emotional competencies in others, we knew we needed to begin by focusing internally within the agency. Early in 2016, PPIE convened an internal, cross-functional workgroup with staff and key leadership from the program management, evaluation, program integration, planning and program development, and program quality departments. The purpose of the workgroup was to develop a systems strategy and implementation plan based on the five leverage points, and to oversee the plan and track progress. Once the implementation plan and common lens and language had been developed and approved, three sub-workgroups were formed to implement the work and track the progress: (a) a training and capacity-building sub-workgroup, (b) a communications sub-workgroup, and (c) an evaluation sub-workgroup. The main workgroup continued to meet quarterly, and its members remained important thought partners and supporters throughout the implementation phase.

PREPARING FOR CHANGE TO PROMOTE THE POSITIVE

During the systems strategy and implementation plan development, the workgroup recognized that if we wanted to see change across the five leverage points, individuals within the system would need to change. We would also need to change by building on our existing knowledge of PYD and aligning our behaviors and mindsets to adopt Promote the Positive as best practice. For example, our common lens and language wouldn't be meaningful or have impact if people didn't use it and integrate it into their work. The same was true for our evaluation tool—if staff didn't know how to accurately and consistently rate the universal indicators, the data would become less informative and applicable. We also recognized that just telling staff and CBO providers to use the common lens and language, tools, and materials would not necessarily change mindsets or behaviors. If we wanted people to change, we would need to develop a strategy and implementation plan that intentionally included activities and roles that encouraged individuals to embrace, adopt, and utilize the change in their day-to-day work. To achieve this, we drew on Prosci's model for individual change, known as the ADKAR model—an acronym for awareness, desire, knowledge, ability, and reinforcement (Hiatt, 2006). We used this model to guide all activities, action items, and roles in the implementation plan for each of the sub-workgroups.

Awareness is the first milestone in the ADKAR model, and it focuses on building an awareness of the need for change. During this stage, it is important to provide information about the nature of the change, how the change is aligned with the mission, how the change will affect the system, what the benefits are for staff, and what the risks are if change does not occur. Based on Prosci's research, executive leaders are the preferred "senders" of communication efforts designed to build awareness (Arnold & Wade, 2015; Hiatt, 2006), so we ensured that leadership actively participated in our communications, starting with the launch event and continuing throughout the process.

Desire, the second element in the model, involves stakeholders having a personal choice and *wanting* to participate and support the change. This was an important but challenging aspect to integrate into our planning because the workgroup and sub-workgroups were not able to fully identify what motivated an individual's desire to change; only people who were familiar with the individual and his or her situation were able to accomplish this task. Recognizing this, we intentionally engaged managers and supervisors, both internally and externally, providing detailed information on how to introduce the common lens and language, and how to utilize the materials and communications to build desire among staff to adopt the concepts.

The third element in the model, knowledge, focuses on how to implement change. The training and capacity-building sub-workgroup began by developing a comprehensive training plan that included scaffolding knowledge based on the three concepts (youth leadership, PYD, and SEL), skill development tailored to the participants' roles, and behaviors needed to adopt and utilize the change.

Ability is the fourth element of the model, representing the demonstrated capacity to implement the change. In our planning, we strategically encouraged staff to create opportunities or activities that would demonstrate their ability to utilize the tools and materials to support their program management practice. We developed a cheat sheet of examples to help staff identify moments or activities where they could provide such opportunities for staff and CBO providers.

Reinforcement, the final element in the model, includes any action or event that strengthens and reinforces the change with an individual or organization. Throughout the planning process, we flagged potential moments where we reinforced the change by celebrating our successes and small wins. We made a conscious effort not to simply move on to the next activity or action. Instead, we built in time to reflect, provide feedback, troubleshoot barriers, and celebrate, as a team and as an agency.

IMPLEMENTING CHANGE TO PROMOTE THE POSITIVE SYSTEM-WIDE

To actualize our envisioned future state of system-wide, asset- and strength-based change, we developed specific, short-term objectives that included internal and external stakeholders. For the first year, we aligned our change objectives with Prosci's ADKAR model, primarily focusing on building awareness, desire, and knowledge. The four change objectives were: (a) *define and name*—shift the focus from a deficit- to an asset-based approach by defining and naming the three interconnected concepts (PYD, SEL, and youth leadership); (b) *promote*—embrace a common lens and language; (c) *identify and enhance*—identify best practices and increase the ability to further enhance those practices in the field; and (d) *build and increase capacity*—increase the capacity of CBOs and DYCD to enhance conditions to build the system, promote positive outcomes, and ensure continuous improvement. To achieve our change objectives, the three sub-workgroups developed and oversaw the implementation of the following activities, materials, and roles.

Training and Capacity-Building Sub-Workgroup

DYCD "In-Practice" Workshop Series for Program Managers

Based on professional experience, education, and facilitation skills, six staff from across DYCD were identified as master trainers. This core group developed all of the interactive content for each workshop and consulted with the training sub-workgroup to ensure that the materials were engaging and aligned with the program manager job role and function.

Throughout the year, we offered voluntary workshops to program managers focusing on (a) building awareness of eight key factors and experiences that promote PYD, and the skills and language to identify and reinforce in the field; (b) building awareness of the competencies for life (SEL) and the skills and language to identify and reinforce in the field; (c) building awareness around leadership as action, not as a position (youth leadership), and the skills and language to identify and reinforce in the field; (d) embedding concepts in program activities, program design, agency climate and culture, and professional development opportunities; and (e) providing strength-based coaching to build capacity and strengthen embeddedness in the field. During these workshops, we intentionally facilitated mixed groups with program managers from different DYCD program areas. This was important because it helped staff gain understanding and buy into the idea that any program could apply all three concepts, irrespective of program type or design.

DYCD Booster Sessions With Program Teams

For a deeper dive into how PYD, SEL, and youth leadership relate to or are aligned with RFP program design and requirements, the master trainers facilitated booster sessions with program teams or units. These sessions were voluntary, and they were facilitated when teams were ready and had expressed an interest in learning more and being more intentional about using the common lens, language, and supportive frameworks.

DYCD Supervisor and Manager Sessions

To build desire for change, the master trainers facilitated activities during management meetings to build managers' awareness, and to demonstrate how to build desire in their staff. The master trainers were also available for consultation and additional strategic planning within units.

DYCD Training for Ambassadors

As part of the communication plan, each program area had a designated ambassador who served as a direct line of communication to each program area and worked to embed the common lens and language into day-to-day activities (e.g., team meetings, check-ins, impromptu discussions, etc.). All ambassadors were trained on similar content (as outlined above for program managers), but all content was tailored to their specific role.

CBO Training for an Organization or Program

Based on requests from CBO providers, the master trainers facilitated a series of trainings out in the field, either with an entire agency or, for larger agencies, with a large group of program staff. Again, all of the content was similar to what was facilitated internally with DYCD staff, but more time was devoted to identifying and naming what they were already doing (our third change objective) and exploring how to further enhance or embed best practices in existing programs. The master trainers intentionally did not suggest a huge overhaul of existing programs.

CBO Provider Training Series for Multi-Site Supervisors

Beyond the Basics was a five-part training series and learning network for 20 multi-site supervisors that focused on utilizing strength-based tools and the PYD, SEL, and youth leadership frameworks to coach staff, provide professional development opportunities, and design programming.

CBO Provider Training for Youth Workers

These training sessions were for less experienced but motivated youth workers, with a focus on enabling them to learn the common lens and language and build self-awareness and knowledge aligned with youth worker core competencies.

CBO Provider Training Provided by TA Partners

Starting in 2017, TA partners were contracted to provide trainings and capacity-building activities to CBO providers focusing on PYD, SEL, and youth leadership. Throughout the year, the master trainers met with TA partners to ensure that the content that was being facilitated aligned with DYCD's common lens, language, and frameworks. In return, TA partners provided feedback on how the common lens, language, and frameworks were being received, as well as questions and barriers identified in the field.

Communications

Promote the Positive Internal Launch Activities

The initiative launch intentionally focused on increasing awareness by building relationships across DYCD units and program areas through a "promote the positive" week, in which DYCD staff engaged in cross-department activities and opportunities for practice sharing. To this end, information exchange, partnership development, and collaboration included interactive activities and workshops, beginning with a presentation to DYCD's senior management and management team. Presentations were followed by a "mindfulness Monday," which utilized art-based activities to broaden knowledge about social and emotional competencies, and a "promote the positive power hour," which provided space for DYCD staff to share PYD practices. Communication team members surveyed DYCD departments to hear how approaches to SEL, PYD, and youth leadership were realized across units. Promote the positive week culminated in an agency-wide scavenger hunt that incorporated PYD principles and SEL practice strategies.

DYCD Ambassadors

To promote a common lens and language throughout the agency, ambassadors were recruited from all DYCD departments. A cohort of 20 ambassadors representing program managers and deputy directors participated in an orientation series, which allowed staff to deeply connect to and understand PYD practices and tools. Ambassadors met bi-weekly and played a key role in internal and external information exchange, peer-to-peer support, and the development of strategies to provide ongoing support and oversight of the implementation plan and actions across the agency.

Focus Groups With CBO Providers

To provide more opportunities for feedback and information sharing between DYCD and CBO providers, DYCD assembled a focus group of CBO program directors and multi-site supervisors from youth services, workforce development, and community services. Twenty directors and multi-site supervisors were selected to participate in two focus group sessions, in which participants identified and shared promising practices around PYD approaches (including social and emotional competencies) to navigate barriers to successful implementation. Participants also engaged in a feedback loop led by DYCD to help inform next steps for the initiative.

CBO Provider Symposium

The Promote the Positive Symposium served as a large-scale external launch of the DYCD's strength-based approach to fostering PYD, SEL, and youth leadership within DYCD-funded programs. The symposium took place at New York University and included keynote speaker Dr. Nadia Lopez, founding principal at Mott Hall Bridges Academy and founder of The Lopez Effect. Facilitated by DYCD master trainers and ambassadors, the symposium included interactive framework presentations titled: *Positive Youth Development: Building on Strengths*; *Social and Emotional Learning: Skills for Life*; and *Leadership Development: Leadership is Action.* Framework presentations were reinforced by deeper dive workshops tailored to meet the needs of youth-serving programs and those focused on workforce development. DYCD TA providers—Morningside Center for Social Responsibility, the Youth Development Institute (YDI), and American Institutes for Research (AIR)—provided these workshops. Deeper dive workshops included time for self-reflection, opportunities to learn practice strategies for embedding PYD and youth leadership principles into program design, and opportunities to learn strength-based approaches to community building. Throughout the event, attendees had the opportunity to participate in a live feedback loop and share workshop experiences on DYCD social media platforms. A total of 360 provider staff attended the event.

SONYC Game Changers

The SONYC Game Changers Project provided an interactive competition and platform for all COMPASS SONYC programs to showcase their leadership skills and community change projects. Beginning in January 2016, SONYC participants were invited to submit their projects (via application) for the opportunity to present at DYCD's youth conference in May 2016. Projects were youth-led, meaningful, and community-relevant, with a focus on one of the following categories: sports and leadership, civic engagement, arts and leadership, and service learning. The culminating event, the Young Citizens Competition, included young people from across DYCD-funded youth service programs and provided a platform for youth participants to showcase their community change projects and share activism stories.

Electronic and Print Materials

In addition to sharing the DYCD's PYD, SEL, and youth leadership frameworks, DYCD created an electronic Promote the Positive flip-book, which includes additional resources to support practice and links to register for DYCD professional development opportunities ("Promote the Positive," 2016a).

Conference Presentations

To share DYCD's Promote the Positive initiative more broadly, DYCD staff facilitated workshops at national conferences including Beyond School Hours, The Network for Youth Success, Partnership for After School Education (PASE), and National After-School Association. At these conferences, DYCD staff shared the PYD, SEL, and youth leadership frameworks, as well as a systemic approach to supporting implementation and continuous quality improvement.

Evaluation

Universal Indicators

As part of a larger initiative to redesign DYCD's evaluation and monitoring tool, the evaluation unit worked closely with the master trainers to develop indicators and accompanying rubrics aligned with the change objectives and the common lens and language.

Tool Development

The evaluation unit also worked with AIR on the development of youth leadership tools such as the provider self-reflection assessment and the youth survey. The self-reflection tool was developed for providers to assess the degree to which they embed youth leadership into existing programming. The survey is designed to gauge young people's (ages 10–14) beliefs about their own youth leadership skills and attributes. The survey has 27 items, plus four demographic items at the end, and takes youth an average of 5–7 minutes to complete. DYCD is working with AIR to develop a high school version of the survey ("Lessons Learned," n.d.). The survey is intended to inform practice at the activity and program levels.[3]

A Year 3 evaluation report revealed that program staff and families agreed that SONYC programs provide opportunities for youth to develop leadership attitudes and skills. Analysis revealed that youth reported high perceptions of their leadership attitudes and skills, with the most favorable responses occurring in the area of inner/self characteristics (motivation, self-awareness, and persistence.)

Common Lens and Language

DYCD supports an array of programs for young people. While they vary in terms of the specific activities offered, the objectives, and the settings, all DYCD programs share a single lens that is reflected in the three interrelated concepts drawn together by Promote the Positive: PYD, SEL, and youth leadership. To promote the positive is to place an emphasis on improving positive outcomes for children, youth, families, and communities by embracing the eight key factors and experiences that promote PYD, and by providing opportunities and supports for all participants to foster social and emotional competencies and leadership skills.

The purpose of a common lens and language is to articulate DYCD's perspective and promote a shared understanding of these concepts. This will enable CBOs that provide services, and the DYCD managers who assess them, to more easily identify program strengths and weaknesses, share best practices, and work together to improve program quality. Ultimately, a clearer understanding of DYCD's expectations regarding critical aspects of program implementation and continuous improvement will benefit all stakeholders.

Below, each concept is briefly outlined, showing how they intersect and overlap. In high-quality youth programs, PYD, SEL, and youth leadership aspects will be seamlessly integrated.

PYD Is an Overarching, Assets-Based Approach

DYCD expects all CBOs to embrace this approach, regardless of program content and specifics. It provides the foundation on which to promote healthy youth development and resilience. To this end, PYD emphasizes eight key factors and experiences: (a) positive social norms; (b) supportive relationships; (c) opportunities to belong; (d) appropriate structure; (e) integration of family, school, and community efforts; (f) opportunities for skill development; (g) opportunities to make a difference; and (h) physical and psychological safety.[4]

SEL Is a Process for Acquiring Competencies

SEL is the *process* through which young people acquire social and emotional competencies (i.e., the knowledge, attitudes, and skills) they need to thrive in school and beyond. These competencies, identified by the Collaborative for Academic, Social, and Emotional Learning (CASEL; "What Is SEL?" n.d.) are:

- *Self-awareness*: The ability to understand and manage emotions.
- *Self-management*: The ability to set and achieve positive goals.
- *Social awareness*: The ability to feel and show empathy for others.
- *Relationship skills:* The ability to establish and maintain positive relationships.
- *Responsible decision making*.

Social and emotional competencies are integral to, and are significant goals and outcomes of, PYD. CBOs must intentionally focus on SEL because social and emotional competencies are among the most significant benefits youth can gain from consistent participation in high-quality programs.

Youth Leadership Builds on PYD and Includes Social and Emotional Competencies

Youth leadership builds on PYD principles, with an emphasis on providing: (a) leadership opportunities within the program, organization, and community; (b) skill building and a capacity for making decisions and solving problems; (c) opportunities to deepen understanding of shared experiences and participate in community projects; and (d) strong youth–adult partnerships (NYC DYCD, 2016).

Youth leadership is seen as having three critical components: *skills* (including social and emotional competencies, communication, active listening, and collaborative skills); *action* (stimulated by the desire and opportunity to acquire and master skills and effect change); and *reflection* (reinforcing what has been learned, feeding confidence, imparting lessons learned, and providing opportunities to identify and respond to new challenges). Both PYD approaches and social and emotional competencies support and sustain youth leadership skills, which, in turn, reinforce the developmental gains nurtured by PYD and SEL, creating a continuing cycle of benefits.

Aligning With NYC Efforts

The DYCD-focused Promote the Positive initiative was well underway when NYC's Department of Education (DOE) and its intermediary, ExpandED, were awarded a planning grant by the Wallace Foundation to develop an approach for districts seeking to create a holistic SEL experience for young people between the school day and OST. DYCD, specifically PPIE and PQI, were asked to be part of the core planning team. DYCD's framework, commitment to the CASEL social and emotional competencies, and approach to engaging staff and providers were seen as a road map for the group in which to ground its approach and response. While NYC was not awarded an implementation grant, DOE and DYCD have embraced the

SEL vision that resulted from this work and will support the vision of joint messaging to families and professional development for teachers, administrators, and community educators.

REFLECTING ON LESSONS LEARNED

While challenges remain, DYCD's success in designing and introducing system changes, and the momentum now underway in terms of staff and stakeholder acceptance, allow assessment of the salient contributing factors.

Invest in Positions and Skill Sets

When rolling out a large-scale transformational initiative, it is critical to employ staff with the skill sets and ability to lead a systems strategy, collaborative planning process, and change methodology. In fact, we would argue that these skills are critical to achieving any type of change, either transformational or project-based. Under the current administration, we have been able to develop innovative positions and hire qualified individuals to support our work, but we have also faced challenges. Since these types of positions (like PPIE's director of program integration) aren't traditionally found in government, upfront groundwork is needed to effectively communicate and establish (a) what the role is; (b) why the role was created; (c) what type of work will be carried out, using what style or methodology; and (d) the role's authority. This is important in order to proactively address resistance, manage expectations, and plan for job tasks to be executed outside of the previous reporting structure. In hindsight, we should have anticipated and planned for these challenges and built in a strategy to not only introduce the new position and role, but to reinforce the goal of the department.

Initially, when hiring for the director of program integration, we included change management skills in the job description but didn't necessarily recruit based on this qualification. Luckily, we ended up hiring someone with experience in process facilitation who was willing to learn more and advance their change management competencies. Moving forward, we will need to be more intentional about recruiting candidates with these skill sets as they have been shown to be very valuable and pertinent in a governmental setting, where things are constantly changing and systems thinking is required.

Focus on the Role of Executive Leadership

Initially, we defined the role of the executive leadership as building awareness through communications and demonstrating support by being visible at large events. In retrospect, there was a missed opportunity to further define the executive leadership role as ensuring that there is a roadmap for *active and sustained* engagement throughout the implementation process. Additionally, there should have been an expectation that managers and executive leadership outside of PPIE would support the people side of change, learning the necessary skills to do so.

Have Patience

If we hadn't employed the ADKAR model, we wouldn't have planned time for building awareness and desire for change, or for identifying and naming best practices in the field. Our inclination was just to build knowledge through training and professional development. Applying this model to our transformational change has been an invaluable lesson and continues to guide thinking and strategy. In addition, for people who are early adopters and want to see change happen quickly, it is helpful to refer to the model to easily explain the process for individual or organizational change.

Don't Underestimate The Need for/Challenge of Culture Change

We found that maintaining a systems thinking mindset was challenging throughout the process. During the planning process, we successfully used tools and habits to maintain systems thinking. However, once implementation involved more of the agency, it was challenging to scale up this thinking. Clearly, a true shift in mindset takes time, and perhaps there is an opportunity to be more intentional about how to change the agency culture, rather than focusing on the people engaged in the activities and trainings.

Press Reset When Needed

During implementation, we were also in the process of updating our data systems and evaluation and monitoring tool. At some point, organizations do experience change fatigue, and we had to take a step back and reassess how often we engaged staff. When planning for the following year, we decided to align our change activities with the new system roll-out and focus on the evaluation and monitoring indicators and the rubrics aligned with the Promote the Positive transformation.

Spend Time on the Numbers

In a numbers-dependent environment, both in government and the nonprofit sector, it is challenging to translate change or transformation into numbers. Since change is people-dependent, we needed to be more intentional about capturing outcomes and outputs that measured individual performance (e.g., did individuals adopt the change?), organizational performance (e.g., did the initiative or project deliver expected results and outcomes?), and change management performance (e.g., did we effectively apply the change management process?). Although we used numbers to document engagement, attendance, and number of people trained, we learned that it would also be beneficial to use numbers to show the impact of the change. To adopt this approach, we would need to capture different types of data and broaden our definition of success and how we report against it.

CONCLUSION

DYCD continues to work to refine its approach to systems change based on lessons learned. Up next is its approach to evaluation and monitoring, including a new application that will allow both desk and mobile use. While not implemented flawlessly, Promote the Positive was the catalyst for this systems realignment and agency-wide review of policies, approach, and indicators. Promote the Positive language is now in all RFPs, all units have developed appropriate indicators, and the agency has significantly increased investment in appropriate professional development for staff and providers. Not bad for 2 years' work.

NOTES

1. At the time, the agency's central task was viewed as administering available city, state, and federal funds to CBOs retained to provide a wide range of high-quality youth and community development programs. DYCD is the local grantee for the federal, anti-poverty Community Services Block Grant (CSBG) and since 2002 has taken charge of youth employment programs, including the Summer Youth Employment program. Under the de Blasio Administration, DYCD's mission and vision were revised following agency-wide strategic planning to focus on advancing equity and promoting collaborations that support holistic services at the neighborhood level (see http://www1.nyc.gov/site/dycd/about/about-dycd/our-mission.page).
2. The program quality monitoring tool and a guide to core competencies for youth work professionals are available on DYCD's website: http://www1.nyc.gov/site/dycd/about/news-and-media/guides-and-manuals.page. Evaluations of the OST initiative are available here: http://www1.nyc.gov/site/dycd/about/news-and-media/reports-plans.page
3. For a brief on the Youth Leadership Development Survey, see http://www1.nyc.gov/assets/dycd/downloads/pdf/17-1033_v05SONYC_Leadership_Survey1-pgr_FNL.pdf
4. An interagency work group consisting of 20 federal departments and agencies reviewed the literature on positive youth development and articulated principles and definitions. See http://youth.gov/youth-topics/positive-youth-development and related links (for example, http://youth.gov/youth-topics/positive-youth-development/key-principles-positive-youth-development; http://youth.gov/youth-topics/integrating-positive-youth-development-programs; http://youth.gov/youth-topics/effectiveness-positive-youth-development-programs).

REFERENCES

Arnold, R. D., & Wade, J. P. (2015). A definition of systems thinking: A systems approach. *Procedia Computer Science, 44*, 669–678.

Hiatt, J. (2006). *ADKAR: A model for change in business, government, and our community.* Loveland, CO: Prosci Learning Center.

Lessons Learned. (n.d.). Retrieved from the Department of Youth & Community Development website: https://www1.nyc.gov/site/dycd/about/news-and-media/lessons-learned.page

NYC Department of Youth and Community Development. (2016, April). *Youth leadership development practices: Program staff self reflection tool.* Retrieved from http://www1.nyc.gov/assets/dycd/downloads/pdf/15-4105_v12Leadership_Practices_SR_Tool%2003739.001.01_FNL.pdf

Promote the Positive: Lead Efforts to Advance Positive Youth Development, Social Emotional Learning and Youth Leadership. (2016). Retrieved from flipsnack website: https://www.flipsnack.com/NYCDYCD/dycd-promote-the-positive-flipbook-for-rfp.html

What Is SEL? (n.d.). Retrieved from CASEL website: https://casel.org/what-is-sel/

CHAPTER 10

THE ROLE OF STATEWIDE AFTER-SCHOOL NETWORKS IN SOCIAL AND EMOTIONAL LEARNING SYSTEMS BUILDING

Ken Anthony

I was driving on Interstate 84 toward Hartford the morning of December 14, 2012, when the news came on. There had been a school shooting in Newtown, about 50 miles from where I was, down the highway to the west. Newtown is an affluent suburb of Danbury, CT, with about 26,000 residents, including authors, athletes, and actors. The median income is $111,022, and 95% of families are Caucasian ("Quickfacts," 2016). The landscape is tree-lined rolling hills, dotted with historic houses. Having visited out-of-school time (OST) programs in this community, knowing that the victims were first graders and teachers that I may have met or spoken with, I had to pull over. Ironically, I could see the state capitol building from where I was. Shocked and saddened, I began wondering what the response would be.

Social and Emotional Learning in Out-of-School Time, pages 165–182

In the days and months that followed the state legislature passed stricter gun control laws, and the conversation about the mental health of the shooter began to identify gaps in the system where he had fallen through the cracks. The larger education conversation was also moving to a more holistic approach to learning. With the new Common Core State Standards being rolled out a couple of years earlier, schools and communities were beginning to make the connection between social and emotional learning (SEL) and the skills needed for youth to be successful under the new standards. The Newtown incident raised the SEL conversation to a statewide and national level, as evidence of the lack of communication between systems became more apparent in the months that followed. Collaboration and coordination became a larger part of the conversation, as the mental health and education fields explored partnerships to meet these needs. In this chapter, I will describe the intermediary and systems-building role the Connecticut After-School Network has played in positioning OST and summer programs to be included in statewide discussions on SEL, as well as practitioner perspectives on implementation of SEL practices within their programs. The chapter concludes with examples from other statewide after-school networks from New Jersey, Utah, and Minnesota, and addresses challenges and barriers faced in SEL-related systems work.

HISTORY OF THE CONNECTICUT AFTER-SCHOOL NETWORK

The Connecticut After-School Network started in 1989 as a collection of after-school providers looking for staff training relevant to the developmental stage of the children they served. Originally the Connecticut School-Age Child Care Alliance, the all-volunteer organization provided professional development to OST providers statewide and held two conferences annually for its membership. Over time, the network affiliated with the National AfterSchool Association (NAA), joining with other similar state organizations, and eventually changed its name to the Connecticut After School Network.

In 2003, Connecticut joined the second cohort of states funded by the Charles Stewart Mott Foundation as a part of its statewide after-school networks (SAN) initiative. Together with funding from the Connecticut State Department of Education, this new core operating support enabled the network to hire full-time staff and greatly increase its work to advance the three primary goals shared by all of the Mott-funded after-school networks:

- creating sustainable partnership structures for policy development,
- supporting statewide policies to secure funding, and
- supporting systems to ensure quality.

Not only did the Connecticut After School Network expand its scope to include policy development at this time, but it also greatly expanded the content of its professional development and training efforts, which continue to be its foundation. Through the relationship with NAA, Connecticut has had several committee members and two board chairs serve in a national role and has been able to be a voice in national conversations around SEL. Being a part of both NAA and the SAN initiative has allowed us to learn from experts from across the country.

This learning network is an invaluable resource in identifying, modeling, researching, and linking communities of practice. The connection to practitioners enables SANs to link the research and practice community and move the field forward. As I stated in my 2017 chapter on research–practitioner partnerships and the role of the statewide after-school networks, "SANs connect with both grassroots and grass-top stakeholders and can convene meetings or work groups as part of their current charge focused on quality, supporting sustainable partnerships, and building internal and external capacity through networks that link stakeholders" (Anthony, 2017, p. 182).

THE SEL LANDSCAPE IN CONNECTICUT

Shortly after the Newtown incident, Connecticut agencies such as the Department of Social Services, Department of Children and Families, and State Department of Education began holding forums to discuss strategies, intended outcomes, and ways to measure success. The Connecticut After School Network's role as an intermediary between state agencies and OST providers gave us an opportunity to highlight the existing practices and work within OST programs statewide that were supporting SEL, but not formally identified as SEL programming.

The Connecticut After School Network focuses in three primary areas: policy and advocacy; systems building efforts that support local and state capacity to deliver high-quality programming; and professional development using national data, practice, and research to inform our efforts. Through its partnership with state agencies, the Connecticut After School Network quickly became an active voice in the early conversations related to integrating SEL into systems. Being present allowed us to highlight findings indicating that children and youth who have participated in OST programs have better social and emotional outcomes, including attendance and behavior (Durlak, Weissberg, & Pachan, 2010). In an effort to guide statewide policy and practice on SEL in OST our 2014 strategic plan had an explicit focus on training and policy supports. More recently, the Connecticut State Department of Education (CSDE) included chronic absenteeism as the fifth indicator (a required, but state selected indicator) in their Every Student Succeeds Act plan (ESSA, 2015). Additionally, the State Board of Education named OST programming as an intervention strategy to support this goal (CSDE, 2017).

Before diving in headfirst, as an organization we had to be clear about our focus, how the SEL work aligned with the vision of the network, and how the SEL work would be incorporated into our work. Michelle Doucette Cunningham, the executive director of the Connecticut After School Network, summarized the process:

> With our history based in child care, we knew that OST programs played an important role in developing all aspects of the whole child, including children's social and emotional skills, but articulating this valuable aspect of programs that work outside the traditional classroom was a challenge because of the varieties of different types of programs and different backgrounds of staff. We often serve as a bridge between schools and community-based organizations, each of which uses a different way of describing social and emotional skills. In addition, depending upon the needs and ages of the children they serve, programs have a vast array of primary program goals. For example, some are focused on building early literacy skills, others on building character, others on keeping children supervised. We need to respect the programs' goals while encouraging them to look beyond academic development or safety and supervision to realize the ways they are already having an impact on children's SEL and developing staff skills to do this more effectively. (M. Cunningham, personal communication, November 4, 2017)

We wanted to have a broad-based, systemic strategy that could resonate with multiple audiences and sectors. This included line staff, supervisors, and program directors as well as school teachers and administrators. Additionally, we reached out to state agencies such as the State Department of Education, Department of Social Services, and Office of Early Childhood, as well as some legislators, to gather thoughts from leaders on the intersection between SEL and OST. Having existing relationships with stakeholders allowed the network to be an integral part of how Connecticut has integrated SEL into existing OST systems. Our efforts have allowed the network to highlight models such as the Consolidated School District of New Britain Summer Enrichment Experience program, which has demonstrated a 40% increase in attendance and an increase in reading scores ("Profile of Success," n.d.).

The summer enrichment experience (SEE) program has typically run for three weeks near the end of summer and expands on the typical summer school model. The district chooses the lowest 20th percentile of children for the program, who then receive an invitation from the superintendent. The morning portion of the program focuses on academic skill building delivered in a classroom setting. After lunch, the children are broken into groups and take part in enrichment programming, co-developed by the district and multiple community-based providers. Certified teachers deliver the morning portion of the SEE program, unlike in its middle school counterpart, the Extreme program, in which certified teachers and community-based staff support and co-teach throughout the day.

SEL AT THE PROGRAM LEVEL

When first talking with providers in the field, I found that they thought of SEL as something extra they would have to add to programming. The term "SEL" immediately drew reactions about program staff members' ability to talk about concepts with the children. The network launched the topic with our 2015 fall conference, "How to Be a Brain Builder," and invited MHA labs to present its skill-building framework (Beller, 2013) in a keynote and workshop. Many participants responded that they were already doing the type of work described in the keynote and that the topic really resonated with them.

COACHING AND LEARNING FOR AFTER-SCHOOL PROFESSIONALS

Coaching and Learning for After-School Professionals Social and Emotional Learning Cohort

Building on the momentum from the conference, the network offered four single-day workshop sessions focused on SEL topics such as de-escalation, an introduction to youth development, and developing "SAFE" programming using the Durlak and Weissberg (2007) model. The sessions—as part of the Connecticut After School Network 2016 Coaching and Learning for After School Professionals (CLASP) cohort, an intensive yearlong experience that involves OST program leaders—examined SEL from the research and practice perspectives. The discussions allowed participants to make a personal connection with the material and explore SEL applications in their own programs.

Session 1

The first session began with some of the research behind SEL. It was evident right away that people came with preconceived notions of what SEL in OST was and how practices were being implemented in their own programs. (This would become even clearer in the second session as we explored various SEL frameworks and participants identified specific practices that supported some of the elements.) Participants also talked about how some components would not fit based on the program design in their organization; this was helpful to know in developing the subsequent sessions and tailoring the content to what the group needed.

Session 2

Like so many aspects of quality in OST, and in education overall, there is no single, unified SEL framework for all providers to rally around. Rather, there is a variety of frameworks with associated strategies for measuring impacts. While the array of options can fracture and confuse the field, it has its benefits, too (Berg et al., 2017; Jones et al., 2017). There is overlap between components of various frameworks, and skills consistently identified across frameworks that support how children and youth connect with their environments (Berg et al., 2017). Every program, every team, and every group of children is different. Attempting to align to a framework is always a challenge. By providing a survey of the most common research-based frameworks, the second session pointed out the unique features of each framework, allowing providers to choose the one that fits best for their program.

Over the four sessions, we used five SEL frameworks to guide the discussions and content. Frameworks included were the American Institutes for Research SEL framework, the Collaborative for Academic, Social, and Emotional Learning (CASEL) framework, the MHA Labs practice guide for its Building Blocks model, the Standards for Practice from the Weikart Center's *Preparing Youth to Thrive* guide, and the Search Institute's 40 developmental assets (MHA Labs, 2015; Search Institute, 2006; "Social and Emotional Learning Practices," 2015; Smith, McGovern, Larson, Hillaker, & Peck, 2016). Once each provider selected a framework, the process of moving to program design and implementation looked remarkably similar. Using Durlak and Weissberg's (2007) SAFE model to discuss activity design allowed us to help bridge research and practice, and provided the practitioner with concrete steps to take in delivering programming with fidelity. It was important that we took some extra time during the second session to cover the SAFE model, as we used this knowledge again in the fourth session when participants developed activities using the SEL framework they chose to work with during session two.

We then shared two concrete strategies focused on behavior management and student engagement adapted by the Connecticut After School Network. We also discussed the Big Idea, Linking, and Teaser (BLT) model, which helped participants practice intentional design, including open-ended questions and reflection that aimed to deepen the relationship between the children and staff. There was also an explicit focus on identifying behavior management strategies and the link with SEL. In this section of the session, we discussed how to connect interventions to SEL, starting with the creation of a problem statement and converting it to a strength and a need using the compliment sandwich model. This helped participants see how they would incorporate SEL linked efforts into their programs. Unfortunately, this portion of the day did not last as long as we had hoped; the second session largely focused on the frameworks, where the conversation remained. As a result, we talked little about applications to practice. However, the result was a vibrant discussion on aspects of the various frameworks and how participants felt about the components. This was a valuable lesson, as it allowed them time to think about and process aspects of the material presented. Through the discussion, they were able to make a link to a chosen framework and make a larger connection to their overall program.

Session 3

By the third session of the cohort, we felt the participants were comfortable with the concepts; we decided to move into how to assess the program for success. One of the key lessons learned was the disconnect between formal assessment language and practice on the ground. (In the book *The Growing Field of Out-of-School Time* [Anthony, 2017], I discuss this dynamic in greater detail.) As we dove deeper into the assessment frame, people grew frustrated, voiced their concerns about assessing SEL, questioned why assessment was needed, asked for multiple breaks, and left feeling confused and disheartened about implementing SEL. We spent the majority of the third session talking about some of these issues and affirmed how participants' experience mirrored some of the feelings of the larger field in assessing social and emotional competencies. One of the key lessons learned for us was to slow the discussion down, allow participants to feel confident and competent with the concept of assessment, and allow them to express their concerns, questions, and feelings related to the topic.

Session 4

With this in mind, when we met for the fourth and final session for 2016, the focus was explicitly on activity design within a program, which was something everyone was familiar with and had a large degree of comfort with. As we walked through the design phase, we intertwined components of the Weikart Preparing to Thrive framework (Smith et al., 2016) with aspects of the activities. When it came time to assess the success of the activity, larger concepts that were part of the framework were integrated, but were layered on top of questions about youth engagement, staff participation, and intentional design. Participants were able to identify with their program through the material, making the concepts we had been discussing real; they were able to see SEL implementation and assessment as more organic elements of the overall program design. It seemed that working in context helped differentiate the last session from the prior ones for participants.

When designing the Connecticut After School Network's conceptual model for how our SEL focus would be developed, we drew from research on the most important attributes of SEL in programming. The frameworks cited above, and the Durlak and Weissberg (2007) SAFE model, were used in the sessions; they provided content that helped bridge the gap between research and practice through anchoring characteristics with fidelity across activities in OST. Participants used what was being learned and applied it to practical applications. This model, when integrated into part of a high-quality program, can lead to improved youth outcomes (Durlak & Weissberg, 2007).

In developing the training, we knew that delivery of the content had to include active participation as a constant, being a key principle of adult learning. This is a standard that the Connecticut After School Network has a strong foundation in, having provided professional development for the past 30 years. This means that in any training course, participants would spend at least 25% of the time trying out, discussing new concepts, and at least 25% of the time exploring, or planning how to implement new knowledge in a practical, boots-on-the-ground way once they got back to their program. Including easy-to-use activities and tools was also a core element of all training. After the completion of the CLASP cohort, we were able to reflect on what did and did not resonate with participants in learning about SEL. One key takeaway was to present an array of frameworks from the start, and allow time for people to explore different elements to find the right fit for their program. Another was to help facilitate program applications of the research, using activity planning as a vehicle for participant learning. We also allowed discussions to move where the group needed them to, and were cognizant of challenges or concerns they were discussing. At the close of the sessions, we would revisit these and see how they were feeling about the issue raised.

The Connecticut After School Network has used this information to create additional training sessions that expand on topics covered in the CLASP cohort. We identified a need for content in one-day training offerings to go much deeper than what is common for training available to the OST field. Thus, we developed a series of "Deep Dive" training sessions to home in on specific subject areas, such as conflict resolution or executive functioning, and develop a robust understanding of the context surrounding the topic, and key research and best practices. Participants were able to connect content to the spectrum of child development and SEL competencies, and explore meaningful ways to adjust adult–child interactions and program planning and implementation to improve outcomes in that area. Needs expressed by providers at our conferences and in our training offerings, insights gained from site visits and quality advising, and periodic surveys of providers helped identify topics for the Deep Dives.

The CLASP program described earlier and Deep Dive training sessions were efforts to make the research-to-practice connection to support the implementation of best practices within the OST system. In the case of CLASP, nine different programs participated, and all left the cohort on the same page with regard to SEL. A major area we addressed in all of our professional development offerings was the challenge of moving from the broadly framed, research-based universal concepts of a framework to the simple, specific, easy-to-implement activities that OST staff can realistically include in day-to-day programming. We found that in order to facilitate meaningful change in programs, we had to be intentional about empowering participants to close the research-to-practice gap and integrate new knowledge into habits of daily program implementation. One of the central components of our SEL work has been teaching programs to embed the attributes of SEL into existing activities in a real-world, hands-on way, and with fidelity.

The Role of the Statewide After-School Network in SEL Systems Building in Connecticut

As a part of its work, the Connecticut After School Network currently provides statewide technical assistance for state-funded after-school grantees through the State Department of Education. As a result, the network started offering SEL training opportunities to state grantees at conferences and workshops. We also discussed the importance of caring adult relationships and implementation of SEL practices at quality advising visits, and connected SEL to fundraising and advocacy strategies across the network. While the efforts sought to create a dialog and help standardize language across programs and audiences, the first iteration of our SEL work also left questions within the system we were trying to nurture. One question was how to evaluate SEL in individuals in OST programs in a time-efficient way and with fidelity across settings.

In the summer of 2015, we conducted a feasibility study on various tools programs could use for measuring SEL. Since the after-school grantees were already using the National Institute on Out-of-School Time (NIOST) APT-O and Q tools, we also reviewed the SAYO (Survey of Academic Youth Outcomes) tool that is part of the NIOST APAS (Afterschool Program Assessment System) suite (among others). The study also used another tool available to the field in a program located in Northwestern Connecticut. Our findings indicated that program staff took four days of the summer program to survey 200 children. In the debrief with the program, it became clear that for them, time would be a significant barrier to performing an SEL assessment during the school year—particularly with the more limited hours an OST program has versus the summer program in which the study was conducted. They also reported that the experience of learning to use a tool was valuable for staff. Measurement and data usage were some of the largest concerns expressed to the program by families. These concerns illustrate a tension in the field with regard to SEL measurement. We want to be able to assess the SEL needs of children to better support them and their families, with an emphasis on relationship building, but need to be able to collect data without interrupting the flow of the program. Likewise, there needs to be consideration given to why we are measuring particular competencies and what these data are for (e.g., individual support, program design, professional development).

Role as the Statewide Intermediary in Connecticut

As mentioned earlier, Connecticut has numerous SEL-related initiatives. Some are at the state level; others are specific to a city, and there are others with a national scope located in higher education settings, such as the Center for Social Emotional Development at Yale in New Haven. Yet for all the "buzz" about SEL, few people know about the work of others, and little is done to coordinate efforts or build synergy for more systemic change.

In Connecticut, the next step in the Connecticut After School Network's SEL work will be addressing systems aspects through an opportunity grant for SANs from the Charles Stewart Mott Foundation. One major aspect of the project focuses on the creation of a new policy council called SEL4CT. This group is composed of nonprofits, schools, state agencies, prevention professionals, and other stakeholders who wish to expand SEL opportunities for children and youth. We plan to send invitations to more than 30 groups and individuals to join, including the Connecticut Association of Prevention Professionals, Connecticut Department of Mental Health and Addiction Services, Child Health and Development Institute of Connecticut, and Yale University School of Medicine. The facilitation role the network will play will help build stronger connections between new and existing partners and OST providers. Our vision for SEL4CT is to build a strong alliance of those individuals and organizations that support expanding SEL for children and youth in all types of settings, including OST, summer, and the school day. We envision a two-tier structure, with a high-level policy council that engages decision makers two or three times per year on big-picture issues, and work groups that meet more frequently, made up of issue experts and program managers, to advance the work in specific areas. While the individuals and groups that choose to participate will determine the work groups, we anticipate at least three different work groups:

- a communications/social media group that will develop and implement a communications plan to advance information about SEL,
- a research/higher education group to coordinate and plan an event highlighting various initiatives at Connecticut colleges and universities, and

- a policy group to catalog existing initiatives, identify issue areas, and examine possible policy initiatives and coordination efforts to improve systems that support SEL.

The work at the Connecticut After School Network also contains linkages to local OST networks, which is similar to other SANs and will be discussed later in the chapter. One such connection that I have written about extensively (Anthony, 2017; Anthony & Morra, 2016) is the Coalition for New Britain's Youth, in New Britain, Connecticut. The collaboration that exists within the local OST system is a model for school and community partnership. Over the past 11 years, the district has increasingly collaborated with community providers during the SEE program offered by the Consolidated School District of New Britain. Strategies for curricular and behavior management alignment were determined prior to the start of the program through meetings and joint professional development. The efforts of this partnership have resulted in national recognition, including a New York Life Excellence in Summer Award in 2016 (National Summer Learning Association, 2016), and the city was twice recognized as an All-American City, in 2016 and 2017, by the National Civic League ("New Britain Is Proud," n.d.).

In 2015, the Coalition and the Consolidated School District of New Britain took part in my exploratory study examining school-and-OST alignment in the areas of communication, sense of partnership, and sharing of academic resources (Anthony & Morra, 2016). This work has been integrated into the OST programming as well. On the whole, the community has been able to get on the same page with regard to quality and holistic supports for children and families. This has included training most of the community providers in the NIOST APT tool for self-assessment, which is one of many quality self-assessment tools available to the field.

The Connecticut After School Network provided coaching and evaluation for the past four years in summer and OST programming, and is a partner in helping improve the OST and summer learning systems in New Britain. Over the past year, the school district and coalition have worked to begin looking at integrating SEL into collective impact efforts. The district has begun using the Pearson Behavioral and Emotional Screening System (BESS) suite of tools to measure the social and emotional competence of students. According to Pearson Education, Inc. (2017), the tool provides a determination of behavioral and emotional strengths and weaknesses across the developmental spectrum, from prekindergarten to Grade 12. The superintendent, Nancy Sarra, intends to train the community providers in the tool and share the results with school and OST staff to develop holistic supports that can help drive student outcomes (academically and socially).

In addition to district efforts, the coalition has brought in the Weikart Center to begin training school, community, and mental health practitioners on the Preparing to Thrive framework (Smith et al., 2016) components. This includes integrating three of the six components identified (emotion management, empathy, problem-solving) into programming and systems work in spring 2018. In an effort to build capacity, a local agency will be conducting the trainings and providing coaching to the OST programs within the city.

The network was instrumental in helping them zero in on the three areas to begin the pilot, and remain involved in conversations about implementation and larger statewide systems work. It is examples such as this that help other communities model and adapt local best practices to build an SEL system within the community. The SANs are able to work within multiple communities within a state, and can be the connector needed to start and nurture critical conversations at a systems level.

The Role of Statewide After-School Networks in Systems Work

The strategic use of statewide OST support networks was a direct result of the Charles Stewart Mott Foundation's investment in developing an infrastructure for technical assistance to OST providers in the late 1990s. However, the foundation had been investing in OST programs for over 80 years, and had an organizational commitment to providing more and better opportunities for children and youth outside of the school day ("The 50 State Afterschool Network," n.d.). They recognized the need for policy and funding streams dedicated to OST programs, as well as building quality in the field, and therefore developed the statewide after-school networks. At the time Connecticut was first funded as part of the SAN initiative, there were only eight other states; all 50 states now have a SAN. Mott's 50-State Afterschool Network allows for cohesive messaging, sharing of best practices, and supporting state and federal OST and summer funding streams, such as the 21st Century Community Learning Center (21st CCLC). According to the Collaborative Communications Group, the key infrastructure elements found in SANs include large-scale change, broad dissemination channels, quality and professional development, data and knowledge, and high return on investment. With the infrastructure provided by the Mott Foundation, SANs have been able to be a primary voice and intermediary for the field at the state and national level. SANs have the unique ability to bring national research, practice, and trends to the local level, and to collaborate on how to apply lessons learned in a local context.

SEL Systems Approaches Through SAN Partnerships

There are now 50 SANs doing similar yet diverse work; this section highlights the work underway in the Utah, New Jersey, and Minnesota networks. Similar to our work in Connecticut, SAN leaders identified pockets of work that were happening at the local and statewide level. One of the common themes across networks was the variety of frameworks used when approaching the work, similar to our experience described earlier. Most network participants have noted that professional development was the starting point for their respective organizations, and that this has led to larger conversations and collaborations. Katie Brackenridge, from the Partnership for Children and Youth in California, describes a statewide technical assistance project focused on SEL supports for staff in Chapter 11. The SANs have also discussed how being an intermediary allows for coordination of a systemic conversation that involves cross-sector collaboration and partnerships.

Utah

Established in 2005, the Utah Afterschool Network connects with over 100 practitioners, advocates, and leaders statewide ("Quality Tool & Research," n.d.). Similar to other statewide after-school networks, in 2008 the Utah Afterschool Network developed a quality self-assessment tool for programs to use that contained four areas: be safe, develop meaningful relationships, learn new skills, and administration ("Quality Tool & Research," n.d.). According to Ben Trentelman, director of operations at the Utah Afterschool Network, the organization provides technical assistance and quality support to over 400 programs using this tool (B. Trentelman, personal communication, November 2, 2017). The section of the tool titled "Developing Meaningful Relationships" has an explicit SEL focus. Though it predates many of the common SEL frameworks, it contains many of the same competencies and allows the Utah afterschool network to offer aligned quality systems support through program observations and cycles of continuous improvement. Having a common tool statewide allows providers to be on the same page, using the same language. Like many other statewide after-school networks, the Utah SAN is able to provide training and guidance to help establish and support future learning communities based on information provided by program self-assessments using the tool.

New Jersey

In an effort to weave policy and practice together to provide access to high-quality OST programs, the New Jersey School-Age Care Coalition (NJSACC) entered into SEL work in 2016. For over 10 years, the network has provided training and technical assistance to New Jersey's fifty-six 21st CCLC programs (E. Grace, personal communication, September 14, 2017).

Working with the SEARCH Institute, Ebony Grace, the director of Expanded Learning Opportunities at NJSACC, participated in a two-day train-the-trainer workshop on the Search Developmental Assets Framework.

Because of this effort, 21st CCLC program directors were required to attend an "Everyone's an Asset Builder" workshop to learn about components of the framework. The SAN used the opportunity of Grace being a part of the White-Riley-Peterson Policy Fellowship to integrate the training into the network's systems work, and provided quality coaching to help funded programs work with the components ("Policy Project 2015–16," n.d.). According to Grace, "21st CCLC grantees were strongly encouraged to utilize the Assets framework to satisfy their SEL program requirements" (E. Grace, personal communication, September 14, 2017). As part of the technical assistance grant with the state, NJSACC is required to

> design and provide training and technical assistance that helps the grantees fulfill program requirements, and also builds the capacity of the program staff which in turn will enhance the quality of the program. We also provide training sessions on best practice strategies for intentional planning, aligning with the school day, creating a youth-centered environment, effective management, summer learning, engaging families, local evaluation methods, and designing program staff professional development. (E. Grace, personal communication, September 14, 2017)

In collaboration with the New Jersey Department of Education, the SAN is able to assess the needs of the grantees at a statewide level during each grant year and determine what trainings would best assist the grantees. The training is a required program element, but there is no specific language regarding SEL. Having an existing contract with the New Jersey Department of Family Development, NJSACC hopes to work with policy makers to offer the training to all programs in the future. The New Jersey SAN is a great example of how the alignment of policy and practice has helped increase competence on the ground. Supporting practitioners through ongoing professional development helps them to make use of the SEARCH Institute framework and understand its elements.

Minnesota

Ignite Afterschool, the Minnesota SAN, highlighted how local work can become statewide through communication and being open to incorporating different frameworks and approaches as part of system-building efforts. Kari Denissen Cunnien, the executive director at Ignite Afterschool, explained how the SAN played a critical role in taking the conversation to a statewide level. She credits the work of Sprockets, a local Wallace Foundation-funded intermediary in St. Paul, Minnesota, with starting the SEL conversation. The city has collaborated with Harvard's Partnerships in

Education and Resilience (PEAR) and provided training to providers using Gil Noam's Clover model.

Other organizations across the state were discussing the topic of SEL also, similar to other states. Dale Blyth, from the Center for Youth Development at the University of Minnesota, had convened a workgroup to develop a white paper on SEL and aligning school and OST time (K. Dennison Cunnien, personal communication, November 2, 2017). Additionally, under guidance from the state education department, schools had begun using the CASEL framework during the school day. Another city was using the MHA Labs framework to train staff in competencies of SEL (K. Dennison Cunnien, personal communication, November 2, 2017).

Cunnien described the role of the SAN as a convener or participant across the various initiatives statewide. One project currently underway is the Pro Pal SEL initiative. This initiative spans the nine-county metro Minneapolis–St. Paul area. As part of the work, they are looking at the way they support OST providers to implement SEL practices as part of the system. This has included listening sessions about frameworks, in which providers discussed whether frameworks made sense across cultural or ethnic groups. Another important finding was the need to build SEL competencies for adults. Through professional development, staff learned foundational knowledge in yearlong training sessions before rolling it out to the children and youth (K. Dennison Cunnien, personal communication, November 2, 2017).

Ignite Afterschool is also part of developing an SEL professional learning community through a collaboration of four intermediaries funded through the United Way: Ignite Afterschool, Brooklyn Bridge Alliance, Sprockets, and the Minneapolis Youth Coordinating Board, which comprises the Minneapolis Afterschool Network. They will be recruiting soon and hope to have people from 8–10 different organizations in two pilot cohorts over 9 months. Participants will explore what SEL means in their organization, analyze frameworks, and develop staff policies and practices to articulate where SEL fits within the program, and what areas need further development. Ignite Afterschool will be the project manager once the program is implemented and will be responsible for convening and coordinating the cohorts.

What matters is intentionality in choosing a framework. According to Dennison Cunnien, you have to "fit a framework to what you need" (personal communication, November 2, 2017). She recommends being aware of the context of who you are serving with a racial equity lens when implementing and assessing SEL. This requires going beyond the "what gets measured matters" standpoint and reflecting on what is good for the children you serve. With the increasing number of SEL tools available for programs to choose from, it is important to use tools that are the best match for the children served. Measuring with fidelity while at the same time developing a relationship with youth is a balance practitioners need to strike. One of the challenges facing wholesale change efforts is often scalability. As discussed, the SAN is able to identify, work with, and lift up local models that are promising, and share ideas statewide by convening partners doing similar work elsewhere. Having a 50-State Afterschool Network has allowed SANs to learn from one another, mirror similar work in other states, share best practices, and collaborate across state lines on SEL and other systems issues.

Challenges and Opportunities Across SANS

In talking with the other SANs to prepare this chapter, we identified some common challenges and opportunities, including frameworks, professional development, and implementing with fidelity. The process was invaluable in generating ideas for how we can move the needle forward in Connecticut. This is a value-add the SANs provide across state lines. Though the context may differ slightly, the ability to share strategies and practices allows other communities to benefit from successful models across the 50-State Afterschool Network. This also allows us to identify holes within the larger systems that SANs can address collectively on the statewide and national policy and training levels.

Some of the things we discussed about SEL included having no consistent statewide measurement and data system. In the examples highlighted above, with multiple frameworks and approaches, finding a common instrument presents a challenge for systems building. The establishment of regional networks that discuss and coordinate policy and professional development, and align SEL practices across settings addresses this need. In thinking about SEL work from a systems context, Ben Trentelman summed it up well:

> Look at what work has already been done in the state. People come to this work overwhelmed, with multiple frameworks available; this is not a unique conversation, communicating with partners to discover what work [that] is being done is essential. What is in place that includes measurement, frameworks, and components? If something exists, be a part of the vision, if nothing exists, be the convener. (B. Trentelman, personal communication, November 2, 2017)

CONCLUSION

SEL provides an opportunity to develop impactful cross-sector collaborations that support holistic development. The Connecticut After School Network has begun offering cross-training to public school teachers and OST teams in the same skills and approaches in order to facilitate smoother and more integrated support of youth. Joint professional development between school and OST professionals helps to get everyone on the same page (Anthony & Morra, 2016).

In the case of New Britain, the district and coalition have coordinated trainings in preparation for the award-winning summer SEE program ("Profile of Success," n.d.). Although this work is still relatively new, it shows great promise. Nevertheless, building strong, collaborative, and mutually respectful relationships between school teams and OST staff can be extremely challenging. According to Bennett (2015), when school districts and community-based organizations have a shared sense of partnership, children do better academically. I would argue that with deeper communication and sharing of academic resources (websites, curriculum, and frameworks), a concerted effort, equal sense of partnership, and well-developed communities of practice, holistic alignment and practice can occur at a systemic level through city-wide collaborative efforts that are already underway.

The role of statewide after-school networks has grown over the past 10 years. Some have merged with existing OST coalitions and have become both Mott SAN initiative and NAA affiliates. This has enabled SANs to play an active role in the field and be a support in national conversations. Through the SANs, practitioners and communities have been able to push back and advocate for policy that will be realistic and impactful on the ground. While there is much variety when it comes to SEL at a systems level, the field is identifying common practices and some degree of agreement on measurement that links school and community partnerships to focus on the whole child.

REFERENCES

Anthony, K. (2017). Exploring the need for research-practitioner partnerships. In H. Malone & T. Donahue (Eds.), *The growing out-of-school time field: Past, present, and future* (pp. 177–194). Charlotte, NC: Information Age.

Anthony, K., & Morra, J. (2016). Creating holistic partnerships between school and afterschool. *Afterschool Matters, 24*/Fall, 33–42.

Beller, L. (2013). *Skill building blocks.* Chicago, IL: MHA Labs. Retrieved from http://mhalabs.org/skill-building-blocks/

Bennett, T. L. (2015). Examining levels of alignment between school and afterschool and associations on student academic achievement. *Journal of Expanded Learning Opportunities, 1*(2), 4–22.

Berg, J., Osher, D., Same, M., Nolan, E., Benson, D., & Jacobs, N. (2017). *Identifying, defining, and measuring social and emotional competencies.* Chicago, IL: American Institutes for Research. Retrieved from https://www.air.org/resource/identifying-defining-and-measuring-social-and-emotional-competencies

Connecticut State Department of Education. (2017). Connecticut Consolidated State Plan Under the Every Student Succeeds Act. Retrieved from https://portal.ct.gov/-/media/SDE/ESSA/august_4_ct_consolidated_state_essa_plan.pdf?la=en

Durlak, J. A., & Weissberg, R. P. (2007). *The impact of after-school programs that promote social skills.* Chicago: University of Illinois at Chicago, Collaborative for Academic, Social, and Emotional Learning.

Durlak, J. A., Weissberg, R. P., & Pachan, M. (2010). A meta-analysis of after-school programs that seek to promote personal and social skills in children and adolescents. *American Journal of Community Psychology, 45*/3–4, 294–309.

Every Student Succeeds Act of 2015, P.L. 114-95, 20 U.S.C. § 6301 (2016)

Jones, S., Brush, K., Bailey, R., Brion-Meisels, G., McIntyre, J., Kahn, J., . . . & Stickle, L. (2017). *Navigating SEL from the inside out: Looking inside and across 25 leading SEL programs: A practical resource for schools and OST providers.* Cambridge, MA: Harvard Graduate School of Education. Retrieved from http://www.wallacefoundation.org/knowledge-center/Documents/Navigating-Social-and-Emotional-Learning-from-the-Inside-Out.pdf

MHA Labs. (2015). *MHA labs practice guide.* Chicago, IL: Author.

National Summer Learning Association. (2016). *2016 New York life foundation excellence in summer learning awards.* Baltimore, MD: Author. Retrieved from http://www.summerlearning.org/wp-content/uploads/2016/10/NYLife-Excellence-Awards-vs7d-update2.pdf

New Britain Is Proud to be a 2016 All-American City by the National Civic League! (n.d.). Retrieved from the Coalition for New Britain's Youth website: http://www.coalition4nbyouth.org/all-america-city.html

Pearson Education, Inc. (2017). *BASC-3 behavioral and emotional screening system* (BASC-3 BESS). San Antonio, TX. Retrieved from https://images.pearsonclinical.com/images/Assets/BASC-3/BASC-3-Rating-Scales-Report-Sample.pdf

Policy Project 2015–16. (n.d.). Retrieved from The Riley Institute Education Policy website: https://riley.furman.edu/education/projects/white-riley-peterson-policy-fellowship/class-2015-16/policy-projects

Profile of Success: Summer Enrichment Experience. (n.d.). Retrieved from the United Way of Central and Northeastern Connecticut website: https://unitedwayinc.org/Profile-of-Success-Summer-Enrichment-Experience

Quality Tool & Research. (n.d.). Retrieved from Utah Afterschool Network website: https://utahafterschool.org/what-we-do/quality

Quickfacts. (2016). Retrieved from the United States Census Bureau website: https://www.census.gov/quickfacts/fact/table/newtowntownfairfieldcounty connecticut/PST045216

Search Institute. (2006). *40 developmental assets for middle childhood.* Minneapolis, MN: Author.

Smith, C., McGovern, G., Larson, R., Hillaker, B., & Peck, S. C. (2016). *Preparing youth to thrive: Promising practices for social & emotional learning.* Washington, DC: Forum for Youth Investment.

Social and Emotional Learning Practices: A Self-Reflection Tool for Afterschool Staff. (2015, September 14). Retrieved from the American Institutes for Research website: https://www.air.org/resource/social-and-emotional-learning-practices-self-reflection-tool-afterschool-staff

The 50 State Afterschool Network. (n.d.). Retrieved from the Statewide Afterschool Networks website: http://www.statewideafterschoolnetworks.net/50-state-afterschool-network

CHAPTER 11

BUILDING CAPACITY FOR SOCIAL AND EMOTIONAL LEARNING AT THE DISTRICT AND STATE LEVEL

Katie Brackenridge

Since 2015, the Partnership for Children & Youth (PCY) has been running an innovative professional learning community (PLC) to help nine school districts in California build their capacity to deliver high-quality social and emotional learning (SEL) across the school day and out-of-school time (OST), including both after-school and summer programs. The work is highlighting key lessons for districts, OST providers, and state-level policymakers.

This chapter is intended to help those interested in building the capacity of districts and OST providers to improve their strategies around SEL, and to implement those strategies consistently across the school day and OST. The goal is for young people to have consistently positive social and emotional experiences all day and all year.

Social and Emotional Learning in Out-of-School Time, pages 183–200

The chapter is organized into four sections. The first sets the context for SEL and OST in California. The second describes the Expanded Learning 360°/365 PLC, and its progress to date.[1] Section three describes lessons learned from the PLC, and the fourth anticipates future challenges and opportunities.

CONTEXT FOR SOCIAL AND EMOTIONAL LEARNING AND OST IN CALIFORNIA

Momentum Around Social and Emotional Learning

California's interest and momentum in SEL is the result of multiple converging pressures and opportunities over the past several years. Before the Every Student Succeeds Act (ESSA) was passed in 2015, California education leaders were already working towards alternative accountability systems that included multiple measures of school success. This movement included 10 of California's biggest school districts, known as the CORE Districts, which secured a federal waiver from NCLB testing requirements in 2013. The waiver included social and emotional outcomes as part of a redesigned accountability structure.

California's education system also welcomed the Common Core State Standards as an opportunity to think more comprehensively about the set of skills and strategies that students need to learn and practice to be effective and productive community members (Carrasco, Glaab, & McLaughlin, 2014). Education leaders acknowledge the link between success in the common core and social and emotional skills (Yoder, 2014, p. 6). Vicki Zakrzewski of the Greater Good Science Center provides the following example about the Common Core emphasis on problem solving:

> Students need to first trust in their ability to solve a problem (self-efficacy) and then work towards that goal. They must be able to focus on the problem rather than get distracted by what the kid on the other side of the room is doing. If they get stuck, students must manage their stress levels by regulating their emotions and, if necessary, ask for help. Staying optimistic throughout the process will help them persevere to the end. (Schonert-Reichl & Zakrzewski, 2014, p. 3)

Recognizing this link, some districts began to look more intentionally at the development of social and emotional skills.

During this same time frame, the state adopted the Local Control Funding Formula (LCFF), which, among other changes, broadens the state's education priorities to include school culture and climate, student engagement, and adherence to the common core, as well as academic achievement ("Local Control Funding," n.d.). These priorities further encourage the integration of SEL into district strategies. This LCFF shift preceded the federal adoption of ESSA, which requires states to define "nonacademic" indicators. With these state and federal policy changes, California schools are well positioned and leading the way on SEL.

Synergy With California's Out-of-School Time System

The California OST community watched these shifts in the national and state education landscape with piqued interest. Aware of the synergy between youth development practice and SEL, statewide advocates and practitioners began thinking about how the state's extensive OST infrastructure and program network could be leveraged to support student success in this new era. Top of mind was the opportunity to partner more authentically with the school day around building the skills, mindsets, and positive behaviors that the OST community has long pushed for.

California's OST community and infrastructure are the most robust in the nation, with $600 million in state funding and another $120 million in federal funds for OST programs. The funding, administered through the California Department of Education (CDE), supports 4,500 school sites across the state serving more than 860,000 students—the vast majority of whom come from low-income families (Hay & Davis, 2017, p. 3). The OST landscape in California includes an extensive infrastructure of technical assistance and a vibrant community of nonprofit youth programs and advocates. While the funding is administered through the education system and heavily influenced by school-day priorities, most of the actual programming is delivered by nonprofit youth organizations. Under the leadership of CDE's Expanded Learning Division, this OST community has had an active voice in establishing and continuously improving a statewide system of support that includes key components like the CDE-endorsed Quality Standards for Expanded Learning programs and a legislated requirement that programs participate in ongoing quality improvement processes. This inclusive and forward-thinking approach has given the state a strong foundation and a network through which to channel new initiatives and priorities, including SEL.

THE EXPANDED LEARNING 360°/365 PROFESSIONAL LEARNING COMMUNITY

The Partnership for Children & Youth—Bridging Practice and Policy

PCY has been deeply immersed in the statewide conversation around SEL for more than 5 years, and has been a leader in OST policymaking and technical assistance for more than a decade. As a nonprofit intermediary, PCY bridges "people, practice, and policy to ensure youth in California's under-resourced communities are successful in school" ("Mission, Vision, and Values," n.d.). PCY provides direct technical assistance to OST and community school initiatives, and links its learning from this on-the-ground work to state and federal policymaking. PCY succeeded in getting four major pieces of after-school legislation passed over the last decade, and is leading multiple statewide committees to strengthen California's systems of support for after-school programs. With a staff composed largely of former practitioners, PCY's approach is both practical and visionary—identifying existing challenges that can be addressed by technical assistance or policy, and predicting future issues, trends, and solutions. PCY rarely operates alone; it is constantly pulling together stakeholders with similar goals and diverse experience and expertise for collaborative initiatives.

With SEL becoming an increasingly hot topic, PCY quickly recognized the significant opportunity for OST providers and advocates to elevate the value of OST programs and reposition their partnership with the school day. Given their leadership role in developing the state's Quality Standards for Expanded Learning Programs, PCY staff were well aware of the synergy between the practices defined in the standards (practices related to, for example, safe and supportive environments, engaging activities, and youth voice) and the emerging state interest in supporting students' social and emotional skills.

The Expanded Learning 360°/365 Professional Learning Community

PCY knew it was not enough to talk about this newfound opportunity—it needed to take action to support deeper partnerships and practice between OST providers and their school-day partners around SEL. Based on the design of its Summer Matters campaign, PCY decided to pull together a PLC of districts from around the state that could take action to improve social and emotional practices, and learn from other districts' experiences.[2] As described by a 2017 American Institutes for Research literature review,

> quality PLCs facilitate participant learning and experiences through a learning cycle. The learning cycle of a PLC engages participants through the examination of practices, implementation of new insights, and reflection on adapted practices. The cycle can be condensed into three core PLC strategies: (1) practice, (2) reflection, and (3) collaboration. (Lopez, Moroney, & Vance, 2017)

The Expanded Learning 360°/365 PLC has convened quarterly since January 2015. The purpose of the PLC is to help districts and their OST partners improve their social and emotional supports, and better align those supports across the school day, after school, and summer to improve students' social and emotional outcomes. Participating districts form teams of four to eight people, with a mix of school-day and OST staff.

The project includes:

- *Four PLC meetings per year.* Each meeting includes a mix of new content from research or expert testimony, cross-district sharing, and team planning time. The content varies based on the needs and interests of the districts, and has included, for example, presentations on these topics:
  - Effective messaging strategies, from the Wallace Foundation and Edge Research
  - Equity issues within SEL, by Professor Shawn Ginwright of San Francisco State University
  - Promising site-based social and emotional practices in the CORE districts, by Heather Hough of the CORE-PACE Research Partnership
- *Development and implementation of a district-specific action plan that describes clear goals and strategies for improved social and emotional practices and alignment.* PCY's technical assistance is grounded in the cycle of quality improvement that guides participants through the process of assessing their work, planning for improvement, and implementing those improvements. Early on, PLC members self-assessed the alignment of social and emotional supports between the school day and expanded learning, identifying strengths and areas for improvement. Since then, district teams have developed annual action plans, implemented the strategies they defined, assessed their progress, and started the annual cycle again.
- *Consulting to support action plan implementation.* PCY contracts with local technical assistance (TA) providers as consultants for the 360°/365 district teams. Consultant support can include coaching, training, facilitation, and materials development to support the action plan strategies. The use of local TA providers is intentional, and based on PCY's understanding that local context (e.g., politics,

culture, relationships) is essential for effective technical assistance. It also reflects PCY's desire to learn from the different strategies of its consultants and to spread SEL-related skill and commitment to diverse partners across the state.
- *Stipends to support PLC participation.* PCY knows that districts and community-based staff are working with constrained budgets and time. Modest stipends ($5,000 in 2017) help ensure that staff can travel to PLC meetings and cover some costs associated with implementing the action plans, like food and materials for trainings and meetings.

Since 2015, seven CORE districts and three non-CORE districts have participated in the PLC. The CORE districts include Fresno, Garden Grove, Los Angeles, Oakland, Sacramento, San Francisco, and Santa Ana. Three non-CORE districts—San Leandro, San Rafael, and Visalia—were also invited to participate to help PCY understand how (and if) the work would be different in districts that are not being held accountable for social and emotional outcomes. Only one district, Garden Grove, has left the PLC since it began.

To date, the 360°/365 PLC has been remarkably impactful. These are some examples of strategies implemented:

- San Leandro Unified School District (SLUSD) included its community-based program provider in joint district trainings around SEL. Similarly, in the Oakland Unified School District (OUSD), the after school programs and SEL offices worked together to deliver SEL trainings to program managers, site coordinators, and line staff.
- San Francisco Unified School District (SFUSD) revised its quality improvement tools, integrating SEL into the Quality Action Plans that its OST providers are required to complete in collaboration with their principals, and shifting language in its guides and resources to more explicitly reference SEL.
- San Rafael City School District (SRCSD) developed a campaign of presentations and site visits to build awareness among district leadership about the role of SEL in student success.
- Los Angeles Unified School District (LAUSD) is working to include SEL in the rubric that is used to assess school site administrators' performance.

The districts have been universally eager to engage in the SEL content, and have in particular appreciated opportunities to gather new ideas, learn from each other's successes and challenges, and have time with their own district teams to plan and reflect.

LESSONS LEARNED FROM THE PLC

The 360°/365 PLC was designed to support the districts' progress in SEL, and at the same time, to surface challenges, ideas, and strategies that could help practitioners in districts and community-based organizations across California and in other states better implement SEL and improve their partnership. This section describes the key lessons learned to date, and can inform the efforts of others interested in implementing practices or policies that support SEL. Lessons learned to date include:

- Lesson 1: Define language.
- Lesson 2: Focus on adult learning.
- Lesson 3: Mobilize and align district-level staff and structures.
- Lesson 4: Scale to state-level action.

Lesson 1: Define Language

Early in this effort, PCY noticed that people's language—the specific words they use—is both a challenge and an opportunity. In the OST field, there has been long-standing agreement that youth development practices support social and emotional outcomes, but practitioners can be hard pressed to identify specific practices or outcomes. This lack of specificity makes it hard to convince skeptical K–12 partners about the value of OST programs. PCY and its partners were eager to leverage the extensive youth development foundation and infrastructure, and to clearly articulate the field's synergy with SEL.

Prior to launching the PLC, PCY brought together a stakeholder group to define specifically how OST practices relate to the social and emotional outcomes that schools were also working toward. Individuals and organizations were intentionally chosen to represent a cross-section of leaders from OST programs, K–12 institutions, and research organizations. The first task of this group was to explore existing social and emotional frameworks and identify which ones were most closely linked to youth development practices. The group looked at frameworks from 13 different organizations and initiatives, including the well-established Collaborative for Academic, Social, and Emotional Learning (CASEL) framework and the newer California-specific CORE framework of social and emotional outcomes. This comprehensive review was based on a commitment to building on existing well-considered, previously researched initiatives.

An extensive process led the group to identify three categories of social and emotional outcomes, and place those outcomes in the school day, family life, and expanded learning environments, as well as political, cultural,

Figure 11.1 Expanded Learning 360°/365 SEL outcomes.

and social contexts that influence them. These outcomes and this framing are graphically represented in Figures 11.1 and 11.2.

With a similar motivation to build on existing work, the stakeholder group also explored how youth development practices (as defined by the California Quality Standards for Expanded Learning) support these social and emotional outcomes. It immediately became clear that each quality standard supports multiple social and emotional outcomes. A "safe and supportive environment," for example, is essential for growth mindset, self-efficacy, social awareness, interpersonal relationships, self-awareness, and self-management. Similarly, one can draw lines between "youth voice and leadership" and growth mindset, social awareness, self-awareness, and other outcomes with little effort. The group was able to connect all six point-of-service quality standards—safe and supportive environment; active and engaged learning; skill building; youth voice and leadership; healthy choices and behavior; and diversity, access, and equity—to all six social and emotional outcomes as described in Figure 11.3 (PCY, 2017).

The resulting report, *Student Success Comes Full Circle* (PCY, 2015), shifts the challenge of vague language to an opportunity, by building off of, and connecting to, existing frameworks. The hope is that K–12 educators and OST providers discover their shared goals and strategies in the more clearly defined language and coherent images of the report. This strategy has come to fruition in varying ways in the 360°/365 districts. Sacramento City Unified School District (SCUSD) adopted the "We Are, We Belong, We Can" framework for its SEL-related staff development, including creating t-shirts that capture the link between social, emotional, and academic goals. This effort to link frameworks is particularly important in California, where the public investment and commitment to OST programs, and quality

Figure 11.2 Expanded learning 360°/365 SEL framework.

standards to support these programs, has been a focus for 5 years. In the OST community, there is little room for new initiatives, but always a desire for deeper connections to the school day.

It is important to note that the group could have simply adopted one of the existing frameworks, like CASEL's, that is widely used. This approach was discussed, but did not get traction. People wanted to dig into all of

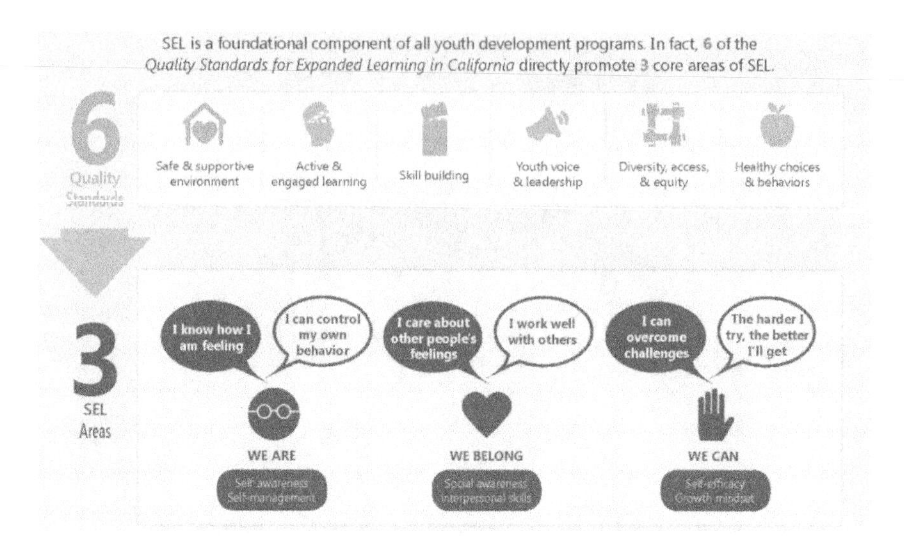

Figure 11.3 Link between California Quality Standards for Expanded Learning and Expanded Learning 360°/365 SEL outcomes.

the frameworks, and identify the social and emotional outcomes that were most relevant to California and OST contexts. The fact that there are multiple frameworks across the country suggests that the impetus to define similar, but unique, approaches, is deep seated. Recognizing this reality, the Expanded Learning 360°/365 initiative has not required adoption of the *Full Circle* (PCY, 2015) report's framework. It has instead focused on encouraging districts and their partners to be explicit and specific about their language around social and emotional outcomes. The PLC districts are therefore working toward different frameworks—including those of CORE, CASEL, and *Full Circle* (PCY, 2015)—depending on their districts' previous decisions.

Continuing its work to connect concepts across language, PCY developed two additional reports. One—*Finding Common Ground* (PCY, 2016a)—highlights SFUSD to illustrate how SEL cuts across multiple efforts within a school district and how intentional communication can help OST providers communicate their work more clearly to their K–12 partners. Specifically, the report links youth development supports and opportunities to Multi-Tiered Systems of Support (MTSS), including Positive Behavior Intervention and Supports (PBIS), as well as to restorative practices, school climate and culture, and the Common Core State Standards.[3] Simple graphics from the SFUSD's OST office (see Figure 11.4) illustrate the connections so that OST staff at multiple levels can see how their work relates to school-day initiatives that they hear about but may never have been directly involved in.

San Francisco Unified School District

Adoption of the District's MTSS Strategy

ExCEL After School Programs is making sure that expanded learning leadership is conversant and comfortable with the same Multi-Tiered System of Support (MTSS) that San Francisco Unified School District uses during the school day. As part of their annual process for building a Quality Action Plan, program leaders are expected to map their offerings to the MTSS structure in three program areas: *Safe and Supportive Culture and Climate, Healthy Active Youth*, and *Aligned Academic Support*. Shared terminology and a common understanding of student support processes help bridge the divide between the school day and after school.

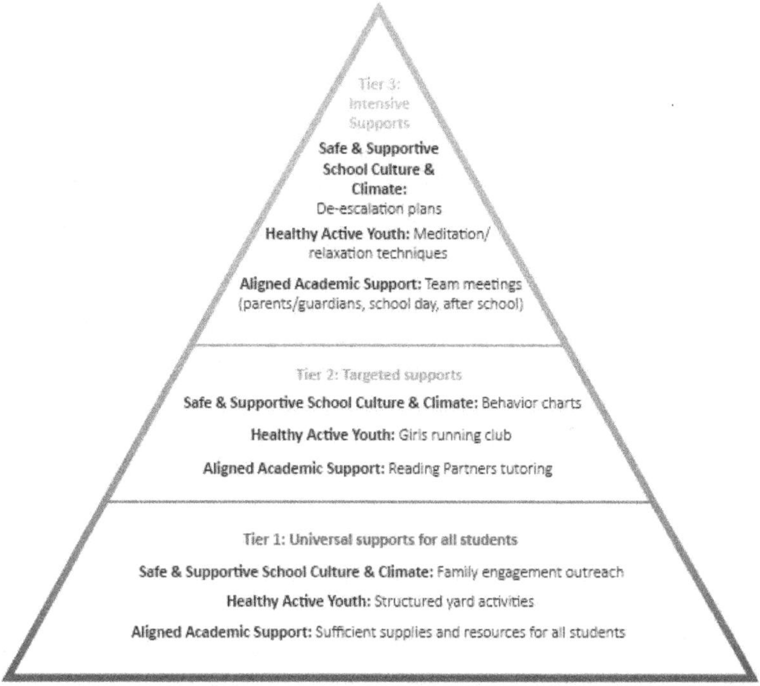

Examples of San Francisco Unified School District's adoption of MTSS strategy within three key program areas.

Figure 11.4 Link between quality standards and MTSS in SFUSD.

Finally, PCY published *Measuring Quality* (PCY, 2016b), a crosswalk of quality assessment tools that are well suited to measuring the point-of-service California Quality Standards that had been linked in *Full Circle* (PCY, 2015) to social and emotional outcomes. This guide was developed to be consistent and explicit about language while helping OST staff choose assessment tools at a time when there were no assessment tools specifically for the California Quality Standards.

Lesson 2: Focus on Adult Learning

During any conversation about SEL in education, the topic very quickly turns to adult skills and experiences. From 2001 to 2015, the No Child Left Behind Act (NCLB; 2001) established an accountability framework based on the results of standardized test scores in reading and math. This emphasis resulted in a narrow focus for schools and teachers on these subjects and test preparation, and the reduction or elimination of other subjects and activities that were not part of the accountability framework (Dee & Jacob, 2010). As a result, both K–12 and OST stakeholders are quick to acknowledge that staff from both sectors have rarely experienced positive social and emotional strategies in action in classrooms. Adding to this dynamic, traditional teacher training programs neither spend time helping teachers develop social and emotional strategies nor emphasize the value of these strategies for supporting student success (Schonert-Reichl & Zakrzewski, 2014). And, of course, everyone carries their own social and emotional experiences into their work environment. Without intentional training and support, people's own social and emotional challenges can play out in their interactions with young people and peers, in some cases making them poor teachers, facilitators, and role models for this content.

Having experienced this conversation many times, PCY was aware that its 360°/365 PLC needed to model social and emotional strategies very explicitly. Fortunately, these strategies align closely with youth development approaches that PCY staff use with young people and adults. For example, the group agreement, engaging activities, and opportunities for voice and input that define a safe and positive learning environment are easily translatable to an intentional SEL environment. These activities were incorporated into the PLC, which resulted in a strong sense of community and rich, honest conversations across and among teams.

Responding to the gap in adult social and emotional skills and preparation, the 360°/365 districts have focused their initial efforts on promoting SEL for adults both at the district and site level. In some cases, this work involved gatherings of adults across departments within a district. SCUSD brought together teams from many of its departments—from student supports to curriculum and instruction to food services—for a four-session PLC. They explored the role of SEL in all of their work, and engaged in cross-department conversations to understand the opportunities for greater synergy. As with the 360°/365 PLC, the SCUSD PLC modeled practices to support social and emotional skills among the adults and explicitly named the practices being used. In OUSD, social and emotional strategies have been embedded in all meetings across the district. Using its "Three Signature SEL Practices," every meeting at OUSD begins with a warm welcome, includes engaging activities, and closes with an optimistic reflection.

OUSD's SEL office has been intentional about training staff at multiple levels so the structure is all-inclusive and thoughtfully implemented.

Most of the 360°/365 districts have invested time and effort into training both OST and school staff. SLUSD invited staff from its OST partner, the Boys and Girls Club of San Leandro, to participate in a district-led SEL training with its school-day teachers. Training side-by-side, teachers and OST staff have a shared experience and language to carry into their work at school sites. A significant challenge for all district/OST partnerships is finding the time for joint training. OUSD is addressing this challenge by taking advantage of professional learning days when school is out. They are paying for additional OST staff hours, and using these full-day opportunities to engage in relationship building, social and emotional exploration, and site-level action planning. Other districts—making the best of the scheduling reality—are having to train people separately, but are making sure to use consistent language and training content across both school-day and OST training.

Of course, training is only part of the professional development toolkit. 360°/365 districts are also eager to observe and coach their teachers and OST staff. Eight of the districts are developing a "look for" tool—an observation tool for SEL practices that they can use to structure coaching sessions around areas of strength and improvement. For many OST staff, this approach is a familiar part of the quality improvement process. For school-day teachers, some districts will need to work through their unions to clarify the role of the observation tool as a low-stakes opportunity for professional development.

For OST providers, districts have worked to explain SEL in the context of the quality improvement process that is required by the CDE in meeting the California Quality Standards. SFUSD incorporated social and emotional practices explicitly into its quality improvement tools and protocols. PCY encourages this link through the infographic (see Figure 11.3) that helps site coordinators and line staff quickly see the connections between the quality standards, the quality improvement process, and SEL.

Lesson 3: Mobilize and Align District-Level Staff and Structures

When the 360°/365 PLC started in 2015, PCY expected that some districts would be able to change practices at the school site level within the first year. In reality, however, every district needed to spend the first two to three years setting up systems and securing commitments at the district level. This dynamic was true even in the CORE districts, where measurement of social and emotional outcomes had preceded the implementation of SEL practices because of the requirements of the NCLB waiver.

These are examples of some of the important actions at the district level:

- Building relationships across departments (including staff in OST, student support services, and curriculum and instruction) and with community-based partner organizations that provide OST programming.
- Creating communication structures and channels across those entities.
- Developing a shared vision and language across district and OST staff, including their community-based partners.
- Mapping multiple SEL-related initiatives and resources across a district so that stakeholders can understand each other's work, find collaboration opportunities, and share each other's tools and strategies.
- Gathering key champions among district leaders to understand and support the work.
- Modeling social and emotional practices with district and community-based staff to begin shifting culture and expectations among the adults.
- Developing and/or collecting assessment, curricular, and training resources in preparation for site-level work.

Interestingly, during the 2017 PLC year, all of the districts started to move toward site-level work, including training plans, PLCs, and greater inclusion of community-based program providers in the planning processes.

One of the biggest surprises of the PLC has been the power of collaboration within and across districts. As mentioned earlier in this chapter, each PLC meeting includes three types of activities: new SEL-related information (research, expert perspective, tools); cross-district sharing; and team reflection and planning time. As evidenced by post-meeting evaluations, this mix is universally well received across the districts. Common feedback is an interest in more team time, with participants lamenting that, even though they work down the hall from each other, team members struggle to find time in busy schedules to reflect on and plan their work collaboratively. Similarly, cross-district conversations have yielded resource sharing (for example, a SEL resource guide from SFUSD has made its way to at least two other districts) and practice sharing (for example, variations on SCUSD's district-wide PLC are showing up in the action plans of other PLC districts).

Lesson 4: Scale to State-Level Action

As described above, the 360°/365 PLC helped PCY understand how SEL could progress through a district system and be a conduit for more authentic partnership between the school day and OST. Through this district-level work, three themes emerged:

- the need to build on existing work rather than create something new;
- the importance of reflecting, learning, and adapting as the work progresses; and
- the power of SEL as a unifying force across multiple stakeholder groups.

These themes have also informed and been reinforced by efforts to create a statewide movement around SEL. As within the PLC districts, the state messaging and guidance around SEL must build on initiatives that are already in motion. OST efforts have to map to the Quality Standards, and school-day efforts have to map to statewide MTSS, PBIS, restorative practices, school climate and culture, and common core implementation. The state-level communication and coalition-building work has to be constantly revisited and adapted as the landscape and policy shift over time. Finally, as in the districts, people and organizations with varying roles and missions are coming together around their desire and the opportunity to consider education and student success more holistically. Defining and leveraging this united voice at the state level is challenging, as various large-scale initiatives struggle for attention and traction with 1,000 districts across the state.

In addition to building PCY's understanding of the social and emotional change process, the PLC provides another important asset for the state-level work. PLC members have fully bought into the value of SEL and the OST role. They are eager to contribute their knowledge, expertise, and experience to the broader statewide planning and awareness building. With this enthusiasm, PCY is able to recruit PLC team members to provide input and examples for tools, reports, and articles; present at conferences, and participate in the statewide planning teams described earlier in this chapter. Their voices are particularly relevant and credible because they have the specific examples and experience to support the concepts around SEL and OST.

Two groups that are planning for state-level action exemplify PCY's role in bridging practice at the local level with policy across the state. The first—the SEL planning team—is a group of 25 OST and K–12 stakeholders brought together by the CDE's Expanded Learning Division to develop recommendations about how the division can promote and support SEL practices and alignment with the school day among its OST grantees. Three PLC members sit on the planning team. The planning team's recommendations include actions that mirror the experiences of the 360°/365 PLC:

- explicitly identifying and describing the social and emotional practices that are already implicitly embedded in the point-of-service quality standards;
- providing training and coaching through regional technical assistance providers in the Statewide System of Support;
- building relationships across different divisions within the CDE, in county offices of education, and in school districts—for example, in early education, English learner, special education divisions, and departments; and
- sharpening communication about SEL resources and tools to grantees across the state.

The planning team's recommendations were released publicly in the Spring of 2018, and the Expanded Learning Division began prioritizing and implementing the recommendations soon thereafter.

A parallel SEL conversation is happening within the California Collaborating States Initiative (CSI) team, which is part of a multi-state CASEL initiative to promote statewide policy around SEL. The CSI team includes several overlapping members with the SEL planning team, and there have been multiple opportunities for the CSI and SEL planning teams to share ideas. The CSI team includes a wide range of organizations—such as CDE, school districts (including four PLC members), county offices of education, a teacher union, universities and other research institutions, advocacy organizations, and foundations. Its work includes these components:

- defining statewide guiding principles for SEL,
- infusing SEL into other statewide conversations like those related to school climate and culture and MTSS, and
- developing a compendium of social and emotional resources.

Because OST stakeholders came to the table understanding the challenges and opportunities of moving SEL through districts, they were able to ensure that OST's role in supporting SEL is infused in each of the emerging CSI strategies.

MOVING FORWARD—ANTICIPATED CHALLENGES AND OPPORTUNITIES

Momentum for SEL and OST in California promises to accelerate over the next few years. The 360°/365 PLC is being evaluated by American Institutes for Research, whose findings will provide inspiration for more regional and local support to help districts and their OST providers partner around SEL.

With their efforts focused on site-level practice change, PLC districts will also have an increasing library of case studies and tools to share with other districts interested in learning from their experience.

Challenges in a large and diverse education system like California are ever-present. The underfunding of school-day and OST programs is a constant threat to quality and stability. California is ranked 42nd among the states in per pupil school day spending ("California Earns a C-Minus," 2016), and the OST funding rate is about a third of the research-based cost of quality. Adding to the funding challenge, "initiative overload" will continue to be a factor as education reform efforts shift and grow. Those working to promote SEL will need to track and adjust their strategies to match changing and emerging initiatives. And of course, changes in national education policy threaten funding sources and guidelines that are foundational to social and emotional programming. Finally, in 2018, California will elect a new governor and new superintendent of public instruction, with their own agendas that also need to be taken into account to move OST and social and emotional strategies forward across the state.

Despite these challenges, California's systems at the local, regional, and state level are well positioned to take advantage of the overall shift in education philosophy toward prioritizing SEL. The state's large investment in OST programming and infrastructure has yielded increasingly high-quality youth development practices across the state. School districts are more aware of the value of this programming and the opportunity to partner around strong, consistent social and emotional practices all day and all year.

Structures like the Expanded Learning 360°/365 PLC are proving to be effective in engaging and uniting district and community staff around a shared vision and strategy for SEL. Their commitment runs deep, including intensive work within their own communities as well as enthusiasm for sharing and influencing other districts across California and the country. These educators are inspired by the opportunity to make change at multiple levels within their school sites and districts, across the OST infrastructure, and throughout the education system.

NOTES

1. Expanded Learning 360°/365 refers to 360 degrees of the child, 365 days a year.
2. For 7 years of the Summer Matters campaign, 12 community teams came together twice each year to gather new information and research about summer learning, plan and reflect on their work, and share experiences with peers. This collective learning process was extremely effective for improving practice and inspiring shared commitment to summer learning. Through its Summer Matters work, PCY staff also honed their skill in creating and sustaining PLCs.

3. Multi-Tiered Systems of Support (MTSS), Positive Behavioral Interventions and Supports (PBIS), restorative practices, and school climate and culture are common strategies in California for organizing student and school-site supports. For more information about these efforts, please follow the embedded links.

REFERENCES

California Earns a C-Minus on State Report Card, Ranks 42nd in Nation. (2016, December 30). Retrieved from the Education Week website: https://www.edweek.org/ew/qc/2017/state-highlights/2017/01/04/california-state-highlights-report-page.html

Carrasco, I., Glaab, L., & McLaughlin, M. (2014). *Implementing Common Core State Standards in California: A report from the field.* Retrieved from http://www.edpolicyinca.org/sites/default/files/PACE%20CCSS%20McLaughlin.pdf

Dee, T., & Jacob, B. (2010). The impact of No Child Left Behind on students, teachers, and schools. *Brookings Papers on Economic Activity.* Retrieved from https://www.brookings.edu/wp-content/uploads/2010/09/2010b_bpea_dee.pdf

Every Student Succeeds Act of 2015, P.L. 114-95, 20 U.S.C. § 6301 (2016)

Hay, J., & Davis, J. (2017). *State of the state of expanded learning in California 2016–2017.* Sacramento: California Afterschool Network.

Local Control Funding Formula Guide. (n.d.). Retrieved from the EdSource website: https://edsource.org/2016/local-control-funding-formula-guide-lcff/89272

Lopez, F., Moroney, D., & Vance, F. (2017). *Introduction to 360°/365 professional learning communities.* Chicago, IL: American Institutes for Research.

Mission, Vision, and Values. (n.d.). Retrieved from the Partnership for Children & Youth website: https://www.partnerforchildren.org/about-pcy

No Child Left Behind Act. Retrieved from https://www.congress.gov/bill/107th-congress/house-bill/1/text

Partnership for Children and Youth. (2015). *Student success comes full circle: Leveraging expanded learning opportunities.* Oakland, CA: Author.

Partnership for Children and Youth. (2016a). *Finding common ground: Connecting social-emotional learning during and beyond the school day.* Oakland, CA: Author.

Partnership for Children and Youth. (2016b). *Measuring quality: Assessment tools to evaluate your social-emotional learning practices.* Oakland, CA: Author.

Partnership for Children and Youth. (2017). *Social-emotional learning in expanded learning.* Oakland, CA: Author.

Schonert-Reichl, K., & Zakrzewski, V. (2014, January 8) *How to close the social-emotional gap in teacher training.* Retrieved from https://greatergood.berkeley.edu/article/item/how_to_close_the_social_emotional_gap_in_teacher_training

Yoder, N. (2014). *Teaching the whole child: Instructional practices that support social-emotional learning in three teacher evaluation frameworks.* Washington, DC: Center on Great Teachers & Leaders at American Institutes of Research.

Zakrzewski, V. (2014, January 22). *How to integrate Social-Emotional Learning into Common Core.* Retrieved from https://greatergood.berkeley.edu/article/item/how_to_integrate_social_emotional_learning_into_common_core

CHAPTER 12

SOCIAL AND EMOTIONAL LEARNING IN OUT-OF-SCHOOL TIME

Public Opinion and Policy Landscape

Jodi Grant and Dan Gilbert

OVERVIEW

From educators and parents to law enforcement and business leaders, a growing number of stakeholders around the country agree that social and emotional learning (SEL) is imperative for future success in school, in the workplace, and in life. In the public realm, popular books and articles focused on SEL and similar abilities have garnered attention nationwide, as have the alarm bells by business leaders regarding the types of skills needed but often lacking among prospective employees.

Media coverage, polling data, and anecdotal evidence from all over the country show that businesses are increasingly mobilizing around the need for SEL-related skills, although there is little agreement between sectors or even organizations around the proper terminology for describing those skills. Prominent business leaders have joined together to assert that the

Social and Emotional Learning in Out-of-School Time, pages 201–219

American education system is not consistently producing students who possess the basic skills needed for success in the workplace. They have begun to urge action to produce more highly skilled individuals, and those skills include SEL-related skills.

Ready Nation is an organization of business leaders who work to strengthen the workforce through policies that affect children and youth. Members of Ready Nation have made positive remarks about SEL in congressional testimony, saying, "In order for American businesses to compete successfully in a global economy, employees must have the knowledge, skills and abilities to be communicators, collaborators and critical thinkers" (Pepper, 2014, para. 15). With leadership that includes former CEOs of Procter & Gamble, Macy's, and Kaiser Permanente, the organization has the ears of members of the U.S. Congress from both political parties and offers a fresh approach to explaining the need for SEL programs and support for them in K–12 schools.

In the education realm, trends towards recognition of SEL receded during the time of No Child Left Behind Act, 2001. With the passage of the Every Student Succeeds Act in December of 2015, SEL has made a resurgence as a number of state education agencies and districts have proposed the integration of SEL standards for students. As of February 2017, four states—Illinois, West Virginia, Maine, and Kansas—have adopted comprehensive, free-standing K–12 standards for SEL, and more states have standards in development. Other states have adopted partial SEL standards or guidelines that only cover up to Grade 3 ("State Scan Scorecard," n.d.).

Adding to this trend is the recent creation of the Aspen Institute's National Commission on Social, Emotional, and Academic Development (NCSEAD), a massive effort focused on engaging and energizing communities and policymakers to fully and thoroughly integrate SEL development in the education system. The NCSEAD has achieved substantial buy in from researchers, policy experts, and educators, and has already released an interim report and a research brief that provide a solid foundation for their work moving forward (Jones & Kahn, 2017; National Commission on Social, Emotional, and Academic Development, 2018). The work of the NCSEAD will culminate in a report that will present specific recommendations for improving the way that social and emotional competencies are developed in youth around the country.

All of this movement is exciting for after-school and summer programs founded in youth development that have long been addressing SEL, often with different names. For decades, out-of-school time (OST) programs have tailored their programming to focus on SEL skills such as leadership, resilience/grit, or collaboration. At the same time, more research has demonstrated that after-school and summer programs support the development of social and emotional skills that lead to greater workforce readiness, and a wide array of new research-based guides, tools, and frameworks for implementing and assessing SEL in the OST field have been published in the past few years.

The rise of SEL in public policy and in our national consciousness has not been without impediments. One of the greatest challenges facing many advocates for SEL is the varied ways in which stakeholders discuss, define, and describe SEL. There are more than a dozen terms commonly used for what we consider to be SEL—noncognitive skills, character, nonacademic skills, and 21st century skills, to name but a few. Those using these terms are often inconsistent in their meaning, and the terms themselves are not always interchangeable. In this chapter, we will not attempt to provide any definitive delineation between these different terminologies, but rather share perspectives on the ways terms and ideas may be perceived by the public, policymakers, and stakeholders.

It is also vital that we recognize that, while interest in supporting SEL seems to be growing in many sectors, SEL remains a hot-button topic in the policy realm. Small but vocal groups, often led by concerned parents, have mobilized against the role of the federal government in supporting, measuring, and evaluating SEL in education. These concerns will be expanded on later in the chapter.

At the federal level, constituents motivated by these concerns have effectively lobbied policymakers to block legislation that could advance research and data collection around SEL. At the state level, a number of legislatures have seen the introduction of policies restricting the collection of SEL data from youth.

This chapter is intended to provide you with a solid understanding of the ever-changing public dialogue and policy landscape around SEL in the OST field. The chapter provides several sections of analysis:

- an overview of existing public opinion polling on issues related to SEL,
- data on parent perspectives collected in the Afterschool Alliance's (2014) *America After 3PM* survey,
- a review of media coverage and cultural critiques of SEL in the public sphere, and
- a summary of federal and state politics and policy related to SEL.

THE STATE OF PUBLIC OPINION

Fortunately for the OST field, there is abundant public opinion polling that bolsters the assertion that the American public strongly supports the availability of and public funding for OST programs, and that support for these programs crosses both party lines and geographic differences, with urban and rural voters agreeing on the importance of quality OST programs.

A March 2017 poll by Quinnipiac University found that American voters overwhelmingly opposed the Trump administration's proposed budget cuts to after-school programs, with an incredible 83% of respondents saying that cutting funding for after-school and summer learning programs was a bad idea, including substantial majorities from both Democrats and Republicans (Malloy & Rubenstein, 2017).

A 2017 Phi Delta Kappa (PDK) International poll focusing on the public's attitudes towards public schools found that there was strong agreement that public schools should provide supports to youth before and after school and during the summer; more than 90% of respondents supported public schools providing after-school programs (PDK International, 2017).

Public Opinion: SEL

Public opinion research that is specifically focused on SEL has proven to be fairly elusive and limited in scope, and does not provide a fleshed-out perspective on the opinions of the general public. One major reason for this is the lack of inter-sector agreement on terminology; many polls focus on things like workforce skills, soft skills, or 21st century skills, but because there is so much confusion around the specific skills that fall under each of these terms, it can be difficult to accurately gauge the level of public awareness of, or support for, SEL.

Further complicating the picture is the fact that the preponderance of polling around SEL seems to focus specifically on whether or not people agree that SEL component skills should be taught during the school day, which is an imperfect proxy for their support for the development of these skills in OST settings. Some adults who may not support the development of social and emotional skills in school settings may be more supportive of the development of these skills in after-school and summer learning programs.

Public Opinion: Workforce Readiness Skills

While there is a dearth of specific polling data around SEL, we have an abundance of data around public support for SEL component skills when those skills are considered through the lens of workforce readiness. Research has also found that a number of skills that are broadly considered to be within the SEL umbrella—critical thinking, collaboration, and creativity—are considered vital by employers (American Management Association, 2012).

By using polling around specific workforce readiness skills as a proxy, we are able to get a more comprehensive view of public support for SEL.

Once this analogy is drawn, it becomes easier to assess public support for SEL. The data available suggest that the public and the private sector see the development of SEL skills as a priority. Below is a sampling of data that reveals public support for the development of these skills:

- A 2013 Gallup poll of American adults found that 80% of those surveyed strongly agreed that the education system should teach critical thinking skills, 78% strongly agreed that the education system should teach communication skills, and significant majorities also strongly agreed that creativity and collaboration were important skills (Lopez & Calderon, 2013).
- A 2013 survey published by Northeastern University & FTI Consulting found that nearly 2 out of 3 Americans surveyed, and almost 3 out of every 4 business leaders surveyed, said that it was *more* important for college graduates to be well rounded and possess broader capabilities such as communication skills and problem solving than to have industry-specific expertise (Northeastern News, 2013).
- A 2017 PDK poll found that 82% of Americans surveyed said that it was highly important for schools to help students develop interpersonal skills, such as being cooperative, respectful of others, and persistent at solving problems (PDK International, 2017).
- A 2017 Business Roundtable survey of its member companies found that critical thinking, problem solving, and communication skills were highly relevant to positions in their companies, but that those same skills were difficult to find in qualified candidates for those positions ("2016 BRT Education," 2017).
- A 2013 PDK-Gallup poll of American adults found that 95% of respondents agreed that schools should teach critical thinking skills, 94% agreed that schools should teach communication skills, and 89% agreed that schools should teach students to set meaningful goals (Bushaw & Lopez, 2013).

The polling data reveal strong underlying support from both the private sector and the general public for a wide array of skills that fall under the SEL umbrella. Viewed in the context of a broader public narrative, these data indicate that the public supports a holistic approach to youth development.

PARENT PERSPECTIVES ON SOCIAL AND EMOTIONAL LEARNING IN OUT-OF-SCHOOL TIME

The findings of the 2014 edition of the Afterschool Alliance's household survey, *America After 3PM,* provide valuable insights on the attitudes of parents around the country toward after-school and summer learning programs' development of a variety of skills that fall within the broad scope of social and emotional development.

America After 3PM (Afterschool Alliance, 2014a) found that parents recognize the value of after-school programs in helping children and youth develop social skills, teamwork, leadership, and critical thinking skills. Seventy-nine percent of all respondents agreed that youth benefit from "[developing] social skills" (Afterschool Alliance, 2014a, p. 11) in after-school programs and 67% agreed that youth benefit from "[gaining] workforce skills such as teamwork, leadership, and critical thinking" (Afterschool Alliance, 2014b, p. 16). Furthermore, 71% of respondents agreed with the statement "after-school programs should... develop workforce skills, such as teamwork, leadership and critical thinking" (Afterschool Alliance, 2014a, p. 27).

America After 3PM (Afterschool Alliance, 2014a) provides strong evidence that the parents who have children in after-school programs value and are satisfied with the nonacademic skill development that is occurring in their child's program. They have recent, firsthand experience with OST programs and are much more likely to believe that programs can help youth in a variety of ways that can be tied directly or indirectly to social and emotional skills, including getting youth excited about learning, developing social skills, reducing the likelihood of engaging in risky behaviors, and developing their leadership, critical thinking, and teamwork skills.

SOCIAL AND EMOTIONAL LEARNING IN THE MEDIA

When considering the ways that public opinion around SEL impacts the politics and policies that relate to it, it is critical that we assess the vital role that media coverage and public discourse around SEL play in influencing public opinion. Public conversations relating to and media coverage of SEL tend to be limited and unfocused, but at the same time the public dialogue around SEL is growing quickly.

A recent search of the Nexis database—the industry standard, with 26,000 news and business sources—shows that the terms *SEL* and *social and emotional learning* are used much more frequently than other terms sometimes seen as synonymous with it, such as *social and emotional development, 21st century skills, character development,* and *soft skills.* The same analysis found that the term SEL is being used more frequently in the news media now than in

TABLE 12.1 Mentions of SEL in the Media

Nexis U.S. Newspapers and Wires Database		
Year	**Mentions of SEL**	**Mentions of SEL in Headlines**
2010	107	4
2013	489	26
2015	818	54

the past, but often not as the leading message in stories. Table 12.1 shows the frequency with which SEL has been mentioned in media in the Nexis database over time.

By contrast, there were more than 6,500 mentions of "after-school program" in the Nexis U.S. Newspapers and Wires database *in just the first quarter* of 2015.

During the time period reviewed, the overlap between coverage of SEL and OST programming has been comparatively small. In 2010, just six of the 107 SEL stories mentioned after-school programs; in 2013, 26 of the 489 SEL stories mentioned after-school programs; and in 2015, 21 of the 818 SEL stories mentioned after-school programs.

SEL is referred to in diverse contexts by the media, often being positioned as a part of the solution to a host of problems afflicting youth and our society. The three terms that most frequently occur in conjunction with SEL are "business," "violence/bully," and "testing."

CRITIQUES OF SOCIAL AND EMOTIONAL LEARNING IN THE PUBLIC SPHERE

There are a variety of critiques that have arisen recently in response to the growing emphasis on SEL-related skills. These critiques vary in nature and origin, coming from concerned parents, academics, and policymakers. A few prominent critiques are elaborated on below:

- Some critics categorically oppose the inclusion of SEL in schools on ideological grounds, arguing that it is an intrusion into what they consider to be exclusively a family matter.
- Some consider the lack of explicitly morality-focused content within the SEL framework to be problematic.
- Academic critics attack the legitimacy of claims relating to the positive impacts of SEL, often focusing on the common theme that SEL research either (a) overinflates the impact of SEL-focused program-

ming, or (b) leaves out key components of what it should mean for programming to be "successful."
- A handful of policymakers and advocates are concerned that measuring the social and emotional development of youth may be incorporated into high-stakes testing systems.

There are also a number of criticisms leveled at particular SEL-related skills, but most of them tend to center around the broad themes discussed above. There is one particular component skill, however, that seems to have drawn some unique criticisms: grit. Attacks upon the pedagogy around grit tend to posit that the current focus, which is frequently centered on helping to develop grit in low-income youth, can prove to be problematic when it is viewed in a historical perspective that values educational equity (Herold, 2015; Strauss, 2016; Tough, 2016).

Critics claim that many proponents of grit are focusing on addressing a nonexistent deficit, in that there is little evidence that low-income youth have *less* grit or mastery of social and emotional skills than their medium- and high-income counterparts. They often further claim that this focus on a "grit deficit" distracts from the fact that low-income youth are frequently in underfunded schools that provide inadequate supports. Because the world of education funding is frequently a zero-sum game (i.e., dollars are provided for one program by taking them away from another), the resources directed towards developing grit can take resources and attention away from the core operations of schools.

While there are exceptions, critiques of SEL typically refrain from claiming that the development of grit, perseverance, and other social and emotional skills is not desirable. The bulk of the critiques tend to focus on the ways that the discussion around developing these skills must reflect context, account for existing research, and not distract from the ever-present need to rectify the education system's existing deficits and inequities.

FEDERAL POLICY: SEL AND OST

While there are no existing federal laws that are specifically focused on SEL, there are a plethora of laws and regulations that touch upon SEL in complex ways that can either provide support or barriers to programs that help youth develop social and emotional skills.

There are two distinct aspects of policy around SEL in OST. First, there is the existing set of laws, regulations, and guidance that determines how SEL can be supported through out-of-school programming. Second are the ongoing efforts of SEL advocates to incorporate SEL-friendly language into future laws and regulations. We will portray the existing policy landscape around SEL—especially around ESSA (2015) and Child Care Development Block Grants (CCDBG, 2014)—and will then move on to the politics that will likely affect future SEL policy initiatives, and discuss how language can help advance or impede those efforts.

Existing Policy Around SEL and OST

The two largest federal funding streams for out-of-school programs are the 21st Century Community Learning Centers, which is authorized in ESSA (2015) and the CCDBG (2014). Both laws were recently reauthorized and include changes that are beneficial to the advancement of SEL in OST. While these laws do not include specific language regarding SEL, they do present opportunities to elevate it.

ESSA (2015) provides flexibility to states around how they can use federal education funding, and there are several ways for OST programs to weigh in on the policies that state and local education agencies develop under the law. The three major avenues within ESSA (2015) that can be used to advance SEL- and OST-friendly policies and systemic supports are (a) new SEL-friendly language in Title II, (b) a requirement that states and districts develop school accountability systems that include a new indicator of school quality or student success, and (c) a new flexible block grant program.

ESSA: New Language in Title II

The purpose of Title II of ESSA (2015) is to increase the effectiveness of educators, in part by providing funding for professional development. New language in Title II provides a potential funding source for SEL-focused programming by allowing Title II funding to be used to support the development of "skills essential for learning readiness and academic success" (ESSA, 2015, p. 129).

After-school staff also have an opportunity to influence the ways that SEL is addressed by Title II–funded teacher preparation programs. To receive grants under Title II, state and local agencies are required to undertake meaningful consultation in developing an application, which includes involvement of "other organizations or partners with relevant and demonstrated expertise in programs and activities" designed to advance teacher training and preparation" (ESSA, 2015, p. 129). OST providers can participate in this consultative process to encourage streamlining professional development training across in-school and out-of-school professionals in areas like SEL through use of consistent language and setting common goals across settings.

ESSA: The Fifth Indicator

ESSA (2015) can also be used to advance SEL through school accountability systems. On top of the four required indicators required for school accountability systems, ESSA introduced a school quality or student success indicator, sometimes referred to as a "nonacademic indicator," or "fifth indicator," that weighs into the accountability systems that states have created. ESSA does not dictate what that indicator should be, and states were given a significant amount of autonomy in identifying the new indicators that have been incorporated in their plans.

After-school and summer learning programs have a long history of tracking indicators that promote academic success, such as student school-day attendance, reducing suspensions, positive behavioral changes like increased homework completion and class participation, school engagement and connectedness, and parent involvement. Research shows that students who regularly attend quality OST programs make gains on these indicators, and many of these indicators are also closely linked to social and emotional competencies. As states continue improving their accountability systems, SEL and OST should both be central components of the discussion.

The new indicators that have gained the most traction in state plans are actually very much linked to student academic success, and include chronic absenteeism and measures of college and career readiness. Many state plans also reflect stakeholder discussions around areas such as school climate and access to a well-rounded education that includes after-school programming. Research tells us that high-quality, SEL-focused OST programs contribute to desirable outcomes in youth, such as positive feelings about their schools and improved school-day attendance rates (Durlak, Weissberg, & Pachan, 2010). These findings are particularly meaningful for states that included chronic absenteeism rates or school climate surveys as part of their new indicators.

ESSA: Student Support and Academic Enrichment Grants

ESSA (2015) includes another new flexible block grant (Title IV Part A), entitled the Student Support and Academic Enrichment (SSAE, 2015) grants. This flexible grant program, authorized for $1.65 billion in fiscal year 2017, is intended to both (a) "provide all students with access to a well-rounded education" (p. 129), and (b) "improve school conditions for student learning" (p. 129), both of which provide states and districts with the opportunity to leverage federal funding towards SEL-related programming.

Title IV Part A (SSAE, 2015) specifically allows funds to be used in a variety of ways that can help advance the social and emotional development of students by providing funding that will help to "establish learning environments that enhance students' effective learning skills" (p. 129). The law allows funds to be used to foster "safe, healthy, supportive" school environments, which research has found to be a foundational requirement for high-quality SEL experiences (Zins, Bloodworth, Weissberg, & Walberg, 2007). The block grant also allows funding to be used to help develop "relationship-building skills, such as effective communication" and "problem solving and conflict resolution" skills (p. 129).

While these funding opportunities are most relevant for OST programs that are operated by or in close cooperation with schools or districts, OST programs and other community organizations may be able to benefit from these funds as well by partnering with schools.

Child Care Development Block Grant

The CCDBG (2014), administered by the Department of Health and Human Services (HHS), is another funding stream for OST programs that support SEL. The law explicitly focuses on the "wellness" of youth served. As research continues to reveal the critical role that SEL plays in the development of youth and as schools pay more and more attention to the ways that SEL bolsters student success, the way that HHS defines wellness may begin to reflect the increasing profile of SEL.

There are opportunities for SEL advocates in OST to advance policy around CCDBG (2014) at the federal level. Legislation requires HHS to provide guidance for state child care agencies and solicit updated state child care plans every 3 years. As of this writing, states are developing their 2018 updated plans, and SEL experts and members of the OST field can provide feedback on those plans to increase the profile and importance of SEL within them.

HHS also has a relatively new Office of Child Care and a new National Center on Afterschool and Summer Enrichment that provide online resources and platforms to advance best practices and highlight how states can help programs to successfully develop children's social and emotional competencies.

The Politics of SEL

Despite broad support in other realms, SEL is a contentious issue in Congress, due to small but passionate groups of activists that oppose government involvement in SEL. The pushback is rooted in the critiques of SEL that were covered earlier in this chapter, and stems from the belief that lessons relating to nonacademic topics such as discipline, self-control, and persistence are best addressed by parents and families alone. These critics oppose the inclusion of any SEL interventions or programs in schools, with some also opposing the implementation and assessment of any kind of SEL supports.

Case Study: The Strengthening Education Through Research Act

A recent example of grassroots opposition to SEL is the unsuccessful effort to pass the Strengthening Education Through Research Act (SETRA, 2013) by the 114th Congress. SETRA was an attempted reauthorization of the Education Sciences Reform Act (ESRA, 2002), which established the Institute of Education Sciences as an independent research arm of the U.S. Department of Education (ED). ESRA (2002) and SETRA (2013) both delineate specific areas of research in education that *may* be undertaken—for example, effective literacy instruction and closing the achievement gap.

When it was originally introduced during the 113th Congress, SETRA (2013) included language that proposed SEL as an acceptable domain of research for the Institute of Education Sciences to pursue. The bill language read: "may include research on social and emotional learning, and the acquisition of competencies and skills, including the ability to think critically, solve complex problems, evaluate evidence, and communicate effectively" (p. 28). This language triggered vocal opposition. Opponents of SETRA frequently cited the work of Dr. Karen Effrem, a pediatrician and researcher who is president of the organization Education Liberty Watch, which, according to its website "supports knowledge-based education that promotes the American Creed, free enterprise, limited government, and the primacy of parental rights" ("Our Mission," n.d., para. 1). Effrem (2016) criticized the SEL provision in SETRA, asserting that it authorized "psychological profiling of our children" and aimed to "collect, analyze, and share the most intimate details about our children—the workings of their minds" (para. 1). Effrem's characterization of the bill galvanized a grassroots opposition that included bloggers with a tremendous social media reach. The messages proved to be very effective, and conservative lawmakers successfully held up final passage of SETRA because of the SEL provision.

The Evolution of Language in ESSA

To avoid scenarios like the one that plagued SETRA, policymakers often adopt language to describe, but not directly mention, SEL in an effort to allow for SEL-related programming to be implemented without raising red flags to its dissenters. During the Obama administration, the U.S. Department of Education tended to use the phrase "noncognitive skills" to describe SEL competencies in both speeches and in programmatic initiatives. Former Secretary of Education Arne Duncan described noncognitive skills as encompassing "grit and self-regulation and executive function, [which] can help children flourish and overcome significant challenges throughout their lifetimes" (Duncan, 2013, para. 69). Under the Obama Administration, noncognitive skills were promoted widely, particularly in early education and college readiness.

Congress initially took a similar approach to describing SEL competencies in 2015 in its bipartisan ESEA reauthorization proposal, the Every Child Achieves Act (2015). This bill was the foundation for ESSA, which was signed into law in December 2015. As the House and Senate negotiated a final bill to reauthorize ESEA, earlier language relating to "'nonacademic' skills" was dropped and lawmakers ultimately decided to replace it with the language "skills essential for learning readiness and academic success" (ESSA, 2015, p. 129). This language is now law.

SEL in Trump's Department of Education

How much support there may be for SEL-focused initiatives under the Trump administration is unknown. During a February 2017 interview, current Secretary of Education Betsy Devos seemed supportive of incorporating more character development programming in schools, which many in the SEL field view as analogous to SEL (Thomas, 2017). It is uncertain whether Secretary Devos's definition of character development is aligned with SEL.

The Carl D. Perkins Career and Technical Education Act

As of this writing, the 115th Congress is working on reauthorizing the Carl D. Perkins Career and Technical Education Act (2006). Among other things, the bill in its current form would include a new focus on employability skills. The bipartisan bill has broad support from the career and technical education community and is popular on Capitol Hill, having already passed the U.S. House of Representatives. Its bipartisan origin is important to note, as this increases its chances of surviving a change of majority control in the U.S. Congress. Specific wins for the SEL community in the most recent version of the bill include the inclusion of "employability skills" as an explicit purpose in the most recent version of the bill:

> The purpose of this chapter is to develop more fully the academic knowledge and technical and employability skills of secondary education students and

postsecondary education students who elect to enroll in career and technical education programs. (House Report 114-728, 2016, p. 46)

The efforts to include language in the bill that is related to employability skills have been viewed favorably by both democrats and republicans. Pro-SEL advocates, such as the Collaborative for Academic, Social, and Emotional Learning (CASEL) and the Committee for Children, have worked closely with House champions on language related to the need to incorporate teaching employability skills as part of a high-quality career and technical education. Furthermore, language from ED's Employability Skills framework includes a number of SEL-related core competencies ("Employability Skills," n.d.). Advocates from the business community—such as the Business Roundtable and the Chamber of Commerce—have also advocated for the inclusion of teaching SEL-related skills in an updated career and technical education curriculum.

STATE POLICY AROUND SEL AND OST

Because of the wide array of ways that SEL is being advanced and obstructed throughout the states, and due to the volatility of the state policies that relate to it, we will not attempt to provide any in-depth exploration of what is occurring in individual states; any summation would become quickly outdated. We will provide a quick overview of the current state of ESSA implementation throughout the 50 states, discuss the opportunity for states to leverage CCDBG (2014) funds to provide SEL-related standards and professional development, and outline one relevant policy trend that is already impacting SEL in some states: student data privacy laws.

ESSA Plans and Implementation

In many states the most significant policy issues relating to SEL and OST are directly related to the implementation of plans around ESSA. States have finalized the statewide accountability systems that include new indicators that often relate either directly or indirectly to SEL.

According to an Afterschool Alliance review of state policies, as of September 2017, at least 32 states and the District of Columbia were moving forward with indicators that included chronic absenteeism rates, and four more were using other measures of student attendance within their state ESSA plans. While chronic absenteeism is not a direct measure of SEL, studies have found that it can serve as a proxy measure for an engaging and secure school environment or for social and emotional competencies, which makes this particular development very promising (Schanzenbach & Mumford, 2016; Tough, 2016). As of this writing, at least 14 states are including other measures that can either impact or be impacted by SEL, such as engagement surveys, behavioral data, and learning environment surveys.

There are a variety of resources that provide additional perspective on the ways that states are implementing SEL in the new ESSA law, including the Learning Policy Institute's April 2017 Report, *Encouraging Social and Emotional Learning in the Context of New Accountability*, which offers guidance for how states and districts can identify helpful measures of SEL (Melnick, Cook-Harvey, & Darling-Hammond, 2017); and CASEL's brief released that same month, *How State Planning for the Every Student Succeeds Act Can Promote Student Academic, Social, and Emotional Learning: An Examination of Five Key Strategies*, which provides valuable insight for how state and local education agencies are leveraging ESSA to improve SEL outcomes for youth around the country (Gayl, 2017).

Child Care Development Block Grants

Many federal laws provide significant flexibility at the state and local levels. The CCDBG permits states to submit plans that highlight how the state agency administering the grants will encourage and develop quality among participating child care providers. States can adopt quality standards that meet the needs and goals of their state. As the law serves children up to age 13, there are often multiple sets of standards and professional development provided for infant care, toddler care, nursery, and school age. State-level efforts to promote standards that incorporate developmentally appropriate SEL practices and professional development opportunities offer a substantial opportunity to provide more youth with intentional SEL skill development opportunities in OST programs.

Student Data Privacy Laws

While states are developing new accountability systems and data collection instruments to help implement new plans under ESSA, there is also a trend in some states that is concerning for advocates of SEL. In many states, there appears to be an effort to sharply limit both the types of data and the quantity of data that schools can collect. According to a September 2016 report by the Data Quality Campaign (2016), between 2013 and 2016, 36 states passed 73 student privacy bills into law. While ensuring that student data are secure is an important priority, many of these student data privacy bills may prevent schools, states, and even OST programs from gathering data, especially SEL-related data, that help them better serve youth.

While many of these laws are intended to prohibit the collection of non-academic data to prevent those data from being incorporated in school accountability systems, it is an unfortunate truth that these laws will have a broader unintended effect of restricting valuable data that are collected by youth-serving organizations.

CONSIDERATIONS MOVING FORWARD

Looking ahead, the political momentum around SEL, both positive and negative, will likely continue to grow. The roles that policy will play in the ever-expanding SEL ecosystem are diverse and critical. Policy will reinforce critical supports for SEL in both school and OST settings through the development and enforcement of critical standards applicable to all states, dictating what skills are developmentally appropriate for youth and encouraging schools and OST programs to work towards those standards. Policy will fund research that will help us understand what the best strategies are for advancing SEL both through curricula and through the development of safe and supportive learning environments. Policy will provide funding for SEL-focused professional development opportunities for school educators and out-of-school staff. And, most importantly, policy will help to ensure that all youth have the opportunity to develop these critical skills by providing funding for high-quality, evidence-based OST programs that help develop SEL competencies.

One of the greatest opportunities for the OST field as it seeks to support SEL through policy may be the chance to engage the business sector in policy development and advocacy around SEL, given that businesses increasingly appear to be advocating for employability skills. Many businesses appear to not yet be aware of the role OST programs play in teaching the skills that they are advocating for, because businesses often use different terminology than after-school advocates. Business leaders that are aware of the benefits of OST programs often understand that OST programming is critical to workforce readiness, and many are willing to help champion programs.

There are cultural and racial issues that are sometimes overlooked in discussions around SEL, and it is important that diverse voices be brought into the conversation. SEL has encountered opposition in certain communities due to the fact that it can be interpreted as advancing one culture's values over others. It is important to be cognizant of the complexities and pitfalls that must be navigated in discussions when dealing with how SEL interacts with factors such as equity, race, class, and culture, and it is vital that specific populations or cultures not be stigmatized or feel stigmatized as a result of the focus on promoting the development of social and emotional skills.

The assessment/data/testing dynamic also requires careful treading. Experts in the field of SEL research generally suggest that comprehensive and/or compulsive measurement of SEL is not yet warranted, and the field should be wary of efforts to measure SEL across the board. We must carefully consider precisely why and how SEL is being injected in both federal and state policy, and whether it is a good idea for states to make schools formally accountable for developing social and emotional skills in their students.

Skills like leadership, teamwork, problem-solving, and communication continue to be ever more popular among businesses, parents, teachers, and policy makers. These are skills that after-school and summer programs continue to cultivate in youth, which is one reason why high-income parents now spend almost seven times as much on these opportunities than low-income parents, who find many of these experiences out of their financial reach (Duncan & Murnane, 2011). If all students are to have an equal chance to succeed academically, socially, and in the workforce, policy must play a large role in helping provide opportunities to develop these skills for all students, and not just those who can afford them.

The state and local momentum behind SEL policy is significant and growing. Many states have incorporated SEL-related measures in their ESSA implementation plans. Meanwhile, both federal and state-level advocates are increasingly drawing attention to the overlap between SEL, workforce readiness, and OST. The challenges and opportunities around SEL have quickly become front-burner issues for supporters of SEL and OST.

REFERENCES

2016 BRT Education and Workforce Survey: Results and analysis (2017, June 7). Retrieved from the Business Roundtable website: https://www.businessroundtable.org/resources/2016-brt-education-and-workforce-survey

Afterschool Alliance. (2014a). *America after 3pm.* Washington, DC: Author. Retrieved from http://www.afterschoolalliance.org/documents/AA3PM-2014/AA3PM_National_Report.pdf

Afterschool Alliance. (2014b). *America after 3pm topline questionnaire.* Washington, DC: Author. Retrieved from http://www.afterschoolalliance.org/documents/AA3PM-2015/AA3PM_Topline_Questionnaire.06.09.15.pdf

American Management Association. (2012). *AMA Critical Skills Survey.* Retrieved from http://www.amanet.org/uploaded/2012-Critical-Skills-Survey.pdf

Bushaw, W., & Lopez, S. (2013). Which way do we go? The 45th annual PDK/Gallup Poll of the public's attitudes toward the public schools. *Kappan Magazine, 95*(1), 9–25. Retrieved from http://pdkintl.org/noindex/2013_PDKGallup.pdf

Carl D. Perkins Career and Technical Education Act of 2006. 20 U.S.C. 2301 (2007)

Child Care Development Block Grant Reauthorization Act of 2014. P.L. 113-186, 42 U.S.C. 9801 (2015)

Data Quality Campaign. (2016). *Student data privacy legislation.* Retrieved from https://2pido73em67o3eytaq1cp8au-wpengine.netdna-ssl.com/wp-content/uploads/2016/09/DQC-Legislative-summary-09302016.pdf

Duncan, A. (2013, July 2). *The charter mindset shift: From conflict to co-conspirators* (Education Secretary Duncan's remarks to the National Alliance for Public Charter Schools 2013 "Delivering on the Dream" conference). Retrieved from https://www.ed.gov/news/speeches/charter-mindset-shift-conflict-co-conspirators

Duncan, G. J., & Murnane, R. J. (2011). *Whither opportunity? Rising inequality and the uncertain life chances of low-income children.* New York, NY: Russell Sage Foundation.

Durlak, J. A., Weissberg, R. P., & Pachan, M. (2010). A meta-analysis of after-school programs that seek to promote personal and social skills in children and adolescents. *American Journal of Community Psychology, 45*(3–4), 294–309. doi:10.1007/s10464-010-9300-6

Education Sciences Reform Act of 2002. 20 U.S.C. 3419 (2003)

Effrem, K. R. (2016, January 4). *Four reasons why student privacy is in grave danger—unless Congress rejects this bill.* Retrieved from http://thepulse2016.com/karen-r-effrem/2016/01/04/13210/

Employability Skills. (n.d.). Retrieved from Perkins Collaborative Resource Network: http://cte.ed.gov/initiatives/employability-skills-framework

Every Child Achieves Act of 2015, S. 1177, 114th Cong. (2015)

Every Student Succeeds Act of 2015, P.L. 114-95, 20 U.S.C. § 6301 (2016)

Gayl, C. L. (2017). *How state planning for the Every Student Succeeds Act (ESSA) can promote student academic, social, and emotional learning: An examination of five key strategies* (CASEL Brief). Retrieved from http://www.casel.org/wp-content/uploads/2017/04/ESSA-and-SEL-Five-Strategies-April-2017-041717.pdf

Herold, B. (2015, January 25). *Is grit racist?* (Weblog). Retrieved from http://blogs.edweek.org/edweek/DigitalEducation/2015/01/is_grit_racist.html

House Report No. 114-728, at 46 (2016) Retrieved from: https://www.congress.gov/114/crpt/hrpt728/CRPT-114hrpt728.pdf

Jones, S. M., & Kahn, J. (2017). *The evidence base for how we learn.* Retrieved from https://www.aspeninstitute.org/publications/evidence-base-learn/

Lopez, S. J., & Calderon, V. J. (2013). *Americans say U.S. schools should teach "soft" skills.* Retrieved from http://news.gallup.com/poll/164060/americans-say-schools-teach-soft-skills.aspx

Malloy, T., & Rubenstein, P. (2017, March 24). American voters want to save Big Bird, Quinnipiac University National Poll finds; Most oppose spending cuts in Trump budget (Rep.). Retrieved from https://poll.qu.edu/images/polling/us/us03242017_Ukux36wm.pdf/

Melnick, H., Cook-Harvey, C., & Darling-Hammond, L. (2017). *Encouraging social and emotional learning in the context of new accountability.* Retrieved from https://learningpolicyinstitute.org/product/encouraging-social-emotional-learning-new-accountability-report?utm_source=LPIMasterList&utm_campaign=357a30710e-Raikes-SEL_2017_04_14&utm_medium=email&utm_term=0_7e60dfa1d8-357a30710e-42332939

National Commission on Social, Emotional, and Academic Development. (2018). *How learning happens: Supporting students' social, emotional, and academic development.* Retrieved from https://www.aspeninstitute.org/publications/learning-happens-supporting-students-social-emotional-academic-development/

No Child Left Behind Act of 2001, P.L. 107-110, 20 U.S.C. §6319 (2002)

Northeastern News. (2013, September 17). *Most Americans and business leaders want colleges to provide a broad-based education.* Retrieved from https://news.northeastern.edu/2013/09/innovation-summit-2013/

Our Mission. (n.d.). Retrieved from Education Liberty Watch website: http://edlibertywatch.org/our-mission/

Pepper, J. E., Jr. (2014). *Expanding access to quality early learning: The strong start for America's Children Act* (Testimony before United States Senate Committee on Health, Education, Labor, & Pensions). https://www.gpo.gov/fdsys/pkg/CHRG-113shrg22610/html/CHRG-113shrg22610.htm

Phi Delta Kappa International. (2017). *Academic achievement isn't the only mission: Americans overwhelmingly support investments in career preparation, personal skills.* Retrieved from http://pdkpoll.org/assets/downloads/PDKnational_poll_2017.pdf

Schanzenbach, D. W., & Mumford, M. (2016). *Lessons for broadening school accountability under the Every Student Succeeds Act.* Retrieved from http://www.hamiltonproject.org/assets/files/lessons_school_accountability_essa.pdf

State Scan Scorecard Project. (n.d.). Retrieved from the CASEL website: https://casel.org/state-scan-scorecard-project/

Strauss, V. (2016, May 10). The problem with teaching "grit" to poor kids? They already have it. Here's what they really need. *The Washington Post.* Retrieved from https://www.washingtonpost.com/news/answer-sheet/wp/2016/05/10/the-problem-with-teaching-grit-to-poor-kids-they-already-have-it-heres-what-they-really-need/?utm_term=.74cff756068a

Strengthening Education through Research Act of 2015. S. 227, 114th Cong. (2015)

Thomas, C. (2017, February 16). *A new direction on education.* Retrieved from https://townhall.com/columnists/calthomas/2017/02/16/a-new-direction-on-education-n2286379

Tough, P. (2016, June). How kids learn resilience. *The Atlantic.* Retrieved from https://www.theatlantic.com/magazine/archive/2016/06/how-kids-really-succeed/480744/

Zins, J. E., Bloodworth, M., Weissberg, R., & Walberg, H. (2007). The scientific base linking social and emotional learning to school success. *Journal of Educational and Psychological Consultation, 17*(2–3), 191–210. Retrieved from http://www.tandfonline.com/doi/abs/10.1080/10474410701413145

CHAPTER 13

SEL

Fertile Ground for Philanthropy

Rebecca Goldberg, Haviland Rummel Sharvit, and Polly Singh

SOCIAL AND EMOTIONAL LEARNING CATCHES ON

A growing body of research highlights that young people need to develop a broad range of skills and capacities beyond academic knowledge to succeed in school, work, citizenship, and life. As a result, the funding community's interest in social and emotional learning (SEL) has grown. Foundations use a wide array of terms to describe SEL, including character development, noncognitive traits and habits, inter- and intra-personal skills, deeper learning, personal success skills, pro-social development, 21st-century skills, and others. For most foundations, the interest in SEL stemmed from conversations with researchers, practitioners, policymakers, youth, and others in the field about their aspirations for young people, the current systems in place to support young people's success, and the gaps that need to be addressed.

Foundations traditionally like metrics, measurement, and evidence, and SEL can be an ambiguous and challenging field for funders that want to assess young people's social and emotional skills. While most consider

Social and Emotional Learning in Out-of-School Time, pages 221–242

these skills essential, it is apparent that the field lacks common terminology, agreed-upon outcomes, and means to assess them.

As the education community increasingly values the role of SEL in young people's development and education, practitioners, advocates, and funders see an opportunity for the out-of-school time (OST) field to share its expertise in youth development as foundational to supporting youth SEL. It is critical for OST practitioners to be well prepared to explicitly support young people's SEL, and it is equally critical to create high-quality environments and programs to support positive youth outcomes. With its youth development approach, the OST field is well positioned to contribute to and provide leadership in the education community on SEL.

FUNDERS GALVANIZE

An early October 2014 convening, titled "Creating Many More Effective Learners" and hosted by the Bridgespan Group, brought together nearly 40 leading researchers, school district leaders, intermediaries, and funders invested in SEL for brainstorming and agenda setting focused on moving the field forward. The conversation continued a few weeks later at the 2014 Grantmakers for Education conference in Miami, where a group of foundations tested the funding community's interest in SEL by hosting a breakfast meeting. Adding this off-program convening to an already packed week of events, the 7:00 a.m. breakfast was scheduled with the hope of getting a handful of foundations to attend. Much to their surprise, over 50 people filled the room. Clearly, SEL had caught on. Foundations didn't yet know what the field needed, or what to call it, but they agreed it was important for supporting young people's success, and that there was value in understanding each other's investments and possibly coordinating.

Following that meeting, a group of foundations came together to fund a landscape survey (conducted by the Parthenon Group in 2015) to better understand the philanthropic community's interest in young people's nonacademic outcomes, the motivations and strategies behind investments in this space, and where foundations were deploying funds.

> "There was a series of conversations and meetings bubbling up among the philanthropic community around these nonacademic youth outcomes. The participants included funders that had been working on education for decades, as well as funders that were newly interested in the space, which ended up being an interesting catalyst," says Itai Dinour, educator portfolio lead at the Einhorn Family Charitable Trust. "It seemed that we had a real interest in minimizing duplication and working together. The first step was to do a landscape analysis (a typical first step in philanthropy) to figure out if we were actually talking about the same thing, what efforts we were funding, and if we

> had an interest in working together." (I. Dinour, personal communication, September 19, 2017)

The survey found that the 73 participating foundations accounted for approximately $285 million in annual grantmaking in support of social and emotional outcomes, spread across multiple age ranges, settings, and activities. Further, 90% of survey respondents stated that their funding in this space would remain steady or increase over the next 10 years, and about half reported plans for a multi-year strategy ranging from 3 to 10 years (EY-Parthenon, 2015).

The most common motivations for foundations to fund SEL initiatives included impacting life success, improving equity, and driving academic success. Zoe Stemm-Calderon, director of education at the Raikes Foundation, explained:

> We recognize that our education system is inequitable. It was designed that way. We are trying to change that. We see understanding the science of learning and development as a critical fuel for those efforts, as well as helping the field understand how to use data... so we can be better at getting better. (Z. Stemm-Calderon, personal communication, September 20, 2017)

Funders were also motivated by the need to support the future workforce, promote holistic youth development, and establish a more complete definition of a quality education.

> "As we were looking at the research on what leads to good outcomes in the workplace and in the education system, it seemed like there was an emergent body of research that suggested there was an important aspect that we might be missing," said Sameer Gadkaree, senior program officer at the Joyce Foundation. "At the Joyce Foundation, we refer to these attributes as personal success skills." (S. Gadkaree, personal communication, September 18, 2017)

The survey found that while there are funders with significant levels of grantmaking across all age ranges, the largest number of funders focus on middle and high school-age youth.

> Research from leaders like James Heckman and SRI International showed that these skills were important across the age and stage continuum, and even for adults, the skills were considered malleable, determinative of life and workplace success, and could be worked on across the spectrum. That was an important consideration for our foundation. (S. Gadkaree, personal communication, as cited in Shechtman, 2016)

Many of the funders focus grantmaking on service delivery and professional development, but funding is also aimed at explicitly supporting field-building research, measurement and assessment, policy and advocacy, evaluation, and promotion and dissemination. The most powerful aspirations for funders to engage in the SEL field involve the spread of evidence-based practices and broader integration with education reform. However, funders have varying ways of measuring success towards those outcomes.

> We think about two different ways of measuring success. Are there instances where we can show something at scale where we move student outcomes? In our work in studying and promoting mindsets, we are potentially talking about tens of thousands of students. We also measure how we are influencing broader policy and thinking, and infusing how we are thinking about personal success skills. (S. Gadkaree, personal communication, September 18, 2017)

While much of the SEL conversation among researchers seemed focused on its role in K–12 education, only about 10% ($29.4 million) of the total funding reported in the survey was targeted to K–12 schools and educators. In contrast, about 27% ($75.6 million) was targeted to after-school, summer, and youth development programs and practitioners, and another 8% ($22.3 million) was targeted to community-based organizations (EY-Parthenon, 2015).

> So many of these broader social and emotional competencies are developed in [OST]. What we are really trying to do is build a system that supports quality in OST, and supporting SEL is part of the definition of quality. At Raikes, we focus on how we can help OST programs continuously improve and get better, primarily in Washington state. (Z. Stemm-Calderon, personal communication, September 20, 2017)

Three national funders that have primarily focused their approach and funding for SEL on the OST field include the S. D. Bechtel, Jr. Foundation, the Susan Crown Exchange, and The Wallace Foundation. Descriptions of each of these foundations' strategies are included below.

Grantmakers for Thriving Youth

With data showing a critical mass of funders in this space and potentially long-term interest in funding SEL (EY-Parthenon, 2015), there was a clear opportunity for the philanthropic community to consider how to coordinate, identify unmet needs, and fill gaps in the funding landscape. The differences in strategy and focus among the funders were not so fundamental that they represented a barrier to potential collaboration, and at the least, coordination.

> What came out of the initial conversations and landscape study was the recognition that funders need to be better coordinated and do more together. For years, we have been funding siloed, competing projects. We need to stop funding that way. We need to step back and recognize that what we all want is to build the equitable education system that our nation requires and our kids deserve, and fund more collaboratively towards that vision. We are part of the problem about why this field is so fractured. (Z. Stemm-Calderon, personal communication, September 20, 2017)

Ultimately, the group developed a steering committee of 16 diverse foundations, now called Grantmakers for Thriving Youth (GTY), that works to advance a comprehensive approach to learning and development that will enable all young people to acquire the skills and capacities needed for success in learning, work, citizenship, and life. The approach is coordinated and collaborative, recognizing the risk of burdening the field with fractured, duplicative initiatives that strain organizational capacity or act at cross-purposes to GTY's goal. The group represents both local and national funders, with individual investment sizes ranging from less than $1 million to greater than $10 million.

GTY members share the belief that positive environments, relationships, and experiences are critical to developing these important skills and capacities, yet structural inequities and other factors prevent many young people from accessing the learning and developmental experiences they need. "One hope was that through the funders collaborative, we could surface policy implications and policies that offer change for communities, districts, states, and even at the federal level" (S. Gadkaree, personal communication, September 18, 2017).

The three main strategies of GTY are to inform and engage the broader philanthropic community, connect and build the capacity of the foundations on GTY's steering committee, and catalyze and influence grantmaking through GTY priority issue workgroups. There are five main workgroups:

- *Adult Practice*: Building the capacity of adults (teachers, principals, OST staff/organizational leaders) across learning settings to foster broad skills and capacities in youth, including scaling/spreading effective practice, addressing the capacity needs of the field's anchor organizations, and supporting networks of practitioners engaging in innovative practice and improvement.
- *Communications*: Changing the narrative around the capacities and capabilities of young people, and engaging in strategic communications to targeted audiences about SEL, including families and policymakers.
- *Equity, Diversity, and Inclusion*: Defining equity, diversity, and inclusion, connecting SEL and equity conversations in the field, and

ensuring all GTY efforts proceed with an understanding and focus on equity.

- *OST*: Delving into challenges/opportunities related to OST, including broadening access to professional development and effective practices, curating/disseminating research and resources, and informing the National Commission on Social, Emotional, and Academic Development (SEAD).
- *Policy*: Building the capacity of the field to advance supportive policies, primarily at state and local levels.

While funders cited the lack of consistent measures of skills as one of the biggest challenges in the field, there is no workgroup focused on measurement under GTY because of the existence of a separate collaborative dedicated specifically to the issue. The Funder Collaborative for Innovative Measurement (FCIM) was formed in 2015 by a funder group that overlaps significantly with members of GTY.

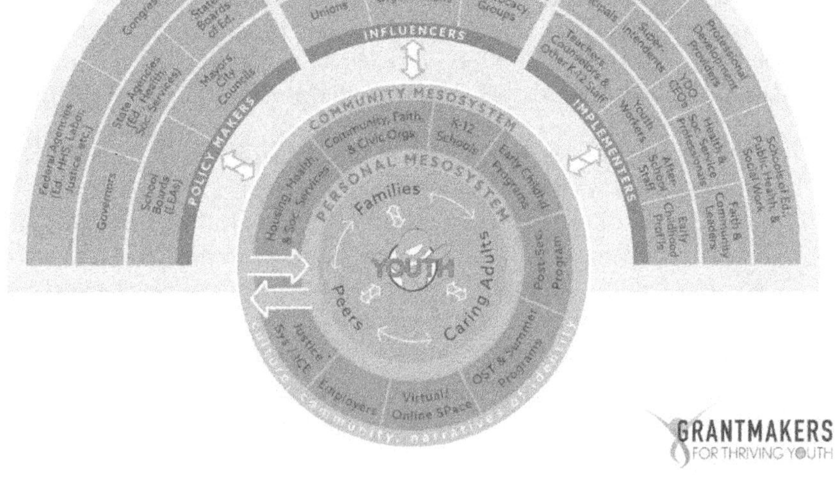

Figure 13.1 Thriving youth ecosystem.

NATIONAL COMMISSION ON SOCIAL, EMOTIONAL, AND ACADEMIC DEVELOPMENT (SEAD)

Launched in 2016, SEAD seeks to advance a new vision of what constitutes success in schools: the full integration of social, emotional, and academic development to ensure every young person is prepared to thrive in school and in life.

> As the funders' collaborative became more interested in figuring out ways to nurture greater collaboration and field building, one of the most concrete examples was the idea of a commission. Many perspectives and voices went into the idea. Soliciting, listening to, and evolving the plan based on feedback from a large community of stakeholders was key. (I. Dinour, personal communication, September 19, 2017)

Drawing on research and promising practices, the commission explores how to make social, emotional, and academic development part of the fabric of every school. Along the way, the commission engages educators, families, community leaders, researchers, and policymakers to identify challenges and opportunities and learn crucial lessons from those engaged in this work.

While the commission is clear on its school focus, it does recognize the broader educational ecosystem that influences young people's success, of which OST programs are a critical component. GTY's OST workgroup shares learnings from the OST field with the commission through introductions to OST leaders and conversations with individual commissioners. Ultimately, the commission will develop a roadmap that points the way toward a future where every child receives the comprehensive support needed to succeed in school, in our evolving 21st-century workplace, and in life.

THREE FOUNDATIONS, THREE APPROACHES

Beneath the different entry points and nomenclature, funders of SEL have a common goal: behavior change on a massive scale among the adults in school and OST settings who educate and support young people, enabling these adults to understand the importance of fostering critical social and emotional skills, and to have the time, resources, knowledge, and skill to integrate the development of social and emotional skills into their work.

> We work with partners that demonstrate what high-quality SEL implementation looks like, while exploring how to best support educators at a larger scale with the resources they need [to] integrate SEL into their daily practices. Collaboration and field building can help create the conditions that make this work possible across the country. (I. Dinour, personal communication, September 19, 2017)

The following case studies highlight how three foundations put this notion into practice, focusing on the OST field.

Investing in Character Development by Improving Adult Practice

The S. D. Bechtel, Jr. Foundation (SDBJR Foundation) envisions a productive, vibrant, and sustainable California that is a model of success and a source of innovation. Our vision is pursued through two programs. The education program focuses on helping young people develop the knowledge, skills, and character to explore and understand the world around them, growing into caring, informed, and productive adults. We support youth and educators in science, technology, engineering, and mathematics (STEM) education and character development, and encourage effective education policy. The environment program concentrates on the management, stewardship, and conservation of the state's natural resources by supporting organizations and partnerships that inform, demonstrate, implement, and advocate for improvements in water management and land stewardship.

Due to the many critical challenges California and the nation face, our board of directors decided to invest the foundation's assets by 2020. We hope to foster the development of models that can become the standard practices of tomorrow, providing support for inspiring projects, enduring partnerships, and high-quality organizations.

SDBJR Foundation's Character Development[1] Strategy

Following the decision to spend down by 2020, we expanded our focus on character development by launching a national strategy. Both in and out of the classroom, adults serve as important mentors and role models who foster positive decision-making and character strengths in youth. For this reason, our focus is on supporting effective adult practice. According to research, the quality of staff preparation and developing meaningful relationships with youth are critical factors that lead to positive social and emotional outcomes (Vandell, Larson, Mahoney, & Watts, 2015).

To develop our strategy, we interviewed our founder and chairman, Mr. Stephen D. Bechtel, Jr., and other board members about their hopes for the foundation's investment in character development. The foundation heard that "character is about perseverance and working hard... being a team player and doing your part, [and] ... having a positive influence on others. These values allow you to be constructive in what you do and improve your effect on the community around you." Based on what we heard from our board members, our character strategy hones in on helping young people develop courage, empathy, fairness, integrity, respect, responsibility, teamwork, and a strong work ethic.

After examining the research, we decided to focus our work primarily on school-aged children, ages 5 to 18, because children and youth begin to develop cognitive complexity during these years, which is critical to character development (Nucci & Turiel, 2009; Walker, Hennig, & Krettenauer, 2000). Additionally, moral character development is additive and nonlinear; character grows and develops across the lifespan (Dawson-Tunik, 2005). Knowing that youth learn about character both during and outside of the school day, we made some key investments to support the exploration of how to infuse SEL practices into school settings and measure young people's progress in developing social and emotional skills. The in-school investments focused on the work of California Office to Reform Education (CORE) districts and the related evaluation work of Policy Analysis for California Education (PACE) at Stanford University. We also support the work of the Collaborative for Academic, Social, and Emotional Learning (CASEL) in guiding California's SEL planning work in the Collaborating States Initiative. Overall, however, our character strategy focuses on the opportunity to develop young people's character in OST settings.

Approach to Grantmaking

Character development was not new to the SDBJR Foundation's grantmaking. However, working at a national level was a new experience. Prior to the decision to spend down, we primarily invested in direct service organizations based in the California Bay Area. With a national focus, our staff identified potential grantee partners, looking primarily at large, sustainable, at-scale youth development organizations that were committed to character development. The strategy began with short-term, introductory grants that supported "shovel-ready" projects, through which we could get to know the organization, visit with its management team, assess its financial health and organizational resiliency, and understand the nature of its relationship with its local affiliates/programs.

Pending the success of those introductory grants and an extensive due diligence process, we then invited proposals for multi-year support focused on adult practice to enhance young people's character development. Grants focus on identifying promising practices that build youth character, and on supporting organizations to translate this knowledge into practice through training and professional development for staff and volunteers. We have taken two general approaches to these grants: the first approach focuses on continuous improvement in support of high-quality adult practice, and the second approach includes grants that have the potential to be transformational for the organization. Continuous improvement grants typically support data collection and research, as well as enhancements to organizations' training and professional development systems. Transformational grants may help an organization with a proven model to serve more youth or may focus internally on building the organization's infrastructure and capacity. These grants often involve organizational culture change.

To reach tens of millions of youth across the country, we selected a set of national organizations[2] that fell into one of three thematic cohorts. The leadership cohort consists of household-name organizations with the greatest reach. The second cohort focuses on sports and play and developing the skills of coaches to support character development and SEL. Lastly, we recognized the unique opportunity that nature provides in helping youth explore their interests and ideas about what's possible and invested in organizations that use nature as a classroom and encourage environmental stewardship.

In addition to the national strategy, we also partner with the California Department of Education Expanded Learning Division and several California-based organizations that support the state's publicly funded OST programs. Collectively, these organizations work to elevate the state's quality standards and continuous improvement efforts while infusing high-quality character development and SEL practices into programs.

Together, the foundation's grantees serve approximately half the school-age youth in the nation.[3]

Research and Influence

In addition to the grants to youth-serving organizations, we supported two important publications to inform practice. We joined several other foundations in supporting a follow-up publication to Paul Tough's 2012 book, *How Children Succeed: Grit, Curiosity, and the Hidden Power of Character.* In 2016, Tough published *Helping Children Succeed: What Works and Why,* a book geared specifically towards educators, with an accompanying online guide to support practice (Tough, 2016). Around the same time, and as we began our character-focused grantmaking, many of the foundation's grantees expressed interest in doing literature reviews to inform their work. Rather than support multiple literature reviews, we sponsored the National Academies of Sciences' National Research Council to host a 2-day workshop in July 2016—titled "Approaches to the Development of Character" and led by researchers in the field—to define character development, discuss emerging research, and debate the merits and challenges of measuring character development in youth (National Academies of Sciences, 2017). We invited our character grantees to the convening and provided space for reflection and peer learning afterwards.

Peer Learning, Collaboration, and Communities of Practice

Following the National Research Council workshop and grantee convening in 2016, our grantees were eager for more opportunities for peer learning. We launched three role-related communities of practice for individuals responsible for program quality, research and evaluation, and oversight of operations and/or a large initiative within the organization. The CEOs of the national organizations also came together in July 2016 and asked to be convened every 6 months. Lastly, we brought together the government relations/policy staff from the grantee organizations, who formed a character coalition with the Afterschool Alliance, Forum for Youth Investment, and the Association of Chamber of Commerce Executives. The coalition focuses on common areas of interest and potential policy collaborations in support of character development, as well as emergent issues, such as defending against public funding threats.

Through the communities of practice, grantees share their experience and strategies for managing scale and expansion across decentralized organizations; collecting and using data for continuous improvement; creating programs that are committed to diversity, equity, and inclusion; and training staff on character development and SEL. Long-term partnerships are being developed utilizing one another's training and curriculum, and several groups of grantees are presenting together at field conferences to share their learning. Many of the grantees are working with some of the same researchers, and we are starting to see more collaboration among the researchers as well. Perhaps most exciting is seeing camaraderie and peer learning among the CEOs as they actively seek out ways to work together and support one another's efforts.

While the SDBJR Foundation's investment is time-limited, its efforts to strengthen the nation's leading youth development organizations (which collectively serve tens of millions of youth) will improve adult practice, leading to more and better character development opportunities for young people for generations to come.

Susan Crown Exchange: Bringing SEL Into Common Practice

At the Susan Crown Exchange (SCE), we believe we have a unique opportunity to help equip the rising generation for success. Founded in 2009, SCE is a Chicago-based foundation invested in shaping an ecosystem of "anytime, anywhere" learning to prepare youth to adapt and thrive in a rapidly changing and highly connected world. Through three primary programs—digital learning, SEL, and catalyst grants—SCE helps identify, codify, and promote high-quality opportunities for young people to learn and grow in OST hours.

Through our work, we identify and leverage current research, best practices, and innovative programming that have demonstrated ability to instill in youth the essential skills they need to thrive. We call our organization an exchange rather than a foundation because of our partnerships with innovative and capable nonprofit organizations that align with our aspirations. In this way, we work to become a hub for ideas, people, and cutting-edge approaches and thinking, where funding is but one element of the process. Our strategies work to bring innovations and expertise into conversation across fields to increase the scale of positive impact on youth. As an organization that is continually learning, these strategies are recalibrated as our knowledge of what's working evolves.

Our focus on OST is intentional. In our view, there is a gap between the demands required for life success and the limited support our education system offers to prepare youth to meet those demands in the workplace and in life. Informal learning environments provide the ideal opportunity to learn and grow through participatory, engaging activities, unhindered by school-day restrictions and pressure to meet standardized goals and prescribed academic benchmarks.

In 2013, SCE conducted a landscape analysis and series of interviews all focused on one question: "What are the skills, dispositions, and experiences that can help put youth on a more positive life trajectory?" What we discovered is that it takes more than academic skills for young people to succeed, and social and emotional development is a key component of that success. We identified pockets of impact and effectiveness, despite the fragmented education system, limited resources, and disparate views about the value of SEL. We also learned that not all informal learning environments are tapping into the opportunities for cultivating SEL with youth, despite the fact that most are working to build more capable and self-aware human beings (Smith, McGovern, Larson, Hillaker, & Peck, 2016).

We also learned that while social and emotional skills can be taught and learned, too many youth today are not getting exposure to the nurturing environments and real-world learning experiences they need to develop them—especially disadvantaged youth. Armed with this knowledge, we built a grantmaking program that works to bring SEL into common practice, specifically in informal learning environments.

Our first effort was to create something called "the SEL challenge"—a process to shed light on how some of the best OST programs work to equip teens with lifelong social and emotional skills. We knew that skills like emotion management and problem solving were critical to success, but less was known about strategies and practices to build these skills. We chose to invest in the field more broadly, rather than hone in on specific programs or services. Teaming up with the David P. Weikart Center for Youth Program Quality and the Forum for Youth Investment, we wanted to study, unpack, and share what exemplar OST programs were doing to help youth develop social and emotional skills.

The SEL challenge brought together experts in youth programming, developmental science, program evaluation, and performance measurement in a 2-year learning community to explore how six social and emotional skill sets—emotion management, empathy, teamwork, responsibility, initiative, and problem solving—are best cultivated in teens. The work was intended to extract and distill the experience and expertise of top-tier youth workers and program leaders into a collective knowledge base, with the ultimate goal of making their practices and principles accessible to the broader field.

Approximately 250 OST programs from all over the country applied, and from these we selected eight exemplar programs in seven cities: AHA! (Attitude, Harmony, Achievement; Santa Barbara, CA); Boys & Girls Clubs of Greater Milwaukee (Milwaukee, WI); The Possibility Project (New York City, NY); Philadelphia Wooden Boat Factory (Philadelphia, PA); Voyageur Outward Bound School (St. Paul, MN); Wyman (St. Louis, MO); Youth on Board (Somerville, MA); and YWCA Boston (Boston, MA). While the programs were distinct, offering activities ranging from wooden boat building to wilderness adventure to musical production, all made a dedicated commitment to SEL and worked with vulnerable youth aged 14–19. The age group and population were critical as we wanted to show that no matter their background or challenges, youth could still develop these skills during their teenage years.

The research team found that with the right combination of responsive practices, staff supports, and curriculum features, youth participants in SEL challenge programs met their objectives in developing social and emotional skills (Smith et al., 2016). This supported previous research asserting that OST programs that operate with the explicit intention of baking SEL practices into their program design have positive impacts on youth that far exceed the impact of programs with no stated focus on SEL (Durlak, Weissberg, & Pachan, 2010).

The findings from the SEL challenge identify promising practices for building social and emotional skills with vulnerable youth that can be applied in any youth-serving program, and provide a method for taking these practices to scale in thousands of OST settings. Accompanying measurement tools were created to track progress as part of a continuous improvement process. We share the practices along with our research, case studies, and measurement and assessment tools in a field guide, *Preparing Youth to Thrive: Promising Practices in Social & Emotional Learning,* available for free at www.selpractices.org (see Figure 13.2).

The suite of tools supports expert practitioners and novices alike in improving the intentionality and impact of social and emotional skill building and assessment. We are taking these practices to scale by partnering with youth-serving organizations and intermediaries across the country to study the nuances of implementation, as well as the challenges and successes of creating a culture that values social and emotional skills. Our aim is that

Figure 13.2

this knowledge will help more organizations embed SEL as an integral component of a high-quality program.

Our interest in building the capacity of adults in OST programs to foster broad skills and capacities in youth has also led us to partner with the Yale Center for Emotional Intelligence on developing strategies for bringing SEL and emotional intelligence training and practices to OST organizations like the Boys & Girls Clubs of America. Additional partners in SCE's SEL portfolio include WINGS for Kids, CASEL, Y-USA, After-School All-Stars, MHA Labs, Center for Youth Engagement, Forum for Youth Investment, Futures Without Violence, University of Minnesota, Youthprise, and others.

We know these efforts represent a small part of the invaluable work being done all over the country to help children succeed. By sharing what we've learned, we hope to stimulate new conversations on the importance of SEL and how we can work together to create stronger, better OST programs for youth, getting them ready for success in the 21st century. We invite you to join the conversation at www.scefdn.org.

The Wallace Foundation: What Can We Learn From Aligning SEL Practices Across Schools and OST Programs?

The New York-based Wallace Foundation is a national philanthropic organization whose mission is to improve learning and enrichment for disadvantaged children and the vitality of the arts for everyone. We work to answer important questions that, if solved, could help strengthen practices and policies within the field. To catalyze this broad impact, we support the development, testing, and sharing of new solutions and effective practices.

Our current work in support of this mission focuses on the following goals:

- Strengthening education leadership to improve youth achievement.
- Improving the quality of and access to OST programs.
- Better understanding the impact of high-quality summer learning programs on disadvantaged children.
- Aligning and improving opportunities for SEL for children across school and OST settings.
- Making the arts a part of many more people's lives by working with art organizations to broaden, deepen, and diversify audiences.
- Expanding arts learning opportunities for children and teens.

Approach to Grantmaking

In all of these areas, we work with our partners to test useful ideas "on the ground," commission research to gather credible evidence on significant innovations, and then publicly share what we have learned to help bring the best ideas to life in ways that benefit children. Our goals are to improve the practices of grantees, offer knowledge to the organizations we do not directly support, and inform policymakers.

How Wallace Draws on Our Experiences

For years, we have supported youth development organizations and helped to coordinate their efforts to create opportunities for children and youth living in low-income urban environments. OST programming is a key component of this work. Although high-quality OST programs can provide children with opportunities for growth and learning, historically the OST field has been fragmented, with many different programs operating in isolation from one another (Browne, 2015). As a result, there is a lack of access to high-quality programs, particularly in urban areas with large numbers of disadvantaged young people (Yamashiro & Rinehart, 2014).

To help address this challenge, Wallace launched the Afterschool System Building Initiative in 2003, which over time brought together key players in 14 cities—including program providers, city agencies, schools, funders, families, and youth—to establish a shared vision of an OST system, adopt quality standards, and collect data to guide improvements. In 2010, the RAND Corporation published *Hours of Opportunity* (see Figure 13.3), a Wallace-commissioned study of the first five cities to take part in the Afterschool System Building Initiative. RAND found a "proof of principle" that OST organizations and institutions within a city could indeed work

Figure 13.3

together to increase access, quality, data-based decision making, and system sustainability (Bodily, 2010).

Because summer is a time when disadvantaged youth lose ground, we have also backed the efforts of districts and their partners to provide high-quality summer learning experiences through our National Summer Learning Project. This 6-year, five-city effort explores whether and how large-scale, voluntary summer learning programs can help improve educational outcomes for children in low-income urban communities. The initiative has developed credible evidence that high-quality programs can lead to measurable benefits in mathematics, reading, and SEL, and has produced guidance on how to achieve those benefits (Augustine, 2013; see Figure 13.4).

In recent years, we have turned our attention to the impact of SEL on youth success. A growing body of research, including the Wallace-commissioned University of Chicago study, *Foundations for Young Adult Success* (see Figure 13.5), has linked social and emotional skills (also known as non-cognitive skills, inter- or intrapersonal skills, soft skills, and character development) to success in school, career, and life (Nagaoka, 2015). However, solid information is still emerging about how school and OST experiences can be strengthened, aligned, and delivered in real-world settings to help children develop these skills. "Evidence points to the importance of building

Figure 13.4

Figure 13.5

SEL as children develop, and that these skills develop over time, in multiple settings," says Will Miller, the president of The Wallace Foundation. "But little is known about social and emotional learning, at scale, in large urban settings and about the potential benefits of schools and out-of-school providers working together" (Wallace Foundation, 2017).

Partnerships for Social and Emotional Learning Initiative

In search of answers, Wallace launched the Partnerships for Social and Emotional Learning Initiative (PSELI) in 2016, a 5-year project that builds on what we have learned from previous initiatives. PSELI brings together urban school districts and OST organizations in six communities to provide disadvantaged children with greater opportunities to develop social and emotional skills such as self-control, teamwork, persistence, and goal setting, and to better understand how schools and OST organizations can collaborate to align and improve those opportunities. The new initiative aims to generate insights into what works and what doesn't in these cross-sector collaborations—knowledge that can be applied to the broader field.

We chose the six communities—Boston, Dallas, Denver, Palm Beach County, Tacoma, and Tulsa—from a larger pool of cities that received planning grants in 2016. They were selected based on their fit with the foundation's dual goals of helping local grantees strengthen their capacity to deliver strong SEL experiences to children, and developing credible new knowledge that will be useful to the field.

PSELI will provide programs to roughly 15,000 children in kindergarten through fifth grade and will involve up to seven Title I elementary school–OST program partnerships in each community. The local partners in each community—a school district and an OST intermediary— will use a continuous improvement process, which involves implementing new practices, reviewing the results, and then incorporating changes based on what has been learned.

In the first year of the initiative, each district/OST intermediary pair in each community will share grants ranging from $1 million to $1.5 million. Participating communities will also receive nonmonetary support, such as inclusion in a professional learning community, regular convenings with other communities in the initiative, supports to integrate SEL data into continuous improvement systems, communications counsel, and other technical assistance provided by national experts such as CASEL, the Forum for Youth Investment, the David P. Weikart Center for Youth Program Quality, and Crosby Marketing Communications.

As with all of our initiatives, we hope to create direct benefits for participating communities, but also to develop credible lessons for the field that can improve practice. We are especially interested in discovering whether the communities see (a) SEL benefits for children; (b) improvements in adult practices, learning environments, and instruction; and (c) stronger partnerships between the school districts and OST providers.

The RAND Corporation will conduct an independent, multi-year research study on whether and how youth benefit from PSELI, and will provide guidance on how such collaborations can be implemented across the field. RAND's research will produce public reports for policymakers and practitioners that shed light on

- what system-level supports school districts and OST organizations need to partner;
- what promotes progress, and what impedes it;
- effective ways to enhance the social and emotional skills of adults in schools and OST programs;
- specific practices and factors that are key to improving children's outcomes,
- what roles partnerships play; and
- outcome evidence on improvements in children's SEL and other measures of youth success.

Meanwhile, the SEL knowledge base continues to expand. In May 2017, a Wallace-commissioned guide to 25 evidence-based SEL programs was released, offering detailed information about the programs' curricular and programmatic features. The aim is to provide practitioners with background information that enables them to make informed choices about which programs are best suited for developing particular skills and competencies. Written by Harvard education professor Stephanie Jones, *Navigating SEL From the Inside Out: Looking Inside & Across 25 Leading SEL Programs—A Practical Resource for Schools and OST Providers* also explains how the SEL programs can be adapted to OST settings. We hope that the lessons learned from the initiative will provide more answers about how schools and OST programs can work in tandem to provide children with SEL experiences, and what impact this has on children (Jones, 2017).

LOOKING FORWARD

With more than 90% of foundations surveyed in the Parthenon Group study projecting a steady or increasing budget for SEL in subsequent years—and a significant amount of the funding going to the OST field—there is an opportunity for OST organizations and practitioners to share their youth development expertise and the ways in which they support young people's SEL (EY-Parthenon, 2015). It is important for OST funders to make the connection between high-quality youth development programs and high-quality environments and practices that foster SEL. As seen through the S. D. Bechtel, Jr. Foundation's strategy, OST organizations must clarify their approaches to supporting SEL and create cultures and environments throughout their networks that consistently encourage staff and volunteers to model social and emotional skills for youth. High-quality SEL programs and practices need to be studied and documented as the Susan Crown Exchange has done, and schools and OST providers must intentionally partner to support young people's success, as encouraged by The Wallace Foundation.

The current public and political environment is ripe for broadening the conversation around youth outcomes, and the OST field should be leading that discussion. For years, funders supporting youth development and SEL have been challenged because these concepts are often treated as peripheral to the core agenda of improving public education. Today, the education community's recognition of (and in some cases, frustration with) the limitations of the current regime of standards and accountability is palpable and rising, and it coincides with increasing public discussion of the research supporting the role of nonacademic outcomes. This confluence of factors creates an opportunity for funders investing in nonacademic youth outcomes to become more integrated with broader philanthropic trends in education, and to attract greater attention and resources for their issues. Yet this promising environment is not without risks, as funders seek to strike the appropriate balance of advocating for a broader definition of youth success without undermining recent reforms around academic standards and assessments that many believe are valuable and important (EY-Parthenon, 2015).

Stemm-Calderon shares that she

> ...hopes that we will continue to coalesce around broader frames, capitalizing on what we know about learning and development and helping the field use that information instead of fighting over narrow frameworks. We know how to build individual programs. We have a lot more to learn about how learning and development happens and how to translate that into practice. The new challenge is how we reimagine the design of an education system that integrates broader skills and strategies. Our aim is an equitable and responsive education system. Our fuel is learning more about how learning and development happens and sharing that learning with the field. And our methods are continuous improvement so we can get better at getting better. (Z. Stemm-Calderon, personal communication, September 20, 2017)

As Stemm-Calderon notes, "this is indeed a fertile time" (Z. Stemm-Calderon, personal communication, September 20, 2017).

NOTES

1. While we do not require our grantees to use specific terminology when referring to our character development work, we generally use "character" and "character development" when talking about our grantmaking strategy. This refers to social and emotional learning, inter- and intrapersonal skills, and other terms for related concepts in the field.
2. The S. D. Bechtel, Jr. Foundation's National Character Initiative grantees include: Big Brothers Big Sisters of America, Boys & Girls Clubs of America, Boy Scouts of America, Camp Fire, Coaching Corps, Girls Inc., National 4-H Council, NatureBridge, Outward Bound, Playworks, Positive Coaching Alliance, Student Conservation Association, and YMCA of the USA.
3. Calculations are based on self-reported numbers from grantee organizations and may include youth who are double-counted if participating in more than one organization.

REFERENCES

Augustine, C. (2013). *Getting to work on summer learning: Recommended practices for success.* Santa Monica, CA: RAND Corporation.

Bodily, S. J. (2010). *Hours of opportunity: Lessons from five cities on building systems to improve after-school, summer, and other out-of-school time programs (Vol. I).* Santa Monica, CA: RAND Corporation.

Browne, D. (2015). *Growing together, learning together: What cities have discovered about building afterschool systems.* New York, NY: The Wallace Foundation.

Dawson-Tunik, T. C. (2005). The shape of development. *European Journal of Development Psychology, 2*(2), 163–195.

Durlak, J. A., Weissberg, R. P., & Pachan, M. (2010). A meta-analysis of after-school programs that seek to promote personal and social skills in children and adolescents. *American Journal of Community Psychology, 45*, 294–309.

EY-Parthenon. (2015). *Preliminary survey output: Non-academic youth outcomes.* Unpublished internal EY-Parthenon report.

Jones, S. (2017). *Navigating social and emotional learning from the inside out.* Cambridge, MA: Harvard Graduate School of Education.

Nagaoka, J. (2015). *Foundations for young adult success: A developmental framework.* Chicago, IL: The University of Chicago Consortium on Chicago School Research.

National Academies of Sciences. (2017). *Proceedings of a Workshop: Approaches to the Development of Character.* Washington, DC: The National Academies Press.

Nucci, L., & Turiel, E. (2009). *Capturing the complexity of moral development and education. Mind, Brain, and Education, 3*(3), 151–150.

Shechtman, N. Y. (2016). *Empowering adults to thrive at work: Personal success skills for 21st century jobs. A report on promising research and practice.* Chicago, IL: Joyce Foundation.

Smith, C., McGovern, G., Larson, R., Hillaker, B., & Peck, S. (2016). *Preparing youth to thrive: Promising practices for social and emotional learning.* Washington, DC: Forum for Youth Investment.

Tough, P. (2012). *How children succeed: Grit, curiosity, and the hidden power of character.* Boston, MA: Houghton Mifflin.

Tough, P. (2016). *Helping children succeed: What works and why.* Boston, MA: Houghton Mifflin.

Vandell, D. L., Larson, R. W., Mahoney, J. L., & Watts, T. W. (2015). Children's organized activities. In M. H. Bornstein, T. Leventhal, & R. M. Lerner (Eds.), *Handbook of child psychology and developmental science* (Vol. 4, 7th ed.). Hoboken, NJ: John Wiley & Sons.

Walker, L. J., Hennig, K. H., & Krettenauer, T. (2000). Parent and peer contexts for children's moral reasoning development. *Child Development, 71*(4), 1033–1048.

Wallace Foundation. (2017, July 24). *New initiative brings together schools and afterschool organizations to foster social-emotional learning in elementary school.* Retrieved from http://www.wallacefoundation.org/news-and-media/press-releases/pages/sel-in-elementary-school.aspx

Yamashiro, N., & Rinehart, J. (2014). *America after 3pm, afterschool programs in demand.* Washington, DC: Afterschool Alliance.

SECTION IV

SEL RESEARCH, MEASUREMENT, AND ASSESSMENT

CHAPTER 14

THE MEASUREMENT OF YOUTH SOCIAL AND EMOTIONAL COMPETENCIES IN OST SETTINGS

Gil G. Noam, Patricia J. Allen, and Bailey Triggs

A substantial body of research has demonstrated that high-quality out-of-school time (OST) programming plays an important role in the development of social and emotional competencies, including positive academic, psychological, and behavioral outcomes in youth (Cooper, Valentine, Nye, & Lindsay, 1999; Darling, 2005; Fredricks & Eccles, 2006; "Helping Youth Succeed," 2006; Lauer et al., 2006; Shernoff, 2010). Moreover, a meta-analysis of OST programs that intentionally focused on promoting social and emotional competencies found that it was possible to identify effective OST programs, and that youth who participated in these programs improved in three key areas: feelings and attitudes, indicators of behavioral adjustment, and school performance (Durlak & Weissberg, 2007). Where there is less clarity is how to measure these competencies: what should we measure, how

Social and Emotional Learning in Out-of-School Time, pages 245–263

should we measure, and how do we use the data we collect to understand what's working in programs and what needs improvement?

In this chapter, we will share the lessons we have learned through partnering with OST program networks over the past decade to integrate social and emotional measurement and practices. We will discuss some of the best practices around measurement adoption and implementation that we have learned through our experiences with partners, and explore areas where we as a field need to learn and grow. We will use our work at The PEAR Institute—Partnerships in Education and Resilience—at McLean Hospital and Harvard Medical School to demonstrate how measures can be used for more than accountability checks or dry evaluations (both are important). To show how these principles apply to real-world practice, we share two case studies of OST program networks that have successfully used social and emotional measures to evaluate program effectiveness, continually improve program quality, and better understand the needs of the youth they serve: Sprockets, a network of OST and summer programs for youth in Saint Paul, Minnesota, and the Boston Summer Learning Project, a citywide network of summer learning programs launched by Boston After School & Beyond (BASB), Boston Public Schools (BPS), and the Boston Opportunity Agenda, in Boston, Massachusetts. In this chapter, we concentrate on citywide networks, because we find they have a commitment to central coordination, measurement, training, and policymaking, and provide a great diversity of program types (e.g., school-based, community-based, generic and specialized, arts, sports, STEM, and more).

APPLYING SOCIAL AND EMOTIONAL MEASUREMENT TO OST

We begin this section with an acknowledgment that there can be ambivalence around using measurement tools in OST. There is a souring around assessment and a fear that the data collected could be used punitively, which adds to the reluctance OST practitioners feel when considering bringing measurement tools into the OST environment (Allen & Noam, 2016). We share this concern but have not concluded that measurement alone is to blame, but rather its type, purpose, and use (or misuse in some cases). Today, everything is measured: the experience of eating a meal in a restaurant, the frequency of flights arriving and departing airports, and the health behaviors of children and adults, to name just a few areas of data collection. The public expects data analysis, prediction, and precision, and technology is allowing for individualized offerings of services and immediate feedback when searches are conducted. This development does not halt in front of the schoolhouse or OST program. Data is here to stay and can have negative or positive impact or any point in between. We propose a different way of thinking about measurement and the use of data in OST that takes a more proactive, positive, and individualized approach. We will first discuss the criteria that are important when selecting an appropriate measurement for OST; second, we will discuss three applications of measurement in OST; and finally, in our case study section we will give more in-depth examples of what this sort of supportive, wraparound training and professional development looks like in practice.

Choosing Robust Tools

When considering which measures to incorporate, it is important that OST programs select robust tools that are aligned to their program and setting, give voice to the youth they serve, support their improvement and evaluation goals, and are grounded in a strong theory or framework of youth social and emotional development. It is important that programs, particularly programs that operate within greater networks or ecosystems within OST, come together around a shared theory or framework that supports the measures they select. A shared theory or framework behind a measure will give all programs a common language with which to share data and lessons learned. Measurement tools can include everything from youth self-report data, to facilitator surveys, to data collected from the families of youth in OST programming, to youth work samples, or observations of the program's quality made by trained evaluators. The measures selected should also be psychometrically strong (see text box for more information). The selected tools should also be flexible enough to use in a variety of settings. OST programs can be conducted anywhere, from a school, to a gym, to a nature center, and the tool selected needs to work in all those venues.

CHOOSING PSYCHOMETRICALLY STRONG TOOLS

It is important to ensure that the chosen tools measure what they are intended to measure (validity) and do so consistently (reliability). There are different types of validity, such as content, construct, concurrent, and predictive validity, and there are different types of reliability, such as internal consistency, test–retest, and interrater reliability. These psychometric properties are affected by many factors, such as difficulty level or length of assessment, so it is important to rigorously test measures through research and practice (for review, refer to Price, 2016).

Adopting a System for Quick and Accurate Reporting

It is important that the tool selected can be incorporated into a larger data system that allows quick, accurate reporting to reduce the burden on staff in both collecting and interpreting data. Collecting data using a youth social and emotional competency measure can be an effective first step for OST programs interested in having a clearer picture of the social and emotional capacities of its youth, but if the data collected aren't reported back to programs until the end of the year, or if the reported data are presented in an unwieldy, overwhelming way that is hard to interpret, they will be of little use to a program.

In addition to the need for rapid and clear reporting, a key factor in the selection of a data system is that it can integrate multiple points of data. For example, selecting a student self-report survey as an OST program's measurement tool will help programs better understand their youths' perspectives, but one source of data will only show one piece of the greater puzzle. In addition to the youth's self-report, it's important to consider the facilitator perspective, as well as the views of the family of the youth, and the observations of trained external program observers or evaluators. Youth work samples, interviews, observation videos, and attendance data can all play an important role in better understanding the strengths and challenges of an OST program and its youth.

Privacy and confidentiality are also important concerns when evaluating any data system that incorporates youth data. All data systems that are considered for use should have protections in place that allow only those who have permission to access the program's data. Strong data security and privacy protections are important—particularly when you consider connecting an OST program's data system to an external one, like a school's student information system. These connections can lead to a greater understanding of youth's social and emotional capacities in a variety of settings and can lead to more targeted support for young people who could benefit from it.

Proactively Using Data

Beyond selecting measurements and a data system to support them, OST programs should proactively use data as a check on their current systems around social and emotional competency building and act on the evidence the data provides to make the adjustments that are needed in meeting the needs of the youth in their program. Fostering proactive use of data starts with training and professional development around the tools and data system. Training includes understanding the administration and results of the tools themselves, but should also focus on the model or framework that underlies the measure to create a common language within and across OST programs.

Applying Measurement to OST

There are at least three ways measurement can be used in the ongoing support of OST programming: (a) as an opportunity to know every child at the beginning of the program and to better customize OST programming to meet the needs of all youth; (b) as an assessment for continuous program improvement, to inform the selection of staff professional development opportunities, and as an assessment of the quality of the programming in general; (c) and as part of a formal evaluation that brings together community members around a common language and to understand the program's impact.[1] In Table 14.1, we describe the three applications of social and emotional measures, their purpose, and the audience for each method. These applications are not presented as à la carte offerings, but as the three essential applications that all OST programs using measurements of social and emotional competencies should employ when planning to collect data. Interestingly, the very same tools can often be used to accomplish the three areas of application we describe in Table 14.1.

KNOWING EVERY CHILD

As noted previously, research on OST programs has found that many young people who attend high-quality programs experience benefits from participating in those programs, but what does it take to create and maintain a high-quality program? A review of OST studies conducted by the American Youth Policy Forum (AYPF) found that quality OST programs

TABLE 14.1 The Three Applications of Measurement in OST

Application	Purpose	Audience
Know every child	To collect data directly from youth via self-report measures to better understand the social and emotional strengths and challenges youth face to better align program curricula and facilitator style to meet the social and emotional needs of youth in the program.	OST program facilitators and staff, youth, teaching partners, families
Continuous improvement	To identify areas where facilitators or staff may benefit from additional professional development and understand strengths and weaknesses of curricula.	OST program directors and staff, families, partners
Understand impact	To determine whether the investments made in the program are generating the intended youth outcomes and identify areas of improvement in the future	Programs, funders, evaluators, researchers, community leaders, families, partners

were dependent on quality staff who developed positive relationships with youth, provided challenging activities, and facilitated youth engagement ("Helping Youth Succeed," 2006). When practitioners have a deep understanding of the tools they are using and the theory behind those tools, they will be able to know every child in their program when the child first enters the program. By using a measurement of youth social and emotional skills that focuses on youth's self-reported strengths and challenges, a facilitator can gain insight into what will motivate the youth to remain engaged and feel connected to the program. Using the measurement can help foster a shared language around social and emotional skills or learning that OST staff can use to communicate both with each other and with the youth they serve.

CONTINUOUS IMPROVEMENT

When we begin working with OST programs interested in incorporating measurement into their program improvement work, we encourage them to go beyond thinking of measurement as only an end-of-the-year evaluation activity. Instead, we believe that in addition to evaluation, continuous improvement is a key use of measurement. This program improvement work is a continuous cycle that can happen while the program is underway, starting with planning, informed by action, checked by data collected during the program, and adjusted during the program to meet youth needs. This process is visualized in our continuous improvement model (see Figure 14.1).

In our two decades of working within OST, we have found that the programs that adopt this approach to continuous improvement engage in the following activities: They choose robust tools, adopt a system for quick and accurate reporting, and proactively use data to know every child, foster continuous improvement, and inform policy and funders.

UNDERSTAND IMPACT

One of the most clear-cut ways to understand an OST program's impact is to use measurement tools to inform a formal evaluation of the program. Before selecting a tool, or a suite of tools, it is important to define how the program intends to measure its impact, and to ensure the tool or tools selected will be able to meet the needs of those goals by providing accurate and informative measurements. Funders, evaluators, researchers, and larger OST networks are always interested in better understanding how investment in OST programming can lead to improved youth outcomes. Is funding being invested in the right strategies and do program facilitators and staff have the right

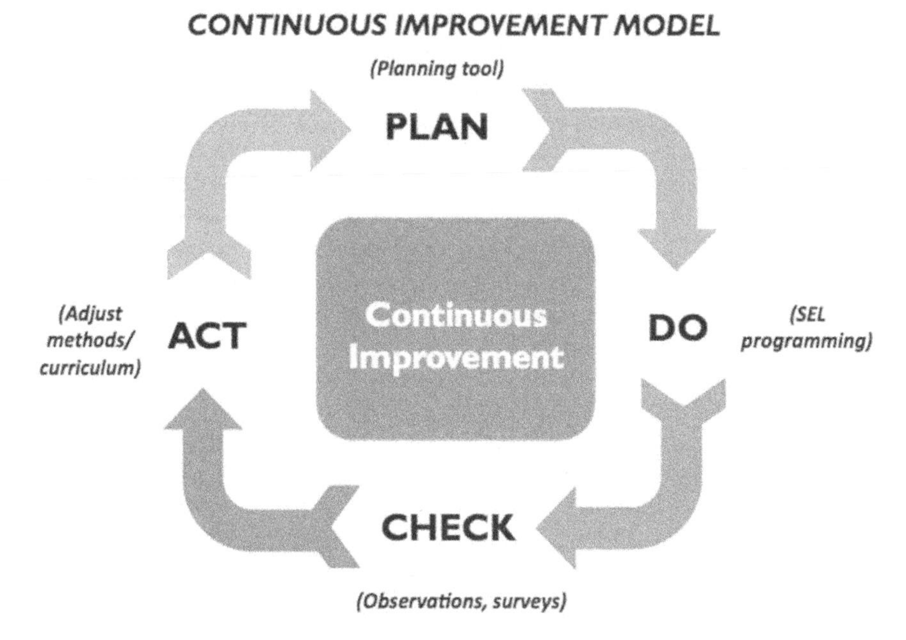

Figure 14.1 Continuous improvement model.

professional development and training opportunities to provide youth with high-quality experiences? Are the programs successfully meeting the needs of the youth they serve, and do they show improvements in social and emotional competencies, program engagement, and academic outcomes?

The benefit of conducting program evaluations is clear, and measures of youth social and emotional competencies are one of many assessment tools that can help OST programs better understand whether they're meeting the goals they set out for themselves at the beginning of the program. For an example of a national evaluation of OST state networks that includes a look at social and emotional competencies (also referred to as 21st century skills), see Allen, Noam, et al., 2017. Beyond measuring the direct impact of participating in an OST program, these measures can also help identify high levels of student need or gaps in program services that could be addressed with additional funding and support.

SPROCKETS AND THE BOSTON SUMMER LEARNING COMMUNITY

Just as we recommend that OST facilitators and staff tailor their program to the needs of their participants, we will share our similar tailored approach to our collaborations with the two OST network partnerships we present in this chapter: Sprockets, in Saint Paul, Minnesota, and the Boston Summer Learning Community (BSLC), in Boston, Massachusetts, which is a collaborative effort between The PEAR Institute and BASB. We have selected these two OST program networks to highlight their strong commitment to building youth social and emotional competencies and to share how they were able to successfully incorporate measurement into their work to evaluate their own efforts, to continuously improve, and to know every child at the beginning of the program. Each organization has deep strengths and has faced challenges along the way, which we will explore in this section. Both organizations were trained in The PEAR Institute's model of social and emotional development, the clover model, at the beginning of our work together, and used our measurement tool, the Holistic Student Assessment (HSA), as well as our data reporting system and professional development, coaching, and training services. This section will briefly describe the clover model and the HSA before further exploring how each organization adapted them to meet the needs of its network.

A Youth Development Foundation: The Clover Model

Starting with a strong model or framework around youth development will help ground any assessment tools or measures an OST program selects in a deeper understanding of youth's social and emotional needs and will help program staff adopt a common language around social and emotional capacities that will improve the program's ability to meet youth needs in this area. There are many models to choose from in this area; one of the more popular ones is the collaborative for academic, social, and emotional learning (CASEL) model, referenced earlier in this book. This section will share the clover model, a model that was designed to be simple and flexible enough to work with a variety of models and frameworks.

The clover model was created by Dr. Gil G. Noam at The PEAR Institute in response to a need he saw for a simple model of youth development that takes a more integrative approach than the linear, stepwise theory of youth development that was popular with stage theorists like Erik Erikson (Erikson, 1950). After two decades of comparative research, including research on various developmental and personality models that incorporate attachment, functionalist, and social-cognitive development theory from Bowlby, Erikson, and Piaget, the clover model was formed (Bowlby, 1969; Erikson, 1950; Piaget, 1954). For a summary of this comparative research, see Noam, Malti, and Karcher (2013). The clover model is also referred to as a developmental process theory (DPT), and comes out of Noam's clinical and developmental theory work. It was designed to function as a compass for educators, youth workers, and families to use in creating a shared language around social and emotional development and learning. The model draws from many research areas and theories as well as classroom and clinical observations to form a clear, unified framework that informs both measurement and program improvement.

The clover model focuses on four domains of development: active engagement, assertiveness, belonging, and reflection (see Figure 14.2). Active engagement represents the time in a young person's life when they have a desire to physically engage with the world through their bodies; assertiveness represents their development of voice and the desire for choice and self-determination; belonging represents their desire to build strong relationships with peers and adults; and reflection represents the desire to explore and make meaning of the world and the self.

The clover model focuses on what Noam has identified as the minimum elements required to describe human social and emotional development, through decades of interviews with youth and longitudinal research (Noam, Powers, Kilkenny, & Beedy, 1990). Each domain is visualized as a distinct "leaf" of a clover, but in practice these leaves overlap like a Venn diagram. While a young person may shift focus from one clover domain to another over the course of development, all domains are present to some degree for youth at all times.

The clover model was first field-tested in the OST world through the Responsive Advocacy for Life and Learning in Youth (RALLY) afterschool program. The RALLY program focused on creating educational environments that helped OST staff build therapeutic elements into their relationship with youth without requiring the hiring of additional therapists. By taking a translational approach, in which research is directly applied to practice and both are informed and strengthened, The PEAR Institute was able to create measurements and coaching and training programs that were informed by the clover model, just as the model itself was informed

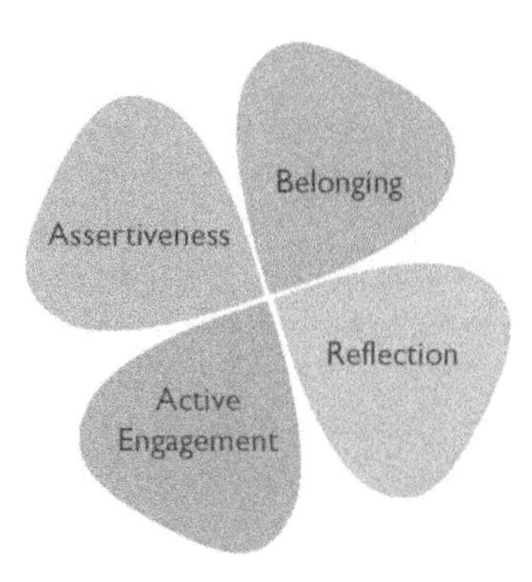

Figure 14.2 The clover model.

by years of practice. The lessons learned piloting the clover model in the RALLY OST program have also been adapted into The PEAR Institute's training and coaching services, which we will describe in the examples of our work with Boston and St. Paul.

The Holistic Student Assessment

The HSA is an evidence-based, student self-report tool that functions as a universal screen to measure social and emotional resilience in youth (Malti & Noam, 2008, 2009, 2016; Noam & Triggs, 2016; see Table 14.2 for a list of the HSA scales and sample items). It is based on the clover model, and interconnects adolescent psychopathology with social and emotional development and resiliencies (Noam, 1996). In keeping with the clover model, the HSA was designed to measure key dimensions of strength and challenge to complement existing assessments of youth risk factors popular in education at the time the tool was developed. The four domains of clover that are represented in the resiliencies section of the HSA measure areas of social and emotional competencies, but can also represent risks of behavioral and emotional problems (Noam et al., 2013). While challenges and risk factors are captured in this measure, the focus of the HSA's interpretation is a strengths-focused one that is designed to help educators identify ways to promote youth's strengths, prevent additional risk, and help educators identify youth who may need additional intervention and individualized support. It is designed this way intentionally because Noam's research has found that holistic measures that address both risk and resiliency can be more effective in engaging students in high-quality, developmentally strengthening educational experiences than measures that only consider risk (Malti & Noam, 2009).

The HSA was piloted in the RALLY program alongside the clover model to ensure it connected effectively to practice (Malti & Noam, 2008). The HSA has also undergone several years of validation research and has become a widely used measure, administered nearly 60,000 times across 22 U.S. states and in 10 countries (Malti, Zuffianò, & Noam, 2017; Noam & Goldstein, 1998; Noam, Malti, & Guhn, 2012). For a more technical dive into the HSA's design and application, see Allen, Thomas, Triggs, and Noam (2017).

When considering using any measure, it is important to ensure it will work well with other measures. In support of the HSA, The PEAR Institute has developed several companion survey variations, including a retrospective student version to measure change throughout the year, a facilitator survey, and a version of the HSA for families of youth. The HSA has also

TABLE 14.2 The 14 Scales of the HSA

Dimension	Scale	Definition	Sample Item
Intra- and Interpersonal Resiliencies	Action Orientation	Engagement in physical and hands-on activities.	I like being physically active and moving my body.
	Assertiveness	Confidence in putting oneself forward and standing up for what one believes.	I defend myself against unfair rules.
	Empathy	Recognition of others' feelings and experiences.	I like to help people with their problems.
	Reflection	Inner thought processes and self-awareness, and internal responsiveness toward broader societal issues.	I try to understand the world I live in.
	Emotional Control	Self-regulation of distress and management of anger.	I react to things so quickly I get in trouble.
	Trust	Perception of other people as helpful and trustworthy.	I trust other people.
	Optimism	Enthusiasm for and hopefulness about one's life.	I have more good times than bad times.
Relationships With Others	Relationships With Peers	Positive and supportive social connections with friends and classmates.	I have friends I can trust.
	Relationships With Adults	Positive connections and attitudes toward interactions with adults.	There are adults I look up to and admire.
Learning and School Engagement	Learning Interest	Desire to learn and acquire new knowledge.	I like to learn new things.
	Critical Thinking	Examination of information, exploration of ideas, and independent thought.	I try to look at a situation in different ways.
	Perseverance	Persistence in work and problem solving despite obstacles.	I keep going with work even when it takes longer than I thought it would.
	Academic Motivation	Incentive to succeed in school, without necessarily including general interest in learning.	I want to be a good student.
	School Bonding	Positive personal connections and the sense of belonging in one's school.	I feel like people understand me at my school.

been used in conjunction with non-PEAR measures and models, as we will describe in our section about our work in Boston and St. Paul.

Data Reporting Systems and Interpretation

Through years of working directly with practitioners to develop the clover model and the HSA, we have learned that the presentation and interpretation of the data is the key to effectively integrating measurement tools into OST programming. HSA data are typically collected at the beginning of the program and are reported back to facilitators within 1 week of their collection so that the data can play an essential role in helping facilitators and staff know every child at the beginning of the program.

In addition to a swift return of the data, The PEAR Institute provides interpretation training and support to each program it works with to ensure the data will be clearly understood and can be used for immediate action within the program. The interpretation sessions include time spent framing the HSA around the clover model and encouraging practitioners to use the data to get to know the youth in their program. It encourages practitioners to stay strengths-focused while interpreting the data and to strive to help youth build balance rather than eliminate behaviors. This approach helps build positive, meaningful relationships. It also helps facilitators and staff to intentionally plan intervention strategies for the youth identified by the HSA as needing higher levels of support.

It is important for any program looking to adopt new measures or models to select ones flexible enough to adapt to the unique needs of the program, while remaining robust enough to maintain quality, so they can be used for bigger-picture norming work across programs as well as long-term evaluations. The clover model and HSA are simply examples of this greater principle. Now that we've laid out the approaches and tools The PEAR Institute uses to support OST programs, we will describe two applications of our work in Boston and St. Paul.

Our Work With Sprockets—Saint Paul

Beginning in 2015, the social and emotional learning (SEL) pilot project is a multi-year collaboration between Sprockets and The PEAR Institute to support the social and emotional development of youth. Sprockets, a network of afterschool and summer programs for youth in Saint Paul, Minnesota, was formed as a collaboration of community organizations, the City of Saint Paul, and Saint Paul Public Schools, and was designed to make Saint Paul a model for community-wide learning. This project includes professionals from youth-serving organizations and schools across the Twin Cities area in a multi-year process of professional learning to increase local SEL capacity. Sprockets exemplifies an OST network that successfully employed an SEL measurement to know every child, continuously improve, and understand its impact, and it serves as a model for other OST programs interested in incorporating SEL more deeply into their work.

The first step in Sprockets' SEL implementation efforts was conducting deep planning around the creation of a cohort of afterschool providers, school districts, and intermediary organizations from St. Paul, Minneapolis; Brooklyn Heights; and Brooklyn Center to work with The PEAR Institute. With a cohort in place, Sprockets was able to take actionable steps toward helping programs deepen their knowledge of SEL through semi-annual, multi-day conferences and monthly cohort meetings. Sprockets programs also began using the HSA to collect youth data that cohort members applied in a variety of ways—for example, as a check on areas where youth had social and emotional strengths and challenges, as a way to explain program impact to the schools they partner with, and in reports to funders on the progress of their programs. These efforts contributed to an increased fluency around SEL within the cohort, and members shared their vast knowledge and experience with each other. In Year 2 of the project, the focus was on putting what the cohort learned into action by building the capacity of the network to support the work locally. Two cohorts were developed to support this effort: the Professional Development and Implementation Cohort, designed to support the implementation of the HSA and clover model; and a Train-the-Trainer Cohort, to prepare local members to become clover facilitators and HSA coaches.

In addition to Sprockets' initiatives around SEL-focused professional development and training, OST programs within the Sprockets network were able to use HSA data to deepen relationships with youth. For example, CLUES, a youth program for Latino/a teens in St. Paul, used the HSA to better support its mentoring program. Mentors and teens, together with CLUES program director and SEL pilot cohort member Tanya Zwald, explored the teens' HSA results as a gateway to learning about the unique strengths, struggles, and dreams of each young person. Zwald shared with us an example of the impact that using HSA data with a young person can have to strengthen a mentoring relationship:

> "I truly think that his mentor came in wondering if it made sense to continue together... and left feeling more connected than he'd ever expected and excited to dig deeper," explained Zwald. "It was so cool to see this young man own and explain who he is, and provide us with an opportunity to build him up and encourage him with ideas for growth. The mentor now has better tools to support and interact with him, and seemed so excited to try them

> out…and I think the student felt more empowered to be his true self and confident to stretch himself."

In that example from the field, an SEL measure was used to "know every child," providing insight into a young person's experience and helping the mentor improve the relationship and select more targeted strategies to improve engagement. In a similar way, our work with Sprockets and the feedback they have shared with us has helped us to gain greater insight into our work as we continue on our own journey of continuous improvement. For example, during both years of the project, the cohort has engaged in deep learning and discussion about cultural responsiveness in SEL. Demonstrating the vast knowledge of the highly diverse Twin Cities area, the cohort has helped give shape to discussions about cultural and linguistic inclusion for HSA and clover trainings nationwide. The result of this collaborative project has been symbiotic, informing The PEAR Institute's work from Boston to Texas and beyond, and has created a strong professional learning community with a deep understanding of how to support social and emotional competencies in youth.

Our Work With the Boston Summer Learning Community

In 2010, The PEAR Institute was invited to join the launch of the BSLC by BASB and BPS in partnership with Boston Opportunity Agenda. The BSLC is a diverse citywide network of summer learning programs that are aligned around the shared goals of closing the opportunity gap for youth in Boston, implementing shared measures across programs, and learning from each other to improve program quality. Over time the community has grown; according to BASB's preliminary report for the 2016 BSLC, the network has served more than 10,000 students through 127 program partners ("The State of Summer," 2016).

The PEAR Institute has provided social and emotional measurements and training support for the BSLC since its inception. Each year, The PEAR Institute administers the HSA to participating programs (the process typically includes two administrations: a pre-survey and a retrospective survey, the HSA-Retrospective). The HSA data collected were combined with other SEL measures to create the Program Report for Improvement & System Measurement (PRISM) that is delivered to programs in the fall. The PRISM is an example of how a measurement tool can be combined with other measures to give programs a bigger picture of "where their program is" in terms of quality, youth engagement, and facilitator strengths and challenges. The PRISM shows a program's specific results across all measurement tools and compares them to the summer cohort as a whole. The PEAR Institute worked closely with BASB to integrate HSA data into the PRISM reporting system so BSLC programs would have a way to review all their data in one place and easily see the importance of considering converging data sources while formulating program improvement strategies.

In addition to data collection and reporting, The PEAR Institute offers on-site coaching services to programs that opt in to the service. This additional coaching support is tailored to the needs of the program and can cover a wide variety of topics. Past coaching services include SEL framework overviews, deeper dives into the program's data, targeted recommendations for youth in need of additional support, research on trauma, action planning, and the piloting of an SEL-focused classroom observation tool. As the needs of the BSLC have evolved over the years, so have the services and support The PEAR Institute provides for the community. Just as the programs focus on continuous improvement, so must the measures and services designed to support these programs. The PEAR Institute's work with the BSLC over the past 7 years has reaffirmed the importance of flexible measurement approaches that OST networks and programs can apply as they see fit to understand the social and emotional competencies of their youth, continually improve, and evaluate impact.

Challenges of Using Measurement in OST

It is important to address some of the challenges that often come up when discussing measuring social and emotional competencies both in general and specifically within OST programming. First, there is the ongoing debate in the field about whether it's possible to accurately measure youth social and emotional competencies, and if so, how. Even researchers who champion teaching social and emotional competencies caution that currently developed measures of social and emotional competencies should not be used for educational accountability due to their limitations and imperfections (Duckworth & Yeager, 2015). While OST programs face different pressures around accountability than schools experience, it is understandable that skepticism remains around how—or whether—to use this type of measurement.

Even the language in this field is cloudy. While the term *social and emotional learning* (SEL) has a measure of popularity in the field, there is not a complete consensus around this terminology. At The PEAR Institute, we believe one of the complications of the term SEL is a misinterpretation of the term that underscores a mistaken belief that youth's social and emotional growth can be addressed with curriculum alone. Our approach is to put the developmental perspective back into the center of the process. By understanding a child's developmental strengths and challenges, educators can be more strategic about which skills should be focused on and how those skills should be approached to lead to the best outcomes. For that reason, in our work we have deliberately chosen to use the term *social-emotional development* (SED), but we see ourselves as part of the larger SEL movement and have refrained from using that terminology throughout this chapter for the sake of consistency within the book.

Even if social and emotional competencies are measurable, is it the best use of an OST program's limited time and resources? The data collection process can be time consuming, particularly for programs with short windows of time to work with youth, and can bring a test-like atmosphere to a program that is consciously working to provide a different experience from the typical school day. To better understand the feelings of OST professionals around data collection, The PEAR Institute conducted the *2016 STEM Learning Ecosystem Leadership Survey on Evaluation and Assessment* (Allen & Noam, 2016). While OST facilitators and staff generally agreed that some level of evaluation and assessment was important to inform program quality, they identified six major challenges: a lack of necessary infrastructure, like a common data system; limited resources, including staff time and funding; a need for common assessments; negative associations with high-stakes testing; stringent data sharing/privacy policies; and disconnects among partners (Allen & Noam, 2016). When considering the question of how social and emotional competency measurement can be effectively used in OST programs, it is important to keep these identified challenges in mind, and not to view them as purely deterrents to measurement, but as inspiration to inform our best thinking around how to create data collection tools and interpretation systems designed to be the most useful for practice.

CONCLUSION

In this chapter, we shared our experiences working with two OST networks to improve their programming and build stronger relationships with the youth they serve. Through these two examples, we have shown that incorporating measurement that focuses on youth social and emotional competencies is possible, but building these types of systems takes time. If you are working to build a system within your own OST program or network of programs, it's important to remember the work described in this chapter took between 2 and 7 years to establish. Though time consuming, it is heartening to see that it is possible for large communities of programs to adopt common measurement tools and use the data to make informed decisions about resource allocation and targeted professional development. We recommend that OST programs do not start from scratch. There are approaches that programs can borrow, try, or modify from others, such as the work we have described in this chapter.

The key to this work is innovation. Research informs only part of the work, and collecting feedback from the field is critical. We have improved our measurements through feedback from our deep partnerships, and they have helped us to design measurement tools and trainings that are better suited for informal/nonformal OST programs. We need to bring the same level of inquiry and reflection to our evaluation and assessment strategies that we hope educators will instill in our children during their OST activities.

NOTE

1. Of course, there is an additional extension of the evaluation process, which entails research, the pursuit of specific hypotheses, and rigorous designs that expand our knowledge and are published in peer-reviewed journals. This last element is not of primary concern for this chapter, though it is an important part of The PEAR Institute's work and the psychometric validation of its tools.

REFERENCES

Allen, P. J., & Noam, G. G. (2016). *STEM learning ecosystems: Evaluation and assessment findings* (Report). Belmont, MA: The PEAR Institute: Partnerships in Education and Resilience. Retrieved from http://stemecosystems.org/wp-content/uploads/2017/01/STEMEcosystems_Final_120616.pdf

Allen, P. J., Noam, G. G., Little, T. D., Fukuda, E., Gorrall, B. K., & Waggenspack, B. A. (2017). *Afterschool & STEM system building evaluation 2016.* Belmont, MA: The PEAR Institute: Partnerships in Education and Resilience. Available at https://www.thepearinstitute.org/afterschool-stem-evaluation-2016

Allen, P. J., Thomas, K., Triggs, B., & Noam, G. G. (2017). *The Holistic Student Assessment (HSA) technical report.* Belmont, MA: The PEAR Institute: Partnerships in Education and Resilience.

Bowlby, J. (1969). *Attachment.* New York, NY: Basic Books.

Cooper, H., Valentine, J. C., Nye, B., & Lindsay, J. J. (1999). Relationships between five after-school activities and academic achievement. *Journal of Educational Psychology, 91,* 369–378.

Darling, N. (2005). Participation in extracurricular activities and adolescent adjustment: Cross-sectional and longitudinal findings. *Journal of Youth and Adolescence, 34,* 493–505.

Duckworth, A. L., & Yeager, D. S. (2015). Measurement matters: Assessing personal qualities other than cognitive ability for educational purposes. *Educational Researcher, 44*(4), 237–251. https://doi.org/10.3102/0013189X15584327

Durlak, J. A., & Weissberg, R. P. (2007). *The impact of afterschool programs that promote personal and social skills* (CASEL Report). Chicago, IL: Collaborative for Academic, Social, and Emotional Learning. Retrieved from https://casel.org/wp-content/uploads/2016/08/PDF-1-the-impact-of-after-school-programs-that-promote-personal-and-social-skills-executive-summary.pdf

Erikson, E. H. (1950). *Childhood and society.* New York, NY: Norton.

Fredricks, J. A., & Eccles, J. S. (2006). Is extracurricular participation associated with beneficial outcomes? Concurrent and longitudinal relations. *Developmental Psychology, 42,* 698–713.

Helping Youth Succeed Through Out-of-School Time Programs. (2006, January). Retrieved from the American Youth Policy Forum website: http://www.aypf.org/publications/HelpingYouthOST2006.pdf

Lauer, P. A., Akiba, M., Wilkerson, S. B., Apthorp, H. S., Snow, D., & Martin-Glenn, M. L. (2006). Out-of-school-time programs: A meta-analysis of effects for at-risk students. *Review of Educational Research, 76*(2), 275–313. doi.org/10.3102/00346543076002275

Malti, T., & Noam, G. G. (Eds.). (2008). Where youth development meets mental health and education: The RALLY approach. *New Directions for Youth Development, 120.* San Franciso, CA: Jossey-Boss.

Malti, T., & Noam, G. G. (2009). A developmental approach to the prevention of adolescent's aggressive behavior and the promotion of resilience. *International Journal of Developmental Science, 3*(3), 235–246. https://doi.org/10.3233/DEV-2009-3303

Malti, T., & Noam, G. G. (2016). Social-emotional development: From theory to practice. *European Journal of Developmental Psychology, 13*(6), 652–665. https://doi.org/10.1080/17405629.2016.1196178

Malti, T., Zuffianò, A., & Noam, G. G. (2017). Knowing every child: Validation of the Holistic Student Assessment (HSA) as a measure of social-emotional development. *Prevention Science, 19*(3), 306–317. https://doi.org/10.1007/s11121-017-0794-0

Noam, G. G. (1996). High-risk youth: Transforming our understanding of human development. *Human Development, 39*(1), 1–17. https://doi.org/10.1159/000278376

Noam, G. G., & Goldstein, L. S. (1998). *The resilience inventory.* Unpublished protocol.

Noam, G. G., Malti, T., & Guhn, M. (2012). From clinical-developmental theory to assessment: The Holistic Student Assessment tool. *International Journal of Conflict and Violence, 6*(2), 201–213. https://doi.org/10.4119/UNIBI/ijcv.276

Noam, G. G., Malti, T., & Karcher, M. J. (2013). Mentoring relationships in developmental perspective. In D. L. DuBois & M. J. Karcher (Eds.), *The handbook of youth mentoring* (2nd ed., pp. 99–115). Los Angeles, CA: SAGE.

Noam, G. G., Powers, S. I., Kilkenny, R., & Beedy, J. (1990). The interpersonal self in life-span developmental perspective: Theory, measurement, and longitudinal case analyses. In P. B. Baltes, D. L. Featherman, & R. M. Lerner (Eds.), *Life-span development and behavior* (Vol. 10, pp. 59–104). Hillsdale, NJ: Erlbaum.

Noam, G. G., & Triggs, B. (2016). Positive developments during the transition to adulthood. In R. A. Scott & S. M. Kosslyn (Eds.), *Emerging trends in the social and behavioral sciences* (pp. 1–15). Hoboken, NJ: John Wiley & Sons. Retrieved from http://doi.wiley.com/10.1002/9781118900772.etrds0416

Piaget, J. (1954). *The construction of reality in the child.* New York, NY: Basic Books.

Price, L. (2016). *Psychometric methods: Theory into practice* (1st ed.). New York, NY: Guilford Press.

Shernoff, D. J. (2010). Engagement in after-school programs as a predictor of social competence and academic performance. *American Journal of Community Psychology, 45*(3–4), 325–337. https://doi.org/10.1007/s10464-010-9314-0

The State of Summer: Preliminary Findings From the 2016 Boston Summer Learning Community. (2016, Fall). Retrieved from the Boston After School & Beyond website: http://bostonbeyond.org/wp-content/uploads/2016/11/Summer-2016-Data-Report.pdf

CHAPTER 15

DESCRIBING AND MEASURING ADULT INSTRUCTIONAL PRACTICE IN OST SETTINGS FOR MIDDLE AND HIGH SCHOOL YOUTH

Kiley Bednar, Karen Pittman, Joseph Bertoletti, Poonam Borah, Stephen C. Peck, and Charles Smith

CONTEXT

Out-of-school time (OST) organizations are defined by their flexibility and their diversity of program content and staffing, both of which facilitate unique responsiveness to youth and community needs. These organizations and programs march to many different drummers. They have different affiliations, different funding models and sources, and different, if interrelated, goals for child and youth development. Our research over the last 10 years in youth development, program quality, and social and emotional learning (SEL) across a wide variety of OST settings reflects the lessons

Social and Emotional Learning in Out-of-School Time, pages 265–283

we have learned in terms of best practices that have a positive impact on children and youth. It has helped us produce a set of measures and instructional practices, along with guidance on designing quality improvement systems that work in a variety of OST networks. We have shown that (a) a set of standards and measures, embedded in a continuous quality improvement approach, can improve program quality; (b) quality improvement is best facilitated at the systems level (OST networks and intermediaries) by enhancing system capacity for measurement and quality improvement; and (c) measuring program quality and child and youth outcomes in a continuous quality improvement system (QIS) offers relevant and useful data for practitioners and systems aimed at improving social and emotional practices and skills.

High-quality programs are linked to increased levels of youth engagement (Akiva, Cortina, Eccles, & Smith, 2013; Naftzger et al., 2013) and gains in academic skills demonstrated in both OST settings (Smith et al., 2015) and the school day (Naftzger, Devaney, & Foley, 2014; Naftzger, Hallberg, & Tang, 2014; Naftzger et al., 2013). We also know that program quality is measureable, malleable, and marketable (Pittman, 2018). Therefore, quality improvement has become one of the primary domains for collaboration that the diverse actors within a local or state OST system can agree on (Smith, 2013). Developing a system-wide approach to quality improvement that is adopted and used by all participating organizations provides a common framework for describing the desired child and youth experiences and for articulating standards for management practices, program quality, and effectiveness that apply regardless of the content of the services and activities offered (Yohalem, Devaney, Smith, & Wilson-Ahlstrom, 2012). A system-wide approach also provides opportunities for cross-age, cross-silo, cross-sector planning and action, allowing for effective blending of public and private resources earmarked for accountability and improvement (Yohalem, Ravindranath, Pittman, & Evennou, 2010).

Building system-wide capacity requires management-level investments. QISs have the dedicated staffing to support routine collection and use of data for continuous improvement and to oversee coordinated training and assessment procedures. Many communities have created or selected *intermediary organizations* to manage quality improvement interventions and provide technical supports necessary for program managers to participate in a QIS. These intermediaries often also provide other quality-related services, such as professional development, assessment, and participation tracking.

In recent years, OST systems that use a QIS have grown in number; as a whole they represent a large social investment in the well-being of youth in Grades 4 through 12. A rough estimate using the Weikart Center's client base as an example puts the total investment in quality improvement for

4,700 sites at over $18 million annually. This investment represents about 4% of the total spending on OST services ($450 million).

Expectations for OST systems have grown along with these investments. Funders are shifting from a focus on defining and setting quality standards, to expecting accountability for service quality and evidence of effectiveness for social and emotional skills and school outcomes. OST systems are now expected to not only have quality standards but to also be equipped to define and demonstrate the level of quality sufficient to achieve desired youth outcomes (Smith, 2013).

This evolution of priorities and questions requires OST systems to respond with more highly elaborated QIS policies that link quality standards and practices more explicitly to the burgeoning research and practice literatures on SEL. This chapter describes the frameworks, interventions, and tools the Forum for Youth Investment's David P. Weikart Center for Youth Program Quality (Weikart Center) has created to support both of these demands.

THE YOUTH PROGRAM QUALITY INTERVENTION

The Weikart Center has developed a proven intervention (i.e., Youth Program Quality Intervention [YPQI]) that is designed to support management-level implementation of continuous quality improvement that operationalizes the QIS approach (Smith et al., 2012). The intervention is anchored in three assumptions. It assumes that the organizational management and staff

1. agree with the basic principles of positive youth development (PYD) and affirm the desire to see PYD reflected in their programming;
2. value an approach that empowers practitioners to assess and improve their craft, through observation, training, support, and reflecting on shared quality standards; and
3. foster a low-stakes or "right stakes" context in which practitioners have the opportunity to reflect on and improve practice within a spirit of continuous quality improvement, not high-stakes incentives such as funding or job security (Smith, 2013).

The intervention supports a site-level continuous quality improvement process that includes three steps: assess, plan, and improve. These steps, in this order, affirm the three assumptions above. The focus on intervention fidelity is at both management and staff levels, reflecting a philosophy that acknowledges the diversity of network members and widespread use of field-developed practices versus evidence-based curricula. A strong QIS has the staffing and structures needed to define indicators, compile data and conduct assessments, use technology to create efficiencies in data use and on-demand training, and provide targeted improvement supports for staff and managers.

The Weikart Center now has more than a decade of experience working with OST systems that have built QISs in the OST sector. Working with dozens of systems (from state departments of education to large local OST intermediaries) over time has allowed the Weikart Center to formally evaluate and "road test" QIS designs, increasing our understanding of what issues can emerge in poorly designed QISs and what designs tend to work best in various systems.

Prime Time Palm Beach County, Inc. (Prime Time) is one of the largest OST systems in the country and was one of the first systems with which the Weikart Center worked. Palm Beach County Quality Standards for Afterschool is the foundation for its QIS. The key components of its QIS system include: (a) quality advisors assigned to assist participating programs in the completion of a self-assessment and (b) the development of an improvement plan. They assist executive directors, program managers, and staff in pinpointing and executing opportunities to improve quality for children and youth, as well as encourage the use of community resources. Primary incentives include funding, access to QIS supports, development of individual skills, and public recognition.

Both the number and quality of programs supported by Prime Time have increased over time. In the 2014–2015 school year, they provided training and assessment services to OST programs at 120 different sites serving 20,000 youth. In that year, more than 70% of sites improved their overall score or maintained a 4.1 or above (5 is the highest score). More than 38% of programs achieved 4.1 or higher on the Youth Program Quality Assessment (PQA) Form A (Smith & Hohmann, 2005). The Youth PQA Form A produces scores for 63 items within 18 scales in four domains: safety, supportive environment, interaction, and engagement. Overall, across programs in the QIS between 2013–2014 and 2014–2015, 64% improved their score and 73% either improved or maintained a 4.1 or higher (Prime Time Palm Beach County, 2015). Not only can quality improve on a case-by-case level, but it can improve and be maintained across large, growing OST systems.

The YPQI is now in use in over 125 networks, reaching over 4,700 sites, over 31,000 staff, and over 400,000 children and youth. Rapid adoption and widespread use of the YPQI demonstrates that measuring and improving OST quality is important, not just for individual programs, but for coordinated OST systems that have decided that quality matters.

QUALITY, EQUITY, AND ADOLESCENT SOCIAL AND EMOTIONAL DEVELOPMENT: THE NEXT FRONTIER

The increased focus on measuring social and emotional skill growth in children and adolescents presents an opportunity to link earlier definitions of program quality based on PYD research and frameworks to more focused definitions of social and emotional skills and adult practice. Recent research showing social and emotional skills as a strong predictor of young adult success has led to a push to understand how to support the SEL skill growth of older adolescents. This push has created a much-needed opportunity to address the different professional development needs of the staff of OST youth programs who, similar to high school teachers, have to integrate SEL practices into more complex, sequenced curricula designed to support mastery of any type of knowledge or skill. The push to acknowledge the value of responding to youth who have experienced trauma with supports, not punishments, has increased the focus on supporting developmentally responsive practice in all systems.

Combined, these new agendas have created a second wave of questions about program quality. What level of quality is needed to achieve significant SEL skill growth? Are current "quality thresholds" adequate to ensure skill growth? Are SEL practices sufficiently specified, assessed, and supported? Can we link quality to outcomes in OST programs? Does quality have a differential impact on high-risk youth? Can we create practical measures that support continuous improvement? Can we create accessible tools and supports for the broader field? Can we create research–practice partnerships to answer these questions? The SEL Challenge, a partnership between the Susan Crown Exchange and the Weikart Center started in 2014, was designed to answer these and other questions.

The SEL Challenge aimed to achieve two ambitious goals. First, to develop *standards* for SEL practice and curate descriptive examples of the *action* that staff and youth actually see in OST settings. Second, to develop a method to take these practices to scale in OST networks by supporting the *measurement of SEL practices and social and emotional skills* (Smith, McGovern, Larson, Hillaker, & Peck, 2016).

The challenge made three contributions to the study of how to support adolescent social and emotional development. The first contribution was in its granularity. The SEL Challenge introduced grounded, granular, universal descriptions and measures of youth skills and adult practices. The initiative's research focused on creating detailed descriptions and measures of the specific staff practices that help structure the context for skill learning and the youth social and emotional skills that are demonstrated and observed in the OST context.

The SEL Challenge's second contribution was to elevate OST work with teens, with a strong but not exclusive focus on disadvantaged teens. In general, an adolescent's ability to self-regulate, for example, to manage emotions, attention, motivation, and behavior to achieve specific purposes is related to a wide range of positive outcomes. We know that social and emotional skills are malleable in adolescence (Pittman, 2018). For some of the youth entering the programs who are considered vulnerable and who have a difficult social and emotional history (e.g., exposure to traumatic events), an intentional intervention that incorporates responsive practices, planned check-ins, safe spaces, and sequenced SEL content may be of particular importance. These types of high-quality environments that blend project-based learning with supportive SEL practices can help adolescents develop agency; for example, to use self-regulatory skills to ignore distractions or to choose environments that have higher developmental potential. The SEL Challenge found that regardless of whether teens were building boats or writing a musical, with the right staff practices, support, and curriculum, youth participants developed social and emotional skills.

The SEL Challenge's third contribution was that it linked quality to outcomes. Linking program quality with outcomes, especially an outcome measure that was developed by practitioners, provides additional information for the field and for programs looking to use data to inform their continuous quality improvement efforts. Linking quality to outcomes also allows us to position the research in a larger picture of neuroscience, learning, and brain development. As QIS systems move toward asking what practices promote the greatest skill gain and how we can target the most appropriate supports to the youth who need them, the research and findings of the SEL Challenge can move us closer to building QISs that are designed to answer these questions.

Methodology for Ensuring Practitioner Engagement

The SEL Challenge was designed to actively engage expert practitioners in qualitative and quantitative research to identify standards for SEL practice across sites and describe performance at each site. Practitioners were involved in every step of the research and development process, from program selection and standards identification to performance measurement and tool development.

This approach to research and practice was key to the development of our validated tool, the Youth PQA. This tool was based on experiences with youth and on best practices developed at a summer camp coordinated by the HighScope Educational Research Foundation. The Weikart Center built on this approach in the SEL Challenge research—by iterating between research and practice and ensuring that the practitioners' experience, wisdom, and expertise were reflected in each stage of development. The full methodology was described in *Preparing Youth to Thrive: Methodology and Findings from the Social and Emotional Learning Challenge* (Smith, McGovern, Peck, et al., 2016). The opportunities for practitioner engagement are summarized below.

Programs were selected through an application process that provided organizations an opportunity to describe specific SEL program offerings (multiple sessions during which the same group of youth and adults meet for a planned learning purpose) that use SEL practices and curriculum to grow social and emotional skills.

Participants were selected, in part, because of their ability to deconstruct their program practices. We used a qualitative approach with participant feedback loops to identify standards for SEL practice. Identification of exemplar practices entailed describing and mapping what happens in the offering, as well as multiple interviews and focus groups with team members and youth. These data were then subjected to an analysis of common themes, reviewed by the challenge practitioners and the Weikart Center, and incorporated into the development of the standards.

Participants were also asked to review the evidence base with us. The published work of Reed Larson and colleagues, summarized in Appendix C of the *Preparing Youth to Thrive* (Field Guide), provided the primary evidence base and a starting framework for development of the application process, the interview questions, and, ultimately, the standards (Smith, McGovern, Larson, et al., 2016). We partnered with Larson because the framework developed by Larson and his colleagues is anchored in the voices of adolescents themselves in hundreds of interviews conducted during this nearly two-decade research program.

Because our intent was to describe curriculum and practice related to learning social and emotional skills, we co-created an SEL learning theory with the practitioners that fit the relatively short time scale of the SEL offerings—less than 1 year in all cases—and the even shorter momentary, daily, and weekly timeframes in which staff practices are delivered. We then reviewed the practices that the expert practitioners described as important, and that were consistent across the challenge offerings, and selected those that were supported in the evidence base to inform the standards for SEL practice.

As part of the performance study, the challenge teams engaged in a continuous improvement process focused on SEL practice. Performance measures were selected to describe the quality of management practices, the quality of instructional practice, and changes in youth SEL-related beliefs and behaviors. We worked with staff to implement performance studies at each of the eight OST sites and engaged them in interpreting the reports developed for their organization and for the SEL cohort, which included comparisons to a normative sample.

Finally, in addition to participation in the SEL Challenge study, we invited the SEL Challenge partners to contribute to outreach and dissemination efforts. Practitioner stories were captured as vignettes that helped describe the standards, and quotes and stories from youth themselves. Case studies describing curriculum and resources in each of the exemplary offerings were developed to provide additional context. These contributions and other resources, activities, blogs, and webinars shared by the expert practitioners were housed on a new website, selpractices.org, along with activities and self-assessment resources. Challenge partners delivered a total of over 50 trainings across the country.

Study Participants, Tools, and Measures

From an initial pool of 250 initial challenge applicants, eight organizations were selected based on several criteria, including a focus on SEL, the ability to clearly describe their program, and evaluation evidence. The eight organizations selected for the Challenge ranged widely, operating in the cities of Santa Barbara, Milwaukee, Philadelphia, New York, St. Paul, St. Louis, and Boston.

In all eight programs selected, SEL went hand-in-hand with complicated and engaging work projects such as creating a service project or boat building. The offering selected by each organization ranged in size from 2 to 5 staff and 11 to 45 youth. The dosage, or amount of participation required by each offering, was intensive in all cases, and varied from 39 to 370 contact hours. Youth participation in the offerings was voluntary. Youth ranged in age from 12 to 19, and the average age was 15. Staff defined their programs as serving many youth who could be considered vulnerable. Their definitions of vulnerable youth varied, and included youth who had few friends, youth who lived in high-stress homes or neighborhoods, youth who were exposed to systematic racism and exclusion, and youth who had been referred by a foster care or juvenile delinquency program.

When developing SEL standards described in the Field Guide, we used the term *standard* to describe practices that (a) appeared across challenge offerings, (b) were described as important by the expert practitioners, and (c) were supported in the evidence base. To convey the essence of the standard, practitioners described what they wanted youth to experience during the offering and what they did to support those experiences. There were 34 standards. Each standard was linked to multiple practice indicators (a total of 60) that describe more specific aspects of the standard (Smith, McGovern, Larson, et al., 2016).

The standards were presented in the Field Guide within the framework of *key youth experiences* and *staff practices*. Our definition of staff practice is broad, and includes momentary staff behavior as well as more enduring structures that the staff can put into place. Key youth experiences help identify the adult decisions and behaviors necessary to increase the probability that youth experiences happen. For example, key youth experiences (e.g., experience a range of emotions) help identify both the staff behaviors (e.g., modeling appropriate use of emotion) and the program structures that the staff put into place (e.g., structured opportunity for sharing) to produce the youth experiences. It is important that both the staff practices and key youth experiences are included in the list of standards for SEL practice.

The standards for SEL practice that were developed during the challenge were organized around six categories, or domains, of SEL practice and skill. The six SEL domains selected are: Emotion Management, Empathy, Teamwork, Responsibility, Initiative, and Problem Solving. Selection of these six domains of practice was based on prior research, the input of the challenge participants, and a desire to discuss SEL practices and skill in plain language (see Figure 15.1).

Examples of standards associated with one of the six domains, Empathy, follow below: Key Youth Experiences:

- *Inequality and Identity.* Youth explore social structure and power in relation to themselves and others.
- *Diverse Perspectives.* Youth share their stories and listen to the stories of others.
- *Acceptance.* Youth practice relating to others with acceptance and understanding.

Staff Practices:

- *Structure.* Staff provide programs with appropriate structure for sharing experience and promoting equity.
- *Modeling.* Staff model empathy skills with youth.

Practice indicators for Empathy include:

- Youth explore effects of stereotypes, discrimination, and social structures (e.g., based on race, gender, class, sexuality, religion, ability).
- Youth develop and share personal stories.
- Youth provide attentive, empathetic listening to the experiences, backgrounds, and perspectives of others (Smith, McGovern, Larson, et al., 2016).

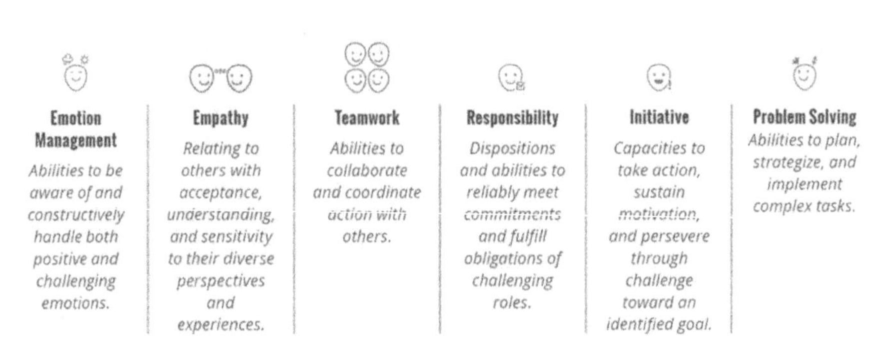

Figure 15.1 Six SEL domains. *Source:* Smith, McGovern, Larson, Hillaker, & Peck, 2016, p. 7. Reprinted with permission.

Although the challenge research methods were focused within each domain, the targeted SEL offerings were found to have common features among all programs. We termed these findings *Curriculum Features.* We use the term curriculum broadly; it is meant to include both the sequence of content and experiences fit to the developmental and learning needs of youth, and also the supports necessary for the instructional staff to implement the sequence (Smith, McGovern, Larson, et al., 2016).

Five categories of features were identified as foundational to the SEL work (see Table 15.1). The challenge's expert practice participants frequently described these features as nonnegotiable underpinnings for the more specific SEL practices described above. All five categories are important, but three, in particular, are worth additional discussion.

One of the most defining contributions of the SEL Challenge is a deeper understanding of the sequence of the programming. Deconstruction of each organization's offerings revealed that there are two sequences at work. The first is the project content sequence (Smith, McGovern, Larson, et al., 2016). Youth are guided along a process where they employ the skills needed to achieve content mastery (e.g., theater production, leading an advocacy campaign). These skills are often introduced in an explicit, specific sequence of steps that build towards mastery.

The SEL Challenge revealed similar, if less explicit, sequencing related to the introduction of opportunities to learn and practice social and emotional competencies. The SEL content sequence, the second sequence, happens in parallel to the project content sequence. The opportunities for challenge and complexity in the SEL content sequence are also fertile ground for experiencing social and emotional skill growth: working with a team, taking responsibility and initiative, solving problems, understanding others, and navigating challenge and positive emotions.

It is important to note that some of the most important practices that adults employ with youth, especially in moments of stress and challenge,

TABLE 15.1 SEL Curriculum Features

Project Content Sequence
• Staff shape the offering work: – with youth input, often requiring youth ownership. – with complex goals and/or a complex sequence of operations. – with repetitive skill practice in diverse contexts.
SEL Content Sequence
• The offerings: – follow a progression through the SEL domains. – are structured for youth to engage their community. • Youth master social and emotional skills and experience increasing agency.
Safe Space
• Staff cultivate: – ground rules for group processes (e.g., listening, turn-taking, decision-making) and sharing of emotions. – a culture around the principles that all are different, equal, and important in which people actively care for, appreciate, and include each other. – a culture where learning from mistakes and failures is highly valued. – consistent routines, activities, roles, or procedures to provide a structured and predictable experience.
Responsive Practices
• Staff: – observe and interact in order to know youth deeply. – provide structure for check-ins to actively listen to and receive feedback from individual youth. – coach, model, scaffold, and facilitate in real time as challenges occur.
Supports for Staff
• The organization: – recruits youth who will benefit from the offering. – includes more than one staff member in every program session with the ability to implement responsive practices. • Staff: – work together before each program session to plan and collaborate on the session activities and regularly debrief following each session to discuss youth progress, staff response, and adjustments for future sessions. – are supported to grow professionally and rejuvenate energy for the work. – are supported by their organization to reflect on and improve their practices through a continuous improvement process.

Source: Reprinted from Smith, McGovern, Larson, Hillaker, & Peck (2016). Reprinted with permission.

are "responsive practices" that contribute to the experience of co-regulation between staff and youth. Co-regulation can be defined as "nurturing, instruction, coaching, and support that will promote optimal self-regulation by the child, while simultaneously buffering against environmental stressors that might diminish regulatory capacity" (Murray, Rosanbalm,

Christopoulos, & Hamoudi, 2015, p. 19). The use of responsive practices keeps the stress and strain of a challenging situation within a comfortable range for the young person, contributing to a sense of safety and the ability to manage one's attention, motivation, emotion, and behavior. The experience of co-regulation leads to an increased ability to self-regulate, which ultimately leads to the experience of agency (Smith, McGovern, Peck, et al., 2016).

One of the key goals of the challenge was to create tools that are useful and can be easily used to take best practices to scale in a variety of settings and programs. This means that the assessments need to reflect what is realistic, relevant, and measurable. In order to test SEL performance measures that could be replicated in a QIS, we focused on both program quality measures and youth outcomes measures, and on program quality measures that could be compared to a larger reference sample.

We began with program quality. Each SEL offering was observed at three points in time using the PQA. Average ratings were used to compare the SEL Challenge offerings to high school and middle school programs in another broadly representative sample of OST programs.

To assess youth engagement, we administered an engagement survey focused on experiences of interest, challenge, and belonging at each of the three time points. Responses were averaged to produce an overall youth engagement rating for each offering.

The Youth Beliefs Survey focused on youth social and emotional skill beliefs, and was also administered at three points in time. This survey included 10 measurement scales across the six domains. Items were drawn from several sources: prosocial and protective indicators (Lippman, Moore, et al., 2014; Lippman, Ryberg, et al., 2014), optimism (Scheier, Carver, & Bridges, 1994), emotional reappraisal and emotional suppression (Gross & John, 2003), and identification of emotions (Schutte et al., 1998).

In addition to the youth surveys, a staff-rated youth behavior measure was also conducted at three points in time (Smith, McGovern, Peck, et al., 2016). This measure included 15 measurement scales across the six domains; it was developed specifically for the SEL Challenge. The items were tailored to reflect practitioner descriptions of skill growth in each domain. The items focused on behaviors that could be observed by staff; that were considered realistic, observable, and important by the expert practitioners; and were seen as behaviors in which youth had skill growth needs and were likely to demonstrate skill change that could be assessed over a short time frame (Smith, McGovern, Peck, et al., 2016).

Finally, the quality of management practices was measured at the end of the program cycle, through a one-time staff and manager survey. The survey focused on accountability, communication, and job satisfaction.

Findings From Performance Studies

With the data collected above, we implemented performance studies at each of the eight OST sites to describe the quality of the SEL practice and youth skill growth in the exemplary offerings. We produced an SEL performance report for each organization that included comparisons to a normative sample, and we engaged challenge teams in a continuous improvement process focused on SEL practice.

There were two types of findings from the performance studies: the quality of staff practices and youth skill change. The quality of staff practice findings are of interest because they offer evidence of validation for the selection of exemplary offerings through the SEL Challenge application process and for the SEL best practice standards that were drawn from these offerings. The standards are more credible if they come from programs that are of unusually high quality and where there is accompanying evidence of youth skill growth (Smith, McGovern, Larson, et al., 2016; Smith, McGovern, Peck et al., 2016).

In the PQA, the SEL Challenge programs scored substantially higher than other OST programs for adolescents, indicating that our selection of expert programs was effective (see Figure 15.2).

Youth outcomes (SEL beliefs and behaviors) increased on average during the challenge project period across all skill indicators (see Figures 15.3 and 15.4). It is important to note that youth who started out lower on these measures increased more over time relative to their peers who started out higher. This finding may not be generalizable to all youth with underdeveloped social and emotional skills. It is possible that the programs attracted vulnerable youth who were more open to the effects of the program experience (Smith, McGovern, Larson, et al., 2016; Smith, McGovern, Peck, et al., 2016). Regardless of the explanation, this finding makes an important

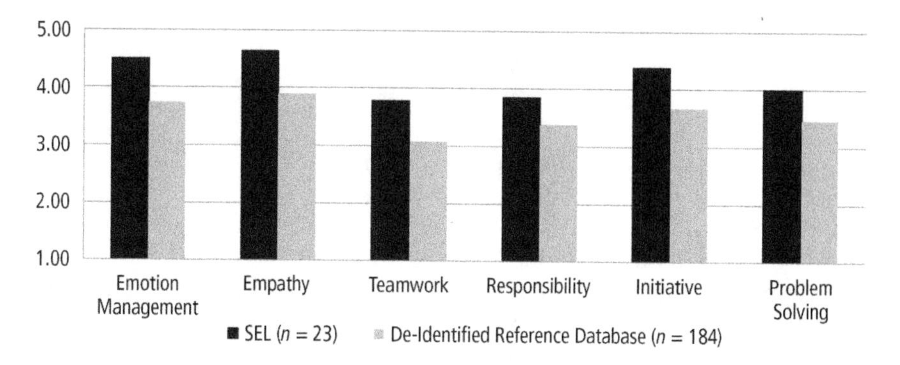

Figure 15.2 Social and emotional program quality assessment by SEL domain. *Source:* Smith, McGovern, Peck, Larson, & Roy, 2016. Reprinted with permission.

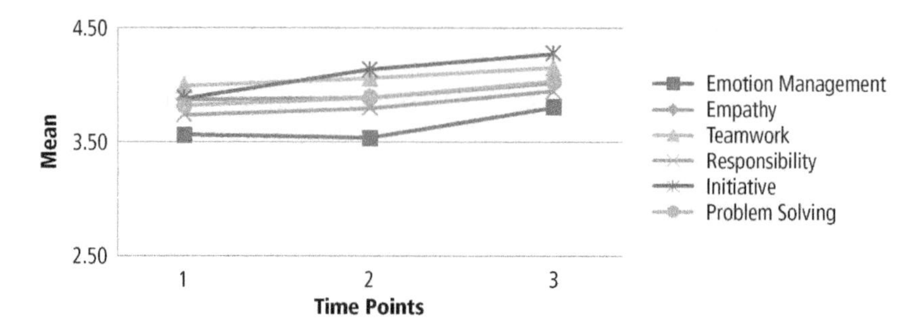

Figure 15.3 SEL belief change. *Source:* Smith, McGovern, Peck, Larson, & Roy, 2016. Reprinted with permission.

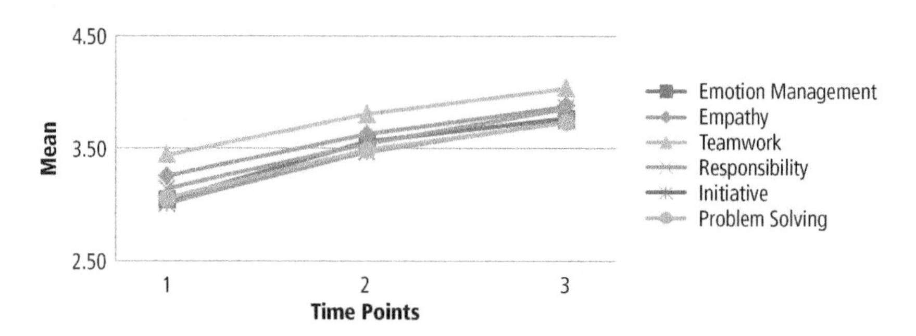

Figure 15.4 SEL behavior change. *Source:* Smith, McGovern, Peck, Larson, & Roy, 2016. Reprinted with permission.

contribution to equity discussions. It suggests that high-quality programs designed for all youth may have enhanced effects on youth most in need of social and emotional skill growth.

DISCUSSION

The SEL standards and measures were designed to fit with an evidence-based continuous improvement intervention or QIS. This approach to building SEL skills is already widely used in the OST field, and there are clear analogies to other sectors. Much of the infrastructure for SEL performance measurement described in this chapter is already available in local and state education agencies and supported in state laws and education agency policies. Further the SEL practices described in the standards have a high degree of overlap with best practices for teaching identified by the learning sciences. The suite of SEL measures developed and used in the challenge, based on the findings of the study, would be appropriate for use in a new or existing QIS (Smith, McGovern, Peck, et al., 2016).

One key outcome of the SEL Challenge study was the ability to describe standards at a consistent and detailed level, based on the experience of the practitioners and informed by research. This detail and consistency facilitates good measurement. And, in general, good measurement facilitates good policy and decision-making.

Beyond the development of descriptive learning theory and practices, the SEL Challenge provided an opportunity to describe how environment and context provide the opportunity for skill-building, with program quality defining context and social and emotional skills as the behavior. Drawing on theory and research focused on individuals developing in context (Roeser, Peck, & Nasir, 2006; Peck, 2007), we adapted the first generation of PQA tools, developed and tested over the past decade, to a body of evidence about learning, neuroscience, and behavior change. Although it is difficult to measure precisely what mental processes are going on in a person's mind, measuring behavior gives us a proxy that can show that SEL is happening.

The SEL Challenge had a major influence on our thinking about the ongoing adaptation of the PQA, one of the most widely used program quality assessment tools. In addition to the traditional scales found in the School Age PQA and the Youth PQA, the revised tool introduces scales for empathy, emotion coaching, problem solving, and mindfulness, and pulling higher-order thinking items and learning strategy items from the Academic Skill-Building/Summer Learning PQAs. Some traditional scales have been adjusted to more clearly differentiate the degrees of quality reflected by the practices (Hillaker et al., 2017).

Finally, the challenge provided an opportunity to better understand what it takes to develop high-quality programs like those that participated in the SEL Challenge. The extensive information gathered about the programs allowed us to identify seven distinguishing features. These features, described in the SEL Technical Report (Smith, McGovern, Peck, et al., 2016), are:

- *Staff and youth diversity.* The challenge offerings were diverse in terms of race/ethnicity and risk. The program staff intentionally recruited diverse youth.
- *Instructional intensity.* All of the SEL offerings were intensive commitments for the youth, ranging between 20 and 75 sessions and between 39 and 370 contact hours.
- *Strong staff qualifications.* Almost all staff had a college degree, and in over half of the organizations, at least one team member had an advanced degree. The organizations had low staff turnover, and lead instructors' tenure ranged between 8 months and 20 years, with one third of the staff in their current position for 5 years or more.

- *Highly collaborative organizational cultures.* SEL Challenge organizations performed higher than a reference group on all measures of culture and climate. In particular, substantially higher performance on both staff-to-manager and staff-to-staff collaborative practices reflect the importance of staff supports identified in the curriculum features and the opportunities to model SEL skills identified in the standards.
- *Exceptionally high-quality instruction.* SEL Challenge offerings were exceptionally high-performing programs, as compared to a normative sample, in terms of both the project curriculum and the quality of staff SEL practices.
- *Low staff-to-student ratios.* Almost all of the exemplary offerings had at least one staff member trained as a social worker or counselor in the setting at all times, and almost all had staff-to-student ratios at or below one-to-eight.
- *Programming with the opportunity for co-regulation with a caring adult.* In addition to use of the SEL practices identified by the standards, the exemplary offerings were characterized by challenging projects, responsive practices, and deep engagement with youth.

Together, these features of high-quality programs produce opportunities for youth to experience success and make mistakes within a safe and structured context, with adults who are responsive and attentive to the youth's needs in the moment and who are aiming to keep the challenge at an optimal learning level for a particular young person. These program features are powerful for all youth, including vulnerable youth, who may struggle with self-regulation or feeling safe and supported.

CONCLUSION

The SEL Challenge offered the opportunity to affirm the impact of high-quality youth programming on youth social and emotional skills, gleaning a detailed understanding of the practices and key youth experiences that contribute to social and emotional skill growth in youth. In the context of the field of youth program quality, the SEL Challenge underscored the link between program quality and youth outcomes, while furthering our ability to measure these concepts within the context of a continuous quality improvement effort. It sets the stage for improving supports for QIS systems aimed at linking program quality and youth outcomes on a larger scale.

Continuing to apply the lessons within a QIS or policymaking context will still require effort and change. Promoting best SEL practices may require not only staff training and development, but adjustments to recruitment or program content, and staff-to-youth ratios that create the need for additional staff. These are changes that organizations and administrators will have to embrace to create space and support for practitioner and youth skills to grow.

Applying these lessons may also require increased coordination among schools and providers to ensure that the most vulnerable youth have the opportunities that youth in the SEL Challenge programs were able to have—opportunities that some adults may consider to be beyond these young people's reach. While beyond the scope of this chapter, we recognize that our efforts to describe and evaluate staff practices and youth skill growth will not achieve their true potential unless we are able to widen our reach and apply the lessons for the benefit of those youth who can be most impacted by this improved understanding.

This research, however, has reinforced our belief that these investments in and by staff and youth are worth it. As highlighted in the Field Guide, the SEL Challenge showed that

> social and emotional skills emerged as youth (and adults) worked through challenges and experienced successes in important personal growth areas such as facing fear, accepting anger, recognizing unfair assumptions made about others learning that errors and failure are necessary and useful, and learning to tough things out, endure setbacks, and persevere through tedious work. (Smith, McGovern, Larson, et al., 2016, p. 15)

In short, participating youth experienced growth in abilities that can help them navigate their worlds, such as recognizing deeply entrenched differences in power, and coming to terms with disadvantage and unequal treatment without succumbing to helplessness.

We hope OST leaders will explore the use of these findings and tools in a variety of ways. Promising avenues include replicating the SEL Challenge in a wider range of communities to identify exemplary programs and expertise; using the standards found in the Field Guide to guide program development; and exploring selpractices.org, which has a suite of discussion and self-assessment tools. Leaders of quality-improvement systems will likely benefit from exploring a continuous quality improvement and evaluation design that uses a program quality measure and a youth outcomes measure to assess change over time, compare program quality to normative samples, or examine more closely the link between program quality and the ability of youth to master social and emotional skills.

REFERENCES

Akiva, T., Cortina, K. S., Eccles, J. S., & Smith, C. (2013). Youth belonging and cognitive engagement in organized activities: A large-scale field study. *Journal of*

Applied Developmental Psychology, 34(5), 208–218. https://doi.org/10.1016/j.appdev.2013.05.001

Gross, J. J., & John, O. P. (2003). Individual differences in two emotion regulation processes: Implications for affect, relationships, and well-being. *Journal of Personality and Social Psychology Bulletin, 85*(2), 348–362. http://psycnet.apa.org/doi/10.1037/0022-3514.85.2.348

Hillaker, B., Akiva, T., Jones, M., Sutter, A., Wallace, L., McGovern, . . . Smith, C. (2017). *Program quality assessment handbook: Social emotional learning.* Ypsilanti, MI: David P. Weikart Center for Youth Program Quality, a division of the Forum for Youth Investment.

Lippman, L. H., Moore, K. A., Guzman, L., Ryberg, R., McIntosh, H., Ramos, M. F., . . . Kuhfeld, M. (2014). *Flourishing children: Defining and testing indicators of positive development.* New York, NY: Springer.

Lippman, L. H., Ryberg, R., Terzian, M., Moore, K. A., Humble, J., & McIntosh, H. (2014). Positive and protective factors in adolescent well-being. In B. Asher, F. Casas, I. Frones, & J. E. Korbin (Eds.), *Handbook of child well-being: Theories, methods, and policies in global perspective* (pp. 2823–2866). Dordrecht, Netherlands: Springer.

Murray, D. W., Rosanbalm, K., Christopoulos, C., & Hamoudi, A. (2015). *Self-regulation and toxic stress: Foundations for understanding self-regulation from an applied developmental perspective* (OPRE Report# 2015-21). Washington, DC: Office of Planning, Research, and Evaluation, Administration for Children and Families, U.S. Department of Health and Human Services.

Naftzger, N., Devaney, E., & Foley, K. (2014). *Summary of analyses related to Nashville After Zone Alliance Program outcomes.* Chicago, IL: American Institutes for Research.

Naftzger, N., Hallberg, K., & Tang, Y. (2014). *Exploring the relationships between afterschool program quality and youth outcomes: Summary of findings from the Palm Beach County quality improvement system.* Naperville, IL: American Institutes for Research.

Naftzger, N., Manzeske, D., Nistler, M., Swanlund, A., Rapaport, A., Shields, J., . . . Sugar, S. (2013). *Texas 21st Century Community Learning Centers: Final evaluation report.* Naperville, IL: American Institutes for Research.

Peck, S. C. (2007). TEMPEST in a gallimaufry: Applying multilevel systems theory to person-in-context research. *Journal of Personality, 75,* 1127–1156.

Pittman, K. J. (2018). Securing the future: Pivoting OST from where and when to how and what. In H. J. Malone & T. Donahue (Eds.), *The growing out-of-school time field: Past, present, and future* (pp. 293–306). Charlotte, NC: Information Age.

Prime Time Palm Beach County. (2015). *Celebrating 15 years of excellence: Annual report 2014–2015.* Retrieved from https://simplebooklet.com/ptannualreport2015

Roeser, R. W., Peck, S. C., & Nasir, N. S. (2006). Self and identity processes in school motivation, learning, and achievement. In P. A. Alexander & P. H. Winne (Eds.), *Handbook of educational psychology* (pp. 391–424). Mahwah, NJ: Erlbaum.

Scheier, M. F., Carver, C. S., & Bridges, M. W. (1994). Distinguishing optimism from neuroticism (and trait anxiety, self-mastery, and self-esteem): A reevaluation of the life orientation test. *Journal of Personality and Social Psychology, 67*(6), 1063–1078. http://psycnet.apa.org/doi/10.1037/0022-3514.67.6.1063

Schutte, N. S., Malouff, J. M., Hall, L. E., Haggerty, D. J., Cooper, J. T., Golden, C. J., & Dornheim, L. (1998). Development and validation of a measure of emotional intelligence. *Personality and Individual Differences, 25*(2), 167–177. https://doi.org/10.1016/S0191-8869(98)00001-4

Smith, C. (2013). *Moving the needle on "moving the needle": Next stage technical guidance for performance based accountability systems in the expanded learning field with a focus on performance levels for the quality of instructional services.* Ypsilanti, MI: Weikart Center for Youth Program Quality, a division of the Forum for Youth Investment.

Smith, C., Akiva, T., Sugar, S., Lo, Y. J., Frank, K. A., Peck, S. C., & Cortina, K. S. (2012). *Continuous quality improvement in afterschool settings: Impact findings from the Youth Program Quality Intervention study.* Ypsilanti, MI: Weikart Center for Youth Program Quality, a vision of the Forum for Youth Investment.

Smith, C., Helegda, K., Ramaswamy, R., Hillaker, B., McGovern, G., & Roy, L. (2015). *Quality-outcomes study for Seattle Public Schools summer programs summer 2015 program cycle.* Ypsilanti, MI: Weikart Center for Youth Program Quality, a division of the Forum for Youth Investment.

Smith, C., & Hohmann, C. (2005). *Full findings from the Youth PQA validation study High/Scope Youth PQA technical report.* Ypsilanti, MI: High/Scope Educational Research Foundation.

Smith, C., McGovern, G., Larson, R., Hillaker, B., & Peck, S. C. (2016). *Preparing youth to thrive: Promising practices for social and emotional learning* (field guide). Ypsilanti, MI: David P. Weikart Center for Youth Program Quality at the Forum for Youth Investment.

Smith, C., McGovern, G., Peck, S. C., Larson, R., Hillaker, B., & Roy, L. (2016). *Preparing youth to thrive: Methodology and findings from the social and emotional learning challenge.* Washington, DC: Forum for Youth Investment.

Yohalem, N., Devaney, E., Smith, C., & Wilson-Ahlstrom, A. (2012). *Building citywide systems for quality: A guide and case studies for afterschool leaders.* Washington, DC: The Forum for Youth Investment and The Wallace Foundation.

Yohalem, N., Ravindranath, N., Pittman, K., & Evennou, D. (2010). *Insulating the education pipeline to increase postsecondary success.* Washington, DC: Forum for Youth Investment.

CHAPTER 16

MEASURING SOCIAL AND EMOTIONAL SKILLS IN OST SETTINGS

Opportunities and Challenges

Neil Naftzger and Sarah Terry

As social and emotional learning (SEL) has gained prominence in education and youth development, the desire to measure the outcomes of SEL work across educational settings has increased (Duckworth & Yeager, 2015; Egalite, Mills, & Greene, 2016; West et al., 2016). However, measurement of social and emotional skills is challenging from both a research and a practice perspective. From a research perspective, competing SEL frameworks and a lack of consensus around the relative importance and malleability of social and emotional skills has complicated the task of measurement. From a practice perspective, we have found that the measures that are available are often difficult to administer and interpret in the context of a typical out-of-school time (OST) program. Furthermore, their findings can be difficult to apply to program practice because the relationship between skill

Social and Emotional Learning in Out-of-School Time, pages 285–302

development and day-to-day experience is complex and often opaque (Yeager, Bryk, Muhich, Hausman, & Morales, 2015).

Despite these challenges, measurement of social and emotional skills has long been an important goal for the OST community. This is driven partly by ambivalence within the sector about using school-related outcome measures to evaluate program activities that are not explicitly academic, and partly by a strong desire to better understand and demonstrate the real value of OST program-based youth development work (Fredricks, Naftzger, Smith, & Riley, 2017; Hurd & Deutsch, 2017). We believe that OST program providers would benefit from social and emotional skill measures that produce data for the following general purposes:

- *Community positioning:* to elevate the work of the OST sector and connect it to important community goals for young people,
- *Performance improvement*: to help providers understand and improve the quality of their work, and
- *Proof of effectiveness*: to provide evidence about the effectiveness of OST programs in changing youth outcomes.[1]

In this chapter, we describe how a research-to-practice partnership between American Institutes for Research (AIR) and Youth Development Executives of King County (YDEKC) has attempted to overcome some of the challenges in measurement by developing an instrument that is both psychometrically sound (valid and reliable from a research perspective) and useful to OST program leaders and staff members for the set of purposes described above.

HOW ARE OST PROGRAMS HAVING AN IMPACT?

We believe that one of the major challenges facing the OST field is policymakers' and funders' inclination to assess OST program efficacy by focusing on how the OST system can potentially advance outcomes that are central to the missions of other systems, in particular the public school system. As a result, OST programs are commonly held accountable for how they contribute to academic performance (as measured by standardized tests), and how they support improvements in other school-related outcomes, such as reducing unexcused absences and disciplinary incidents. However, a lingering question persists among those who have spent substantial time in OST programs: How well do these outcomes align with how OST programs design and deliver programming?

For the past 15 years, a research and evaluation team at AIR has been studying the impact of OST programs on participating youth, particularly those funded by the 21st Century Community Learning Centers (21st CCLC) program (Naftzger, 2017; Naftzger et al., 2013). While this work has focused primarily on how programs support the achievement of desirable school-related outcomes, reflecting the stated goals of the 21st CCLC program (e.g., improved academic achievement, school-day behaviors, etc.), the team at AIR has come to the conclusion that the primary ways in which OST programs are likely supporting positive youth development are largely going unmeasured. After interviewing site coordinators running OST programs in a variety of states (and as part of a number of different projects), we found that programs have a tendency to describe their most positive impacts on participating youth as falling within one of the following categories, many of which are associated with SEL:

- Belonging/Mattering
  - Youth experiencing a sense of belonging and connectedness through positive and supportive relationships.
- Youth Agency
  - Youth developing positive mindsets and beliefs about their capacities, including confidence and a sense of self-efficacy.
  - Youth cultivating cognitive tools such as strategic thinking, which Larson and Angus (2011) describe as a capacity to craft and implement a course of action to achieve specific goals.
- Interest Development and Sense of Self
  - Youth having the opportunity to experience new things, which supports both identity development and young people's ability to make sense of themselves and the world around them.
  - Youth developing interest in domain-specific content areas, such as science, technology, engineering, and mathematics (STEM) and the arts.
- Self-Management
  - Youth developing schema to manage cognition and emotion.
- Sense of Purpose
  - Youth gaining an understanding of why and what they do with their lives matters.

SURVEYS AS A MECHANISM FOR MEASURING OST PROGRAM IMPACT

What is common across the above categories is that they explicitly reference skills, attitudes, and beliefs that are important to positive youth development, but are challenging to observe in a way that helps us understand how they are influencing youth behaviors and actions. For example, young people may attend school more frequently because they feel more connected to school, thanks to the friends they have made while participating in OST activities; they may enroll in an honors physics class in high school because they became interested in science while participating in an OST STEM program; they may work harder to master challenging academic content as a result of their experiences solving difficult problems in an OST setting; or they may participate in a service learning project focused on the environment because of their experiences in a summer learning program that emphasized the importance of environmental stewardship. We would argue that a key measurement challenge for the OST field is being able to better document growth in the skills, beliefs, and attitudes affected by participation in OST programs, and to describe how these changes may lead to the types of behaviors and actions described in the above set of examples. Starting in early adolescence, we believe the most direct way to access this kind of information is to question youth directly. Surveys are the most feasible mechanism for doing this.

For example, in a recent study conducted by AIR, a series of youth in Grades 4 to 9 served by 21st CCLC-funded programs in Washington state were asked to choose the top three ways in which they believed they had been affected by their participation in the programs. Of the 13 options listed for respondents, youth reports of impact were found to be concentrated in three primary areas (Naftzger & Sniegowski, 2018):

This program has helped me

- discover things I want to learn more about,
- find out what I like to do, and
- feel good about myself.

In this case, youth-reported program impacts related both to interest development and the development of a positive self-concept. While documenting these outcomes is useful in its own right, a critical question remains: How do these experiences affect how youth engage in other learning environments, including school and other OST programs? In other words, what are the cascading effects that may result from youth-reported program impacts in these areas? Generally, across the OST field, we would hypothesize that positive experiences in OST programs associated with the list of unmeasured youth outcomes detailed previously could result in the following types of observable youth behaviors in other settings, both within the confines of the OST program and in other learning environments during the school day:

- *Greater engagement in learning*, with new-found interests potentially leading youth to perceive academic content as more relevant than they did previously;

- *Enhanced levels of perseverance and effort*, which could be driven by future goals linked to new-found interests, or an improved sense of self-efficacy driven by successes they had in undertaking work or projects in an OST program where they had the opportunity to experience a sense of agency;
- *Positive interpersonal skills* resulting from interactions with peers in the program and an enhanced capacity to manage emotions and cognition honed through interpersonal interactions taking place during the OST program; and
- *Enhanced capacity to employ critical thinking/problem-solving skills* afforded through OST offerings that give youth the opportunity to experience challenges and a sense of efficacy and agency in overcoming those challenges.

While many of these behaviors may be directly observable by teachers and OST activity leaders, we believe that the extent to which these behaviors can be observed is largely context-dependent. That is, certain settings are going to afford more opportunity than others for youth to try out and showcase newly minted interests, beliefs, attitudes, and skills. As mentioned previously, for many OST programs, the dominant context of interest is the school-day learning environment, reflecting key stakeholder expectations and formally defined performance metrics specified by funders.

Efforts to reduce the impact of context on measuring the presence of social and emotional skills, attitudes, and beliefs may be an additional advantage of youth reports. While efforts to observe behaviors are completely dependent on the context in which those behaviors are being observed, youth reports allow youth to make a more global assessment of functioning that is less dependent on context, allowing them to potentially identify skills, attitudes, and beliefs that are stable and enduring, rather than situational in nature. For example, as noted previously, youth interest in STEM may be sparked and nurtured through participation in an OST program. In such cases, we would argue that youth are in a better position to report on this than adults who are trying to infer interest development by collecting data on behaviors hypothesized to be indicative of interest. Our feeling is that youth reports over time hold more promise in demonstrating the enduring nature of a given set of attitudes, beliefs, perceptions, and self-assessed presence of skills than a reliance on context-dependent, observed behaviors.

While there are a number of potential advantages associated with using youth reports to collect data on OST outcomes, there are certainly challenges and limitations associated with this measurement approach. Youth may not always be motivated to answer questions based on careful consideration and reflection, and they may lack the capacity to accurately self-evaluate on the skills, attitudes, and beliefs they are asked about. As youth enter early adolescence, they start developing enhanced analytic and cognitive processing skills that make survey measurement more viable, but that does not necessarily mean they will be motivated to engage in these processes in a serious and thoughtful manner. In addition, while we believe there are some advantages associated with youth reports in being able to document more stable and enduring attitudes, beliefs, and perceptions, what is happening within a youth's life at the time a survey is taken can influence how he or she responds, potentially demonstrating more variation in these outcomes across time than exists in reality. Like most efforts to measure social and emotional skills, a reliance on youth reports is characterized by both opportunities and challenges that warrant careful consideration and examination. YDEKC and AIR's effort to develop a youth survey assessing SEL-related outcomes over the past several years is representative of this balancing act.

DEVELOPMENT OF A SURVEY TOOL FOR USE IN AN OST NETWORK

YDEKC is a member-led coalition of youth-serving organizations in the Seattle area. It was established in 2011 with the mission of building and unifying the local youth development sector. To do this, YDEKC pairs an internally focused approach—consisting of network building and leadership and organizational development—with cross-sector work aimed at raising the profile of the youth development sector among external partners. The measurement of social and emotional skills, attitudes, and beliefs has played a central role in both of these approaches from the beginning. Internally, the process of defining a set of common outcomes and measurement approaches has provided a diffuse set of providers with a unifying framework for talking about their impact. Externally, the articulation of these outcomes has helped partners in other sectors (K–12 education in particular) to better understand the unique contribution of OST programs to school-related outcomes.

YDEKC's measurement work has evolved considerably over time. While youth development practitioners have always guided the work, it was initially catalyzed by an external need. In 2011, YDEKC began to work closely with the Road Map Project, a then-nascent collective impact initiative aimed at dramatically increasing educational attainment in the region by the year 2020.[2] Much of the Road Map Project's early work centered on establishing indicators of student success, essentially data points that could be tracked over time to monitor progress toward the project's 2020 goal. Most of the resulting "on-track" indicators were academic, but the project also identified a set of "contributing" indicators that were more holistic in nature. Two of these—the percentage of students motivated and engaged to succeed in school and the percentage of students exhibiting 21st-century skills—lacked clear definitions and associated measures. Since both of these indicators seemed closely aligned with the work of OST program providers in YDEKC's network, YDEKC assumed responsibility for establishing operational definitions and measurement approaches.

YDEKC began by convening a group of OST thought leaders from the Road Map Project region to conduct a comprehensive literature review on the topics of youth motivation and engagement and 21st-century skills. The group ultimately identified and named a set of components (or constructs) to represent these concepts:

- *Future Orientation:* Positive beliefs about the future; ability to set goals and monitor progress.
- *Self-Efficacy and Mindsets:* A belief that effort will bring success, and a belief in one's own capacity to succeed.
- *Perseverance/Grit:* A tendency to persist through challenges and sustain interest over time.
- *Self-Management:* The ability to assess and regulate feelings, emotions, and behaviors.
- *Belonging:* The perception of acceptance and support in schools, programs, and community.
- *Interpersonal Skills:* The ability to communicate effectively and work with individuals representing diverse points of view.
- *Creativity:* The ability to think creatively and restructure ideas to make a new contribution.
- *Critical Thinking:* The ability to apply prior skills and knowledge to new circumstances, reflect, and problem solve.

Measuring Motivation and Engagement in Schools

The task of measuring these constructs at the population level raised several issues. First, the work group concluded (after a thorough review) that no existing instrument adequately captured the constructs the group had identified. Second, the question of when, where, and how to assess all of the young people in the Road Map region's seven school districts presented huge practical and logistical challenges. YDEKC's work group ultimately decided to create a self-report survey that could be administered to students in the seven Road Map school districts along with school climate surveys. By creating a custom instrument, the group could ensure alignment with their outcomes framework. By piggybacking on an existing process (most school districts were already using student surveys for middle and high school students), they could get close to the population-level indicator to which the group had originally aspired.

The work group created an instrument called the Student Engagement and Motivation Survey (SEMS) by adapting scales from the research literature and from tools that local practitioners had found useful in their work.[3] An initial version of the SEMS was pilot tested with 6,000 students in the Renton School District in December 2012. This pilot provided preliminary evidence of the survey's reliability, and of its potential to increase understanding of youth motivation and engagement at the school, district, and aggregate levels. YDEKC developed a revised version of the student survey in the Spring of 2013 and expanded its use to other Road Map region school districts during the 2013–2014 school year.

Bringing Measurement to OST Programs

As the SEMS was being administered in schools, YDEKC shifted its focus to OST settings. Population-level measurement of the kinds of social and emotional skills, attitudes, and beliefs addressed by the SEMS was useful for external positioning. It had the potential to elevate the importance of social and emotional skills in the broader community, and to raise the profile of youth development, given its longstanding focus on these skills. However, the providers in YDEKC's network wanted a tool that could help them both improve their practice and prove that their work was having a positive impact on young people.

In 2013, YDEKC began working with the Weikart Center for Youth Program Quality to adapt the SEMS to OST settings. YDEKC convened a cohort of member organizations who were already involved in the Youth Program Quality Initiative (YPQI) led by School's Out Washington—a statewide intermediary organization and YDEKC's fiscal sponsor. One goal of this group was to pair data from YDEKC's OST survey with data on program quality and youth engagement in programming to test the underlying relationships in the Weikart Center's Quality-to-Outcomes theory of change, which posits that sustained participation in high-quality OST programs leads to the development of inter- and intra-personal skills that are broadly applicable and lead to better outcomes in other settings (Smith et al., 2012). Another goal was to meet YDEKC members' needs with a valid and reliable youth outcome measure that could produce meaningful data for program improvement and impact evaluation.

The first step in bringing the SEMS to OST settings was to revisit the set of constructs originally identified by YDEKC's work group. Since school engagement and motivation was no longer the central organizing principle behind the survey, YDEKC asked providers for additional input on

(a) the skills, attitudes, and beliefs that were most important to them, and (b) the skills, attitudes, and beliefs that they felt their programs influenced most directly. This initially led to an expansion of the list of constructs to include additional youth development outcomes (health awareness, civic engagement), but eventually resulted in a smaller "core" set of constructs: academic identity,[4] future orientation, mindsets, self-management, and interpersonal skills.

The first version of YDEKC's OST program-based Motivation, Engagement, and Beliefs Survey was administered to 345 youth in 27 programs in the spring of 2013. The results were presented to program staff alongside program quality data from the Youth Program Quality Assessment (YPQA) in June 2013. The Weikart Center's analysis found some association between quality services and youth outcomes and led to some key recommendations for improving the tool:

- Isolating program impact would require either a pre/post design or the use of a comparison group of young people not involved in programming.
- Since youth self-ratings tend to be very positive overall, it may be necessary to focus on lower-scoring youth in order to use the data for improvement.

Although YDEKC did not feel that pre/post measurement was feasible for most providers, it was clear that changes were warranted. Providers wanted information that tied program activities more closely to outcomes. They also wanted information on program impact that OST funders and other community stakeholders would find convincing. For this, YDEKC believed that additional work was needed to both improve the usefulness of the tool, and to more fully demonstrate its reliability (consistency as a measure) and validity (the extent to which it actually measured what it purported to measure). At this time, YDEKC entered into a partnership with AIR to further refine and pilot the survey tool. As the statewide evaluator for Washington's 21st CCLC, AIR had the ability to survey a large group of young people year after year, and to match survey data to school records from the state's data warehouse.

Validating the Survey for Broader Use

AIR administered revised versions of YDEKC's Engagement, Motivation, and Beliefs Survey to fourth through 12th graders in 21st CCLC programs each year between 2014 and 2017. The number of young people increased incrementally each year, and in 2017, more than 4,000 young people took the survey. Since the survey was largely unchanged between 2015 and 2017, and a subset of youth took it in at least 2 years during this period, year-to-year comparisons were possible for the first time.[5] In addition, AIR undertook a study with funding from the Washington State Office of Superintendent of Public Instruction (OSPI) and the Raikes Foundation called the Washington Quality to Youth Outcomes Study to explore the relationship between observed OST program quality, as measured by the YPQA, and pre/post youth outcomes, as measured by YDEKC's survey in Fall 2016 and Spring 2017. Each of these projects has afforded the AIR research and evaluation team the opportunity to address a series of questions. First, how is YDEKC's survey tool functioning from a reliability and validity standpoint? Second, how is youth functioning on the survey scales related to other key outcomes, including those associated with the school day?

Revising the Tool to Better Meet Provider Needs

Starting in Fall 2013, AIR began working with YDEKC and OSPI to further refine the tool for use with the state's 21st CCLC programs. The goal of these efforts was to improve the psychometric functioning (reliability and validity) of the tool, add items that provided youth with the opportunity to reflect on how they had benefited from program participation, and provide centers funded by 21st CCLC with information about how the youth they served were progressing in terms of key social and emotional skills, attitudes, and beliefs linked to school and work success. A revised version of the tool, with new items pertaining to perceived program impact, was piloted in Spring 2014 in 38 centers funded by 21st CCLC. Results from the 2014 pilot resulted in a series of substantial modifications to the survey. Based on these revisions, three types of scales were created and used on the final version of the survey:

1. *Items pertaining to youth's sense of belonging and engagement in the 21st CCLC program.* The purpose of these items was to obtain authentic feedback from youth on their experiences in the 21st CCLC program they were enrolled in during the school year. Examples of items of this type included: "I feel proud to be part of my program;" "This program helps me build new skills;" and "What we do in this program is challenging in a good way."
2. *Items pertaining to youth's sense of how they may have been affected by participation in the program.* The purpose of these items was to explore the extent to which youth believed the program may have helped them in terms of developing positive academic behaviors and better self-management skills. Examples of items of this type included:

"This program has helped me to become more interested in what I'm learning in school;" and "This program has helped me get better at staying focused on my work."

3. *Items pertaining to how youth reported functioning in a series of areas related to positive youth development.* The purpose of these items was to gauge how youth described their progress in four key areas: (a) academic identity, (b) positive mindsets, (c) self-management, and (d) interpersonal skills. Examples of items appearing on these scales included: "Doing well in school is an important part of who I am" (academic identity); "I can solve difficult problems if I try hard enough" (mindsets); "I can calm myself down when I'm excited or upset" (self-management); and "I work well with others on group projects" (interpersonal skills). Many of the findings described in the sections that follow focus on these scales because they represent the primary mechanism by which the YDEKC OST survey attempts to measure youth functioning in SEL-related areas.

WHAT DO WE KNOW ABOUT THE RELIABILITY AND VALIDITY OF THE TOOL?

Since its 2015 revision, we have found the YDEKC Engagement, Motivation, and Beliefs Survey to function well from a psychometric perspective in terms of (a) content validity (assessed by examining the technical quality of the items); (b) structural validity (scales were found to measure a single construct); (c) substantive validity (the rating scale used on the survey is functioning well); (d) generalizability (how reliable the measures are); and (e) external validity (responsiveness/sensitivity to detect both changes in youth functioning over time and hypothesized differences in subgroups taking the survey; Naftzger, 2016). The main takeaway from this work is that the reliability and psychometric validity of a youth report tool should be established before using it to assess youth outcomes. OST practitioners should ask that this evidence be provided before making use of a given tool or measure.

One additional note is warranted before turning our attention to the ways in which social and emotional skills (as measured by YDEKC's survey tool) were related to other key data about OST programs and the youth in question. For most of the analyses described below, we focused on youth who had room to improve on a given survey scale. Although this varied by scale, in general, approximately half of survey respondents were excluded from analyses because they were already functioning at a relatively high level on the scale in question. As pointed out later, this characteristic of the survey may limit how the tool can be used to inform program improvement and outcome evaluation efforts.

To What Extent Was Youth Growth on Survey Scales Associated With OST Program Quality, Youth Engagement, and Youth Experiences in Programming?

Addressing this question was a key goal of the study undertaken with support from OSPI and the Raikes Foundation. OST program quality was measured by conducting program observations using a series of items from the YPQA suite of tools. To collect youth engagement data, we administered a paper youth experience survey at the end of OST programming, which youth completed on 2 days each week during 1 week a month, for up to 6 months during the 2016–2017 school year. Four items from these surveys were used to create an engagement measure: (a) "Were today's activities interesting?"; (b) "Were today's activities important to you?"; (c) "Did you enjoy today's activities?"; and (d) "Did you have to concentrate to do today's activities?" Finally, summative youth experiences in programming were collected on the youth survey administered at the end of the school year. This survey contained scales pertaining to youth perceptions of their relationships with adults and other youth in the program, and the extent to which youth felt they had opportunities to engage in activities that would allow them to experience a sense of agency.

While we did *not* find that YPQA scores (program quality) and average youth engagement in programming were directly related to growth on the scales represented on the YDEKC survey tool, we found evidence to support the following sequence of events:

- Higher YPQA scores were associated with higher reported average engagement in programming on a day-to-day basis.
- Higher levels of engagement in day-to-day programming were related to more positive youth descriptions of their summative and cumulative experiences in programming at the end of the school year, both in terms of positive peer interactions and more frequent opportunities for agency.
- More positive youth-reported peer interactions and greater opportunities for agency were found to be associated with greater growth on the youth development outcomes examined through the YDEKC survey.

In this sense, we found a sequence of significant relationships connecting program quality to positive youth experiences in programming to improvement on the outcomes measured by the YDEKC survey tool. In addition, while higher YPQA scores were not found to predict improvement in youth development outcomes directly, they were found to strengthen the relationship between (a) positive youth-reported peer interactions and greater opportunities for agency, and (b) growth on the youth development outcomes examined. In this sense, higher YPQA scores strengthened the relationship between positive youth experiences in programming and growth on the pre/post outcomes examined.

This sequence of events is fairly compelling and suggests that growth on the YDEKC scales pertaining to SEL development seems to be related to a set of program characteristics and youth experiences we would expect to precede growth in these areas.

Was Youth Growth on Survey Scales Correlated With the Number of Days Youth Attended 21st CCLC Programming?

In undertaking both the Washington Quality to Youth Outcome Study and our evaluation work with OSPI (in relation to the statewide 21st CCLC program), we tested the hypothesis that the more regularly youth participate in programming, the more apt they are to show improvement on the SEL outcomes represented on the YDEKC survey. In this case, we have found consistent evidence that youth who participate for 60 days or more are significantly more likely to show growth on the SEL-related scales found on the survey. For example, in the Washington Quality to Youth Outcomes Study, youth attending programming for 60 days or more were more apt to show significant improvement on the academic identity, positive mindset, and self-management scales of the survey, compared to youth attending programming at lower levels (Naftzger & Sniegowski, 2018).

We saw similar results when we examined growth on the survey scales for youth taking the survey in the Spring of 2015 and 2016 as part of the Washington 21st CCLC evaluation. In this case, youth attending 60 days or more during the 2015–2016 programming period demonstrated significantly higher growth on the positive mindset, self-management, and interpersonal skills scales, compared to similar youth attending programming at lower levels (Naftzger, Sniegowski, & Vinson, 2017). Each of these findings is consistent with what we would expect in terms of the relationship between program attendance and youth growth on this set of SEL outcomes.

Was Youth Functioning on Survey Scales Correlated With School-Related Outcomes?

When collecting youth survey data as part of the statewide evaluation of the Washington 21st CCLC program, we took steps to capture the unique statewide identifier for each youth, allowing survey response data to be linked to school-related demographic and outcome data housed in OSPI's data warehouse. We used these data to assess whether there was a relationship between the SEL outcomes measured on the youth survey and the following school-related outcomes:

- state assessment scores in reading,
- state assessment scores in mathematics,
- number of school-day absences,
- number of school-day disciplinary incidents, and
- number of intervention days associated with school-day disciplinary incidents.

Overall, we found youth functioning on each of the four SEL-related constructs to be significantly related to multiple school-related outcomes in the manner predicted, with higher survey scores associated with more desirable school-related outcomes in all cases where a significant relationship was found to exist (Naftzger et al., 2017).

IMPLICATIONS FOR FURTHER DEVELOPMENT OF THE TOOL

At this point, the evidence establishing the validity of the YDEKC Engagement, Motivation, and Beliefs Survey as a measure of social and emotional skill development in OST programs is generally positive. We have repeatedly shown the tool to function well from a psychometric perspective, as described above. Overall, we have found scores from the YDEKC youth survey to be positively correlated with youth reports of their summative and cumulative experiences in OST programming, levels of youth attendance in programming, and a series of school-related outcomes, all in the manner hypothesized. In addition, while we did not find a direct relationship between the degree of improvement on the scales in question and (a) YPQA scores obtained from external observation of programming, and (b) youth-reported levels of daily engagement in programming, we were able to identify a chain of significant relationships that linked program quality and youth engagement in programming with youth summative experiences in programming and growth on the YDEKC survey outcomes. Overall, our sense is that the YDEKC Engagement, Motivation, and Beliefs Survey is a promising tool. However, there is room for additional study to further validate the tool as a measure of social and emotional skills, attitudes, and beliefs. In particular, there are opportunities to establish the convergent validity of the tool by deploying it in concert with other validated measures oriented at assessing the same domain of constructs to ensure estimates of youth functioning are largely consistent across tools.

IMPLICATIONS FOR PRACTICE

Although evidence of the reliability and validity of the YDEKC Engagement, Motivation, and Beliefs Survey has continued to grow, questions about its practical utility remain. In terms of the three purposes described at the beginning of this chapter, the survey has proved most useful for community positioning. Providers in YDEKC's network have largely appreciated the common language provided by YDEKC's outcomes framework, and as SEL has gained traction in Washington's K–12 education system (the state adopted SEL benchmarks in 2016), OST providers have been involved in policy, planning, and implementation discussions at many levels.

From a provider perspective, the value of the survey for program improvement and proof of impact is less clear. In order for program staff to use data on youth skills for program improvement, they must see a link between program activities and skill development. This link can be elusive when the skills in question are not explicitly taught, but instead are built and practiced over time and across experiences. It is imperative that survey data are interpreted in light of an overall theory of change and alongside other program-relevant data.

Proof of impact is similarly challenging. Many OST providers lack the resources to administer individually identifiable surveys on a pre/post basis to document growth. Even if they could do this, it would be difficult to say with certainty that growth is due to a particular program or intervention. Young people have a range of experiences every day, and the impact of the experiences they have in their OST program cannot be reliably untangled from the impact of their experiences at home, in school, and in the broader community. Additionally, the majority of youth who take the YDEKC Engagement, Motivation, and Beliefs Survey score in the highest response categories *before* they participate in programs, leaving little or no room to grow. Any accounting for change over time would need to focus on lower-performing youth, further complicating the collection, analysis, and interpretation of data.

Finally, self-report measures have inherent limitations. As Duckworth and Yeager (2015) point out, a number of potential sources of bias make their use for program evaluation or accountability problematic. When rating their own attributes, some young people may respond in ways that are socially desirable rather than honest or true. Others may rate themselves *more* stringently when they are in an environment characterized by high expectations, or when they are surrounded by high-performing peers (West et al., 2016). The same kind of effect is often seen in pre/post self-ratings, where individuals rate themselves lower after a program experience has shifted their frame of reference. In these cases, the results of self-report surveys may show decline, even if the respondents' skills have improved. On a measure like YDEKC's Engagement, Motivation, and Beliefs Survey, where most young people rate themselves very positively before they have participated in programs, program effects are particularly difficult to discern.

WHERE DO WE GO FROM HERE?

From a research point of view, additional work still needs to be done to align youth experiences in OST programming with measures that best reflect the manner in which youth are being affected by participation in these programs. In order to move this work forward, additional thought is required on how best to measure youth experiences in programming, and how to use this information to formulate hypotheses around how these experiences are likely to translate into the development of social and emotional skills, attitudes, and beliefs. By necessity, these studies will involve a very close examination of what programming looks like and relatively frequent assessment of the types of subjective experiences youth are having. For this reason, researchers should consider focusing on a small number of diverse, high-quality programs. In addition, there is a need to improve our understanding of how changes in youth attitudes, beliefs, and perceptions of their skills and capabilities affect how youth approach tasks in other learning environments over time, and what this means for the longer-term development of youth attending OST programs.

From a practitioner point of view, valid and reliable measures of social and emotional competencies are only part of the equation. It is also important that these measures are useful in a typical program context for positioning, program improvement, and/or proof of impact. In the cases of program improvement and proof of impact, practitioners should orient their program-level theories of change around SEL principles. When program activities are explicitly framed as skill-building opportunities, the implications of skill measures for program practice, and the relationship between program participation and skill development, become clearer.

Often, programs need considerable support around data collection and use in order to effectively tie new and evolving social and emotional skill measures to practice. Over time, YDEKC has invested a great deal of effort in providing this kind of support. In addition to running long-term cohorts focused on measurement, YDEKC has developed an online toolkit of measurement-related resources and offers a five-part training series on program evaluation processes generally. While these activities are not tightly focused on the survey measures that YDEKC and AIR have developed, they provide programs with a practical framework and an evaluative context in which these measures might prove useful.

Finally, OST practitioners can continue to benefit from the increasing prominence of social and emotional skills in discussions focused on the aims of education and workforce development. The OST field's long-standing focus on these kinds of skills can and should earn OST leaders a voice in policy discussions related to SEL. Hopefully they can use this voice to strengthen SEL practice across sectors, and to work in strong partnership with schools to improve outcomes for young people.

NOTES

1. These purposes were identified through Youth Development Executives of King County's early work with the David P. Weikart Center for Youth Program Quality (Weikart Center); see David P. Weikart Center (2015) for a more detailed discussion of this work.
2. The Road Map Project goal has recently been revised as follows: "*By 2020,* we will increase equitable policies and practices in our education systems and dramatically improve outcomes for children and youth, from cradle through college and career; so that: *By 2030,* we will eliminate the opportunity and achievement gaps impacting students of color and low-income children in South King County and South Seattle, and 70 percent of the region's youth will earn a college degree or career credential" (Community Center for Education Results, 2018, para. 3).
3. All of the source material for the SEMS was either in the public domain or was used with the permission of the original author.
4. The concept of academic identity was added after the first version of the SEMS was finalized. It refers to a young person's sense of himself/herself as a learner, particularly in a school setting.
5. During this time, YDEKC has continued to offer the survey tool to member organizations. However, the youth surveyed by providers in the YDEKC network have not been included in AIR's analysis unless they are also part of the 21st CCLC evaluation.

REFERENCES

Community Center for Education Results. (2018). *Vision, values, and goals.* Retrieved from http://roadmapproject.org/the-project/vision-values-and-goals

David P. Weikart Center for Youth Program Quality. (2015). *Youth service providers build a tool to measure their impact (Seattle, Washington).* Ypsilanti, MI: Author. Retrieved from http://cypq.org/content/youth-service-providers-build-tool-measure-their-impact-seattle-washington

Duckworth, A. L., & Yeager, D. S. (2015). Measurement matters: Assessing personal qualities other than cognitive ability for educational purposes. *Educational Researcher, 44*(4), 237–251. http://doi.org/10.3102/0013189X15584327

Egalite, A. J., Mills, J. N., & Greene, J. P. (2016). The softer side of learning: Measuring students' non-cognitive skills. *Improving Schools, 19*(1), 27–40.

Fredricks, J. A., Naftzger, N., Smith, C., & Riley, A. (2017). Measuring youth participation, program quality, and social and emotional skills in after-school programs. In N. L. Deutsch (Ed.), *After-school programs to promote positive youth development* (pp. 23–43). Cham, Switzerland: Springer International.

Hurd, N., & Deutsch, N. (2017). SEL-focused after-school programs. *The Future of Children, 27*(1), 95–115.

Larson, R. W., & Angus. R. M. (2011). Adolescents' development of skills for agency in youth programs: Learning to think strategically. *Child Development (82)*1, 277–294. doi:10.1111/j.1467-8624.2010.01555.x

Naftzger, N. (2016). *Motivation, Engagement, and Beliefs Survey validation report.* Washington, DC: American Institutes for Research.

Naftzger, N. (2017, July 28). Guest blog: Q&A with an afterschool researcher [Blog post]. Retrieved from http://www.afterschoolalliance.org/afterschoolSnack/Guest-blog-Q-A-with-an-afterschool-researcher_07-28-2017.cfm

Naftzger, N., Nistler, M., Manzeske, D., Swanlund, A., Shields, J., Rapaport, A., & Sugar, S. (2013). *Texas 21st Century Community Learning Centers: Year two evaluation report.* Naperville, IL: American Institutes for Research.

Naftzger, N., & Sniegowski, S. (2018). *Exploring the relationship between afterschool program quality and youth development outcomes: Findings from the Washington Quality to Youth Outcomes Study.* Washington, DC: American Institutes for Research.

Naftzger, N., Sniegowski, S., & Vinson, M. (2017). *Washington 21st Century Community Learning Centers program evaluation: 2015–16.* Chicago, IL: American Institutes for Research.

Smith, C., Hallman, S., Hillaker, B., Sugar, S., McGovern, G., & Devaney, E. (2012). *Development and early validation evidence for an observational measure of high quality instructional practice for science, technology, engineering, and mathematics in out-of-school time settings: The STEM supplement to the Youth Program Quality Assessment.* Washington, DC: Forum for Youth Investment.

West, M. R., Kraft, M. A., Finn, A. S., Martin, R. E., Duckworth, A. L., Gabrieli, C. F., & Gabrieli, J. D. (2016). Promise and paradox: Measuring students' non-cognitive skills and the impact of schooling. *Educational Evaluation and Policy Analysis, 38*(1), 148–170.

Yeager, D., Bryk, A., Muhich, J., Hausman, H., & Morales, L. (2015). *Practical measurement.* San Francisco, CA: Carnegie Foundation for the Advancement of Teaching.

SECTION V

CONCLUSION

CHAPTER 17

CLOSING COMMENTARY

Karen Pittman

More often than not, stories about young people who have successfully beaten the odds dealt them by their families, schools, and communities credit out-of-school time (OST) programs. These are the places where youth find safety and structure, build relationships, and get challenged to pursue interests, hone skills, and make a difference.

I was one of those kids whose demographic profile did not accurately predict my life success. I was a Black girl, growing up in a low-income, single-parent family in Washington, DC, attending public schools in the 1950s and 1960s. I clearly "beat the odds" associated with my gender, race, class, and family status. I was reminded of this frequently in college by well-meaning classmates and professors who remarked on how well rounded and well prepared I was. Their consistent surprise surprised me. I didn't think I had beaten the odds. I wasn't held up as the exception in my school, church, or youth orchestra. I did what was expected of me. I worked hard to use the opportunities I was given to learn, grow, and contribute. The incongruity between my actual readiness for college and the expectation that I would struggle because of my background helped me form the question that has guided my career: What did the adults in my school, church,

Social and Emotional Learning in Out-of-School Time, pages 305–313

youth organization, neighborhood do that *changed the odds* for me and the majority of my peers?

My journey towards answering this question started in 1970 when I was hired to be a counselor at the High Scope Educational Camp for Teenagers, a residential camp setting that brought 80 teens from diverse backgrounds together for a summer of free-choice learning. High Scope's Perry Preschool Project paved the way for the creation of the Head Start program and underpins the Early Childhood Program Quality Assessment and Training tools that are used around the world. The camp and the foundation served as the practical research and training lab for David Weikart, High Scope's founder, and his team of researcher-educators. It was the training ground not only for me, but for several of the Forum for Youth Investment's current and former staff, including Dr. Charles Smith, founder and, until recently, director of the Weikart Center for Youth Program Quality, which is part of the Forum (Weikart, 2004).

I'm sure by this point you are wondering why my personal and professional past are relevant to the task I was assigned, which was to reflect on the future of OST. I was asked to ponder the future of OST in the closing chapter for the *first* volume in this series (Pittman, 2018). In that chapter, I documented my reasons for arguing that it is time for us to find language that elevates the contributions the OST field has to make from the domains of "where and when" youth spend their time to the domains of "how and why" youth learn and develop.

This chapter picks up where that chapter left off. It is shorter, bolder, and obviously more personal. I started with this history to remind younger readers that the contributions we have made as youth workers predate the language we currently use to describe who we are and what we do as a field. Variations on the terms "out of school" and "social and emotional skills" have eclipsed the term "youth development," which, until fairly recently, was used to describe both the profession (youth development work/youth work) and the approach.

THE NEED FOR CHILD AND YOUTH DEVELOPMENT-CENTERED VERSUS ORGANIZATION-FOCUSED LEADERSHIP

There is no comparison between where OST research, policies, systems, and networks are now and where they were 30 years ago. The reality, however, is that, until recently, the advances we have made have often been linked to savvy case-making and justified positioning of OST as the solution to pressing problems that other systems are charged with addressing, such as child care, safety, crime reduction, behavioral risk management, academic achievement, and workforce readiness.

A constant thread throughout these negotiations has been the argument that OST programs and practitioners are equipped to address these other problems because we put youth first. Our overarching mission is to support their overall well-being and development. The recent focus on social and emotional skill building, especially by K–12 educators, provides us with an opportunity to explain how and why we naturally integrate social and emotional skill building into the work we do to encourage young people to explore, experience, and even master everything from the arts to advocacy to academics, if that is where their passion lies.

It is time to get credit for the work we have done to prioritize social and emotional competence, coordinate community programming, and adopt robust standards of practice that reflect the diversity of OST partners. We have to take great care, however, not to present OST as the unique embodiment of all of these goals. The winds are blowing in our direction. Hubris should be our enemy.

To be successful going forward, I believe OST leaders should do three things: claim the intersection of these three overlapping drivers as the true north that describes the work of our field; actively acknowledge the value and expertise that other systems, organizations, and fields have brought or are now trying to bring into each component; and consider adopting a new descriptor that better reflects the intersection and decouples us from a particular system and time frame.

MAKING THE CASE (AGAIN) FOR PURPOSE-DRIVEN YOUTH WORK

In 2004, I wrote an article for *New Directions for Youth Development,* fittingly titled "Reflections on the Road Not (Yet) Taken: How a Centralized Public Strategy Can Help Youth Work Focus on Youth" (Pittman, 2004). I encourage readers to locate not only the article but the entire Winter 2004 volume (Garza, Borden, & Astroth, 2004), which was devoted to professional development for youth workers. In addition to my concluding article (there is a pattern here), this volume included articles on the history of professional development for youth workers in the United States, the move to define common competencies for entry-level workers, and the roles that local intermediaries, national organizations, and higher education can play in supporting the continued professionalization of the field. I've taken the liberty of quoting segments of the opening paragraphs of the article directly:

> As a formal observer of youth development for the last fifteen years, I am pleased to say that youth work in the United States has made great progress in creating and institutionalizing the basic elements of a mature professional development system and purpose-driven field. Topics such as youth worker competencies, links to higher education, professional support networks, adequate recognition and compensation for skills, and career ladders for growth have not only been debated but, as documented in the articles in this volume, have been addressed at the state and local levels across the country. There have even been glimpses of promise at the national level as these issues have been taken up by policy researchers, national intermediaries, and government agencies. In recent years, I have to admit to increased concerns that the field may be gaining momentum but losing focus as efforts to refine definitions of the youth development "field" and of youth worker competencies appear to be more centrally focused on the realities of "where" and "when" youth workers do their work, rather than on the "what" and "how" of youth work—definitions that, for me, lead directly to the elements of youth work that distinguish it from the related professions of teaching and counseling or social work. (Pittman, 2004, pp. 87–88)

I had three reactions as I reread these paragraphs. First, chagrin. I had forgotten that I had used the "where/when" versus "what/how" framing at least 14 years ago. Second, sadness. It was disheartening to recognize that progress on some of the gains I was pleased to report has slowed or been sidetracked. Third, resolve. I was reminded that change is slow and rarely linear, and that opportunity does knock twice if you wait long enough.

Fifteen years ago, we were on the cusp of helping youth workers and youth development organizations define what effectiveness meant to them and the youth with whom they worked. But we were not making headway on scale (increasing our capacity and mandate to serve more youth) or sustainability (developing larger, more stable sources of public funding). The OST movement pushed us hugely ahead on the second goal. But, as I feared, it muddied the waters on the first. The pendulum swung away from a focus on the "what and how" distinctions needed to advance a profession to the "when and where" distinctions needed to develop delivery infrastructure. The pendulum is now swinging back. One of the main roles that grey hairs like me play is to remind us (a) that we have been here before, and (b) that we still have unfinished business. I return to my conclusions from the 2004 article:

> My strong sense is that, after more than a decade of field-building work in the US, what is lacking is the external validation and broad-based, cross-sector demand for high quality youth work that can only come from a clear and deep public understanding of the value of the work and a firm national commitment to adequately compensate the workers. My sense is that while it may seem expedient to garner this validation by tapping adults' concerns and fears about the challenges of "unused time" it is wiser to take the time to en-

gage the public, policy makers, and practitioners in richer discussions of the challenges of "untapped potential." (Pittman, 2004, p. 89)

LESSONS FROM ACROSS THE POND

Each time I am asked to reflect on the future of our field, I find myself reflecting on the lessons the United Kingdom has learned over the decades and wondering if the time is right, again, to bring them back into the discussion. The bulk of my 2004 article is devoted to reflections on the U.K.'s youth work system. In the decade prior to writing that article, I immersed myself in learning how other countries, specifically the United Kingdom, figured out how to nurture a national commitment to operationalizing child and youth development not just as a goal, but as a distinctly defined approach articulated through an integrated set of policies, programs, and professional development supports designed to manage and support a diverse set of providers (Davies & Gibson, 1967; Nicholls, 1997; Gilchrist, Jeffs, & Spence, 2001).

The United Kingdom is not the United States, so let me address the skepticism up front. There are many good reasons, starting with sheer size, for assuming that strategies that work in the United Kingdom will not translate easily to our realities. There are six good reasons, however, to use their experiences (which have been replicated to some extent across the commonwealth countries) to help us think outside the box.

Professional Clarity

Youth work is defined as distinct from but equal to teaching, counseling, and social work. The defining characteristics of youth work are most visible at the point of encounter with young people. Compared to these other professions, youth choose to be involved with youth workers, who, in turn, focus on helping youth build relationships and skills to better connect with the community. Youth work starts where young people are and encourages them to be critical and creative in their responses to the world. It focuses on the whole person and is concerned with how youth feel, not just what they know and can do. It focuses on interests, experiences, and perspectives, acknowledging but not leading with identified problems. It complements school and college-based education by encouraging youth to identify nonformal opportunities to fulfill their potential.

Developmental Clarity

Youth work is not only distinct from teaching, counseling, and social work, it is also distinct from playwork. Playwork is "based on the recognition that children and young people's capacity for positive development will be enhanced if given access to the broadest range of environments and play opportunities" (Playwork Principles Scrutiny Group, 2004, p. 1). The key purpose of youth work, in contrast, is to facilitate young people's personal, social, and educational development; to help them gain a voice, influence, and place in society as they transition from dependence to independence (Smith, 2013). There is developmental clarity and overlap in the distinction between playwork (focused primarily on pre-teens) and youth work (focused primarily on teens and young adults) from which we can benefit.

Setting and Activity Neutrality

Youth work, like play work, literally meets young people where they are—in schools, community organizations, parks, malls, housing projects, hospitals, jails. Some of these are places specifically created for young people; some are places where the community meets and goes about its business. Youth work engages young people in a variety of activities, from drama to recreation to social advocacy. The specific activities, however, are "merely the medium through which [the] experience which leads to personal and social development is offered" (Department of Education and Science, 1987, p. 4). This explicit decoupling of the profession from the setting and activity highlights the value youth workers (and play workers) bring to any setting, including to schools during the day.

Local Service Integration

National and community commitment to youth work is realized through the concept of a youth service—"a complex network of providers, community groups, voluntary organizations and local authorities" that shares a set of youth work values (Department for Education and Skills, 2002, p. 6). The local authorities are responsible for ensuring that there is a youth service for their area, and for working with all partners to ensure that adequate, equitable, high-quality supports are available.

National Quality Oversight

The quality of youth work in individual local authorities and national voluntary youth organizations is monitored and evaluated through inspections of annual youth service action plans, which include information on key priorities and target groups, strategies for achieving outlined goals and objectives, involvement of youth in planning, and partnerships with public-sector and private organizations. Plans have to include a clear statement about youth work methods and approaches that shows how the youth work complements formal education in promoting and assessing the overall development of youth. The government created the National Youth Agency (NYA) and charged it with developing specific standards of youth work that must be achieved by all local authorities, demonstrated through their plans and through oversight of youth worker training (NYA, 2000). The roles and responsibilities of the NYA have shifted over the decades, but its focus on strengthening practice is reflected in the three goals listed on its website: *championing youth work in all its many forms*—incubating new approaches, celebrating its many thousands of practitioners; *professionalising youth work*—training youth workers, setting occupational standards; and *enabling youth work*—making it happen through our networks of front-line youth work providers ("About the National Youth Agency," n.d.).

Consistently Qualified Staff

At the core of the system is a cadre of well-trained, visibly deployed youth workers—full-time, part-time, and volunteer. All youth workers are expected to hold appropriate qualifications (linked to specific types of youth work), though pathways to credentials are varied. Competencies can be built on the job, through formally certified employer training programs, or through institutions of higher education. Workers with all levels of formal education are eligible for certification. Training programs, wherever developed, are reviewed and centrally certified through the NYA against a set of job descriptions and worker competencies agreed upon by managers and workers. This means that vocationally and academically trained youth workers have equally portable degrees that can be used to apply for jobs and can be pegged to common descriptions and compensation histories.

CONCLUSION

My greatest regret is that we do not, in this country, have an allied youth field, in which the professionals who work with youth have joined forces to define what we do with and for young people in our own terms, and to defend our approach to the researchers, practitioners, and policymakers who monitor and manage systems (Pittman, Irby, & Ferber, 2001).

I believe it is time to try again. Operating largely in the out-of-school domains, we have demonstrated the value of expanding "where" and "when." We have demonstrated that it is possible to establish and sustain local and state structures to coordinate providers, set standards, and advocate for funds to ensure community-based learning opportunities when school is not in session. It is now time to demonstrate the value of the practitioners by supporting efforts to codify "what and how" lessons to create a field of adult practice that focuses on modeling, teaching, and enabling SEL through active reflection and engagement.

The articles in this volume easily demonstrate that we have the capacity to lead. Co-editors Devaney and Moroney have done a masterful job of organizing a truly encyclopedic set of chapters into a coherent whole. My charge in this concluding chapter reinforces their opening message that it is time for us to both build upon our strong history of supporting youth development, and share our story so we can be leaders in the SEL movement.

The verdict is still out, however, on whether we have the motivation to lead. For the first time in more than a decade, the pendulum has swung back to where we have always been— prioritizing the need to support children's SEL. These calls are coming from all systems and sectors, from higher education to juvenile justice to business (Krauss, Pittman, & Johnson, 2016). But the OST field, by name, is tethered to K–12 education. And as Devaney and Moroney wisely note, there are good reasons to worry "that SEL will be perceived as the latest trend in education, something that could go away at the whim of key leaders, rather than something that is foundational and historically embedded in the work of high-quality educators and youth workers" (Devaney & Moroney, this volume, p. 4).

We have two choices as I see it. We can jump on the bandwagon and ride the wave, or we can run ahead to guide the way. Coming up from behind is never easy, but if there was ever a time to try, it is now. Let's offer up our stories and research about how and why we integrate SEL into the work we do with children and youth as a way not to promote our OST organizations, but to promote the spread of intentional youth work practice.

REFERENCES

About the National Youth Agency. (n.d.). Retrieved from the National Youth Agency website: https://www.nya.org.uk/about-us/

Davies, B., & Gibson, A. (1967). *The social education of the adolescent.* London, England: University of London Press.

Department for Education and Skills. (2002). *Transforming youth work: Resourcing excellent youth services.* London, England: Author.

Department of Education and Science. (1987). *Effective youth work: A report by HM inspectors.* London, England: Department of Education and Science. Retrieved from http://www.infed.org/archives/gov_uk/effective_youth_work.htm

Garza, P., Borden, L. M., & Astroth, K. A. (Eds.). (2004). Professional development for youth workers [Special issue]. *New Directions for Youth Development, 104.* https://doi.org/10.1002/yd.93

Gilchrist, R., Jeffs, T., & Spence, J. (2001). *Essays in the history of community and youth work.* Leicester, England: Youth Work Press.

Krauss, S. M., Pittman, K. J., & Johnson C. (2016). *Ready by design: The science (and art) of youth readiness.* Washington, DC: The Forum for Youth Investment.

National Youth Agency. (2000). *National occupational standards for youth work.* Leicester, England: Author. Retrieved from http://www.most.ie/webreports/Fatima%20reports/Youth%20Services/National%20occupation%20standars-ds%20for%20youthworkuk.pdf

Nicholls, D. (1997). *An outline history of youth and community work and the union 1834–1997.* Birmingham, AL: Pepar.

Pittman, K. J. (2004). Reflections on the road not (yet) taken: How a centralized public strategy can help youth work focus on youth. *New Directions for Youth Development, 104,* 87–99.

Pittman, K. J. (2018). Securing the future: Pivoting OST from where and when to how and what. In H. J. Malone & T. Donahue (Eds.), *The growing out-of-school time field: Past, present and future* (pp. 293–306). Charlotte, NC: Information Age.

Pittman, K., Irby M., & Ferber T. (2001). Unfinished business: Further reflections on a decade of promoting youth development. In P. L. Benson & K. J. Pittman (Eds.), *Trends in youth development* (Outreach Scholarship Series, Vol. 6). Boston, MA: Springer.

Playwork Principles Scrutiny Group. (2004). *The playwork principles.* Retrieved from http://www.playwales.org.uk/login/uploaded/documents/Playwork%20Principles/playwork%20principles.pdf

Smith, M. K. (2013). *What is youth work? Exploring the history, theory and practice of youth work.* Retrieved from www.infed.org/mobi/what-is-youth-work-exploring-the-history-theory-and-practice-of-work-with-young-people/

Weikart, D. P. (2004). *How High/Scope grew: A memoir.* Ypsilanti MI: High/Scope Press.

ABOUT THE EDITORS

Elizabeth Devaney is the director of the Center for Social and Emotional Learning at the Children's Institute in Rochester, NY. In that role she coordinates research and capacity building related to social and emotional learning (SEL) in Out-of-School Time programs, schools, and early childhood centers across the state of New York. Devaney co-chairs Rochester's Expanded Learning Time Collection Action Network and its subcommittee focused on developing an SEL framework for the ELO community. Devaney has over 15 years of experience in implementing and studying programs designed to support youth outside of schools hours as they grow and develop socially, emotionally and academically. Prior to the Children's Institute, she was a researcher at the American Institutes for Research (AIR) where she studied the implementation and impact of high quality afterschool programs with a particular emphasis on the intersection between research and practice. Devaney has co-authored several guides for afterschool and school-based practitioners, including *Beyond the Bell®: A Toolkit for Creating Effective Afterschool and Expanded Learning Programs* and *Sustainable Schoolwide Social and Emotional Learning (SEL): Implementation Guide and Toolkit.* Previously, she served as deputy director of the Providence After School Alliance where she developed and implemented a quality improvement system for the state of Rhode Island and oversaw the organization's research and evaluation activities. She was also a project director at the Collaborative for Academic, Social, and Emotional Learning (CASEL). Devaney was a William T. Grant Foundation Distinguished Fellow recipient in 2009. She received her Master's degree in social policy from the Heller School at Brandeis University.

Social and Emotional Learning in Out-of-School Time, pages 315–316

Deborah A. Moroney, PhD is a managing director at American Institutes for Research (AIR), and she serves as the director of the Youth Development and Supportive Learning Environments practice area. Dr. Moroney's research and practice experience is in SEL and youth development. Dr. Moroney is the architect of a collaborative method for the design of dual purpose (improvement and demonstration) evaluation frameworks. She has worked with national multi-site programs including the YMCA of the USA, Boy Scouts of America, and Every Hour Counts. Additionally, Dr. Moroney serves as the principal investigator of city and statewide evaluations including a collaborative project with the Partnership for Children and Youth in California and the citywide evaluation for School's Out New York City. She serves as member of the Afterschool Technical Assistance Collaborative for the C. S. Mott Foundation's statewide afterschool networks. Dr. Moroney's work demonstrates a value in bridging research and practice. She serves on the editorial board of *Afterschool Matters* and she has authored practitioner and organizational guides using both research findings and practitioner input. Dr. Moroney was a co-author of the fourth edition of the seminal afterschool resource, *Beyond the Bell: A Toolkit for Creating Effective Afterschool and Expanded Learning Programs*. Dr. Moroney has authored numerous chapters and publications on social and emotional development and assessment, including *Ready to Assess*. Prior to joining AIR, Dr. Moroney was a clinical faculty member in educational psychology at the University of Illinois at Chicago in the Youth Development Graduate Program. Dr. Moroney holds a PhD and MEd from the University of Illinois at Chicago.

ABOUT THE CONTRIBUTORS

Patricia J. Allen, PhD, is the manager of research and evaluation at The PEAR Institute: Partnerships in Education and Resilience and an instructor in psychiatry at Harvard Medical School. She was awarded a PhD in Experimental Psychology from Tufts University in 2013 after gaining expertise in behavioral neuroscience research. She focused her postdoctoral work on the concept of translational medicine in the Stuart T. Hauser Clinical Research Training Program in biological and social psychiatry (T32, NIMH) through Judge Baker's Children Center in Boston, MA. She manages the implementation and development of PEAR's quantitative assessments that measure outcomes of youth participating in programs that emphasize social-emotional learning (SEL) and science, technology, engineering, and math (STEM). She is currently involved with several national evaluation efforts to collect evidence of SEL and STEM learning to help ensure that young people across the country have positive, high-quality experiences when they participate in out-of-school time activities.

Ken Anthony, EdD, is the director of professional development and research for the Connecticut After School Network. Being in the field for the past 25 years, Ken has worked as a front line staff, site supervisor, program director, district coordinator, to his current position for the past 10 years. His primary role at the network is to oversee training, professional and leadership development, program consultation, quality advising, and support research efforts. Published in the *Journal of Expanded Learning Opportunities* and *Afterschool Matters Journal,* Ken has also authored a chapter on Research–Practitioner Partnerships in the book *The Growing Out-of School Time Field,*

Social and Emotional Learning in Out-of-School Time, pages 317–330 published by Information Age Publishing. He holds a bachelor's degree in psychology with a concentration in child development from Southern Connecticut State University; a master's degree in human services with a concentration in organizational management and leadership from Springfield College, and was part of the inaugural class of White-Riley-Peterson Policy Fellows. Ken completed his doctorate in educational leadership at the University of Hartford in 2015, where he researched expanded learning practices that build sustainable relationships and partnerships between school and afterschool program staff.

Kiley Bednar helps people who work with youth do that work better. At the Weikart Center, she provides technical assistance to clients across the country, including clients with a focus on social emotional learning. Previously, she oversaw the Forum for Youth Investment's training programs—including the Ready by 21 Webinar Series and Ready by 21 Institutes—as well as coordinated the national Children's Cabinet Network. Kiley began her career as a Lutheran Volunteer Corps member in Seattle, WA, where she led a neighborhood meal program and advocated for insurance coverage for youth aging out of foster care. Then, in Illinois, she coordinated a statewide Violence Prevention Youth Advisory Board, developed service-learning opportunities at the Interfaith Youth Core, and oversaw an educational summer camp at Northwestern University. Kiley received her BA in Psychology from Illinois Wesleyan University and her MA in Social Service Administration from the University of Chicago.

Joe Bertoletti leads the David P. Weikart Center's team of project managers and trainers that support quality improvement system building efforts across 135 networks. His favorite part of this role is designing customized pathways to help systems build quality improvement systems that are specific to their needs and goals. Prior to joining the Weikart Center in 2007, Joe had 8 years of youth development experience that included work in traditional after-school, therapeutic wilderness, and adventure-based educational programs. Joe earned a master's of social work degree from the University of Michigan, a Master of Science in Industrial Engineering from Pennsylvania State University, and a Bachelor of Science in Mechanical Engineering from the University of Illinois.

Dale A. Blyth, PhD, is currently senior consultant to CASEL. Formerly a professor in the College of Education and Human Development at the University of Minnesota where he served as Howland Endowed Chair in Youth Development Leadership. For 15 years he was associate dean and director of the Extension Center for Youth Development. Prior to that he was the director of research and evaluation at Search Institute and on the faculty of Cornell University and Ohio State University. He co-developed the Center for Adolescent Health at the American Medical Association and was a Research Scientist at the Boys Town Center for Youth Development. Dr. Blyth has co-authored a book, as well as authored many chapters and articles and helped found the Society for Research on Adolescence as well as several journals. His experience includes bridging research and practice to shape the fields of youth development and non-formal learning to make a difference.

Poonam Boorah's passion for equity and education began as she worked in various low income schools during her undergraduate and post graduate years in India's North East. After her master's from the University of Delhi, she worked as a classroom teacher for a few years in New Delhi. Her interest lies in understanding the impact of community based education especially in historically marginalized and conflict prone regions. Sustainable and organic organizational improvement that builds learning communities is her mantra for growth. Most recently, she has earned a Master of Arts in Educational Leadership and Policy from the University of Michigan. During this time she also volunteered in various after-school programs and interned with preservice teacher education programs.

Katie Brackenridge is an SEL advisor to the Partnership for Children and Youth. As vice president of programs until 2018, Katie oversaw PCY's five program initiatives, including the Summer Matters campaign, Expanded Learning 360°/365, Community Schools, HousEd, and Technical Assistance. In this role, Katie has worked with hundreds of district and community-based youth programs to improve quality, build sustainability and implement innovative practices in after-school and summer programming. Katie also supports PCY's work to develop and improve policies that make expanded learning programming more accessible and effective. Over her career, Katie has worked at almost every job in the expanded learning field—from high school tutor to line staff to program director to executive director to technical assistance provider to policy developer and advocate. With this deep experience, Katie constantly works to ground statewide policy and action in practices that make a real difference for students and families in their communities.

Katie Brohawn, PhD, is the vice president of research at ExpandED Schools. There, she leads the research department, helping establish the organization's research and evaluation priorities in order to raise service quality and inform policy, and supporting the organization to make data/research-driven continuous improvement, with special attention to relevant research in expanded learning time. She oversees all data collection and analysis (including SEL data) for all of ExpandED Schools' initiatives, and oversees the external evaluation of over thirty 21st Century Community Learning Center after-school program grants. Prior to joining ExpandED Schools, Katie served at the NYC Department of Education as the director of research and evaluation in the Research and Policy Support Group where she oversaw the external evaluations of large-scale initiatives, such as the roll-out of the Common Core and designed and implemented internal evaluations of DOE pilot programs. She holds a BA in Neuroscience from Connecticut College and a PhD in Psychology from Tufts University.

Mary Ellen Caron, PhD, is the CEO of After School Matters, one of the nation's largest and most successful providers of after-school and summer programming for high school teens. Previously, she was commissioner of Chicago's Department of Family and Support Services, where she managed the transition of several human services departments while providing support for Chicago's residents. At the Chicago Board of Education, she was special assistant to Arne Duncan, utilizing her background in education to serve Chicago Public Schools. Dr. Caron was the founding principal of Frances Xavier Warde Elementary School and worked many years as a teacher. She earned her PhD in Educational Leadership and Policy from Loyola University, her master's degree in elementary education and Type 75 certificate from Concordia University, and her undergraduate degree from Rosary College. She currently serves on the boards and advisory committees for multiple youth- and education-related organizations throughout Chicago.

Christina Dandino is currently the director of the Greater Rochester After-School Alliance (GRASA), an initiative of Rochester Area Community Foundation. GRASA provides a set of quality standards, a system for reaching these standards through assessment, technical assistance, and resources; as well as professional development opportunities and networking events for OST professionals across the community. Chris has over 30 years' experience in the youth development planning, programming, funding, and policy arena within the public and private sector. She is actively involved in planning and collaborative activities within the community including ROC the Future, the local area collective impact initiative, the School Climate Advisory Committee to the Rochester City School District Board of Education, and the Greater Rochester Health Foundation Social and Emotional Health Implementation Task Group. She was educated at the State University of New York at Geneseo (BA) and Syracuse University (master's in social work) and is New York State certified in elementary education.

Carinne Deeds directs the United Way for Greater Austin's efforts to promote social and economic opportunity for Austin families. This includes serving as a backbone leader for the community and overseeing the organization's 2-Gen funding portfolio. Previously, Carinne served as a senior policy associate at American Youth Policy Forum in Washington, DC, where she developed learning events, products, and policy and practice guidance to inform the development and implementation of policies that affect young people. Her main areas of expertise included after-school and out-of-school time systems, workforce development, social and emotional learning (SEL), employability and college and career readiness, the Every Student Succeeds Act, and strategies to support opportunity youth. Carinne previously served as the Bryna and Henry David Fellow at the Ray Marshall Center for the Study of Human Resources. She has also worked for various after-school programs in the United States and West Africa. Prior to her work with nonprofits, Carinne was a kindergarten English teacher in Bangkok, Thailand and an ESL instructor in Austin, Texas. Carinne holds a bachelor's degree in communication studies from The University of Texas at Austin and a master's in public affairs from the Lyndon B. Johnson School of Public Affairs at UT Austin.

Dan Gilbert joined the Afterschool Alliance in July 2014. As a project manager, Dan directs the alliance's work around social and emotional learning (SEL), works to advance the alliance's outreach and messaging efforts, manages the alliance's webinar offerings, coordinates activities and collaborative efforts with partner organizations, and plans and implements projects including performing research and writing and disseminating reports for stakeholders at the national, state, and local level. Dan has experience working for Massachusetts state government, European Parliament, and political campaigns, and most recently worked at the Alliance for Excellent Education's Center for Digital Learning & Policy. Dan has a master's in public administration from the Trachtenberg School at The George Washington University and a bachelor's degree in political science from Northeastern University in Boston.

Rebecca Goldberg joined the S.D. Bechtel, Jr. Foundation in 2013 as a program officer in the education program. Her focus is on supporting high quality OST programs in California and nationally that embed character building and SEL into their youth development practices. Her grant portfolio focuses on quality improvement, dissemination of evidence-based practices, capacity building, and growth strategies. Rebecca brings experience supporting OST programs and adult practice from her role as regional strategies director for California School-Age Consortium, a statewide after-school intermediary where she led workforce development initiatives. At a community based organization in Los Angeles, she served as director of career and workforce development and was responsible for program development, employer engagement, and career pathways including the Energy Pathway, Promo Pathway, and Urban Teacher Fellowship/CA Teacher Pathway. Rebecca earned a Bachelor of Arts in Religion from Colgate University. She serves as a local board member for Playworks in San Francisco and is on the steering committee of Grantmakers for Thriving Youth chairing the OST Work Group.

Jodi Grant is executive director of the Afterschool Alliance, a public awareness and advocacy organization working to ensure that all students have access to quality, affordable after-school programs. The Afterschool Alliance educates the public, the media, and policy makers about the enormous potential of quality after-school programs and how programs across the country are inspiring children and creating opportunities for them to succeed academically, socially, and professionally. Grant oversees all aspects of the Afterschool Alliance's work—setting its goals and strategies for reauthorization of the Elementary and Secondary Education Act, working with the field to help programs tap into federal funding streams, and supervising research to help stakeholders support, create, and expand quality after-school programs. Grant served as director of work and family programs for the National Partnership for Women & Families. She served as general counsel to the Senate Budget Committee and as staff director for a Senate Committee. Her legislative accomplishments include expanded support for the child tax credit, the Child Health Insurance Program, and class size reduction. She served as liaison to the National Governors' Association, where she worked closely with Republican and Democratic governors. Grant graduated from Yale University and received her law degree from Harvard University. She currently serves as a trustee of the America's Promise Alliance, and on the steering committee of the Coalition for Community Schools.

Leona Hess, PhD, is a change leader, systems thinker, and experiential facilitator with extensive experience in planning for, creating, and implementing training and professional development solutions to support transformational change. As senior director of program integration at the NYC Department of Youth and Community Development, she created structures and interactive experiences to engage and enable the agency to design and implement social emotional learning, positive youth development and youth leadership frameworks, common language and lens, trainings and capacity building opportunities for staff and community-based organization providers. A transformational educator, she recently joined the Icahn School of Medicine at Mount Sinai as the director of strategy and equity education programs where she is leading a structured process for managing and leading the content, process, and people side of transformational change related to Icahn's Racism and Bias Initiative. Dr. Hess holds a PhD from Columbia University, a MSW from NYU, and a BS from George Washington University.

Jessica Jarahain Jackson has over 15 years of experience in the field of youth development and education. Jessica joined the Department of Youth and Community Development in 2015 as the deputy director of program quality and innovation in the Comprehensive After School System (COMPASS NYC) unit. Her work included tool development for quality programming, capacity building for agency and program staff, facilitation of internal and external work groups, and CBO planning and support. Most recently, Jessica transitioned to the director of planning, program integration, and evaluation where her work will continue to build the capacity of agency staff through universal frameworks, systems integration, and data-informed decision-making. Through both domestic and international nonprofit experience as well as her years in school leadership, Jessica has developed a passion of ensuring youth have trained, caring, effective professionals to build opportunities and positive outcomes for every child. Jessica has a BA in Counseling from Bloomsburg University and is pursuing a MA in Youth Studies from CUNY.

Bridget Durkan Laird is the CEO of WINGS for Kids. WINGS is an award winning after-school social and emotional education program. It has received numerous accolades including: 4-star rating by Charity Navigator; featured by Edutopia, as a "School that Works"; featured in Mario Morino's "Leap of Reason" and Paul Bloom's "How to Scale Your Social Venture." Bridget has been with WINGS since 1998. Through the years, Bridget has helped to develop all aspects of the organization, from program/curriculum development to spearheading grant and research applications to growth strategies, replication, and scaling. During this time, she was working toward efforts to bring SEL to the forefront of education today. Bridget took over as CEO in 2011. Since her tenure, WINGS has increased the number of kids served by 300%. She has an undergraduate degree in parks and recreation from North Carolina State and a master's degree in education, from Concordia University.

Jennifer Brown Lerner manages the policy efforts of the National Commission on Social, Emotional, and Academic Development. She is also responsible for developing partnerships on behalf of the commission's efforts. Previously, Jennifer served as the deputy director of the American Youth Policy Forum, where she managed the organization's work on a wide range of issues that ensure all students graduate ready to succeed in college and careers. Prior to joining AYPF, Jennifer worked as a classroom teacher and communications officer for a number of schools in the Boston area. Her career began supporting the creation of a Summerbridge (now Breakthrough Collaborative) site in Atlanta, Georgia. Jennifer received her BA from the University of Pennsylvania and her MA from Teachers College, Columbia University.

Jolie Logan joined WINGS for kids in 2016 as the chief development officer. She is the former CEO of the Charleston nonprofit Darkness to Light and brings experience in fundraising, partnership development, and grants management to the position. While president and CEO of Darkness to

Light, a nonprofit working to prevent child sexual abuse, Jolie led development and business strategy, growing the organization's revenue by 44%. Jolie holds a bachelor's degree from Converse College and a graduate certificate in organizational psychology from The Chicago School of Professional Psychology.

Joseph L. Mahoney, PhD, is a senior research scientist at the Collaborative for Academic, Social, and Emotional Learning (CASEL) and research professor in the Department of Psychology at the University of Illinois at Chicago. His research has focused on understanding how out-of-school time affects youth development across school, family, and community settings. He currently collaborates on CASEL's efforts to make scientific evidence related to social and emotional learning useful for practitioners and used in practice to support high-quality learning environments. Prior to joining CASEL, he was an associate professor in the Department of Psychology at Yale University and a professor in the School of Education at the University of California, Irvine. He received the Society for Research in Child Development's Distinguished Congressional Policy Fellowship and served as lead education council for U.S. Senator Jeff Bingaman. He earned his PhD in Psychology through the Center for Developmental Science at the University of North Carolina at Chapel Hill.

J. Tyler McCormick is a passionate youth practitioner and advocate with over a decade of experience in organizational design and management, quality youth program evaluation and oversight, and coalition building between community stakeholders, educational institutions, and city government. Ms. McCormick is currently a senior director of education and youth development for CAMBA, Inc. In her previous roles, J. Tyler served as an arts content specialist for the Comprehensive After School System (COMPASS NYC) and a program manager for Beacon Community Centers with the Department of Youth and Community Development (DYCD). Prior to working with city government, Ms. McCormick served as the director of youth development for the Association to Benefit Children (ABC). Ms. McCormick has a deep commitment to designing youth programs that catalyze authentic community engagement to achieve collective impact. Ms. McCormick has a BA in Art History/Visual Arts from Barnard College and an MSEd from Bank Street College.

Elizabeth Mester, a graduate of College of Charleston's Arts Management program, first entered the nonprofit sector in an administrative and programming role at the former Creative Spark Center for the Arts. Her passion and empathy for others fueled her move to WINGS for kids, an organization that teaches K–5 at-risk kids the skills they need to rise above the obstacles they're born into—skills like self-management, responsible decision-making, and how to build healthy relationships. Since 2008, Liz has worked in various roles at WINGS, thriving while WINGS was expanding. From director of development to now director of communications and engagement, Liz is charged with identifying, connecting, and engaging individuals who care about kids, our community, and our future. Liz is a 2012 Charleston Regional Business Journal's "40 Under 40" winner and is the former VP of professional development for the Association for Fundraising Professionals Lowcountry Chapter.

Neil Naftzger is a principal researcher working on after-school and youth development initiatives at American Institutes for Research (AIR). An experienced evaluator and researcher within the field of after-school programs, Naftzger has spent more than a decade designing and conducting evaluations and research studies in the after-school and out-of-school time arena that involve the collection and analysis of data in various forms, particularly in relation to the 21st Century Community Learning Centers (21st CCLC) program. Naftzger studies both the impact of youth-serving programs on various outcomes and the role program quality plays in this process. Naftzger has been the principal investigator on research grants from the Charles Stewart Mott, William T. Grant, Raikes, and National Science Foundations and on statewide evaluations of the 21st CCLC programs in New Jersey, Ohio, Oregon, South Carolina, Texas, and Washington.

Gil G. Noam, EdD, PhD, Habil, is the founder and director of The PEAR Institute: Partnerships in Education and Resilience at Harvard University and McLean Hospital. An associate professor at Harvard Medical School focusing on prevention and resilience, Dr. Noam trained as a clinical and developmental psychologist and psychoanalyst in both Europe and the United States. He has published over 200 papers, articles, and books in the areas of child and adolescent development as well as risk and resiliency in clinical, school, and after-school settings. He also served as the editor-in-chief of the journal *New Directions for Youth Development: Theory, Practice, and Research* with a strong focus on out-of-school time. Dr. Noam has a strong interest in translating research and innovation to support resilience in youth in educational settings.

Stephen C. Peck, PhD, received a BA in Psychology from the California State University, Long Beach in 1985; an MA in Experimental Social Psychology from the University of Montana, Missoula in 1990; and a PhD in Personality Psychology from the University of Michigan, Ann Arbor in 1995. From 1995 to 2016, he worked as a research investigator and assistant research scientist at the University of Michigan's Achievement Research Lab, Research Center for Group Dynamics, Institute for Social Research. He began working as a consultant to the David P. Weikart Center for Youth Program Quality in 2005 and became a regular employee (i.e., Sr. Research Fellow) in 2016, following his retirement from the University of Michigan. His primary research interests focus on multilevel person-in-context models of lifespan development using both psychological and transdisciplinary approaches to theory and method development and the integration of variable- and pattern-centered theoretical, measurement, and statistical models.

Luis A. Perez, LMSW, has been driving the development of high-quality summer enrichment in the Greater Rochester by increasing access throughout the community since Summer 2010. Engaging a host of community partners that include colleges and universities, local early childhood providers, educational institutions, and funders—in summer 2017 the emerging consortium included twenty sites and served 1,200 students. Previous to current assignment, Mr. Perez served as an assistant professor of social work and the director of graduate social work field education at Roberts Wesleyan College. Prior to that he served as the executive director of HOPE Initiatives Community Development Corporation. Mr. Perez's interests include positive youth development, mentoring children of prisoners, faith-based initiatives and prisoner re-entry. He received his master's degree in social work (MSW) from Roberts Wesleyan College.

Karen J. Pittman is president and CEO of the Forum for Youth Investment, a national nonprofit, nonpartisan "action tank" that combines thought leadership on youth development, youth policy, cross-system/cross-sector partnerships and developmental youth practice with on-the-ground training, technical assistance, and supports. Karen is a respected sociologist and leader in youth development. Prior to co-founding the forum in 1998, she launched adolescent pregnancy prevention initiatives at the Children's Defense Fund, started the Center for Youth Development and Policy Research, and served as senior vice president at the International Youth Foundation. Karen was involved in the founding of America's Promise and directed the President's Crime Prevention Council during the William Clinton administration. Most recently, Karen received the Lifetime Achievement Award from Partners for Livable Cities, joining previous awardees such as President William Clinton and Lady Bird Johnson. Karen was recently selected to join the National Commission on Social, Emotional, and Academic Development with the Aspen Institute.

Hillary Salmons has led the Providence After School Alliance (PASA), a public–private nonprofit organization whose mission is to expand and improve quality after-school, summer, and expanded learning opportunities for the youth of Providence for 13 years. She is responsible for PASA's community engagement, management, planning, and long-term development and sustainability. Hillary has worked closely with three mayors, five superintendents, and over 100 community groups to manage a high quality after-school system that has served 14,000 middle school youth—connecting 30% of Providence's middle school youth and 400 high school youth each year to real hands-on learning experiences that are steeped in youth development practices. Hillary has been a national advocate for building quality after-school systems having hosted 4 annual City Symposiums in Providence inspiring 40 cities to replicate components of PASA's systems model, as well as an active leader of the Every Hour Counts board. Prior to PASA, Hillary led the Health and Education Leadership for Providence (HELP) coalition of the city's nonprofit colleges and hospitals that focused on improving the health and education of the children of Providence. While there, she worked to establish numerous systemic health and education initiatives which continue to this day. Hillary worked in Japan for 8 years with Refugees International, as well as in New York City as a deputy director at CAMBA, a Brooklyn community development organization. She has an MA in Public Administration from the University of Oklahoma and a BA from Harvard University. She currently serves on the board of the Learning Community Charter School and is president of the Workforce Board's Youth Council.

Polly Savitri Singh is a senior program officer at The Wallace Foundation (www.wallacefoundation.org). Wallace is a national foundation, based in New York, with a mission to foster improvements in learning and enrichment for disadvantaged children and the vitality of the arts for everyone. During Polly's 16-year tenure at Wallace, she has been involved in a range of projects dedicated to building Wallace's capacity, the capacity of our grantees, and the OST field. Polly is a member of the Partnerships for Social and Emotional Learning initiative implementation team and manages two grantee communities. Polly managed the Strengthening Financial Management initiative: oversight of 24 Chicago OST grantees receiving financial management training, and led the project to develop strongnonprofits.org, where the tools and resources are among the Top 10 downloads from Wallace's website every month. Polly holds a BA from Hamilton College, and an MPA from Baruch.

Haviland Rummel Sharvit is the executive director at Susan Crown Exchange (SCE) (www.scefdn.org), a national foundation with a mission to help youth develop skills needed to succeed and thrive in a rapidly changing, highly connected world. Haviland manages the organization's strategy and grantmaking in digital learning and social and emotional learning. Prior to joining SCE she served as a senior consultant to nonprofit organizations in the areas of strategic planning and fund development. She has worked with a variety of nonprofits across sectors including cultural institutions, human service agencies, education and innovation groups, and healthcare organizations. Haviland serves on the Metro Board of Metropolitan Family Services, one of Chicago's first and largest human services agencies, and on the advisory board of After School Matters. Haviland holds an MBA in Strategic Management and Corporate Social Responsibility from George Washington University and a BS in Communications from Boston University.

Charles Smith, PhD, is the owner and principal consultant at QTurn. Charles spent the past decade as founder and executive director of the David P. Weikart Center for Youth Program Quality and as a senior vice president at the Forum for Youth Investment. Charles has 20 years of experience supporting organizations to design, implement, and validate quality improvement systems (QIS) in the education and human services fields.

Chris Smith has created, scaled, and led cross-sector partnerships in education and workforce development for over two decades. Under his leadership, Boston After School & Beyond has developed a nationally recognized model of summer learning that improves student outcomes, built a citywide program performance measurement system, and cultivated a network of 150 programs serving more than 15,000 students. Previously, Chris worked at the Boston Private Industry Council, where he collaborated with business leaders to integrate work and learning in order to help thousands of students graduate, with universities on Boston's first-ever study of college graduation rates of Boston Public Schools students, and with legislative leaders to address the dropout rate in Massachusetts. Chris began his career at the U.S. Department of Education in Washington, DC, where he coordinated partnerships for the secretary of education. A native of Worcester, MA, Chris earned a BA in American Studies from Trinity College in Hartford, CT and an MBA from Babson College in Wellesley, MA.

Carla Stough-Huffman currently serves as the coordinator of professional development and OST program quality for the Greater Rochester After School Alliance (GRASA) in Rochester, NY. Carla has more than 30 years of professional and personal experience working with youth and the families, agencies, and institutions that support them. Armed only with a BA in Developmental Psychology and an insatiable quest for knowledge, she has created a crazy-quilt career path that includes program design and development, assessment and evaluation, grant writing and, her favorite, training design and delivery. When not engaging others in educational, entertaining workshops or feeding her own brain, Carla devotes her free time to her greatest passions, writing and reading.

Sarah Terry is the research and evaluation manager for Youth Development Executives of King County (YDEKC). Her work focuses on building the measurement and evaluation capacity of YDEKC's member organizations. Prior to joining YDEKC, Sarah worked as a research and instruction librarian at several colleges and universities and as a reference librarian for the New York Public Library. Sarah holds a Master of Public Administration and a Master of Library and Information Science from the University of Washington in Seattle.

Saskia Traill, PhD, is the senior vice president at ExpandED Schools, dedicated to its mission of closing the learning gap by increasing access to enriched education experiences. Saskia leads the organization's research and policy efforts in expanded learning, including focuses on social and emotional learning, high school programs, and opportunities for children to engage in quality science, technology, engineering, and math (STEM). Prior to working at ExpandED Schools, Saskia was a program manager for the Insight Center for Community Economic Development, working to build state systems for early care and education. She has authored and co-authored articles for peer-reviewed journals, policy briefs, and reports on a range of issues, including family economics, how to fund innovative education strategies, and how to ensure education that sparks future innovation and opportunity. She received her BA from Columbia University and a PhD in research psychology from Stanford University.

Bailey Triggs, MS, is the senior manager of communications and knowledge management at The PEAR Institute: Partnerships in Education and Resilience at Harvard University and McLean Hospital. Prior to her work at Harvard, Bailey served as the communications director of the Children's Safety Network, a national injury and violence prevention resource center funded by the Health Resources and Services Administration of the U.S. Department of Health and Human Services, centered at the Education Development Center. She holds a master's degree in public relations from Boston University.

Roger Weissberg, PhD, is University/LAS Distinguished Professor of Psychology and Education and NoVo Foundation Endowed Chair in Social and Emotional Learning and at the University of Illinois at Chicago. He is also chief knowledge officer of the Collaborative for Academic, Social, and Emotional Learning (CASEL), an organization committed to making evidence-based social and emotional academic learning an essential part of education. For over 35 years, he has trained scholars and practitioners about innovative ways to design, implement, and evaluate family, school, and community interventions. Weissberg has authored over 250 publications focusing on preventive interventions with children. He has received several awards including: the American Psychological Association's Distinguished Contribution Award for Applications of Psychology to Education and Training, the Society for Community Research and Action's Distinguished Contribution to Theory and Research Award, and the "Daring

Dozen" award from the George Lucas Educational Foundation for being 1 of 12 people who are reshaping the future of education. He is a commissioner on the National Commission on Social, Emotional, and Academic Development and a member of the National Academy of Education for contributions to education research and policy.

Denice Williams joined the Department of Youth and Community Development in 2005. Currently, she serves as deputy commissioner for the Bureau of Planning, Program Integration, and Evaluation. The bureau was launched by DYCD Commissioner Chong in 2015 to maximize DYCD investments and improve the customer experience and outcomes through streamlined, coordinated service delivery. Denice served as assistant commissioner for the Comprehensive After School System of New York City (COMPASS NYC). Denice joined COMPASS in 2010 after serving as head of the DYCD's Capacity Building Department for 5 years. Under Denice's leadership, COMPASS grew from $92 million initiative serving 58,000 to a $247 million initiative with 813 programs serving 86,000 young people. Prior to joining DYCD, Denice served as deputy executive director of Community Resource Exchange, a renowned management consulting group serving NYC's nonprofit sector. She is a graduate of Pace University and NYU's Wagner School of Public Service.

Jill Young, PhD, has over 10 years of experience in nonprofit research and evaluation. She is currently the senior director of research and evaluation at After School Matters in Chicago, Illinois, where she leads research and evaluation efforts for 25,000 after-school and summer program opportunities for teens each year. Previous to After School Matters, Dr. Young worked as a statistical analyst at University of Chicago and as a research manager at Northwestern University. She graduated from Drake University with honors, earning her BA in Journalism and Mass Communication. She earned her MA and PhD in Research Methodology from Loyola University Chicago. Recently, she was awarded a distinguished alumni award for professional achievement, service to society, and service and support to the School of Education at Loyola University Chicago.

CPSIA information can be obtained
at www.ICGtesting.com
Printed in the USA
BVHW042003121218
535281BV00006B/37/P